INSIDER DEALING

INSIDER DEALING

Law and Practice

Sarah Clarke

BA (Hons) (Law) (Dunelm)
Barrister of the Inner Temple
Serjeants' Inn Chambers

UNIVERSITY PRESS

OXFORD
UNIVERSITY PRESS

Great Clarendon Street, Oxford, OX2 6DP,
United Kingdom

Oxford University Press is a department of the University of Oxford.
It furthers the University's objective of excellence in research, scholarship,
and education by publishing worldwide. Oxford is a registered trade mark of
Oxford University Press in the UK and in certain other countries

© Sarah Clarke 2013

The moral rights of the author have been asserted

First Edition Published in 2013

Impression: 1

All rights reserved. No part of this publication may be reproduced, stored in
a retrieval system, or transmitted, in any form or by any means, without the
prior permission in writing of Oxford University Press, or as expressly permitted
by law, by licence, or under terms agreed with the appropriate reprographics
rights organization. Enquiries concerning reproduction outside the scope of the
above should be sent to the Rights Department, Oxford University Press, at the
address above

You must not circulate this work in any other form
and you must impose this same condition on any acquirer

Crown copyright material is reproduced under Class Licence
Number C01P0000148 with the permission of OPSI
and the Queen's Printer for Scotland

Published in the United States of America by Oxford University Press
198 Madison Avenue, New York, NY 10016, United States of America

British Library Cataloguing in Publication Data
Data available

Library of Congress Control Number: 2013937376

ISBN 978–0–19–967295–0

Printed in Great Britain by
CPI Group (UK) Ltd, Croydon, CR0 4YY

Links to third party websites are provided by Oxford in good faith and
for information only. Oxford disclaims any responsibility for the materials
contained in any third party website referenced in this work.

FOREWORD

For over 30 years, insider dealing has been unlawful in this country, and for nearly 80 years, it has been unlawful in the United States. The law now in force here reflects and implements the 1989 EU Insider Dealing Directive. It is, like so many other laws, complex. It can catch the unwary, as well as the dishonest, and may result in significant terms of imprisonment for the offender and significant reputational damage for employers. The fact, as the author points out, that some argue that insider dealing is positively beneficial to the market, will be of little comfort as the prison doors clang shut and the inevitable confiscation order bites. Most will agree with the author that insider dealing is simply 'cheating'.

Sarah Clarke's book is a 'must' for all those directly or indirectly involved in financial markets, whether as compliance officers, traders, accountants, or lawyers. Each of these can 'have significant information that he or she knows but other market participants don't'. Disclosure of that information whether dishonestly or unwarily on the 18th tee can lead to prosecution or civil proceedings. A compliance officer in any company linked to the financial markets will be failing in his or her responsibilities if a copy of this excellent book is not readily available. Accountants and lawyers need the book to avoid insider dealing and to advise those caught up in an investigation or in criminal or civil proceedings. Regulators will find the book invaluable. Judges required to try insider dealing cases or hear final or interlocutory appeals in insider dealing cases (as I have had to do), will likewise find the book invaluable.

The book has the added advantage of explaining in Chapter 2 to those not closely involved in the financial markets how the markets work—from ordinary dealing through to spread betting.

I recommend the book enthusiastically to anyone at risk of insider dealing or those involved in advising on potential insider dealing. Sarah Clarke is to be congratulated.

The Right Honourable Sir Anthony Hooper
Associate Member Matrix Chambers

PREFACE

My aim in writing this book is to provide a thorough, practical, and straightforward guide to this complex area of law. This book deals with the development of the criminal insider dealing regime (Part V of the Criminal Justice Act 2003 ('CJA')), and offers an analysis of the current law and a guide to the issues of practice and procedure that arise in such cases. It also deals similarly with the civil market abuse regime contained in Part VIII of the Financial Services and Markets Act 2000 ('FSMA'), although it is deliberately confined to the insider dealing types of behaviour which amount to market abuse contained in s 118(2)–(4) of FSMA, rather than the four other ways in which market abuse can be committed. This ensures that the book remains true to its purpose—to provide a thorough yet focused treatment of insider dealing law as it arises in the criminal and civil context.

Historically, insider dealing prosecutions and market abuse proceedings relating to insider dealing type conduct, have been few and far between. This was due to the complexity of the law, the difficulty of the issues and the negligible success rate. In 2000, the responsibility for taking action in respect of insider dealing was given to the newly created Financial Services Authority ('FSA') which was given the power to bring prosecutions for the criminal offence, or bring civil proceedings for market abuse. However, it was not until the arrival of Margaret Cole as Director of the FSA's Enforcement Division in 2005 that the FSA (now the Financial Conduct Authority, 'FCA') began instituting criminal insider dealing prosecutions and civil market abuse proceedings in earnest. At this time, I had recently commenced employment in the FSA's Enforcement Division as a Technical Specialist and In-House Counsel, where for the next six years I advised on and acted in a number of these cases for the FSA. What was striking during this period, was how little jurisprudence and legal text or reference material there was on this subject. A good deal of the jurisprudence that now exists was created during this time.

Since my return to private practice at Serjeants' Inn Chambers in 2011, I have had the privilege to see these cases from both sides. The reality is that not only are insider dealing and market abuse cases increasing in number, they are also increasingly wide-ranging and increasingly serious. What this means is that ever larger numbers of practitioners, firms, and individuals are coming into contact with insider dealing investigations and proceedings, either as advisers, suspects, employers of suspects, subjects, defendants, applicants, or witnesses. This book aims to provide these persons, the lawyers, and compliance specialists who advise

Preface

them and the judges and tribunal panel members who try them, with a route map through the practice and procedure of an insider dealing investigation and prosecution or civil action for market abuse. In so doing, I have sought to provide a comprehensive guide to insider dealing legislation—both criminal and civil—combined with a practical approach to the topic and to identify the challenges for both sides that are inherent in these cases. In short, what I have aimed to do is write the text book that I would have liked to have read seven years ago and had by my side during the intervening years.

The Law is as stated at 1 July 2013.

Sarah Clarke
1 July 2013

ACKNOWLEDGEMENTS

It is trite but true to say that this book would not have been possible without the help and support of a number of people. Firstly, I would like to thank David Ormerod QC for encouraging me to write it in the first place, and Nick Green QC for goading me to actually get on and do it. Eva Anderson, my talented, committed, and organised researcher and assistant who single-handedly obtained and marshalled the vast quantity of source material from which this book was written. A number of people were kind enough to review and critique various sections of this book including Michael Bowes QC, Therese Chambers, Richard Atterbury, and Paul Laffan. Particular thanks must go to Tom Epps of Brown Rudnick LLP for reviewing many of the Chapters in this book from an experienced defence solicitor's perspective and providing valuable suggestions and new angles so that these chapters properly reflect the views and issues that are pertinent to both sides; and to Sarah Wallace of Irwin Mitchell Solicitors for her advice on certain defence issues. Thanks should also go to Mr Justice Simon, His Honour Judge Jeffrey Pegden QC, and His Honour Judge Anthony Leonard QC who between them are responsible for a good deal of the current jurisprudence on the criminal law of insider dealing, and who have all been supportive of the writing of this book as have Peter Carter QC and my former boss and mentor David Kirk. My thanks are also due to Oxford University Press, and in particular to Roxanne Selby, Eleanor Walter, Amy Jones and Emma Brady for their wise advice, support, and patience through the various stages of this book from conception to completion. Thanks must also go to my clerks Nick Salt and Lee Johnson of Serjeants' Inn Chambers who have given me the space to write this book, never doubted I could do it, and kept my practice going in the meantime. Lastly but importantly—family and friends. My parents in particular father Peter Clarke, who, following retirement from a successful career in the City, has been a valuable and unswerving supporter, advisor, and proof-reader; my children Marcus and Tilly who have cheerfully and good-naturedly brought themselves up while I wrote this book, and my dear friends His Honour Judge Alistair McCreath, the Honorary Recorder of Westminster, and Patricia Lynch QC for encouraging, supporting, and occasionally cajoling me to keep going whenever I started to flag or lose heart. Finally, to Keith Mathieson and Desmond Browne QC for the reasons you know.

CONTENTS

Table of Cases   xix
Table of Legislation   xxv
List of Abbreviations   xxxi

1. **Introduction to Insider Dealing**
    1. Introduction   1.01
    2. What is insider dealing in practical terms?   1.02
    3. The value of information in determining pricing   1.15
    4. The prevalence of insider dealing in the UK today   1.22

2. **Trading on the Financial Markets—Essential Principles for Insider Dealing Cases**
    1. Introduction   2.01
    2. Shares   2.02
    3. UK stock exchanges   2.11
    4. Availability of information and stock market pricing   2.16
    5. The price of shares   2.23
    6. Investors   2.26
    7. Contracts for difference   2.33
    8. Spread bets   2.47

3. **A History of Insider Dealing Legislation in the UK**
    1. Introduction   3.01
    2. Relevant developments in the US   3.02
    3. Economic theory   3.03
    4. The UK's response to insider dealing   3.12

4. **The European Insider Dealing Directive**
    1. Introduction   4.01

2.	The Relationship between the Insider Dealing Directive and Part V of the CJA	4.02
3.	The background to the Insider Dealing Directive	4.04
4.	The Proposal	4.08
5.	The Insider Dealing Directive—Recitals	4.25

5. Part V of the Criminal Justice Act 1993: The Criminal Offences (s 52 CJA)

1.	Introduction	5.01
2.	Part V of the CJA—an overview	5.02
3.	The offence	5.07
4.	Insider dealing (s 52(1) CJA) (the 'primary' offence)	5.16
5.	The secondary offences	5.21

6. Inside Information (s 56 CJA)

1.	Introduction	6.01
2.	The statutory definition of inside information	6.02
3.	Identifying the inside information	6.03
4.	Relating to particular securities or issuers (s 56(1)(a) CJA)	6.10
5.	Specific or precise (s 56(1)(b) CJA)	6.22
6.	Information which has not been 'made public' (s 56(1)(c) CJA)	6.64
7.	The evidential practicalities of proving that information has not been 'made public'	6.95
8.	Likely to have a 'significant effect' on price (s 56(1)(d) CJA)	6.111
9.	Price-affected securities	6.129

7. Insiders (s 57 CJA)

1.	Introduction	7.01
2.	Meaning of 'insider'	7.02
3.	The elements of knowledge	7.03
4.	Inside information at the time of dealing	7.10
5.	An inside source	7.16
6.	Categories of insider	7.19

Contents

8. Securities and Regulated Markets

    1. Introduction — 8.01
    2. The correct analysis — 8.02
    3. Securities — 8.03
    4. Regulated markets — 8.29
    5. Securities other than shares — 8.37

9. Dealing

    1. Introduction — 9.01
    2. Dealing (s 52(3) CJA) — 9.02
    3. Acquisitions and disposals (s 55(1)–(3) CJA) — 9.06
    4. Procuring an acquisition or disposal (s 55(4) CJA) — 9.11
    5. Professional intermediaries — 9.20

10. Territorial Scope (s 62 CJA)

    1. Introduction — 10.01
    2. Primary insider dealing offence (s 62(1) CJA) — 10.02
    3. Secondary 'Encouraging' and 'Disclosing' offences (s 62(2) CJA) — 10.05
    4. The scope of s 62 CJA — 10.06

11. Statutory Defences

    1. Introduction — 11.01
    2. Statutory defences to the primary insider dealing offence (s 53(1) CJA) — 11.02
    3. Statutory defences to the secondary 'Encouraging' offence (s 53(2) CJA) — 11.17
    4. Statutory defences to the secondary 'Disclosing' offence (s 53(3) CJA) — 11.19
    5. Special defences — 11.23
    6. Statutory defences—legal and evidential burden on the defence — 11.42

12. Prosecution of Insider Dealing Offences

    1. Introduction — 12.01
    2. Prosecuting bodies — 12.02

3. Consent for prosecution	12.05
4. Prosecution of other offences connected to insider dealing	12.09
5. Conspiracy or substantive counts	12.13
6. Summary proceedings: venue and time limit	12.21

13. Penalties and Sentencing

1. Introduction	13.01
2. The penalty for offences of insider dealing (s 61 CJA)	13.02
3. Court of Appeal sentencing authorities	13.04
4. Sentences imposed in recent insider dealing cases	13.16
5. Disqualification of company directors	13.17
6. Confiscation issues in insider dealing cases	13.19
7. Other FCA proceedings	13.28

14. Insider Dealing—The Civil Market Abuse Regime

1. Introduction	14.01
2. Legislative background	14.02
3. Legal and source materials	14.12

15. The Civil Offences

1. Introduction	15.01
2. Part VIII of FSMA	15.02
3. Qualifying investments and prescribed markets	15.13
4. Territorial scope	15.32

16. Section 118(2) FSMA; Behaviour—Insider Dealing

1. Introduction	16.01
2. Section 118(2) FSMA	16.02
3. Insider	16.05
4. Dealing or attempting to deal	16.14
5. 'On the basis of'	16.16
6. Inside information	16.28
7. Section 118(2) FSMA behaviour—safe harbours	16.66

17. Section 118(3) FSMA; Behaviour—Improper Disclosure

1. Introduction — 17.01
2. Section 118(3) FSMA behaviour — 17.02
3. Section 118(3) FSMA behaviour—safe harbours — 17.10

18. Section 118(4) FSMA; Behaviour—Misuse of Information

1. Introduction — 18.01
2. Section 118(4) FSMA behaviour — 18.02
3. The regular user — 18.17
4. 'Generally available' — 18.18
5. 'Based on' — 18.19
6. 'Relevant information' — 18.20
7. Standards of behaviour — 18.22
8. Section 118(4) FSMA—safe harbours — 18.23

19. Market Abuse—Statutory Defence and Power to Impose Penalties

1. Introduction — 19.01
2. Statutory defence (s 118A(5) FSMA) — 19.02
3. Power to impose penalties in cases of market abuse (s 123 FSMA) — 19.06
4. Penalties imposed in market abuse cases — 19.28

20. Market Abuse Proceedings—Article 6 ECHR and the Burden and Standard of Proof

1. Introduction — 20.01
2. Status of market abuse proceedings under Article 6 ECHR — 20.02
3. Burden and standard of proof in market abuse proceedings — 20.12

21. Detection and Referral to Enforcement

1. Introduction — 21.01
2. The FSA — 21.02
3. The FSA—attitude to enforcement — 21.07
4. Insider dealing prosecutions—the statistics — 21.08
5. The PRA and the FCA — 21.10

6.	Detection of insider dealing and market abuse	21.20
7.	The Enforcement and Financial Crime Division	21.34
8.	The process by which cases are referred to Enforcement for investigation	21.36
9.	Cases in which other authorities have an interest	21.38

22. The Enforcement Investigation

1.	Introduction	22.01
2.	Allocation to a case team	22.02
3.	Powers of investigation	22.03
4.	Notification of an investigation	22.06
5.	Use of statutory powers to require the production of documents, the provision of information, or the answering of questions	22.09
6.	Powers under the Regulation of Investigatory Powers Act 2000	22.17
7.	Protected items (s 413 FSMA)	22.18
8.	Banking confidentiality (s 175(5) FSMA)	22.20
9.	Sanctions for failure to comply (s 177 FSMA)	22.21
10.	Use of information	22.25
11.	Search warrants	22.34
12.	Interviews	22.40
13.	Witness statements	22.51

23. Criminal Proceedings

1.	Introduction	23.01
2.	The decision to commence criminal proceedings	23.02
3.	Factors which may influence the decision	23.05
4.	Co-operation agreements	23.15
5.	Plea discussions	23.29
6.	The role of the RDC Chairman	23.31
7.	Instituting criminal proceedings	23.35
8.	Restraint proceedings	23.38
9.	Issuing a caution	23.39
10.	Decisions not to prosecute	23.41

24. The Enforcement Process—Market Abuse Proceedings

1.	Introduction	24.01
2.	Range of enforcement actions	24.02
3.	Informal enforcement action	24.03
4.	Formal enforcement action	24.09
5.	The enforcement process	24.21
6.	The Executive Settlement Process	24.45
7.	Civil proceedings	24.57
8.	Publicity	24.59

25. The Future

1.	Introduction	25.01
2.	New European legislation	25.02
3.	The Draft Regulation	25.06
4.	The Draft Directive	25.24
5.	Conclusion—the next five years	25.28

Appendices

Appendix 1:	Glossary of Terms Commonly Encountered in Insider Dealing Cases	291
Appendix 2:	Legislation	
	A. Insider Dealing Directive (Dir 89/592/EC)	296
	B. Criminal Justice Act 1993, Part V	301
	C. Criminal Justice Act 1993, Schedule 2	306
	D. Insider Dealing (Securities and Regulated Markets) Order 1994 (SI no 187) (as amended)	308
Appendix 3:	Financial Services and Markets Act 2000, Part VIII (as amended)	312
Appendix 4:	FSMA 2000 (Prescribed Markets and Qualifying Investments) Order 2001	322

Index   325

TABLE OF CASES

UNITED KINGDOM

Arch Financial Products LLP v FSA, Upper Tribunal [2013] All ER (D) 67 . . . . .24.61
Attorney General's Reference (No.1 of 1975), Re [1975] 61 Cr App R 118, CA. 9.17
Atwal v Massey 56 Cr App R 6, DC. 7.04

B v Chief Constable of Avon and Somerset Constabulary [2001] 1 WLR 340 . . . . . . 20.16, 20.23
Bolton Engineering Co v Graham [1957] 1 QB 159 . . . . .5.11

Chase Manhattan Equities Ltd v Goodman [1991] BCLC 897 . . . . .9.12
City Index Ltd (t/as FinSpreads) v Balducci [2011] EWHC 2562. . . . . 8.20

Fleurose v The Securities and Futures Authority Ltd [2001] EWCA Civ 2015 . . . . . . 20.06–20.08
Flintshire CC v Reynolds 170 JP 73, DC. 7.04
FSA v Da Vinci Invest Ltd [2011] EWHC 2674 . . . . .24.58

H, Re [1996] 1 All ER 1 . . . . 20.15, 20.23
Han v Customs and Excise Commissioners [2001] EWCA Civ 1040 . . 20.04–20.09, 20.16, 20.25

In R v Goodman [1993] 97 Cr App R 210 . . . . .13.17
In re B (Children) [2008] UKHL 35 . . . . .20.19

Lennards Carrying Co v Asiatic Petroleum [1915] AC 705. . . . . .5.11

Mackie (Thorold) v HM Advocate, 1994 JC 132; 1995 SLT 110; 1994 SCCR 277. . . . . 6.21, 6.38

Official Receiver v Stern [2001] 1 All ER 633; [2000] 1 WLR 2230. . . . . 20.07

Percival v Wright [1902] 2 Ch 401 . . . . 3.12, 3.15

R (McCann) v Crown Court at Manchester [2002] UKHL 39, [2003] 1 AC 787. . . . . 20.23
R (on the application of Clegg) v Secretary of State for Trade and Industry [2002] EWCA
    Civ 519; [2002] All ER (D) 114 . . . . .22.15
R (on the application of Uberoi and another) v City of Westminster Magistrates' Court
    [2008] EWHC 3191 (Admin) 21.03
R v Adam Buck, Unreported, Southwark Crown Court, Mr Justice Simon, 9 May
    2012. . . . . 6.58–6.60, 6.61
R v Allpress [2012] UKSC 51. . . . . 13.20, 13.24
R v Andrews Weatherfoil [1972] 56 C App R 31 CA. 5.11
R v Anjam Ahmad, Unreported, Southwark Crown Court, His Honour Judge Rivlin QC,
    the Honorary Recorder of Westminster, 22 June 2010 . . . . .13.27, 23.26–23.28
R v Asif Nazir Butt [2006] EWCA Crim 137, CA 12 Jan 2006 . . . . 13.08–13.11
R v Beale, Judson, Masters, Butt and Coleman, Unreported, Southwark Crown Court, His
    Honour Judge Elwen, 17 Mar 2004 . . . . .8.16–8.19, 8.20

Table of Cases

R v Calvert, Unreported, Southwark Crown Court, His Honour Judge Testar,
  7 May 2010 .... 6.40, 6.123, 7.35, 13.20, 13.21
R (Canada Inc.) v Financial Services Authority [2011] EWHC 2766. (Admin) 24.62
R v Christopher McQuoid, Court of Appeal (Criminal Division) 10 June 2009, [2009]
  EWCA Crim 1301, [2010] 1 Cr App R (S) 43. .... 1.02, 13.12–13.16
R v Clark [1998] 2 Cr App R (S) 95 .... 13.10, 13.16, 13.24
R v Coren and Greenwood, Unreported, (but see FT (London, 24 Jan 1990)) 7.11
R v Cross [1990] 1 Cr App R 115 .... 11.14, 11.42, 11.43
R v Dickinson, Unreported, (but noted (1982) 3 Co Law 185) 7.21
R v Dougall [2012] EWCA Crim 1048 .... 23.27
R v Fisher 4 BCC 360. .... 7.34
R v Geoffrey Collier, Unreported (but see 'Bang Goes a Scandal', Sunday Times (London,
  16 Nov 1986); 'Collier's Rise and Fall', Independent (London, 2 July 1987); 'Mischief
  that may stop the Market's Heart' Financial Times (London, 2 July 1987)) 7.30
R v Gooding, Unreported, (but see FT (London, 2 Mar 1990)) 11.06
R v Goodman, In, [1993] 97 Cr App R 210 .... 13.17
R v Goodman, Unreported (but see FT (London, 1 May 1991 and 16 June 1992)).......... 9.12
R v Gray [1995] 2 Cr App R 100, CA 6.121
R v Greenfield 57 Cr App R 849 CA. 12.15
R v Griffiths [1966] 1 QB 589 .... 12.15
R v Holyoak, Hill and Morl Financial Times (London, 28 Oct 1989) 7.06
R v Jenkins, Unreported, (but see FT (London, 18 July 1987)). 7.23
R v John Morris Cross [1990] 91 Cr App R 115. .... 7.21
R v Jones (J) 59 Cr App R 120 CA 12.15
R v Kean and Floydd, Unreported, (but see FT (London, 7 June 1991)) 7.29
R v Littlewood and others, Unreported, Southwark Crown Court, His Honour Judge
  Anthony Leonard QC, 10 Jan 2011 .... 1.08, 5.12, 7.31, 7.35
R v Littlewood and others, Unreported, Southwark Crown Court, His Honour Judge
  Anthony Leonard QC, 2 Feb 2011. .... 1.09, 13.20
R v Malcolm Calvert, Unreported, Southwark Crown Court, His Honour Judge Testar and
  a Jury, 16 Feb to 11 Mar 2010. .... 6.07, 6.30, 6.123, 7.35, 23.22–23.25
R v May [2008] UKHL 28. .... 13.20
R v McQuoid and Melbourne, Unreported, Southwark Crown Court, His Honour Judge
  Testar and a Jury, 9 to 27 Mar 2009 . ... 6.16
R v Montila and others [2004] UKHL 50 [2005] 1 Cr App R 26; [2005] 1 Cr App R 26 .... 8.22
R v Mustafa and others, Unreported, Southwark Crown Court, His Honour Judge Pegden
  QC and a Jury, 5 March to 23 July 2012. .... 6.08, 6.09, 6.32, 6.40, 6.106, 6.109, 6.127,
                                                7.32, 7.35, 8.23, 11.16, 11.21, 11.47, 11.49
R v Neel and Matthew Uberoi, Unreported, Southwark Crown Court, His Honour Judge
  Testar and a Jury, Oct to 6 Nov 2009 . ... 6.16, 6.66, 6.122, 9.14–9.18, 12.06
R v Neil Rollins [2010] UKSC 39, Supreme Court. 12.10–12.12
R v Neil Rollins, Unreported, Southwark Crown Court, 16 to 26 Nov 2010 .... 6.31, 11.49
R v Power and Carlisle, Unreported, His Honour Judge Wadsworth QC,
  24 Feb 2009. .... 6.53–6.57, 6.61
R v Paul Milsom, Unreported, Southwark Crown Court, His Honour Judge Pegden QC,
  7 Mar 2013 .... 13.27, 23.29–23.30
R v Richard Joseph, Unreported, Southwark Crown Court, His Honour Judge Pegden QC
  and a Jury, 30 Jan to 11 Mar 2013 .... 6.09, 6.128, 7.32, 12.20
R v Rigby and Bailey [2006] EWCA Crim 1653 .... 13.10
R v Rooney [2010] EWCA Crim 2. .... 13.20, 13.25
R v Rupinder Sidhu, Unreported, Southwark Crown Court, His Honour Judge Gledhill
  QC and a Jury, 28 Nov 2011 to 15 Dec 2011 .... 7.09, 7.35, 8.23, 13.24, 13.27

R v Sanders and others, Unreported, Southwark Crown Court, Mr Justice Simon,
　20 June 2012 . . . . 1.10, 1.12, 5.13, 5.25, 6.42, 6.58, 6.106, 6.119,
　　　　　　　　　　　　　　　　　　　　　　　　6.124, 7.12–7.15, 8.23, 8.33, 8.40, 13.18
R v Smith, Spearman and Payne [2003] EWCA Crim 2893. 13.05–13.07
R v Spearman and others [2003] EWCA Crim 2893 . . . . 13.10
R v Staines and Morrissey [1997] 2 Cr App R 426 . . . . 6.43–6.47, 6.49, 6.52, 6.57,
　　　　　　　　　　　　　　　　　　　　　　　　　　　　　6.58, 6.60, 6.61, 11.20
R v Stebbing, Unreported, (but see Accountancy, September 1991, 12) 11.15
R v Thomas Ammann, Unreported, Southwark Crown Court, His Honour Judge Anthony
　Leonard QC, 15 Nov 2012. . . . . 10.08
R v Thomas Ammann, Christina Weckewerth and Jessica Mang, Unreported, Southwark
　Crown Court, His Honour Judge Anthony Leonard QC, 24 May 2012 . . . . . . 10.07–10.11
R v Uberoi, Unreported, Southwark Crown Court, His Honour Judge Testar,
　7 July 2010. . . . . 13.20
R v Watts The Times (London, Apr 14, 1995) CA 12.15
R v Waya [2012] UKSC 51. . . . . .13.22, 13.23, 13.26
Re Dellow's Will Trusts, Lloyds Bank Ltd v Institute of Cancer Research [1964] 1 All ER
　771 773, [1964] 1 WLR 451. . . . . .20.15
Re H [1996] 1 All ER 1 . . . . 20.15, 20.23

Sheldrake v DPP [2004] UKHL 43, [2005] 1 AC 264, [2005] 1 All ER 237, [2004] 3 WLR
　976 (14 Oct 2004), House of Lords 11.44
Spreadex v Battu [2005] EWCA Civ 855 . . . . 8.20, 8.21
Spreadex Ltd v Sekhon [2008] All ER (D) 329 (May). 8.20

Tesco Supermarkets Ltd v Nattrass [1972] AC 153. . . . . .5.11
The Queen on the Application of the FSA v MM, AR and AK [2010] EWCA
　Crim 1151 . . . . 7.37–7.41
The Queen on the application of Matthew Francis Uberoi, Neel Akash Uberoi v City of
　Westminster Magistrates' Court, Administrative Court, 2 Dec 2008, [2008] EWHC
　3191 (Admin), 2008 WL 5044304 . . . . 12.06, 21.03

Verrier v DPP [1967] 2 AC 195, HL 12.15

Warner v Commissioner of Police of the Metropolis [1969] 2 AC 256 . . . . .7.04
Westminster City Council v Croyalgrange Ltd 83 Cr App R 155 . . . . .7.04

FSA CASES

Alexei Krilov-Harrison Final Notice, 3 Nov 2009 . . . . .19.08
Andre Jean Scerri Upper Tribunal Case 0016, 21 May 2010. . . . . .16.45
Andrew Osborne Final Notice, 15 Feb 2012. . . . . 5.29, 17.07–17.08
Arif Mohammed v FSA FSMT, Case 012, 29 Mar 2005. . . . . 16.41–16.45, 20.15
Atlantic Law LLP and Andrew Greystoke v FSA Upper Tribunal, 1–10 Mar 2010 . . . . 20.21

Bertie Charles Hatcher Final Notice, 13 May 2008 . . . . .18.14

Canada Inc and Peter Beck v FSA Upper Tribunal, 2 Aug 2011 . . . . .24.61
Christopher Parry Final Notice, 16 Oct 2009 . . . . .19.27

Darren Morton Final Notice, 6 Oct 2009 . . . . 19.23–19.27
Darwin Lewis Clifton and Byron Holdings Limited Final Notice, 27 Jan 2009. . . . . .19.12
David Einhorn Final Notice, 15 Feb 2012 . . . . 16.22–16.23, 16.56, 19.19–19.22

David Isaacs Final Notice, 28 Feb 2005 . . . . .18.13
David Massey v FSA Upper Tribunal, 2nd Feb 2011 . . . . 16.36, 16.49, 16.50

Eurolife Assurance Company Ltd v FSA (26 July 2002) 24.62

Philippe Jabre and GLG Partners LP FSA Final Notice, 1 Aug 2006 . . . . 15.09, 16.44, 16.70

Greenlight Capital Inc Final Notice, 12 Jan 2012 . . . . .5.10, 15.12

James Parker v FSA FSMT, Case 037, 18 Aug 2006 . . . . 16.68–16.69, 20.06–20.09, 20.17
Jason Smith Final Notice, 13 Dec 2004 . . . . 18.08
Jeremy Burley Final Notice, 19 July 2010 . . . . .19.11
John Shevlin v FSA Case 060, 12 June 2008 . . . . 16.09
John Shevlin Final Notice, 1 July 2008 . . . . .16.12
Jonathan Mallins Final Notice, 20 Dec 2005 . . . . .18.12

Karpe and others v FSA FIN/2010/0019 . . . . 24.62

Mark Ainley v FSA Upper Tribunal Decision, 13 July 2012 . . . . .20.24–20.25
Michael Thomas Davies Final Notice, 28 July 2004 . . . . 18.09

Nicholas James Kyprios Final Notice, 13 Mar 2012 . . . . .15.30

Paul Davidson and Ashley Tatham v FSA FSMT Case 031, 16 May 2006 . . . 20.04–20.05, 20.09,
 20.12, 20.16, 20.17
Perry John Bliss Final Notice, 13 Dec 2010 . . . . .19.10
Peter Bracken Final Notice, 7 July 2004 . . . . .18.10

Richard Ralph and Filip Boyen Final Notices, 12 Nov 2008 . . . . 23.09–23.14
Robert Middlemiss Final Notice, 10 Feb 2004 . . . . .18.11
Robin Chhabra and Sameer Patel v FSA FSMT Case 072, 29 Dec 2009 . . . . 18.15, 20.22
Robin Mark Hutchings Final Notice, 13 Dec 2004 . . . . 18.08

Sonaike v FSA (13 July 2005) 24.62

William James Coppin Final Notice, 7 Dec 2010 . . . . .19.10

EUROPEAN UNION

Ipourgos Ikonomikon v Georgakis [2007] All ER (EC) 1106; [2007] ECR I-3741; [2007] 2
 BCLC 692; [2007] 3 CMLR 4; [2007] CEC 891 . . . . .11.10–11.11

Jahn v Germany (2006) 42 EHRR 1084 . . . . 13.23

Markus Geltl v Daimler AG Judgment of the European Court (Second Chamber) of
 28 June 2012 C-19/11 . . . . .16.32

Pressos Compania Naviera SA and others v Belgium, judgment of 20 Nov 1995,
 ser A no 332, 23, ... 13.23

Spector Photo Group NV and Chris Van Raemdonck v Commissie voor het Bank-, Financie-
 en Assurantiewezen (CBFA) Case C-45/08; [2010] All ER (D) 125 (Feb) 16.17–16.19,
 16.22–16.23

Table of Cases

UNITED STATES

In re Cady, Roberts & Co, 40 SEC 907 (1961) 913 .... 3.02

SEC v Texas Gulf Sulphur Co, 401 F 2d 833 (1968) 3.02
Securities and Exchange Commission v Arnold McClellan and Annabel McClellan,
    Case No 10-cv-5412 WHA (ND Cal, filed Nov 30 2010) 1.14
Securities and Exchange Commission v Raj Rajaratnam et al, US District Court Southern
    District of New York 09 Civ 8811 (JSR) 1.07
Speed v Transamerica Corp, 71 F Supp 457 (D Del 1945) 3.02

USA v Annabel McClellan, US Northern District Court of California, No CR 10-0860
    (WHA) 1.14
US v Carpenter 791 F 2d 1024 (2nd Cir 1986) 6.85
United States v Raj Rajaratnam, 09 CR 1184 (RJH) (SDNY) 1.07
US v Winans 612 F supp 827 (1985) 6.85

TABLE OF LEGISLATION

UNITED KINGDOM

Companies Act 1948 .... 3.14, 3.16
  s 195............................. 3.13
Companies Act 1967 .... 3.16
  s 25.............................. 3.16
  ss 2–9............................ 3.16
Companies Act 1980
  Pt V 3.01, 3.31–3.36, 3.37
Companies Act 1985
  s 442(1) 22.15
  s 741(2).......................... 7.21
Companies Act 2006
  s 251(1).......................... 7.21
Company Directors Disqualification
  Act 1986
  ss 1–2........................... 13.17
Company Securities (Insider Dealing)
  Act 1985........ 3.37–3.40, 5.02, 5.04,
             6.70, 7.29, 7.34, 11.43
  s 1(3) 7.34
  s 8 .... 3.37
  s 9 ....7.17
  s 10........................6.23, 6.47
  s 10(b) 6.68
Coroners and Justice Act 2009........ 23.17
Criminal Justice Act 1987
  s 12(3) 3.37
Criminal Justice Act 1993 .... 3.38, 4.03,
     5.04, 5.33, 6.24, 6.25, 6.77, 6.113,
     6.115, 7.07, 8.01, 8.28, 8.39, 16.47
  s 7 ....8.33, 8.45
  s 9 ....8.33, 8.45
  s 52 .... 4.16, 5.06–5.34, 6.19,
               6.84, 6.86, 11.39
  s 52(1) 5.07, 5.15, 5.16–5.20, 6.51,
        6.129, 7.10, 9.03, 10.08, 10.10,
        11.07, 12.10, 13.05, 18.14
  s 52(2) 6.51, 7.10, 10.04–10.05, 13.18
  s 52(2)(a) 5.07, 5.15, 5.21–5.25, 6.129,
                 9.04, 19.07
  s 52(2)(b) 5.07, 5.15, 5.24,
              5.26–5.34, 17.04
  s 52(3) 4.21, 5.16, 9.02–9.05,
                  9.20, 9.22
  s 53............. 5.20, 11.01, 11.42, 11.46

  s 53(1) 11.02–11.16
  s 53(1)(a) 11.03–11.06
  s 53(1)(b) 11.07–11.11
  s 53(1)(c)............ 11.12–11.16, 11.47,
                  11.49, 12.19
  s 53(2) 11.17–11.18
  s 53(2)(b) 11.18
  s 53(3) 9.22, 11.19–11.22
  s 53(3)(a) 11.20, 11.21, 11.47
  s 53(3)(b) 11.22
  s 53(4) 11.23
  s 53(6) 11.03
  s 54 .... 4.21, 8.01
  s 54(1) 6.17
  ss 55(1)–(3)................. 9.05–9.10
  s 55(2)(b) 9.09
  s 55(3)(b) 9.09
  s 55(4) 9.10
  s 55(5) 9.16
  s 56 .... 4.18, 6.01–6.129, 7.02
  s 56(1) 6.03, 6.07,
                 6.21, 6.33, 6.69
  s 56(1)(a) 6.10–6.21
  s 56(1)(b) 6.22–6.63
  s 56(1)(c) 6.64–6.94, 6.97, 6.110
  s 56(1)(d) 6.111–6.128
  s 56(2) 6.129
  s 56(3) 6.111
  s 57............. 4.13, 6.86, 7.01–7.41
  s 57(1)(a)........................ 7.35
  s 57(2) 7.02, 7.15, 7.16, 7.19, 7.20
  s 57(2)(a) 7.17–7.18
  s 57(2)(a)(i).............. 7.19, 7.21–7.24
  s 57(2)(a)(ii) 7.19, 7.25–7.32
  s 57(2)(b) 7.19, 7.21, 7.33–7.41
  s 58 ....6.71, 6.73, 6.74
  s 58(1) 6.71, 6.73, 6.74
  s 58(2)(a)–(d)........... 6.74, 6.76–6.83
  s 58(3)(a)–(e) 6.75, 6.87–6.94
  s 59.....................4.21, 9.23, 9.26
  s 59(2) 9.24, 9.25
  s 59(3)(a) 9.25
  s 59(3)(b) 9.25
  s 59(4) 9.25
  s 60 .... 8.29
  s 60(2) 6.11

s 60(3)(a)	6.12	Financial Services and Markets Act	
s 60(3)(b)	6.13	2000	8.20, 12.02, 14.04, 14.11, 14.12–14.18, 15.02, 21.03, 21.04, 21.07, 22.01, 22.33
s 60(4)	6.17, 6.19, 6.20, 6.21		
s 61	13.02–13.03		
s 61A	12.21	s 1C	21.16
s 61(2)	12.05, 12.06	s 1D	21.16
s 62	10.01–10.11	s 1E	21.16
s 62(1)	10.02–10.03, 10.09, 10.10	s 1F	21.16
s 62(2)	10.04–10.05	s 1H(3)	21.16
s 63	11.39–11.41	s 1I	21.16
s 63(1)	11.40, 11.41	s 2	21.04, 21.05
s 116	23.25	s 2(4)	21.05
Pt V	1.01, 3.43, 4.01, 4.02–4.03, 4.11, 5.01–5.34, 6.66, 8.01, 8.33, 8.35, 8.45, 8.46, 9.01, 9.06, 9.20, 9.21, 12.07, 14.03, 14.10, 15.04, 16.39, 22.05, 25.28, App 2B (p 301–5)	s 3	21.04
		s 3A	21.04
		s 5	21.04
		s 6	21.04
		s 55	24.19
		s 55J	24.02, 24.19
Sch 1	11.01, 11.23, 11.24, 11.25–11.27, 11.29, 11.42, 11.46	s 55Q	24.19
		s 55(7)	24.02
Sch 1(2)	11.28–11.32, 11.34	s 56	24.02, 24.14, 24.29
Sch 1(3)	11.33–11.34	s 56(4)	24.15
Sch 1(5)	11.35–11.38	s 56(7)	24.15
para 5(2)	11.37	s 63	24.02, 24.16
Sch 2	4.21, 6.17, 8.01–8.24, 8.25, 8.30, 8.34, App 2C (p 306–7)	s 66	24.20
		s 66(3)	24.02
Criminal Justice Act 2003	6.95	s 118	14.12, 14.14, 15.03, 15.13, 15.29, 24.21
s 67(c)	7.39		
Criminal Law Act 1977		s 118(1)	15.01, 15.03–15.04, 15.07, 15.28, 16.23, 19.13
s 1	12.13		
Criminal Law (Consolidation) Scotland Act 1995		s 118(1)(a)(i)	15.14
		s 118(1)(a)(ii)	15.14
s 44(2)	22.50	s 118(2)	15.01, 15.04, 15.15–15.25, 15.28, 16.01–16.84, 18.01, 18.06, 18.07, 18.08, 18.14, 19.11, 19.13, 19.19, 19.23, 24.58
Criminal Procedures and Investigations Act 1996	6.95, 6.96, 6.108		
s 3(1)(a)	6.98		
s 5	6.98		
s 6	6.98	s 118(3)	5.30, 15.01, 15.04, 15.15–15.25, 15.28, 17.01–17.12, 18.01, 18.07, 18.08, 19.09, 19.11, 24.58
s 6A(1)	6.98		
s 6B	6.98		
s 7A	6.100	s 118(4)	15.01, 15.04, 15.22, 18.01–18.23, 24.58
Pt II	6.95, 6.96		
		s 118(4)(a)	18.06
Data Protection Act 1998	22.32	s 118(5)	15.21
		s 118(6)	15.21
Financial Services Act 1986	3.41–3.43, 8.20	s 118(7)	15.21
s 47	6.85, 14.03	s 118A(1)	15.01, 15.35
s 177	3.42	s 118A(5)	19.01, 19.02–19.05
Pt VII	3.42	s 118B	16.05
Financial Services Act 2012	21.10, 21.14, 21.15	s 118B(a)	16.06
		s 118B(b)	16.06
s 1A(1)	21.15	s 118B(c)	16.11
s 1B(2)	21.16	s 118B(e)	16.08
s 1B(3)	21.16	s 118C	16.28, 16.50
Sch 12	22.39	s 118C(2)	16.28, 16.29, 16.37

s 118C(3)	16.61	s 352	22.25, 22.28
s 118C(4)	16.64	s 381	24.57
s 118C(5)	16.30	s 387(2)	24.35
s 118C(5)(b)	16.36	s 391	24.63
s 118C(6)	16.47	s 391(1)	24.32
s 118C(7)	16.63	s 394(1)	24.32
s 118C(8)	16.38	s 394(3)	24.34
s 119(1)	14.13	s 394(7)	24.33
s 123	15.05, 19.06–19.27, 20.13, 22.50, 23.23, 24.02, 24.21, 24.29, 24.41	s 395	24.24
s 123(1)	15.05, 19.01, 19.06	s 397(1)	13.10
s 123(1)(b)	15.05, 19.07–19.13	s 401	12.11, 12.12
s 123(2)	19.01, 19.14–19.27	s 401(2)	12.11
s 123(2)(a)	19.16, 19.24, 19.25	s 402	12.11, 12.12
s 123(2)(b)	19.16, 19.19, 19.22	s 402(1)	12.03, 12.07
s 123(3)	19.06	s 402(1)(a)	12.03, 12.04
s 126	24.29, 24.32	s 413	22.18–22.19
s 128	24.41	Pt IV	24.02
s 128(4)	24.43	Pt VI	19.03
s 130A(1)	15.13	Pt VIII	1.01, 5.10, 14.02, 14.05, 14.10, 15.02–15.12, 22.04, 24.01, 25.28 App 3 (p 312–21)
s 130A(3)	14.06, 15.06, 15.28, 16.14, 16.62, 18.02, 18.17	Pt XI	22.03
s 132	14.18	Sch 6	20.24
s 133	24.43	Sch 15, Pt 1	22.12
s 165	21.10–21.12	Fraud Act 2006	12.12
s 168	22.34		
s 168(2)	22.04, 22.05, 22.06, 22.07, 22.13, 22.14–22.15	Human Rights Act 1998	11.44, 24.21
s 168(2)(a)	22.04	Interpretation Act 1978	
s 168(2)(b)	22.04	Sch 1	5.10, 5.21
s 170	22.06		
s 170(3)(a)	22.06	Perjury Act 1911	
s 170(4)	22.06	s 5	22.50
s 173	22.13, 22.14–22.15, 22.41	Police and Criminal Evidence Act 1984	
s 174	20.10, 22.09, 22.50	s 16	22.36, 22.49
s 174(5)	22.15	Proceeds of Crime Act 2002	12.09, 13.19, 21.25, 24.58
s 175	22.16		
s 175(5)	22.16, 22.20	s 6(4)(c)	13.20
s 176	22.34	s 327	12.12
s 176(5)	22.35	s 327(d)	12.10
s 176(8)	22.39	s 328	12.12
s 177	22.21–22.24, 22.44	s 328(e)	12.10
s 177(2)	22.23	Pt 2	23.38
s 177(3)	22.21, 22.23	Pt 5	23.20
s 177(4)	22.22, 22.23		
s 177(5)	22.23	Regulation of Investigatory Powers Act 2000	22.17, 24.33
s 205	24.02		
s 206	24.02		
s 206A	24.02, 24.20	Serious and Organised Crime and Police Act 2005	23.22, 23.26
s 348	22.25, 22.27		
s 348(2)	22.26	s 71	23.17, 23.19
s 348(4)	22.26, 22.27	s 72	23.17, 23.20
s 348(5)	22.27	s 73	13.27, 23.17, 23.21, 23.26
s 349	22.28	s 74	23.17, 23.21

Serious Crime Act 2007
  Pt 2 .... 5.15

Theft Act 1968 .... 3.37

SUBORDINATE LEGISLATION

Criminal Procedure Rules 2005
  (SI 2005 no 384)
  r 14.2 .... 12.15
FSMA (Disclosure of Confidential
  Information) Regulations 2001 S.I.
  (2001/2188) 22.25, 22.28, 22.29,
                              22.31, 22.33
  reg 7 .... 22.25, 22.28, 22.29
FSMA (Market Abuse) Regulations
  2011 (SI 2011/2928)
  reg 2(2) 15.04, 18.02
FSMA (Prescribed Markets and
  Qualifying Investments) Order
  2001 (SI 2001/996) 15.13, 15.21,
  16.15, App 4 (p 322–4)
  Art 4(1) 15.15
  Art 4(2) 15.22
  Art 5 .... 15.26
  Art 5(2) 15.27
FSMA (Recognized Auction Platforms)
  Regulations 2011
  (SI/2011/2699) 15.21, 16.06
Financial Services and Markets Tribunal
  (Legal Assistance) Regulations
  2001 (SI 2001/3632) 20.10

Insider Dealing (Securities and
  Regulated Markets) Order 1994
  (SI 1994/187) 4.21, 4.23, 6.17, 8.01,
                     8.03, 8.25–8.28, 8.40,
                     App 2D (p 308–11)
  Art 2 .... 8.27
  Art 4 .... 8.28, 8.36, 8.39, 8.42, 8.43–8.46
  Art 5 .... 8.37
  Art 6 .... 8.37
  Art 7 .... 8.37
  Art 8 .... 8.37, 8.38, 8.42, 8.45
  Art 9 .... 8.30
  Art 10 .... 10.04
  Sch 1 .... 8.30, 8.35, 8.41
Insider Dealing (Securities and
  Regulated Markets) (Amendment)
  Order 1996 (SI 1996/1561) 8.26
Insider Dealing (Securities and
  Regulated Markets) (Amendment)
  Order 2000 (SI 2000/1923) 8.26

Insider Dealing (Securities and Regulated
  Markets) (Amendment) Order 2002
  (SI 2002/1874) 8.26, 8.34
  Art 2(2) 8.30

Perjury (Northern Ireland) Order 1979
  Art 10 (SI 1979/1714) 22.49

Traded Securities (Disclosure)
  Regulations 1994 (SI 1994 no 188) ... 6.76
Treaty of Lisbon (Changes in
  Terminology) Order 2011
  (SI 2011/1043) 8.28
Tribunal Procedure (Upper Tribunal)
  Rules 2008 (SI 2008 No 2698) 24.62

EUROPEAN UNION

Commission Directive 2003/124/EC of
  22 December 2003 implementing
  Directive 2003/6/EC of the
  European Parliament and of the
  Council as regards the definition
  and public disclosure of inside
  information and the definition of
  market manipulation 14.07, 16.31,
                              16.33, 16.52
  Art 1(1) 16.33, 16.35, 16.53
Commission Directive 2004/72/EC
  of 29 April 2004 implementing
  Directive 2003/6/EC of the
  European Parliament and of
  the Council as regards accepted
  market practices, the definition
  of inside information in relation
  to derivatives on commodities,
  the drawing up of lists of insiders,
  the notification of managers'
  transactions and the notification of
  suspicious transactions Art 7 ..... 21.26
Council Directive 79/279/EEC of 5 Mar
  1979 coordinating the conditions
  for the admission of securities to
  official stock exchange listing 4.10
Council Directive 80/390/EEC of 17
  March 1980 coordinating the
  requirements for the drawing up,
  scrutiny and distribution of the
  listing particulars to be published
  for the admission of securities to
  official stock exchange listing 4.10
Council Directive 82/121/EEC of 15 Feb
  1982 on information to be published
  on a regular basis by companies the

shares of which have been admitted to official stock-exchange listing 4.10
Council Directive 89/592/EEC of 13 November 1989 coordinating regulations on insider dealing ('Insider Dealing Directive') . . . . . . 4.01–4.28, 5.03, 5.34, 6.26, 6.115, 7.03, 9.02, 14.09, 16.18, 25.29, App 2A (p 296–300)
Art 1(1) 4.18, 6.02, 6.24, 6.70
Art 1(2) 4.21, 4.23, 8.14
Art 2 . . . . .4.13, 4.14, 5.08
Art 2(1) 4.15, 7.03, 7.24, 9.02, 11.10, 11.12
Art 2(3) 9.02
Art 2(4) 11.40
Art 3 . . . . 4.14
Art 4 . . . . 4.13, 4.14
Art 5 . . . . 4.23, 10.06
Art 7 . . . . 6.76
Art 8 .12.04, 12.08

Directive 2003/6/EC of the European Parliament and of the Council of 28 Jan 2003 on Insider Dealing and Market Manipulation (Market Abuse) 14.07–14.11, 14.12, 15.02, 15.18, 15.23, 16.18, 16.20, 16.31, 16.48, 16.66, 16.71, 16.78, 16.82, 18.01, 21.25, 21.26, 25.01, 25.07, 25.08, 25.27
Art 1(3) 15.26
Art 2(1) 16.16, 16.17, 16.19, 16.21
Art 4 . . . . 16.09
Art 9 . . . . 21.25
Art 17(2) 16.55

Directive 2004/39/EC of the European Parliament and of the Council of 21 April 2004 on markets in financial instruments amending Council Directives 85/611/EEC and 93/6/EEC and Directive 2000/12/EC of the European Parliament and of the Council and repealing Council Directive 93/22/EEC. 15.23, 15.27, 25.08
Art 4(14) 15.18
Art 4(15) 15.24
Art 4(18) 15.26
Art 47. . . . . .15.19
Art 69 . . . . 15.26

UNITED STATES

Securities Act 1933
  s 5 . . . . 8.43
Securities and Exchange Act 1934 . . . . . . 3.02
Securities and Exchange Act 1934
  s 10. . . . . 3.02

TREATIES AND CONVENTIONS

European Convention on Human Rights
  Art 6 . . . . .20.01–20.25
  Art 6(1) 20.02
  Art 6(2) 11.44, 11.46, 16.21, 20.02, 20.04, 20.10
  Art 6(3) 20.02, 20.04, 20.10
  First Protocol, Art 1 . . . . 13.23

Treaty of Rome 1957
  Art 67. . . . . .4.02, 4.04

LIST OF ABBREVIATIONS

ACPO	Association of Chief Police Officers
AIM	Alternative Investment Market
BIS	Department for Business Innovation and Skills
CESR	Committee of European Securities Regulators
CFD	Contracts for Difference
CJA	Criminal Justice Act 1993
CJA 2003	Criminal Justice Act 2003
COB	FSA's Conduct of Business Sourcebook
CPIA	Criminal Procedure and Investigations Act 1986
CPS	Crown Prosecution Service
CSA	Company Securities (Insider Dealing) Act 1995
DEPP	FSA's Decisions Procedures and Penalties Manual
DOCIR	Financial Services and Markets Act 2000 (Disclosure of Confidential Information) Regulations 2001
DOJ	US Department of Justice
DPA	Data Protection Act 1998
DTI	Department of Trade and Industry (now the Department for Business Innovation and Skills (BIS)
DTR	UKLA's Disclosure Rules and Transparency Rules
EA	Emissions Allowances
EC	European Community
ECHR	European Convention on Human Rights
ECJ	European Court of Justice
EFCD	Enforcement and Financial Crime Division (FSA)
EG	FSA Enforcement Guide
ESD	Enforcement Submissions Document
ESME	European Securities Markets Expert Group
EU	European Union
EU ETS	EU Emissions Trading System
FBI	Federal Bureau of Investigations
FCA	Financial Conduct Authority
FRN	Floating Rate Notes
FSA	Financial Services Authority
FS Act 2012	Financial Services Act 2012
FSMA	Financial Services and Markets Act 2000
FSMT	Financial Services and Markets Tribunal
FT	Financial Times
ICAP	Intercapital (*see also* ISDX)
IDD	Insider Dealing Directive 1989

IDO	Insider Dealing (Securities and Regulated Markets) Order 1994 (as amended)
IPO	Initial Public Offering
IR	Investigation Report
ISDX	ICAP Securities and Derivatives Exchange
LSE	London Stock Exchange
MAD	Market Abuse Directive 2003
MAR	Code of Market Conduct
MiFID	Markets in Financial Instruments Directive 2004
MOU	Memorandum of Understanding
MTF	Multilateral Trading Facility
NASDAQ	National Association of Securities Dealers Automated Quotations, a US computerised system for trading in securities
NDA	Non-Disclosure Agreement
NOMAD	Nominated Adviser
NYSE	New York Stock Exchange
OFCOM	Office of Communications
OFEX	Off Exchange Market
OTC	Over the Counter
OTF	Organised Trading Facility
PFL	Preliminary Findings Letter
PIR	Preliminary Investigation Report
PLUS-DX	PLUS Derivatives Exchange (now known as the ICAP Securities and Derivatives Exchange (ISDX)
PMQI	Financial Services and Markets Act 2000 (Prescribed Markets and Qualifying Investments) Order 2001
POCA	Proceeds of Crime Act 2002
RAPR	Recognised Auction Platform Regulations 2011
RDC	Regulatory Decisions Committee
RINGA	Relevant Information Not Generally Available (s 118(4) Market Abuse—Misuse of Information)
RIPA	Regulation of Investigatory Powers Act 2000
RIS	Regulatory Information Service
RNS	Regulatory News Service
SABRE II	Surveillance Analysis of Business Reporting System
SDM	Settlement Decision Maker
SEC	Securities and Exchange Commission
SFA	Securities and Futures Authority
SFO	Serious Fraud Office
SIB	Securities and Investments Board
SOCPA	Serious Organised Crime and Police Act 2005
STR	Suspicious Transaction Report
SUP	FSA Supervision Manual
SYSC	FSA Handbook—Senior Management Arrangements, Systems and Controls
Tribunal	Financial Services and Markets Tribunal or Upper Tribunal (Tax and Chancery Chamber)
UKLA	UK Listing Authority

1

INTRODUCTION TO INSIDER DEALING

1. Introduction	1.01	3. The value of information in		
2. What is insider dealing in		determining pricing	1.15	
practical terms?	1.02	The Efficient Capital Market Hypothesis	1.17	
Ivan Boesky	1.03	4. The prevalence of insider dealing		
Raj Rajaratnam	1.06	in the UK today	1.22	
The *Littlewood* case	1.08	The Market Cleanliness Statistic	1.22	
Sanders and others	1.10	Tougher enforcement action	1.25	

1. Introduction

Insider dealing is a criminal offence in the UK under Part V of the Criminal Justice Act 1993 ('CJA').[1] It is also a civil offence under the market abuse regime contained in Part VIII of the Financial Services and Markets Act 2000 ('FSMA').[2] This Chapter covers what insider dealing is from a practical perspective, with reference to some real-life examples. It also considers the value of information in determining pricing, and deals with the prevalence of insider dealing in the UK markets today, as shown by the Market Cleanliness Statistic developed by the Financial Services Authority ('FSA'). It concludes by considering the FSA's tougher Enforcement regime and the current and likely future effects of this strategy under the new Financial Conduct Authority ('FCA'). **1.01**

2. What is insider dealing in practical terms?

An insider dealer aims to beat the system by trading on significant information that he knows but other market participants don't. The insider dealer thereby profits from the fact that the price at which he is buying or selling securities does not reflect the information that he holds. In this way, the insider dealer is aiming to beat the odds or at least move them significantly in his favour. **1.02**

---

[1] See Chapters 5 to 13.
[2] See Chapters 14 to 20.

In essence, it is cheating.³ And the rewards can be huge as some of the more infamous cases demonstrate.

*Ivan Boesky*⁴

1.03 In the 1980s, Ivan Boesky was one of New York's most successful and renowned risk arbitrageurs. He had amassed a multi-million-pound fortune by betting on corporate takeovers—essentially taking stakes in companies in the expectation that the companies would be taken over and that he would benefit from the corresponding rise in the share price. For many years, Mr Boesky epitomised the material and acquisitive culture of the 1980s. He even wrote a book on the secrets of arbitrage.⁵ It is said that the character of Gordon Gekko in the film *Wall Street*⁶ was based on him (at least in part). Boesky made a famous speech on the positive aspects of greed at the University of California (Berkeley) School of Business Commencement Ceremony in which he has been quoted as saying, 'I think greed is healthy. You can be greedy and still feel good about yourself.'⁷

1.04 His father-in-law, Ben Silberstein, apparently once described him as having 'the hide of a rhinoceros and the nerve of a burglar'.⁸ Perhaps these qualities were also ultimately his downfall, because it turned out that Mr Boesky's millions were not based wholly on his acute financial judgement and timing. In fact, he relied on a network of paid informants, mostly financial professionals involved in takeover negotiations, who fed him information about forthcoming corporate takeovers in return for a percentage of the profits from his trades. As with the rhinoceros, it appears that subtlety was not his strong point as Mr Boesky would commonly take huge positions in a stock just days before a takeover announcement.

1.05 His downfall came when one of his paid informants—Dennis Levine—turned informer on him. Mr Boesky ultimately struck a deal with the US Federal Authorities, in which he informed on other participants in his network of informants and provided evidence via covert tape recordings and wiretaps. Mr Boesky agreed to pay a $100 million fine; however, as part of the deal he was allowed to close out his positions by selling an estimated $1.6 billion in stocks and other assets,

---

³ See remarks of the Lord Chief Justice in *R v Christopher McQuoid*, Court of Appeal (Criminal Division) 10 June 2009, [2009] EWCA Crim 1301, [2010] 1 Cr App R (S) 43.
⁴ Myles Meserve, 'Meet Ivan Boesky, the Infamous Wall Streeter who inspired Gordon Gekko', *Business Insider* (26 July 2012).
⁵ Ivan F Boesky, *Merger Mania: Arbitrage: Wall Street's Best Kept Money-Making Secret* (Holt Rinehart & Winston 1985).
⁶ Oliver Stone (dir), *Wall Street* (20th Century Fox 1987).
⁷ Speech at the School of Business Administration Commencement Ceremony, University of California (Berkeley), May 1986.
⁸ Christopher Byron, 'The Phantom of Wall Street: How Ivan Boesky's Bitter Legacy Hauns Mike Milken and His Firm', *New York Magazine* (4 December 1989, reprinted 1 Apr 2012).

and also pay debts in advance of his fraud charges being made public. Ultimately, in 1987, Mr Boesky was sentenced to three years' imprisonment but served only twenty-two months. Thereafter he retired to his California mansion to live a quiet life as an exceptionally wealthy man.

Raj Rajaratnam

In 2009, Raj Rajaratnam was declared the 236th richest American by Forbes magazine, with an estimated net worth of $1.8 billion. He owned and ran a multibillion dollar New York hedge fund called the Galleon Group. In October 2009, he was arrested by the Federal Bureau of Investigation (FBI) on allegations of insider trading. It was alleged that he ran a vast network of friends and associates—corporate insiders who leaked him inside information upon which Galleon then traded. **1.06**

Mr Rajaratnam was convicted of criminal conspiracy and securities fraud charges[9] and was sentenced in October 2011 to eleven years' imprisonment (the largest sentence ever imposed for insider dealing in the US). In addition, the US Securities and Exchange Commission ('SEC') obtained judgment against him for $92.8 million.[10] Total financial penalties (civil and criminal) came to over $150 million. He is currently appealing his criminal conviction and the financial penalties imposed. **1.07**

The *Littlewood* case

Husband and wife team Christian and Angie Littlewood, together with their co-conspirator (Helmy Omar Sa'aid) were arrested in 2010 following a lengthy FSA investigation. In January 2011, the three pleaded guilty at Southwark Crown Court to eight counts of insider dealing which brought them approximately £590,000 in profits.[11] **1.08**

Inside information about forthcoming takeovers was leaked by Christian Littlewood who worked as a senior investment banker, to his wife Angie and Mr Sa'aid, a family friend, both of whom traded on the information. Christian Littlewood was subsequently jailed for 40 months, with the other two receiving suspended sentences of two years' imprisonment respectively.[12] Subsequently, the Littlewoods were ordered to pay confiscation orders totalling £1.5 million.[13] **1.09**

---

[9] *United States v Raj Rajaratnam*, 09 CR 1184 (RJH) (SDNY).
[10] *Securities and Exchange Commission v Raj Rajaratnam and others,* US District Court Southern District of New York 09 Civ 8811 (JSR); 'SEC Obtains Record $92.8 Million Penalty Against Raj Rajaratnam' Securities and Exchange Commission Release 2011-233.
[11] *R v Littlewood and others*, unreported, Southwark Crown Court, His Honour Judge Anthony Leonard QC, 10 Jan 2011. FSA/PN/062/2011.
[12] *R v Littlewood and others*, unreported, Southwark Crown Court, His Honour Judge Anthony Leonard QC, 2 Feb 2011. FSA/PN/018/2011.
[13] *R v Littlewood and others*, unreported, Southwark Crown Court, His Honour Judge Anthony Leonard QC, 20 Aug 2012. FSA/PN/082/2012.

Sanders and others

1.10 In May 2012, James Sanders, director of now defunct brokerage firm Blue Index Ltd ('Blue Index'), his wife Miranda Sanders, and his colleague James Swallow pleaded guilty at Southwark Crown Court, to a total of eighteen counts of insider dealing.[14]

1.11 Miranda Sanders' sister, Annabel McClellan, passed inside information to the Sanders, on mergers in the US, where her husband was a partner in Deloitte's M&A division in San Francisco. James Sanders then traded on the information and also encouraged the clients of Blue Index to trade. He also disclosed information on some of the stocks to his co-director James Swallow who also traded.

1.12 Total profits generated by the defendants were approximately £1.9 million, while the total profits generated by the clients of Blue Index were approximately £10.2 million. James Sanders was subsequently sentenced to four years' imprisonment with the other two each receiving ten months' imprisonment.[15]

1.13 The case was significant for being the most serious insider dealing case prosecuted in the UK to date and also for being the first to involve a parallel investigation by the US SEC and US Department of Justice ('DOJ'), together with the FBI.

1.14 Annabel McClellan reached a 'no admissions' settlement with the SEC which included the payment of a $1 million fine.[16] All claims by the SEC against her husband were dismissed. She also pleaded guilty to a charge brought by the DOJ and served an eleven-month prison sentence without parole.[17]

3. The value of information in determining pricing

> Gordon Gekko, the infamous anti-hero of the film *Wall Street* said, 'the most valuable commodity I know of is information'.[18]

1.15 All markets depend on information. Information is what determines the price of the commodities being traded. This is as true for the market stall-holder as it is in the world's financial centres. Information is as much a valuable commodity in these markets as in any other.

---

[14] *R v Sanders and others*, unreported, Southwark Crown Court, Mr Justice Simon, 20 June 2012. FSA/PN/060/2012 & FSA/PN/067/2012.

[15] *R v Sanders and others* (n 14).

[16] US Securities and Exchange Commission, Litigation Release No 22139, 25 October 2011, *Securities and Exchange Commission v Arnold McClellan and Annabel McClellan*, Case No 10-cv-5412 WHA (ND Cal, filed 30 Nov 2010).

[17] US, Northern District Court of California, before ALSUP J, *USA v Annabel McClellan*, No CR 10-0860 (WHA).

[18] *Stone* (n 6).

Prices are not determined in a vacuum. The value of something is determined by how many people want to buy and how many want to sell at a particular time. If more people want to buy than sell, then the price goes up. Conversely, if there are more sellers than buyers, then this will drive the price down. Information is what drives those buyers and sellers in that it helps them to decide what a commodity is worth at the time or is likely to be worth in the future. **1.16**

The Efficient Capital Market Hypothesis

In a perfect market, all available information about a commodity and its future prospects is equally available to all market participants, and therefore fully and instantly reflected in the commodity's price. This recognises that information, and equal access to information by all investors, is key to the fundamental fairness and equality of the free market. **1.17**

In the context of the financial markets, this is referred to by economists as the 'Efficient Capital Market Hypothesis'. This concept was brought to the world's attention by the famous economist Eugene Fama who described it thus: **1.18**

> The primary role of the capital market is the allocation of ownership of the economy's capital stock. In general terms, the ideal is a market in which prices provide accurate signals for resource allocation: that is, a market in which firms can make production-investment decisions, and investors can choose among the securities that represent ownership of firms' activities under the assumption that security prices at any time 'fully reflect' all available information. A market in which prices always 'fully reflect' available information.[19]

For this to work in practice, securities markets need to be perfectly efficient in reflecting information about stocks and the stock market as a whole. In such a perfect world, information would be quickly disseminated and incorporated into the price of a stock without delay. **1.19**

This way, market participants could be confident that the price they are paying represents the 'real' value of the security, because the real value would have been set by the market on the basis that all information relating to that security had been made public and equally available, and therefore factored into the share price by all **1.20**

---

[19] See Eugene Fama, 'Efficient Capital Markets: A Review of Theory and Empirical Work' (1970) 25 J Fin 383. For other articles on this topic see Ronald J Gilson and Reinier H Kraakman 'The Mechanisms of Market Efficiency' (1984) 70 Va L Rev 549; and Daniel R Fischel, 'Efficient Capital Markets, the Crash and the Fraud on the Market Theory' (1988–89) 74 Cornell L Rev 907. The current world financial crisis, coupled with several high-profile financial scandals, has caused most to question whether an efficient capital market has ever existed or is indeed even possible. For an interesting article on the Enron scandal in this context see Jonathan R Macey, 'Efficient Capital Markets, Corporate Disclosure and Enron' (2003–04) 89 Cornell L Rev 394. See also Gill North and Ross P Buckley, 'A Fundamental Re-Examination of Efficiency in Capital Markets in Light of the Global Financial Crisis', (2010) 33 UNSWLJ 714.

market participants. In a macro sense, this benefits the economy by improving its allocation of capital investment and by decreasing price volatility. In a micro sense, investor confidence increases, and the firm itself also benefits from accurate pricing of its securities through reduced investor uncertainty.

1.21 However, in the real world, a range of other factors operate to disrupt this perfect scenario. These factors include transaction costs, information which is not freely or readily available to all investors and disagreement among investors about the value and implications of the information that is available. These factors give rise to opportunities for the insider dealer to profit from the inequality of access to information that he holds, but other market participants do not.

4. The prevalence of insider dealing in the UK today

The Market Cleanliness Statistic

1.22 The evidence suggests that insider dealing is prevalent today. The FSA, responsible for monitoring standards in the UK financial markets until 1 April 2013, used what it termed the 'Market Cleanliness Statistic', to measure the prevalence of insider dealing prior to important corporate announcements. Since 2008, the Market Cleanliness Statistic has been included in the FSA's Annual Report. It will continue to be used by the FSA's successor, the Financial Conduct Authority ('FCA').

1.23 The Market Cleanliness Statistic analyses the share price movements in the two days prior to regulatory announcements, in order to identify movements that are abnormal. From this, it calculates the percentage of all announcements with abnormal pre-announcement price movements. This is known as the 'market cleanliness measure', and provides a measurable indicator of the extent of insider dealing.

1.24 Until 2010, the market cleanliness measure was around 30 per cent. However, in 2010 and 2011, this significantly declined to 21.2 per cent and 19.8 per cent respectively, the lowest levels since 2003. The FSA's last Annual Report (2012–13) noted that the level had dropped to 14.9 per cent in 2012. The FSA commented that this drop coincided with its greater emphasis on pursuing market abuse enforcement action, and in particular, its increased emphasis on criminal prosecutions and civil proceedings, coupled with higher financial penalties.[20]

---

[20] FSA Annual Report 2011/2012. See also 'Challenging the culture of market behaviour', Speech by Jamie Symington, Head of Wholesale Enforcement, FSA at the City and Financial Market Abuse Conference, London, 4 Dec 2012. See also FSA Annual Report 2012–13.

Tougher enforcement action

This tougher Enforcement approach is likely to continue. Tracey McDermott, the current Director of the Enforcement and Financial Crime Division ('EFCD') of the then FSA, said in November 2012: **1.25**

> Our current work to tackle insider dealing is a world away from where it was five or six years ago. Since 2009 we have seen twenty-one convictions, confiscation orders totalling more than £2.2m, prison sentences of up to forty months. On the civil side we have imposed penalties of £24.5 million (£18.5 million of which was imposed on individuals) and prohibited seventeen people for market abuse. This tough approach will continue.[21]

It will be interesting to see whether this continues to be reflected in the market cleanliness statistic in the coming years. **1.26**

Despite the inroads made by the FSA, it is plain that insider dealing is still happening in a large percentage of cases. This is not surprising given the potential for huge rewards and the difficulties in detection. What is clear is that from a legal perspective, insider dealing is an area that will continue to see increased FCA Enforcement action in the form of investigations and civil and criminal litigation. **1.27**

---

[21] 'Combating Financial Crime: Key themes and Priorities for 2013', Speech by Tracey McDermott, Director of the Enforcement and Financial Crime Division at the APCIMS Conference, 15 Nov 2012. See also, 'The Changing Face of Financial Crime', Speech by Martin Wheatley, FCA Chief Executive, at the FCA Financial Crime Conference and 'Keynote Address: Financial Crime in the FCA World', Speech by Tracey McDermott, Director of the FCA Enforcement and Financial Crime Division, at the FCA Financial Crime Conference, both published 1 July 2013.

2

TRADING ON THE FINANCIAL MARKETS—ESSENTIAL PRINCIPLES FOR INSIDER DEALING CASES

1. Introduction	2.01	Other sources of information	2.22
2. Shares	2.02	5. The price of shares	2.23
Ordinary shares	2.04	Market makers	2.23
Preference shares	2.06	Share trading example	2.25
Redeemable shares	2.08	6. Investors	2.26
Selling shares to outside investors	2.09	Trading strategies	2.28
3. UK stock exchanges	2.11	7. Contracts for difference	2.33
LSE Main Market	2.13	Shared CFD example: long trade	2.40
The Alternative Investment Market	2.14	Shared CFD example: short trade	2.40
ICAP Securities and Derivatives Exchange	2.15	An unsuccessful CFD trade	2.41
4. Availability of information and stock market pricing	2.16	Limiting losses	2.42
		8. Spread bets	2.47
Regulatory information services	2.20	Spread bet example	2.53

1. Introduction

2.01 This Chapter describes the essential principles of trading on the financial markets that are commonly encountered in insider dealing cases, including types of trading, the UK exchanges, and commonly encountered trading strategies.[1]

2. Shares

2.02 In the simplest terms, when a new company is formed, its owners put cash (referred to as 'capital') into the business to start it up and keep it going. In return for this,

---

[1] For a more in-depth analysis of company law see generally Brenda Hannigan, *Company Law* (OUP 2012); Charles Wild and Stuart Weinstein, *Smith and Keenan's Company Law* (Longman 2011); Paul Davies, *Gower and Davies' Principles of Modern Company Law* (Sweet & Maxwell 2008).

the company issues shares to its owners (often referred to as 'securities', 'equities' or 'stock'), which represent their ownership rights over the company's assets and their share of the income as the business develops. The amount of shares in a company is known as its 'share capital'.

2.03 As the company grows and develops, it may require more capital to purchase assets, expand, or generally finance its trading. The company's owners can go to the bank for a loan, or it may be more advantageous to raise capital by issuing further shares in the company and selling them. The price or value of a company's shares should reflect the value of the company's assets and business. In the UK, there are several different types of shares. The most common types are described below.

Ordinary shares

2.04 The most common type of share in a company is the 'ordinary share'. Ordinary shareholders can receive income from the company in the form of a dividend per share, which is paid by the company to the shareholders on an annual basis.

2.05 If the company is doing well, then the dividend may increase; however, if it is doing badly, then the dividend may reduce or be cut entirely. An ordinary shareholder usually also has certain other rights, such as being able to vote at company meetings. However, usually the main reason for an external investor to buy ordinary shares in a company is for the shares to increase in value so that he can make a profit on his initial investment.

Preference shares

2.06 Preference shares typically carry a right that gives the holder preferential treatment when dividends are distributed to shareholders. Shares in this category have a fixed value, and usually the shareholders have rights to their dividend ahead of ordinary shareholders. If the company is wound up, preference shareholders are likely to be repaid the par or nominal value of their shares ahead of ordinary shareholders.

2.07 If a dividend cannot be paid in any one year, the dividend in relation to these shares will be carried forward to successive years. These are known as 'cumulative preference shares'.

Redeemable shares

2.08 Redeemable shares come with an agreement that the company can buy them back at a future date, which can be at a fixed date or a date chosen by the company.

Selling shares to outside investors

2.09 If the company's shares are owned only by its founders, management, or private investors, then it is a 'private company'. If, however, the company decides to raise finance by issuing shares and selling them to outside investors or to the general public, then it will need to re-register as a public company. A public company sells shares to outside investors by way of an Initial Public Offering ('IPO'). If the company is still fairly small, then it may choose not to be listed on a stock exchange; but once it reaches a certain size, and in order to attract a wider range of outside investment, it may seek to have its shares traded on a stock exchange, and thereby become a 'listed company'.

2.10 Once a company's shares are listed on a stock exchange, it becomes easier to raise capital from a wider range of investors because the stock exchange provides a trading platform upon which the company's shares can be bought and sold, and also from which the company can sell further issues of its shares. This is known as a 'public offering' or 'placing'.[2]

3. UK stock exchanges

2.11 Modern stock exchanges are electronic trading systems that enable persons to trade in shares either directly with each other on an order-driven basis, or with market participants, under the overall regulatory umbrella of the particular stock exchange's rules and its regulatory requirements.

2.12 There are three principal UK stock markets. The London Stock Exchange ('LSE') Official List or Main Market, the Alternative Investment Market ('AIM'), which is also run by the LSE and ICAP Securities and Derivatives Exchange ('ISDX').[3]

LSE Main Market

2.13 In order to list on the Main Market, a company must comply with stringent requirements and regulations. In general terms, a company has to have a minimum of 25 per cent of its shares in public hands; a trading record of at least three years; and must comply with the rules of the UK Listing Authority ('UKLA'). Today, the main market has around 1800 companies with a total market capitalisation of more than £3500 billion.

The Alternative Investment Market

2.14 The Alternative Investment Market, known as AIM, was launched by the LSE in the mid-1990s to appeal to smaller, newer companies that may not have the track

---

[2] See Eilis Feran, *The Principles of Corporate Finance Law* (OUP 2008).
[3] See Michael Blair QC, George Walker, and Stuart Willey, *Financial Markets and Exchanges Law* (OUP 2012). For a simple guide to the City, see William M Clarke, *How the City of London Works: An Introduction to its Financial Markets* (Sweet & Maxwell 2008). See also Glen Arnold, *The Financial Times Guide to the Financial Markets* (FT Guides 2011).

record of those on the Main Market. As such, it has more flexible requirements. It does not require any minimum percentage of shares to be in public hands; a company does not need a trading record to list on AIM, and admission documents do not have to be submitted to the LSE or the UKLA. A company that wishes to list on AIM has to appoint a broker and a Nominated Adviser ('NOMAD'), which is an LSE-approved adviser whose role it is to manage the admission of the company to AIM and ensure that the regulatory requirements have been met.[4]

ICAP Securities and Derivatives Exchange

The ICAP Securities and Derivatives Exchange, known as 'ISDX', is a London-based stock exchange which provides a range of fully listed and growth markets. ISDX allows a company to raise capital on its primary market, and investors are able to trade in the company's shares on an active secondary market. The requirements for listing are not as stringent as those on the other markets, and therefore companies may start here with a view to moving up to AIM or the Main Market in the future.   **2.15**

4. Availability of information and stock market pricing

The share price in the market at any point in time should reflect the supply and demand for the shares. Supply and demand is in turn affected by the available market information, such as the announcement of the company's results, or more unusual events such as mergers and acquisitions activity, or a placing, as well as overall market conditions, political events, and other factors outside the company's control. A company's share price should therefore reflect all these factors.   **2.16**

The market reacts to new information by adjusting the price of the company's shares to reflect its reaction to the information. This may not happen immediately while the market digests the information, but pretty quickly the price will be adjusted up or down to reflect the new supply and demand for the shares resulting from the market's reaction to the news.   **2.17**

Before a company's shares are first allowed to be traded on a stock market, it has to publish a Listing Prospectus which contains detailed information about the company, its business, and its financial situation. The purpose of a Listing Prospectus is to provide all relevant information that a prospective investor needs to decide whether or not to invest in the company.   **2.18**

Once a company has listed on a stock market, there is a continuing obligation on it to make available to the market all price-sensitive information in a timely manner.   **2.19**

---

[4] For a full treatment of the AIM market, see Keith Hatchick et al, *The Alternative Investment Market Handbook* (Jordan Publishing 2002).

The timely provision of information to the market is fundamental to the operation of an orderly market.

Regulatory information services

2.20 The continuing obligations of a UK listed company to announce information are contained in the UKLA's Disclosure Rules and Transparency Rules ('DTR').[5] These DTR require a company to publish as soon as possible, through a Regulatory Information Service ('RIS') (an approved newswire service), any price-sensitive information which directly concerns the company and which is not already known to the market. A company is able to delay an announcement, if making the information public would prejudice its legitimate interests (for example, if the matter is still under negotiation or public disclosure would be likely to affect its outcome). However, once the matter is agreed, an announcement must be made as soon as possible.

2.21 Once an announcement has been made via the RIS, it will be quickly picked up by the press and internet media. Often, a company will send a press release to certain journalists at the same time as the RIS announcement is made. Research analysts at the investment firms that cover the company or its sector will also closely monitor all announcements. Research analysts will also produce reports on the companies they cover, expressing views on whether a company is a good investment, and these will be sent to the firm's investment clients.

Other sources of information

2.22 Alongside all this information, there is usually a good deal of rumour and speculation circulating in the market at any given time. This may be little more than internet chat room, or bulletin board, gossip or it may receive wider coverage in the more mainstream press. If the rumours concern an actual event (such as negotiations for a takeover or merger), then it may be that there has been a 'leak'. Depending on the nature and timing of the leak, the company in question may be forced to make an announcement either confirming or denying the rumours.

5. The price of shares

Market makers

2.23 In many stock markets, a listed company will usually have at least one market maker dealing in its shares. A market maker is a firm that accepts the risk of holding a certain number of shares in a particular security in order to facilitate trading.

---

[5] FCA Handbook of Rules and Guidance.

Market makers normally quote a share price in terms of a 'bid' and 'offer' price. The bid price is the price at which the market maker will buy a given number of shares on an immediate basis. The offer price is the price at which the market maker will make an immediate sale of a given quantity of shares. The 'mid' price falls exactly between these two and is the price usually quoted in the newspapers.

Market makers are obliged to quote a bid and offer price for a given, minimum number of shares. This makes the market much more liquid, because it means that anyone wanting to buy or sell those shares will be able to do so immediately. As with any other type of trading, the market maker is looking to buy the shares at a lower price than he is able to sell them at, and thereby profit from the difference. For this reason, the bid price will always be lower than the offer price. The difference between these two prices is called the 'spread'. The size of the spread will usually depend on whether a share is 'liquid' (regularly traded), in which case the spread will be smaller, or 'illiquid' (thinly traded), in which case the spread tends to be wider. **2.24**

What this means from an investor's perspective is that for him to make a profit, the offer price when he comes to sell his shares needs to be higher than the bid price at which he bought them. The effect of this can be illustrated by the following simple example: **2.25**

Share trading example

> Tesco plc is trading at a mid-market price of 100p. The market maker is offering a bid / offer spread of 95p / 105p.
>
> Mr B buys 1000 shares at 105p (£1050). On top of this, he will also have to pay commission to his broker and stamp duty.
>
> One month later, the mid price has increased to 105p. The market maker adjusts his spread to 100p / 110p. If Mr B were to sell now, he would make a loss, because the best price he can get for his shares is 100p—ie: 5p lower than the price at which he bought them.
>
> Mr B therefore decides to hang on. He is lucky. Two weeks later, Tesco announces positive financial results. The mid price goes up to 130p. The market maker adjusts his spread to 125p / 135p. Mr B therefore sells his shares at 125p and makes a gross profit of £200. The market has moved 30p, but due to the spread, Mr B's profit equates to a move of only 20p.

6. Investors

There are a wide range of investors who buy and sell shares. At one end of the spectrum are the major financial institutions, such as insurance companies and **2.26** pension funds, and at the other end is the private individual investor.[6] Most private investors will typically use a stockbroker as the intermediary who will actually undertake the purchase or sale of the shares in question on their behalf.

2.27 The introduction of sophisticated electronic trading systems has provided some investors with the ability to trade directly through their stockbrokers instead of using a market maker. These systems allow potential buyers and sellers to put their orders directly into the system, and these are then automatically matched together. This works well for frequently traded (liquid) stocks; but illiquid stocks (which are not frequently traded) will still need a market maker to make a market in the stock and thereby facilitate trading.

Trading strategies

2.28 Investors will buy or sell shares on the basis of their view of the available information, their financial resources, investment goals, and attitude to risk, or for many other reasons. Some traders determine their trading strategy by a detailed analysis of the economic situation of the share or commodity (Fundamental analysis) or use an approach that concentrates on price charts and market patterns as a way of predicting price movements (Technical or Chartist analysis).

2.29 Some investors are more interested in the dividend income from the shares, while others are more concerned with capital growth. Some argue that there is a difference between 'investing' and 'trading'. 'Investing' is when an investor buys a share with a view to a longer term capital return or dividend income stream. 'Trading', on the other hand, is the buying and selling of an asset to obtain a short-term profit. A trader has no particular desire to own the underlying asset; his only interest is profit.

2.30 A trader uses market movements to try to maximise his return by buying shares and by selling shares he actually owns, or by the practice of 'short selling'. A 'long trade' is where a trader buys an asset with the expectation that it will rise. In an equity trade, this would mean buying the actual shares.

2.31 A 'short trade' is where the trader sells an asset that he does not own in the expectation that the price will fall and he can buy the asset back at a cheaper price and thereby 'cover' his short position.

2.32 Short selling is a particular trading mechanism used in a falling market. In summary, a short seller will borrow shares from someone who owns them (usually an institutional investor who is a long term holder of the shares) and then sell them

---

[6] For an accessible guide to investing in the UK Financial Markets, see Glenn Arnold, *The Financial Times Guide to Investing: The Definitive Companion to Investment and the Financial Markets* (FT Guides 2009); see also Dominic Connolly, *The UK Trader's Bible: The Complete Guide to Trading the UK Stock Market* (Harriman House 2005); David Stevenson, *Investing in shares for Dummies* (John Wiley & Sons 2012).

immediately. His aim is that the price will fall and he will be able to buy back the shares at a lower price and then return them to the lender, thereby profiting from the difference in price.

7. Contracts for difference

In modern global markets, it is no longer necessary to buy actual shares. Derivative products such as Contracts for Difference ('CFDs'), which track the market price of the shares, can be used instead. A CFD mirrors the value of an underlying asset, allowing an investor to trade that asset without actually having to own it. CFDs can be used to trade a wide range of financial products including shares, commodities, indices, and foreign exchange.[7] 2.33

A CFD is a contract between two parties (typically a broker and client) to settle for cash the difference between the opening price and closing price of a specific referenced underlying security, for example an equity. The size of a CFD position is quoted as being equivalent to a number of shares. The price of a CFD is based upon the price of the underlying instrument. The result of the trade is the difference on closure between the opening price and the closing price. 2.34

CFDs allow a trader to trade 'long' or 'short'. In an equity trade, this would mean buying or selling the actual shares. With a CFD, however, rather than buying or selling the actual shares, the trader opens a position by posting 'margin'—a percentage of the total value of the shares he wants to bet on. 2.35

The client will open a position with a CFD broker to buy or sell in a particular product, for example an equity. If the client believes the price of the equity, ie stock, will rise, then he will 'buy'; and if he believes that the price will fall, he will 'sell'. Rather than pay the full value of a transaction, the client only needs to pay a percentage[8] of the total value of the transaction when opening the position. This is called 'Initial Margin'. This margin allows leverage or 'gearing', which means that a trader can access a larger amount of shares for a smaller amount of money than he would be able to do if he was actually buying or selling the shares themselves. 2.36

In order to keep the position open, the client must make sure that the margin is maintained at the level required by the broker. If the trader's position moves 2.37

---

[7] CFDs are currently available in the United Kingdom, Hong Kong, The Netherlands, Poland, Portugal, Germany, Switzerland, Italy, Singapore, South Africa, Australia, Canada, New Zealand, Sweden, Norway, France, Ireland, Japan, and Spain. They are not permitted in the United States, due to restrictions by the US Securities and Exchange Commission ('SEC') on over-the-counter ('OTC') financial instruments. For a much more thorough treatment of Derivatives, see Edmund Parker, *Equity Derivatives: Documenting and Understanding Equity Derivative Products* (Globe Law and Business 2009).
[8] Typically this percentage ranges between 5 and 30 per cent.

against him so that he is below the required margin level on a trade, then he will be subject to a 'margin call' and he will have to pay additional money into his trading account to keep the position open or he may be forced to close his position (called 'closing out').

2.38 The CFD broker charges commission on a CFD trade which is calculated on the value of the total position not the margin paid. Because the client does not actually own the underlying shares, he does not have to pay stamp duty. However, gains on CFDs are taxable (and losses are tax deductible.)

2.39 The trader's ability to gear his investment by trading on margin, combined with no stamp duty, make the CFD an ideal instrument for short-term trading. However, the geared nature of a CFD means that both profits and losses can be magnified.

2.40 The geared nature of CFD trading, coupled with the fact that the trader does not need to purchase the underlying shares, makes this an attractive choice for an insider dealer, as he can take advantage of magnified profits while enjoying the relative certainty that the trade is unlikely to move against him.

Share CFD example: long trade

> **Burberry Group plc is currently trading at 250–250.5p**
>
> *Trader A* believes that the price of Burberry Group will rise and places a trade to buy CFDs equivalent to 10,000 shares at 250.5p. The total value of the contract would be £25,050. However, he only needs to post initial margin of 10% (£2505).
>
> The commission on the trade is £50.10 (£25,050 x 0.20%), but because he is trading in CFDs there is no stamp duty to pay.
>
> A week later, *Trader A*'s prediction is proved correct, and Burberry Group rise to 260–260.5p, and he therefore decides to close his position. He therefore sells 10,000 CFDs at 260p (£26,000). The commission on this trade is £52 (£26,000 x 0.20%).
>
> The profit on the trade is calculated as follows:
>
> | | |
> |---|---|
> | Opening level | 250.50p |
> | Closing level | 260.00p |
> | Difference | 9.50p |
> | Profit on trade (9.5p x 10,000) | £950 |

> **Overall profit**
> To calculate the overall profit, the trader must take into account the commission and daily financing charges on the trade (interest calculated and charged on a daily basis on the contract value).

Profit on trade	£950.00
Commission	-£102.10
Finance charge	-£25.00
Overall profit on the trade	£822.90

Share CFD example: short trade

Sage Group plc is currently trading at 600–601p.

Trader B believes that Sage is overvalued and is going to fall. He therefore places a trade to sell CFDs equivalent to 1000 shares at 600p. The total value of the contract is £6000. He posts initial margin at 10% (£600).

The commission on the trade is £12 (£6000 x 0.20%).

A week later, *Trader B*'s sprediction proves correct and Sage falls to 530–531p. He decides to close his position. He therefore buys 1000 Sage Group CFDs at 531p, and pays £10.62 commission.

The profit on the trade is calculated as follows:

Opening level	600.00p
Closing level	531.00p
Difference	69.00p
Profit on trade (69p x 1000)	£690.00

Overall profit

To calculate the overall profit, the trader must take into account the commission and financing charges on the deal. With a short position, the financing charge is actually credited to the trader.

Profit on trade	£690.00
Commission	-£22.62
Financing charge	+£7.40
Overall profit on the trade	£674.78

An unsuccessful CFD trade

2.41 The nature of geared trading is that, if a trade goes against him, the trader is potentially exposed to the full amount of the loss that he would have suffered if he had actually owned the underlying shares:

Burberry Group plc is currently trading at 250–250.5p.

Trader A believes that the price of Burberry Group will rise and places a trade to buy CFDs equivalent to 10,000 shares at 250.5p. The total value of the contract would be £25,050. However he would only need to post initial margin of 10% (£2505).

The commission on the trade is £50.10 (£25,050 x 0.20%), and because he is buying CFDs, there is no stamp duty to pay.

A week later, *Trader A*'s prediction proves incorrect, and Burberry Group has in fact fallen to 220–220.5p. He therefore decides to close his position. He sells 10,000 CFDs at 220p (£22,000). The commission on this trade is £44 (£22,000 x 0.20%).

The loss on the trade is calculated as follows:

Opening level	250.50p
Closing level	220.00p
Difference	-30.50p
Loss on trade (30.5p x 10,000)	£3050

Overall loss

To calculate the overall loss the trader must take into account the commission and financing charges.

Loss on trade	£3050.00
Commission	£94.10
Financing charge	£25.00
Overall loss on the trade	£3169.10

Limiting losses

2.42 In order to limit his potential losses, it is possible for a client to place a 'stop loss' on a CFD trade.

2.43 A stop loss is a price level set by the client on a particular trade at which the trade should be closed out. A stop loss can be 'guaranteed', which means that the broker guarantees that the trade will be closed out at the desired price. The broker charges a fee for this service which is charged up front—even if the stop does not ultimately need to be exercised.

2.44 A 'non-guaranteed' stop triggers an order to close the trader's position once the selected level has been reached. The broker will use 'best endeavours' to achieve closure; however, should it not be possible, perhaps because the market moves very quickly, then closure may only be achieved at a worse, and sometimes much worse, level than the level selected. This is known as 'slippage'. There is usually no charge for a non-guaranteed stop.

Trailing stops track the client's position while the market moves in his favour, allowing the client to lock in profits without the need to frequently re-adjust his stop level. Trailing stops are non-guaranteed, and there is usually no charge for this service. **2.45**

A limit order is an instruction to take profit by closing the position if the price moves to a specified level in the client's favour. This enables the client to realise a pre-selected level of profit. **2.46**

8. Spread bets

Spread betting, like CFDs, also enables a client to invest in the fortunes of a certain share without actually buying it. Spread betting in the financial markets has grown significantly in recent years and spread betting organisations will now accept bets on a large number of quoted UK and foreign shares, as well as a wide range of other situations such as sporting events, election results and movements in a particular financial index.[9] **2.47**

With a spread bet, the client is able to bet not just on whether the share will go up or down but on the extent to which it does so. When an investor wants to place a spread bet on the price of a share, he will approach a spread betting company to obtain a quote for a bet that the price of a particular share will rise or fall by a particular date in the future. This is quoted in terms of a bid and offer price, the difference between these being 'the spread'. **2.48**

The spread is based on the current market bid and offer quotation for the actual share and will usually also have the spread betting company's commission and financing charges wrapped up in the spread. This means that the spread will in most instances be wider than the spread for the underlying share or a CFD. **2.49**

The client will place a spread bet by betting an amount of money per unit change in the price of the underlying share. Typically this will be an amount in pounds (or dollars) per 'point'. A point is usually a 1p (or 1 cent) movement in the underlying share price. **2.50**

As with a CFD, if the client thinks that the underlying price of the security on which the spread bet is based will rise, he takes out an 'up' bet (also called going 'long'). The price at which the up bet starts is the higher buy price of the spread. **2.51**

---

[9] For an accessible guide to spread betting see Stuart Fieldhouse, *The FT Guide to Financial Spread Betting* (FT Guides 2011). See also Malcolm Pryor, *The Financial Spread Betting Handbook: A Guide to Making Money Trading Spread Bets* (Harriman House 2007).

The length of the bet will typically be for a fixed period, or it may be a rolling bet which rolls over each day until it is closed. At any time up to the end of the period, the investor may close out the bet by making a 'down' bet (also called a 'closing' bet) for the same amount per point. If the 'down' price at any point in time exceeds his opening 'up' price then he can close the bet at a profit.

2.52 If the client thinks a share is going to fall in value, he will make a down bet (also called going 'short'). This opens at the lower sell price and is closed out by an up bet at the higher buying price. In both cases, as with CFDs, the initial margin is payable as a percentage of the value of the overall trade. Similarly, the client may be subject to a margin call if his position moves against him.

2.53 As with CFDs, a client can protect his position by putting in place a guaranteed or non-guaranteed stop loss. Like CFDs, there is no stamp duty to pay. As spread betting is considered to be a form of gambling, profits on a spread bet are tax free in the UK, but on the other hand losses are not tax deductible.

Spread bet example

> **Burberry Group plc is currently quoted in the market at 249–251p, with a mid-market price of 250p.**
>
> *Trader A* believes that the price of Burberry Group will rise. The spread betting company with which he has his spread betting account is offering a spread of 248–252p.
>
> *Trader A* therefore places an 'Up' bet on Burberry Group at £10 per point at 252p. This is the equivalent of buying 1000 shares at £2.52. He is required to post a 10% margin (252 x £10 x 10% = £252).
>
> The market moves in *Trader A*'s favour, and Burberry Group's share price has risen to 280p. The spread betting company has therefore adjusted its spread to 278–282p.
>
> *Trader A* therefore decides to close his position. He places a 'Down' bet on Burberry Group at 278p.
>
> The profit on the trade is calculated as follows:
>
> | | |
> |---|---|
> | Opening level | 252p |
> | Closing level | 278p |
> | Difference | 26p |
> | Profit on trade (26 x £10 stake) | £260 |

However, if the trade has gone against him, and the price of Burberry Group has fallen to 220p, then the spread betting company will also adjust its spread accordingly—perhaps to 218–222p.

Trader A decides to close his position. He therefore places a Down bet on Burberry Group at 218p. His loss is calculated as follows:

Opening level	252p
Closing level	218p
Difference	-34p
Loss on trade (34 x £10 stake)	£340

2.54 This example demonstrates the risk inherent in spread betting. Not only does the gearing effect magnify potential losses, but also the size of the spread means that the trader does not obtain the full benefit if the price moves in his favour, but he will suffer a greater loss if the price moves against him. In the example above, a movement of 30p in the mid market price in the trader's favour results in a £260 profit; however, a movement of 30p against him results in a loss of £340.

3

A HISTORY OF INSIDER DEALING LEGISLATION IN THE UK

1. Introduction	3.01	The Justice Committee Report	3.20
2. Relevant developments in the US	3.02	The Stock Exchange and Takeover Panel Joint Statements	3.24
3. Economic theory	3.03	Privatisation	3.27
Henry Manne	3.04	Part V of the Companies Act 1980	3.31
The prevailing view	3.10	The Company Securities (Insider Dealing) Act 1985	3.37
4. The UK's response to insider dealing	3.12		
The Jenkins Report	3.14	The Financial Services Act 1986	3.41
The Panel on Takeovers and Mergers and the Stock Exchange	3.17		

1. Introduction

3.01 From the vantage point of the twenty-first century, there is general agreement that insider dealing is reprehensible, affects the cleanliness and integrity of markets, and damages investor confidence. It is also generally agreed that insider dealing should be the subject of legislative prohibition. But it was not always so. Insider dealing did not become a criminal offence in the UK until 1980 with the enactment of Part V of the Companies Act 1980. This Chapter summarises the most important developments in the history of insider dealing legizlation which led up to the criminalisation of insider dealing in the UK.

2. Relevant developments in the US

3.02 In terms of legislation to prohibit insider dealing, the US was ahead of the UK by some fifty years.[1] The Securities and Exchange Act 1934 ('1934 Act') created the

---

[1] For a compact summary of US Insider Dealing Regulation during this period, see Dennis C Hensley, 'Securities Regulation—Trading by Insiders—*SEC v Texas Gulf Sulphur Co* 401 F 2d 833 (2d cir 1968)' (1969) 10 Wm & Mary L Rev 755.

Securities and Exchange Commission ('SEC'). The SEC was President Franklin D Roosevelt's response to the Stock Market Crash of 1929 and the Great Depression that followed. It is a federal agency that has primary responsibility for enforcing the federal securities laws and regulating the US securities industry, markets, and exchanges. The SEC is able to bring civil enforcement actions against individuals and companies for violations of securities law, insider trading, and company violations. Under powers delegated by s 10 of the 1934 Act, the SEC enacted Rule 10b-5(3) which prohibited fraud or deceit in connection with the purchase or sale of securities. This rule was swiftly interpreted by US courts to provide a right of civil action to victims of insider trading.[2] By 1961, the SEC was using Rule 10b-5(3) as the basis for imposing and enforcing sanctions for insider trading,[3] and in 1968, the US Courts upheld this approach in the case of *SEC v Texas Gulf Sulphur Co*.[4]

3. Economic theory

Economic theorists have long been divided over whether insider dealing represents a vice or a benefit to the financial system. **3.03**

Henry Manne

In 1966, Professor Henry Manne published his book *Insider Trading and the Stock Market*[5] to a storm of criticism and debate.[6] In this work, Manne put forward the revolutionary hypothesis that insider dealing was, in terms of economic efficiency, positively beneficial.[7] **3.04**

Manne identified two principal ways in which insider trading benefitted society and / or the company whose stock the insider trades. **3.05**

---

[2] *Speed v Transamerica Corp*, 71 F Supp 457 (D Del 1945). Critics have suggested that Rule 10b-5(3) was never intended to address the issue of insider dealing and that, instead, the prohibition was developed through federal rule-making and judicial interpretation rather than through legislative action. See Stephen Bainbridge, 'A Critique of the Insider Trading Sanctions Act of 1984' (1985) 71 Va L Rev 498. See also Carlton and Fischel, 'The Regulation of Insider Trading' (1983) 35 Stan L Rev 857, 884 n 90; Dooley 'Enforcement of Insider Trading Restrictions' (1980) 66 Va L Rev 1, 55–69; Easterbrook, 'Insider Trading, Secret Agents, Evidentiary Privileges, and the Production of Information' (1981) Sup Ct Rev 309, 317–20.
[3] *In re Cady, Roberts & Co*, 40 SEC 907 (1961) 913.
[4] *SEC v Texas Gulf Sulphur Co* (n 1). See also 'Insider Trading on the Open Market: Non-disclosure and Texas Gulf Sulphur' (1969) 42 So Cal L Rev 309.
[5] Henry Manne, *Insider Trading and the Stock Market* (Free Press 1966).
[6] See S Bainbridge, 'Manne on Insider Dealing', UCLA School of Law, Law and Economics Research Paper Series, Research Paper No 08-04. See also Henry Manne, 'In Defense of Insider Trading' (1966) 44(6) Harv Bus Rev 113, which summarised his arguments for the Harvard Law Review. See also J A C Hetherington, 'Insider Trading and the Logic of the Law' (1967) 3 Wis L Rev 720.
[7] See also Henry Manne, 'Insider Trading: Hayek, Virtual Markets and the Dog that Did Not Bark' (2005) 31(1) J Corporation L 165.

3.06 First, he claimed that insider trading causes the price of the traded security to move towards the price that it would have achieved had the inside information been made public. On this basis, he claimed, traders, society, and the company benefit from increased price accuracy.

3.07 He described how this would work in practice. Individuals who possess material non-public information begin trading. Their trading has only a small effect on the price. Other traders then become aware of this trading through tips, leaks, or by market observation, and they too begin trading. As the volume of trading increases, the price continues to steadily increase and other traders enter the market. The cumulative effect of this pattern is to increase (or decrease) the share price to the level it would have achieved had the inside information been publicly disclosed at the outset. Without this, Manne argued, the stock price would remain at an artificial level until the public disclosure of the information, whereupon it would rapidly rise (or fall). Therefore, insider trading actually operates as a replacement for the public disclosure of information, and smooths out rapid price fluctuations.[8]

3.08 Secondly, Manne argued that insider trading was an efficient way to compensate a company's entrepreneurs for having created the information in question in the first place. He argued that this meant that the company benefitted directly, and society benefitted indirectly, from the fact that entrepreneurs[9] have a financial incentive to create information of value to the company.[10]

3.09 Manne's hypothesis was in turn robustly criticised and lauded by economists and legal scholars alike.[11] Manne responded at length to his critics over subsequent years,[12] thereby fuelling the vigorous academic debate that in some quarters continues to rumble on.[13]

The prevailing view

3.10 Manne's hypothesis relies wholly on principles of economic theory. This approach has little time for the 'moral' viewpoint, expounded by many of his critics, that

---

[8] See also Leo Herzel and Leo Katz, 'Insider Trading: Who Loses?' (1987) 165 Lloyds Bank Rev 15.
[9] Manne drew a distinction between entrepreneurs and mere managers for whom a salary was an appropriate method of compensation.
[10] David Haddock, 'Academic Hostility and SEC Acquiescence: Henry Manne Insider Trading' (1999) 50 Case W Res L Rev 313, 314.
[11] Two essays are referred to by Manne himself as being particularly hostile to his arguments—John A C Hetherington, 'Insider Trading and the Logic of the Law' (1967) Wisc L Rev 720; and Roy A Schotland, 'Unsafe at Any Price: A Reply to Manne, Insider Dealing and the Stock Market' (1967) 53 Va L Rev 1425.
[12] Henry Manne, 'Insider Trading and the Administrative Process' (1966–67) 35 Geo Wash L Rev 473 which focused on the federalisation of SEC Disclosure Rules. In 'Insider Trading and the Law Professors' (1969–70) 23 Vand L Rev 547, Manne replied to Schotland's (n 11) and Hetherington's (n 11) criticisms.
[13] Manne (n 7).

insider dealing is morally reprehensible, unfair, and unethical and, in effect, 'cheating'.[14] However, it is this moral viewpoint that has prevailed and which underpins much of the insider dealing legislation in the US and (many years later) the UK.

In the UK, the 1989 Trade and Industry Select Committee's Report into Company Investigations[15] summed it up thus:

3.11

> Insider dealing damages the operation of open markets. The insider dealer is misusing information he has received, breaching a fiduciary duty to his employers or clients and stealing a march on other investors. Investors and consumers cannot have confidence in markets affected by insider dealing. In the end what is at stake is the reputation at home and abroad of the UK financial system.

4. The UK's response to insider dealing

For many years, the case of *Percival v Wright*[16] (1902) represented the prevailing view of the UK Courts on insider dealing. In this case, Mr Justice Swinfen Eady held that company directors who bought or sold the shares of their company while in possession of price-sensitive information, owed no fiduciary duty to disclose this information to the other party to the transaction.

3.12

The first post-war discussion of the topic of insider dealing came with the Report of the Cohen Committee ('the Committee') in 1945.[17] It formed part of the Report's consideration of 'financial relations between companies and directors'. The Committee considered that it was 'improper' for directors to trade in the shares of their companies when in possession of specific inside information.[18] However, the Committee's suggested solution to this was simply that directors should be required to disclose their trades in the shares of their companies.[19]

3.13

The Jenkins Report

The first suggestion that legislation was an appropriate mechanism to combat insider dealing, came with the Report of the Company Law Committee of the Board of Trade,[20] known as the 'Jenkins Report', which was presented to Parliament

3.14

---

[14] As Brenda Hannigan put it, 'It is fair to say that nothing infuriates the economists more than this falling back to moral imperatives.' See Brenda Hannigan *Insider Dealing* (2nd edn Longman 1994) 12.
[15] HC 36 1989/90, para 158.
[16] *Percival v Wright* [1902] 2 Ch 401.
[17] Report of the Committee on Company Law Amendment, Cmd 6659, 1945 (Chair: Mr Justice Cohen).
[18] Report of the Committee on Company Law Amendment (n 17) para 86.
[19] Report of the Committee on Company Law Amendment (n 17) para 87. This proposal was later enacted in the Companies Act 1948 s 195.
[20] Cmnd 1749 (5 Jan 1960). The Committee was chaired by Lord Jenkins.

in June 1962. The terms of reference of the Committee, however, had little to do with insider dealing, but were in fact to review and report upon the provisions and workings of the Companies Act 1948. The Report dealt with the duties and responsibilities of company directors[21] and insider dealing in this context.

3.15 The Report concluded that the principal in *Percival v Wright* was wrong:[22]

> We have come to the conclusion that the law should protect a person—whether or not a member of the company or companies concerned—who suffers loss because a director has taken unfair advantage at his expense of a particular piece of confidential information about the company or any other company in the same group in any transaction relating to the securities of such companies.

3.16 Although some of the recommendations made by the Jenkins Report were implemented by way of a couple of later statutes,[23] the recommendations relating to insider dealing by company directors were not. However, the debate continued, and public concern grew. In 1970, Professor Louis Loss[24] described the mood:

> There can be no doubt that the public today thinks of both the market pool and the insider trading coup as aspects of Nineteenth Century capitalism that are on a par with sweatshops and David Copperfield.[25]

The Panel on Takeovers and Mergers and the Stock Exchange

3.17 In the 1970s, responsibility for policing insider dealing rested with the Panel on Takeovers and Mergers ('the Panel') and the Stock Exchange. The Panel was established in 1968 on the initiative of the Bank of England in response to a series of takeovers in the 1960s that had attracted much public criticism.[26] Its purpose was to ensure compliance with the City Code on Take-Overs and Mergers ('the City Code') and to deal with violations.

3.18 The City Code did provide some restrictions on insider dealing in the context of takeover or merger activity in that it prohibited dealing in the shares of offeror or offeree companies by any person privy to the preliminary takeover or merger

---

[21] Cmnd 1749 (n 20) ch III.
[22] Cmnd 1749 (n 20) para 89.
[23] The Companies Act 1967 made a number of amendments to the Companies Act 1948. The Committee's recommendations on share options were enacted by s 25 of the Companies Act 1967 and ss 27–29 of that Act substantially enlarged a director's duty to disclose dealings in his company's shares.
[24] BS (U of Pa); LLB (Yale); AM (hon) (Harv); William Nelson Cromwell Professor of Law, Harvard University. See Louis Loss, 'The Fiduciary Concept as Applied to Trading by Corporate Insiders in the United States' (1970) Mod L Rev 34. This article sought to explain to the UK how insider dealing in the US had developed.
[25] Loss (n 24) 36.
[26] See D Prentice, 'Take-over Bids—The City Code on Take-Over and Mergers' (1972) 18 McGill Law Journal 385. See also Mark A Spitz, 'Recent Developments in Insider Trading Laws and Problems of Enforcement in Great Britain' (1989) 12(1) Boston College Int'l and Comp L Rev, art 10.

discussions or to an intention to make an offer, during the period of the discussions, until the announcement of the offer (or termination of discussions). However, the Panel lacked any legal powers of interrogation or ability to require the production of documents, and its efficacy in investigating and taking action for violations of the code was thus rather hampered.[27]

3.19 The Stock Exchange was responsible for conducting investigations into suspicious stock price movements. The Stock Exchange's rules required its members to assist an investigation and also empowered the Stock Exchange to take disciplinary proceedings against its members. However, it too was hampered by the fact that it lacked the power to enforce co-operation with its investigations and compel the provision of information.[28] The fact that the Panel relied on the Stock Exchange to conduct investigations into alleged breaches of the City Code underlines the practical difficulties faced by both bodies.

The Justice Committee Report

3.20 Despite the Panel's rather sedentary attitude, public concern continued to build and, by 1972, had assumed sufficient importance to justify a Justice Committee Report[29] (the 'Report'), dedicated to the topic of insider dealing. The Report proposed that insider dealing should be made a criminal offence where it took place through a stock exchange, punishment being imprisonment or an unlimited fine.[30]

3.21 The response to this Report was mixed. Maurice Kay, writing in the Modern Law Review expressed the concern that:

> it would be unwise to introduce a prohibition on insider trading before some attempt to prognosticate the economic repercussions of such a prohibition has been made.[31]

3.22 However, not all commentators shared this view. In 1972, veteran journalist Graham Sarjeant published an article in the *Sunday Times Business News* under the banner headline, 'Hands Up a Man who Isn't an Insider Trader'.[32] The article stated that insider trading:

> is the stuff of which many merchant banks and city operators generate their share-dealing profits and in it is the life-blood of the short-term trading that makes

---

[27] GK Morse, 'The City Code on Takeovers and Mergers—Self Regulation or Self Protection?' (1991) J Bus L 509.

[28] A case dealt with by the Stock Exchange in 1971 illustrates how insider dealing was viewed and dealt with at the time: 1971/4 The Takeover Panel, Stock Exchange Dealings in the Course of a Take-Over Situation, 2 April 1971. See also Douglas W Hawes, T Peter Lee, and Marie-Claude Robert, Insider Trading Law Developments: An International Analysis (1985) 14 Law & Pol'y Int'l Bus 335, 378–79.

[29] The Justice Committee under the Chairmanship of Sir William Goodheart, 'A Report by Justice, Insider Trading' (1972).

[30] Goodheart (n 29) paras 31–36.

[31] Maurice Kay, 'The Justice Report on Insider Trading' (1973) 35(2) MLR 167.

[32] *Sunday Times Business News* (5 Nov 1972).

brokerage business profitable. Far from being an occasional wickedness, it is an integral part of city life.

3.23 A similar view was echoed by the Financial Editor of the *Sunday Times* who came up with the famous description of insider dealing as 'the crime of being something in the city'.[33]

The Stock Exchange and Takeover Panel Joint Statements

3.24 The cry for legislative action for the criminalisation of insider dealing was taken up by the Stock Exchange and the Takeover Panel which issued a Joint Statement in 1973 calling for criminal sanctions in respect of insider dealing ('Joint Statement').[34] In response, the 1973 Companies Bill proposed the criminalisation of insider dealing and some limited civil sanctions.[35] However, the dissolution of Parliament in 1973 meant that this Bill did not progress and was quietly dropped.

3.25 In 1977, the Stock Exchange and the Takeover Panel issued a second Joint Statement[36] ('the Statement'), which made a number of recommendations, including that those involved in a takeover negotiation should establish security procedures in order to protect the confidentiality of inside information and ensure that all parties were aware of the importance of this. The Statement also set out the circumstances in which the Takeover Panel would expect an announcement to be made of a takeover.

3.26 The next significant event was a 1977 White Paper entitled 'The Conduct of Company Directors',[37] which again proposed legislation to make insider dealing a criminal offence. Another Companies Bill[38] was introduced into Parliament in 1978. This Bill proposed the criminalisation of insider dealing but again fell by the wayside upon the dissolution of Parliament.

Privatisation

3.27 By 1979, the Conservative Government had taken office and had embarked upon its policy of privatisation of nationalised industries. Margaret Thatcher's memoirs demonstrate her personal crusade against State ownership which she regarded as the bastion of corrosive socialism[39]:

> Privatisation ... was fundamental to improving Britain's economic performance. But for me it was also far more than that: it was one of the central means of reversing

---

[33] *Sunday Times* (4 February 1973).
[34] February 1973 Stock Exchange and Takeover Panel Joint Statement on Insider Dealing.
[35] Companies Bill 1973, cls 12–16. For a summary of the legislative history see Gil Brazier, *Insider Dealing* (Routledge-Cavendish 1995) ch 4.
[36] The Takeover Panel and the Stock Exchange Panel on Takeovers and Mergers Joint Statement, Announcement of Price-Sensitive Matters 1977/4, 14 Apr 1977.
[37] Cmnd 7037, 1977, para 22.
[38] Companies Bill 1978, cls 57–63.
[39] Margaret Thatcher, *The Downing Street Years* (Harper Collins 1993) 676.

the corrosive and corrupting effects of socialism … Just as nationalisation was at the heart of the collectivist programme by which Labour Governments sought to remodel British society, so privatisation is at the centre of any programme of reclaiming territory for freedom.

3.28 Between 1982 and 1986, the privatisation agenda cut a swathe through the nationalised industries as the Government sold off such entities as Jaguar, British Telecom, the remainder of Cable and Wireless, and British Aerospace, Britoil, and British Gas. This was the era of Thatcher's 'popular capitalism' as depicted in the famous 'Tell Sid' advertising campaign of 1986, which encouraged individuals to buy shares in the Initial Public Offering ('IPO') for British Gas Corporation when it floated on the Stock Exchange.

3.29 In 1984, the privatisation of British Telecom, the largest single floatation in the Stock Market's history, demonstrated how successful the Conservative Government had been at turning households of ordinary people into share-owners. The Government mounted an extremely successful campaign of TV and press advertising to attract the small private investor. The floatation was an outstanding success and proved that small investors were prepared to invest in privatisation initiatives, particularly where (as here), the shares were offered at an attractive discount.[40]

3.30 In the late 1980s and early 1990s, the Conservative government was enjoying its third election victory and took the opportunity to roll out its most aggressive privatisation programme to date. This programme included British Steel, British Petroleum, Rolls Royce, British Airways, and water and electricity utilities. The privatisation agenda continued well into the 1990s with the final sell-off of British Coal, Powergen, National Power, and British Rail.

Part V of the Companies Act 1980

3.31 For the Conservative Government's privatisation agenda to have any prospect of success, private investors had to be persuaded to buy shares in the newly privatised companies. This brought the debate on insider dealing legislation back into sharp focus.[41]

3.32 Cecil Parkinson[42] then a Junior Trade Minister, told the House of Commons in 1979:

---

[40] See Marko Kothenburger, Hans-Werner Sinn, and John Whalley, *Privatization Experiences in the European Union* (MIT Press 2006).
[41] See Raymond Hughes, 'A case of frustration for the DTI', *FT* (28 Nov 1989): 'The act was brought in to ensure that the Thatcher dream of a share-owning democracy, with millions of new shareholders recruited through the privatisation of British Telecom, British Gas and the like, was not sullied by City professionals and others in the know getting an advantage over the shareholder in the street.'
[42] HC Deb, Companies Bill, 22 Oct 1979.

It is the Government's ambition to see that as many people as possible own shares in the company in which they work and to see a much wider spread of share ownership. It is essential that such small shareholders develop confidence in the market and do not feel that they are at the mercy of the unscrupulous. Therefore, there is general agreement that insider dealing should now be made a criminal offence.

3.33 Following a swift public consultation, Part V[43] of the Companies Act 1980 ('the Companies Act') came into force on 23 June 1980. For the first time in the UK's history, insider dealing was now a crime. The mood was summed up by T Peter Lee the then Deputy Director-General of the Panel on Takeovers and Mergers:

> At last insider trading in the UK is a crime! It took us nearly fifty years to catch up with the United States in this respect—but, you may say, that is par for the course in all aspects of our life.[44]

3.34 The Companies Act made it a criminal offence for individuals who were knowingly connected with a company either at the time of the dealing or at any time within the preceding six months, and individuals who received information from these connected individuals, to deal in securities in circumstances where they possessed 'unpublished price-sensitive information'. Such persons were also prohibited from counselling another person to deal or from communicating the unpublished price-sensitive information to anyone who might reasonably be expected to deal in the relevant securities.

3.35 The Companies Act also prohibited individuals connected with one company from dealing on the basis of unpublished price-sensitive information in the securities of another company, if they had acquired the information because they were connected with the first company.

3.36 The then Department of Trade was tasked with the carrying out of investigations, although it was heavily dependent on the LSE to provide evidence and intelligence. T Peter Lee stated, with a fair degree of perspicacity:

> it is the deterrent effect that advocates of the legislation see as the main purpose of this law. If the experience of other countries—eg France, Australia, Singapore—is anything to go by, the chances of more than a few prosecutions in the next few years are remote. But, of course, the deterrent effect cannot be judged by this criterion.[45]

The Company Securities (Insider Dealing) Act 1985

3.37 The insider dealing provisions in the Companies Act 1980, were later consolidated into an Act of their own—the Company Securities (Insider Dealing) Act 1985 ('CSA'). On the one hand, this might be said to be reflective of the seriousness of the crime. On the other, the maximum penalty following conviction on indictment

---

[43] Sections 69–73.
[44] T Peter Lee, 'Law And Practice with Respect to Insider Trading and Trading on Market Information in the United Kingdom', (1982) 4 J Comp Corp L and Securities Reg 389.
[45] Lee (n 44) 390.

was only two years' imprisonment (and/or an unlimited fine[46]), placing this offence significantly below the maximum penalties available for other offences that might be considered to be reasonably close relatives (such as fraud and theft[47]).

In essence, the CSA attempted to criminalise insider dealing by primary insiders (those connected with the company) and secondary insiders (who had received the information from a primary insider). It also prohibited an insider from counselling or procuring another to deal and from improperly disclosing inside information. In practice, however, the drafting of the legislation was tortuous in the extreme and was described as providing 'a form of obstacle race for the prosecution'.[48] And so it proved, because there were only a handful of prosecutions between 1980 (when insider dealing first became a crime) and 1993 (when the CSA was replaced by the current insider dealing legislation, the Criminal Justice Act ('CJA'), as these statistics demonstrate:[49] **3.38**

Alleged cases of insider dealing reported to the DTI by the stock exchange between 1987/88 and 1992/93

Year	Cases reported
1987/88	29
1988/89	33
1989/90	21
1990/91	8
1991/92	11
1992/93	2
Total	104

Insider dealing prosecutions between 1987/88 and 1992/93

Year	Cases	Prosecutions	Convictions	Acquittals
1987/88	3	3	3	0
1988/89	1	1	0	1
1989/90	10	14	4	10
1990/91	1	2	2	0
1991/92	5	8	3	5
1992/93	1	5	4	1
Total	21	33	16	17

---

[46] CSA, s 8.
[47] The maximum penalty for offences of theft being seven years' imprisonment and Obtaining by Deception ten years (Theft Act 1968). The maximum penalty for Conspiracy to Defraud is ten years' imprisonment (s 12(3) CJA 1987).
[48] See Hannigan (n 14) 58.
[49] House of Commons Library, Research Paper 93/8, 27 Jan 1993, The Criminal Justice Bill (Bill 104 of 1992/93). These two tables were included in the Paper. Only 104 cases were reported during

3.39 Critics pointed to the apparent reluctance of the Department of Trade and Industry ('DTI') to devote resources to insider dealing cases and its consequent focus on the small scale, opportunistic insider dealer rather than the rumoured sophisticated networks of City insiders who were widely regarded as the real villains.[50]

3.40 But it was a start. And it fitted in well with the increasingly intensive legislative focus on the financial services industry as a whole. The 'Big Bang' of 27 October 1986 heralded the introduction of screen-based electronic trading together with other measures designed to ensure London's place as the leading financial centre in Europe; but it also meant that the City had to be seen to be properly regulated.[51]

The Financial Services Act 1986

3.41 The 1986 Financial Services Act ('FS Act') established a wholly new regulatory structure for the UK financial services industry. The Securities and Investments Board ('SIB') became the overarching regulator, and a number of self-regulating organisations were given responsibility for particular aspects of the financial services industry.

3.42 The FS Act also remedied a key problem with the CSA which was that it did not provide investigating authorities with any specific investigative powers.[52] Section 177 of the FS Act provided for the power to appoint investigators, compel the production of documents or information, conduct compulsory interviews, and require any other assistance.[53]

3.43 This helped the investigative process, but of course did little to overcome the difficulties inherent in the CSA's drafting. Despite this, the CSA remained in force for

---

the whole fifteen-year period. Of these, less than a third resulted in prosecutions and a spectacular sixteen convictions.

[50] There was at least one City Professional prosecuted. Geoffrey Collier, director of Morgan Grenfell was convicted of making £22,000 by dealing on the basis of inside information about a takeover deal he was working on. For a thorough analysis of the early cases brought under the Companies Act and the CSA see Spitz (n 26). One MP—a Mr Jenkin, observed during the House of Commons debate upon the introduction of the Criminal Justice Bill to the House (HC Deb, Commons Standing Committees A&B, Official Report Session 1992–93, vol II, p 140), 'The number of convictions under the existing legislation is no reflection upon its efficiency or effectiveness in delivering its purpose. It is a curious test of the law that it should be shown to be working only if it can be proved that enough people have broken it.' Mr Jenkins was at the time a City Professional.

[51] See LCB Gower, '"Big Bang" and City Regulation' (1988) 51(1) MLR 1. See also RCH Alexander, *Insider Dealing and Money Laundering in the EU: Law and Regulation* (Ashgate 2007) 12.

[52] See the Roskill Report, 'Financial Services in the United Kingdom', Cmnd 9432, para 3.1. See also the Fraud Trials Committee Report, 1986, para 1, 'If the Government cherishes the vision of an equity owning democracy, then it also faces an inescapable duty to ensure that financial markets are honestly managed and that transgressors in those markets are swiftly and effectively discovered, convicted and punished.'

[53] Part VII of the FS Act also made other fairly minor amendments to the CSA.

eight years until it was finally replaced by the current version of the UK's criminal insider dealing law—Part V of the CJA. The impetus for this was not—as one might expect—a recognition of the domestic need for a legislative overhaul, but was in fact down to irresistible pressure being brought to bear from another source altogether: Europe.

4

THE EUROPEAN INSIDER DEALING DIRECTIVE

1. Introduction	4.01	Prohibitions	4.14
2. The Relationship between the Insider Dealing Directive and Part V of the CJA	4.02	Inside information	4.17
		Securities and markets	4.19
		Territorial scope	4.22
		Monitoring and enforcement	4.24
3. The background to the Insider Dealing Directive	4.04	5. The Insider Dealing Directive—Recitals	4.25
4. The Proposal	4.08		
Insiders	4.12		

1. Introduction

4.01 This Chapter focuses on the 1989 European 'Directive to Co-Ordinate Regulations on Insider Dealing', which is known as the 'Insider Dealing Directive' ('IDD').[1] The IDD is important because the UK's current insider dealing criminal legislation—Part V of the Criminal Justice Act 1993 ('CJA') was enacted in order to implement the requirements of the IDD into domestic law. Understanding the IDD is therefore key to understanding the CJA. This Chapter therefore deals with the background to the IDD and focuses on the rationale behind certain of the key provisions that in turn informed the drafting of Part V of the CJA.

2. The Relationship between the Insider Dealing Directive and Part V of the CJA

4.02 The impetus for further legislative reform of the UK's criminal insider dealing legislation came from within the European Community ('EC'). Article 67 of the

---

[1] Council Directive 89/592/EEC, 13 Nov 1989.

Treaty of Rome² which established the European Economic Community, provided that Member States should gradually remove restrictions and abolish discriminatory treatment affecting capital movements between them, to the extent necessary for the proper functioning of the Common Market. In 1989, the Council of the EEC agreed upon a 'Directive to Co-Ordinate Regulations on Insider Dealing', which eventually became the IDD.³ On 1 March 1994, the UK implemented the IDD into domestic law by enacting Part V of the CJA.

The IDD is a 'minimum harmonisation' directive, which means that it set down a minimum standard with which all Member States were required to comply in implementing it into their domestic law. In providing this minimum threshold, the IDD was directly responsible for shaping, and to a large extent prescribing, the scope and wording of Part V of the CJA. The IDD is in effect the bedrock upon which the CJA rests. Understanding the IDD is therefore a critical pre-requisite to understanding the CJA and provides an important aid to the interpretation of many of its sections. Beyond the minimum harmonisation threshold, Member States were free to implement more onerous requirements in their law, and in some instances in relation to the CJA, this is precisely what happened. **4.03**

3. The background to the Insider Dealing Directive

Europe's legislative response to the issue of insider dealing can be traced back to the 1966 Segre Report on 'The Development of a European Capital Market'⁴ ('the Segre Report'). The purpose of the Segre Report was to study the problems confronting capital markets in the European Community and make recommendations on the integration of those markets, with a view to achieving a European Capital Market.⁵ **4.04**

Chapter 11 of the Segre Report dealt with the need for improvements in the quality and quantity of information made available to investors.⁶ The Segre Report recognised that the problem of ensuring the equal availability of information to investors was a particularly important aspect of the development of a European securities market. Inequalities in the availability of information would mean that **4.05**

---

  ² 25 Mar 1957.
  ³ Council Directive (n 1).
  ⁴ The Development of a European Capital Market, Report of a Group of Exports Appointed by the EEC Commission, Nov 1966. The Group was chaired by Professor Claudio Segre, Director for Studies, Directorate-General for Economic and Financial Affairs of the EEC Commission.
  ⁵ Article 67 of the Treaty of Rome establishing the European Economic Community provided that Member States should gradually remove restrictions and abolish discriminatory treatment affecting capital movements between them, to the extent necessary for the proper functioning of the Common Market.
  ⁶ The Segre Report (n 4) ch 11: 'Operation of a European Securities Market: Information for the public, dealing in and movement of securities'.

investors would not have confidence in the market as a whole, which in turn would impede the development and effective functioning of a European market. The Segre Report also acknowledged the need to deal with the problem raised by 'the operations of directors or executives dealing in the securities of their own companies ("insider trading").'[7]

4.06 Little was done to implement the Segre Report's recommendations until the 1970s when there were a couple of fairly half-hearted attempts to approach the issue from a Company Law angle. In 1970 and 1975, the EC produced drafts of a proposed 'Statute of the European Company',[8] which attempted to introduce a European Code for Companies that included provisions for mandatory registration of an insider and recovery by a company of profits made by insiders on short-term positions. The proposals met with resistance from several of the Member States, particularly Germany,[9] and were quietly dropped.

4.07 In 1977, the European Commission ('the Commission') took a different approach and issued a formal recommendation to the Member States for a European Code of Conduct relating to transactions in transferable securities.[10] This contained principles relating to the improper use of price-sensitive information, together with more general principles regarding access to information by the public.[11] This was largely ignored by many Member States, and responsibility thereafter passed to the Directorate-General XV for Financial Institutions and Taxation.[12] A working party was duly established which spent the best part of the next ten years looking at the issue. However, as with the UK and the US, it was the exponential growth of the international securities markets in the 1980s, together with a number of major insider trading scandals that were the impetus for meaningful change.[13]

---

[7] The Segre Report (n 4) 30.
[8] OJ 1970 C 124/1, as modified Supplement 4/75. For a summary of events, see Klaus J Hopt 'The European Insider Dealing Directive' (1990) 27 Common Market L Rev 51.
[9] Joseph Blum, 'The regulation of insider trading in Germany: Who's afraid of self-restraining?' (1986) NW J Int'l L & Bus 507. See also PL Davies, 'The European Community's Directive on Insider Dealing: From Company Law to Securities Markets Regulation?' (1991) 11 Oxford J Legal Stud 92 for a discussion on the Company Law versus Securities Law approach in the UK.
[10] Commission Recommendation of 25 July 1977, OJ 1977, L 212/37, with Annex: European Code of Conduct Relating to Transactions in Transferable Securities; text correction in OJ 1977, L 294/28.
[11] Commission Recommendation (n 10) L 294/28, supplementary principles 8–9.
[12] Hopt (n 8).
[13] For example, in France, it was the Pechiney insider dealing scandal surrounding Pechiney SA's $1.26 billion acquisition of US firm Triangle Industries Inc in November 1988. See Steven Greenhouse, 'Modest Insider-Trading Stir Is a Huge Scandal in France', *New York Times* (30 Jan 1989); Leslie A Goldman, 'The Modernization of the French Securities Markets: Making the EEC Connection' (1992) 60(6) Fordham L Rev, art 12; SEC Litigation Release No 15429 / 4 Aug 1997; SEC Litigation Release No 16058 / 11 Feb 1999. See also the *Liechtenstein Norgren* case—SEC News Digest, Issue 90-173, 6 Sept 1990; USDC SDNY, 89 Civ 7667 (JMC) (LR-12603).

4. The Proposal

European legislative action began in earnest on 21 May 1987, when the Commission published a Proposal for a Council Directive co-ordinating regulations on insider trading[14] ('the Proposal'). **4.08**

The problem being faced in Europe at the time was that Member States had each responded in different ways to the insider dealing issue. For example, by then, Denmark, France, and the UK had all adopted insider dealing legislation. Belgium, Ireland, and Holland were also in the process of finalising their legislation on insider trading. Germany had introduced rules under which market participants voluntarily undertook not to exploit inside information in their possession, yet there was no sanction for breaches of these rules. However, the other Member States had not introduced any rules or regulations to deal with the insider trading issue and it appeared, had no plans to do so.[15] **4.09**

The Commission therefore took the view that it was necessary for rules and regulations to be co-ordinated at Community level in order to ensure the creation of an efficient and fair European Securities Market, described at paragraph 2 of the Proposal as 'a step towards the setting up of a European capital market'. The Commission also considered that the Proposal for an IDD would form an important addition to the Directives that already existed in the Securities field.[16] **4.10**

The Proposal is worthy of some consideration because it explains the thinking behind the final version of the IDD and, in turn, therefore informs much of the drafting of Part V of the CJA which was the UK's means of implementing the Directive into its domestic law. **4.11**

Insiders

On the definition of insiders, the Proposal noted that there were two possible approaches. The first option was a narrow approach, which would limit the reach of the IDD to what it referred to as 'primary insiders' who, by virtue of their profession **4.12**

---

[14] COM(87) 111 final OJ 1987 C 153/8.
[15] COM(87) (n 14) para 2.
[16] Council Directive 79/279/EEC of 5 Mar 1979 coordinating the conditions for the admission of securities to the official stock exchange listing OJ No L 66, 16 Mar1979; Council Directive 80/390/EEC of 17 Mar 1980 coordinating the requirements for the drawing-up, scrutiny and distribution of the listing particulars to be published for the admission of securities to official stock exchange listing 3OJ No L 100, 17 Apr 1980; Council Directive 82/121/EEC of 15 Feb 1982 on information to be published on a regular basis by companies the shares of which have been admitted to official stock-exchange listing 4OJ No L 48, 20 Feb 1982; the proposal for a Directive on information to be published when major holdings in the capital of a listed company are acquired or disposed of OJ No C 351, 31 Dec 1985.

or occupation, are in a fiduciary relationship with, or have a duty of confidentiality towards, the company whose shares are in question.[17]

4.13 However, it was decided that such a definition would be too limited, particularly in cases which concerned international securities markets and the modern deregulated markets, where there was perceived to be a real risk that individuals, whether acting on their own account or otherwise, could procure privileged information from primary insiders and trade on it to their own, or others' advantage. The Proposal referred to such persons as 'tippees'.[18] For this reason, the Commission proposed that the IDD adopt the broader approach to the definition of an insider and cover both primary insiders and tippees (secondary insiders).[19] Therefore Articles 2 and 4 of the IDD defined a primary and secondary insider in these terms. In due course, this would be reflected in s 57 of the CJA.

Prohibitions

4.14 The Proposal, and in due course, Articles 2 and 3 of the IDD, defined the prohibitions to be placed on a primary insider—namely that he should be prohibited from taking advantage of inside information by buying or selling transferable securities either directly or through another person. Primary insiders were also to be prohibited from disclosing inside information to a third party unless the disclosure was made in the normal course of exercising their profession or duties and also from using inside information to recommend a third party to buy or sell transferable securities. Article 4 imposed the same prohibitions on secondary insiders, who knowingly obtained their information from primary insiders.

4.15 The prohibition was proposed to cover only the 'taking advantage of' inside information, ie, if the insider's decision to buy or sell has been taken in light of that information. In due course, this would be reflected in Article 2(1) of the IDD which provided that insiders should be prohibited from '[t]aking advantage of that information with full knowledge of the facts'.

4.16 Section 52 of the CJA reproduced these prohibitions as the criminal insider dealing offences under UK domestic law.

Inside information

4.17 The Proposal stated that for information to qualify as 'inside' it had to meet a series of conditions:[20]

1. The information must be unknown to the public, ie, not yet published.

---

[17] COM(87) (n 14) s II/1—Commentary.
[18] COM(87) (n 14) s II/1—Commentary.
[19] COM(87) (n 14) s II/1—Commentary.
[20] COM(87) (n 14) s II/1—Commentary.

2. It must be of a sufficiently specific nature. The Proposal considered therefore that a simple rumour could not be regarded as inside information.
3. It must relate to one or more issuers of securities or to one or more securities. The Proposal took the view that this condition was wide enough to cover information concerning an issuer, whether originating from within the issuer (for example, an increase in profits) or outside it (for example, a bid to take over the issuer launched by another company). It was also sufficient to cover information on the situation or prospects of one or more securities and information which was likely to influence the market as such (the example given being the decision of a central bank to alter the discount rate.)
4. The information must be likely to have a material effect on the price of the security or securities in question. According to the Proposal this meant that not all information that was unknown to the public was necessarily inside information. It observed that otherwise managers or directors or even most of the employees of a company would never be able to buy or sell the securities of their companies since they would always have information which had not been published.

4.18 These Proposals were adopted by Article 1(1) of the IDD and in due course would be reflected in s 56 of the CJA.

Securities and markets

4.19 The prohibitions were proposed to apply to transactions in securities 'admitted to trading on the stock exchange market'.[21] This meant not just the official market but also parallel or secondary markets.[22] However the Proposal considered that the transaction did not necessarily need to be carried out on the stock exchange market itself. Off-market transactions should also be covered if carried out through a professional intermediary such as a bank, stockbroker, or dealer.[23] However, the prohibition should not go so far as to include face-to-face transactions outside a stock exchange in which a professional intermediary was not involved.

4.20 The Proposal stated that to fall within the prohibitions, transactions had to be carried out in 'transferable securities' which included 'securities usually traded on the stock exchange market such as shares and debt securities but also traded options relating to such securities.'[24]

---

[21] COM(87) (n 14) s II/3—Commentary.
[22] COM(87) (n 14) s II/3—Commentary. The examples given were the 'Second Marché' in France or the Unlisted Securities Market in the United Kingdom.
[23] COM(87) (n 14) s II/3—Commentary.
[24] COM(87) (n 14) s II/3, Draft Article 5.

4.21 These Proposals were adopted by Article 1(2) of the IDD and in due course would be reflected in ss 52(3), 54, 59 and Schedule 2 of the CJA, and the Insider Dealing (Securities and Regulated Markets) Order 1994.[25]

Territorial scope

4.22 The Proposal stated that where a transaction is carried out on the stock exchange market, the competent Member State is clearly that in which the stock exchange in question is located or is being operated.[26] As regards the prohibitions relating to disclosing inside information and encouraging dealing, the Proposal took the view that the competent Member State should be the State in which the insider is resident.[27]

4.23 These Proposals were adopted by Articles 1(2) and 5 of the IDD, and in due course would be reflected in s 62 of the CJA and the Insider Dealing (Securities and Regulated Markets) Order 1994.[28]

Monitoring and enforcement

4.24 The Commission considered it essential that each Member State designate supervisory authorities to effectively monitor application of insider dealing rules and that these authorities be provided with all necessary investigative and disciplinary powers.[29] In the UK, the designated body was initially the then Department of Trade and Industry, and in due course the Financial Services Authority ('FSA'). As of 1 April 2013, the FSA was replaced by a new, designated body—the Financial Conduct Authority ('FCA').

5. The Insider Dealing Directive—Recitals

4.25 The Opinion of the Economic and Social Committee ('The Committee') was sought on the draft directive. In its Opinion of 16 December 1987,[30] the Committee supported the Proposal in principle.[31] Thereafter, the Final version of the IDD was published on 13 November 1989.[32]

---

[25] SI 1994/187.
[26] COM(87) (n 14) s II/5.
[27] COM(87) (n 14) s II/4.
[28] SI 1994/187.
[29] COM(87) (n 14) s II/6.
[30] OJ No C 153, 11 June 1987, 8 and OJ No C 277, 27 Oct 1988, 13. The European Parliament was also consulted, OJ No C291/54.
[31] OJ No C 153, 11 June 1987, 8 and OJ No C 277, 27 Oct 1988, para 1.3.
[32] Council Directive 89/592/EEC. (A modified draft had previously been published on 4 Oct 1988 (COM(88) 549 SYN 85, OJ 1988 C 277/13). For an analysis of the IDD's provisions, see Hopt (n 8). See also Takis Tridimas, 'Insider Trading: European Harmonisation and National Law Reform' (1991) 40(4) ICLQ 919.

4.26 The Recitals (preamble) to the IDD introduce the main provisions (the Articles), and present the reasons for their adoption. They do not have legal force as such and do not usually feature in the national legislation implementing the Directive in question. However, they are an aid to understanding the Directive, in particular by clarifying the meaning of certain words. In litigation, the European Court and domestic Courts may take the Recitals into consideration in ascertaining the intentions of the European Council and the European Parliament when drafting the Articles.[33]

4.27 The Recitals to the IDD are broadly drafted and focus overwhelmingly on the importance of the securities markets and the perception that insider dealing undermines investor confidence and therefore affects the smooth operation of those markets. In so doing, they demonstrate once and for all that the 'morality' and 'investor confidence' arguments had won the day in Europe's economic thinking.[34] It had taken a long time, and had required the explosion of global capital markets, together with some major insider dealing scandals, but by 1989 the IDD demonstrated unequivocally that the view of the European legislators was firmly in the camp that propounded the threat posed by insider dealing to the integrity of European markets.[35]

4.28 On this, the UK was in agreement, and the IDD provided the UK Government with a reason to completely overhaul the unworkable Company Securities (Insider Dealing) Act 1995 ('CSA') and replace it with a newer, sleeker, and simpler version altogether. Thus we have Part V of the CJA, which was enacted in 1993 and remains the UK's criminal insider dealing legislation to this day.

---

[33] Joint Practical Guide, Guide of the European Parliament, the Council and the Commission for persons involved in the drafting of legislation within the Community institutions, para 10.
[34] See Hopt (n 8).
[35] For a discussion of the effect of globalisation see Thomas J Ramsdell, 'The EEC Directive on Insider Trading: Will There be a Cure by 1992?' (1990–91) Am U J Int'l & Pol'y 637. For an analysis of the implementation of the IDD by European Member States see R C H Alexander *Market Abuse and Insider Dealing* (Ashgate 2007).

5

PART V OF THE CRIMINAL JUSTICE ACT 1993

THE CRIMINAL OFFENCES (s 52 CJA)

1. Introduction	5.01	5. The secondary offences		5.21
2. Part V of the CJA—an overview	5.02	Encouraging dealing ('Encouraging')		
3. The offence	5.07	(s 52(2)(a) CJA)		5.21
4. Insider dealing (s 52(1) CJA) (the		Disclosing inside information		
'primary' offence)	5.16	('Disclosing') (s 52(2)(b) CJA)		5.26

1. Introduction

5.01 This Chapter provides an overview of Part V of the CJA. It then sets out the three ways in which an offence of insider dealing can be committed (insider dealing, encouraging dealing, and improperly disclosing inside information). For each offence, there is a sample draft Indictment Count and also a flow chart that sets out the elements that must be proved.

2. Part V of the CJA—an overview

5.02 Part V of the CJA consists of only thirteen sections (ss 52–64): thirteen sections to criminalise the entire spectrum of insider dealing offences does not seem very many and one might be forgiven for thinking that the law is therefore fairly straightforward. Unfortunately, this is not the case, although at the time of its enactment, it was undoubtedly an improvement on its predecessor the Company Securities (Insider Dealing) Act 1985 ('CSA').[1] Part of the reason for its complexity is the

---

[1] Anthony Nelson, the Economic Secretary to the Treasury in introducing the redrafted Bill, stated that the aim was to, 'make the legislation clearer, while not substantively changing its scope'. (HC Deb, Commons Standing Committees A&B, Official Report Session 1992–93, vol II, col 133).

difficulty inherent in drawing a line between criminal activity on the one hand, and not placing a stranglehold on legitimate market practice on the other. This was summarised during the Parliamentary debates by Anthony Nelson, then the Chief Secretary to the Treasury, giving the views of the Government:

> Not only must we crack down on insider dealing but we must be seen to be doing so effectively and must send the right deterrent messages to the financial services industry. Furthermore we must not inhibit unreasonably the legitimate practices and expertise of those in the City of London and the financial services industry in general. The industry is extremely important to our economy and employs very many people.[2]

5.03 Another reason is that Part V was enacted in order to implement the minimum requirements of the Insider Dealing Directive 1989 ('IDD') and this of itself provided something of a straightjacket for the legislative draughtsmen. The IDD required Member States to implement it into their domestic law by 1 June 1992. The UK was slightly behind the curve in relation to this as the Criminal Justice Bill was not introduced into Parliament until October 1992. There was then a further consultation targeted towards interested parties in the City, including the Stock Exchange, the Confederation of British Industry, the Law Society, and the British Merchant Banking Securities Housing Association.[3] Thereafter the Bill was radically redrafted before being considered by the Standing Committee of the House of Commons in June 1993.

5.04 The CJA received the Royal Assent on 27 July 1993. Part V was brought into force on 1 March 1994 and its predecessor the CSA was repealed in its entirety at that point.

5.05 A House of Commons Library Research Paper[4] on the Criminal Justice Bill summarised the aim of Part V of the CJA as:

> Put simply the law has to do three things. First it has to define an 'insider'. Secondly, it has to define what sort of information it is that insiders cannot deal with. Lastly, it has to define what they cannot do with that class of information.[5]

5.06 This is broadly what Part V does. But given its history, it was perhaps inevitable that it would achieve this in a rather tortuous (and at times, rather opaque) way as is demonstrated in the following chapters.

3. The offence

Section 52—The offence

(1) An individual who has information as an insider is guilty of insider dealing if, in the circumstances mentioned in subsection (3), he deals in securities that are price-affected securities in relation to the information.

---

[2] HC Deb (n 1) vol II, col 150.
[3] HC Deb (n 1) col HC Deb (n 1) col 133.
[4] House of Commons Library, Research Paper 93/8, 27 Jan 1993, The Criminal Justice Bill (Bill 104 of 1992/93).
[5] House of Commons Library (n 4) 21.

(2) An individual who has information as an insider is also guilty of insider dealing if
  (a) he encourages another person to deal in securities that are (whether or no that other knows it) price-affected securities in relation to the information, knowing or having reasonable cause to believe that the dealing would take place in the circumstances mentioned in subsection (3); or
  (b) he discloses the information, otherwise than in the proper performance of the functions of his employment, office or profession, to another person.
(3) The circumstances referred to above are that the acquisition or disposal in question occurs on a regulated market, or that the person dealing relies on a professional intermediary or is himself acting as a professional intermediary.
(4) This section has effect subject to section 53.

5.07 Section 52 creates three separate ways in which the offence can be committed by 'an individual who has information as an insider'. These are insider dealing (s 52(1)), encouraging dealing (s 52(2)(a)), and improper disclosure of inside information (s 52(2)(b)). In reality, each of these amounts to a separate offence, and they are therefore treated as such within this book, in which they are described as the 'primary offence' (insider dealing) and the 'secondary offences' (encouraging or disclosing).

5.08 The first matter of note is that the prohibition in s 52 CJA applies only to 'individuals'. On the face of it, this means that liability for a s 52 offence does not extend to corporate structures. This is consistent with Article 2[6] of the IDD which provides that:

(2) Where the person referred to in paragraph 1 [the insider] is a company or other type of legal person, the prohibition laid down in that paragraph shall apply to the natural persons who take part in the decision to carry out the transaction for the account of the legal person concerned.

5.09 It also accords with the recommendation in a 1989 Department of Trade and Industry ('DTI') Consultative Document which suggested that it was more appropriate [for the CJA] to focus on individuals who misuse financial information, and that attempting to cover the actions of companies in general would result in unnecessary complication.[7]

5.10 Restricting section 52 CJA offences to 'individuals' was plainly a deliberate decision. Had Parliament intended to extend the ambit of the offences contained therein to legal persons then it would have been open to it to instead use the word 'person', which under Schedule 1 of the Interpretation Act 1978, includes a 'body of persons corporate or unincorporated'. This was precisely the course adopted in the market abuse regime under Part VIII of the Financial Services and Markets Act 2000

---

[6] Council Directive 89/592/EEC.
[7] DTI Consultative Document, 'The Law on Insider Dealing' (Dec 1989) para 2.29. See also Brenda Hannigan, *Insider Dealing* (2nd edn Longman 1994) 90.

('FSMA'),[8] under which companies have been held liable for market abuse committed by its senior personnel, under principles of attribution.[9]

5.11 For those who represent companies whose employees are under investigation for insider dealing offences, this should represent a degree of comfort. It has always been difficult to establish corporate liability for criminal offences. Under the well established 'identification principle'[10] of corporate criminal liability, a company can only be held criminally liable if it can be shown that the 'acts and state of mind' necessary to commit the offence, can be attributed to the directing mind of the company, ie, the board or the people at the most senior levels of the organisation.[11] Added to this is the fact that s 52 CJA appears on its face to exclude corporate liability in any event.

5.12 Does this mean that a company could never face a criminal prosecution for insider dealing? Perhaps in most cases, the issue will simply not arise. This may be because the individual(s) under investigation do not fall within the identification principle. For example, a manager in the Corporate Broking Department of a merchant bank (as in the *Christian Littlewood* case[12]), who abuses the inside information he obtains as a result of his role, is never going to be considered the 'directing mind and will' of the corporate entity by which he is employed. However, might the position be different in a case where the corporate entity is central to, and an essential part of, the alleged insider dealing?

5.13 This was precisely the situation that occurred in the case of *R v Sanders and others*.[13] Here, the defendant (James Sanders) was the founder and director of a contracts for difference ('CFD') brokerage named Blue Index Ltd ('Blue Index') and also ran the business on a day-to-day basis. James Sanders and his wife Miranda, who was also a co-defendant, obtained inside information on forthcoming takeovers of US companies from Miranda's sister in the US whose husband held a senior position in the Mergers and Acquisitions team at Deloitte in San Francisco, and worked on the deals in question. The defendants traded on the information for their own accounts and, in addition, a strategy was put in place by James Sanders whereby the clients of Blue Index were encouraged to trade in the same stocks through their accounts at Blue Index. The purpose of this strategy was to benefit Blue Index through the commission earned on these trades and also to make the

---

[8] See Chapter 15 The Civil Offences, Section 2, para 15.07.
[9] See Chapter 15, Section 2, paras 15.09–15.12; *GLG Capital Partners*, Final Notice 1 Aug 2006; *Greenlight Capital Inc*, Final Notice 15 Feb 2012.
[10] *Lennards Carrying Co v Asiatic Petroleum* [1915] AC 705; *Bolton Engineering Co v Graham* [1957] 1 QB 159 (per Denning LJ); and *R v Andrews Weatherfoil*, 56 C App R 31 CA.
[11] *Tesco Supermarkets Ltd v Nattrass* [1972] AC 153.
[12] *R v Littlewood and others*, unreported, Southwark Crown Court, His Honour Judge Anthony Leonard QC, 10 Jan 2011. FSA/PN/062/2011; 2 February 2011. FSA/PN/018/2011.
[13] Unreported, Southwark Crown Court, Mr Justice Simon, 20 June 2012. FSA/PN/060/2012 & FSA/PN/067/2012.

company a more attractive sale prospect (which would ultimately have benefitted the defendants).

5.14 Applying the identification principle to this scenario would ordinarily operate to open up the possibility of criminal proceedings against the corporate entity as well as the individuals, although whether, in practice, the entity is ultimately prosecuted will depend on several factors, including the application of the two-stage test in the Code for Crown Prosecutors.[14] However, for the reasons set out above, it appears conclusive that s 52 CJA would preclude the prosecution of Blue Index for insider dealing.

5.15 It might, however, (at least theoretically) be possible to allege a conspiracy to commit insider dealing in which the company is named as a party, and it would also be possible to prosecute under s 52 CJA the individuals who procure a company to deal, as well as those who deal as agents for a company.[15] An individual might also be liable for assisting or encouraging a corporation to commit an insider dealing offence under Part 2 of the Serious Crime Act 2007. In practical terms, however, such issues will, in virtually all cases, be more illusory than real. In the Sanders case, for example, the prosecution took a straightforward approach and simply prosecuted the individuals for offences under ss 52(1), 52(2)(a), and 52(2)(b) CJA. Blue Index's permissions to conduct regulated activities were removed by the Financial Services Authority ('FSA') at the time the initial arrests were made,[16] which had the effect of putting the company out of business, precipitating its quick descent into insolvency, and winding up proceedings. In most instances, it is the regulatory and reputational implications that will be of greater and more relevant concern to a company whose employees become the subject of an insider dealing investigation, than the threat of a criminal prosecution.

4. Insider dealing (s 52(1) CJA) (the 'primary' offence)

5.16 The Primary offence, in essence, amounts to the deliberate abuse by an insider of the information that he holds, by dealing in the securities with which the information is concerned, at the expense of other market participants who do not have access to the same information. The offence is encapsulated in ss 52(1) and 52(3) CJA. These sections are then informed by the remaining sections of Part V CJA which define the meaning of the specific terms contained in ss 52 and also provide for limitations on such matters as the territorial scope of the offence.

5.17 Sample indictment:

Statement of Offence

Insider dealing, contrary to Section 52(1) of the Criminal Justice Act 1993.

---

[14] Code for Crown Prosecutors 2013.
[15] See Chapter 9.
[16] See Chapter 24, Section 2, para 24.02 & Section 4, para 24.18.

Particulars of Offence

XY between the ... day of ... 20 ... and the ... day of ... 20 ..., being an individual who had information as an insider which related to a proposed takeover of a particular issuer of securities, namely Z Ltd, dealt in securities that were price affected securities in relation to that information.

5.18 The various elements that have to be proved in for this offence are set out in Figure 1.

5.19 As the flow chart demonstrates, the offence involves a number of specific elements, each of which must be proved. The requirements are disjunctive and questions of fact—firstly, prove that the defendant had information as an insider and, secondly, prove that he dealt in securities in one of the ways set out. Note that it is not necessary to prove that the individual dealt *because of* the inside information, or *in reliance* upon it, although it may be difficult in practice to conceive of an insider dealing case in which the defendant's dealing has not occurred as a direct result of, or in reliance on, his inside information.

5.20 Once the necessary elements of the offence have been proved to the criminal standard, it is then for the defendant to raise one of the statutory defences set out in s 53 CJA. If he does raise a s 53 defence, then there is a legal and evidential burden on him to prove that defence on the balance of probabilities.[17]

5. The secondary offences

Encouraging dealing ('Encouraging') (s 52(2)(a) CJA)

5.21 The Encouraging offence is committed when an insider 'encourages' another person to deal in securities that are price-affected by his information, in circumstances in which he (the insider) either knows or reasonably believes the dealing will take place. Note that the offence is deliberately drafted to encompass the encouraging of any 'person'. 'Person' is defined in the Interpretation Act 1978 (Schedule 1) as including a 'body of persons corporate or unincorporated', and the offence therefore applies to the encouraging of legal persons such as companies as well as the encouragement of individuals. For example, if the insider in question is a Director of a company and rather than trading himself, he encourages his company to trade in the shares about which he has inside information, then he would be liable under s 52(2)(a).

5.22 Sample indictment:

Statement of Offence

Insider dealing, contrary to Section 52(2)(a) of the Criminal Justice Act 1993.

---

[17] See Chapter 11, Sections 1–5 (for the statutory defences) and Section 6 Statutory defences— legal and evidential burden on the defence.

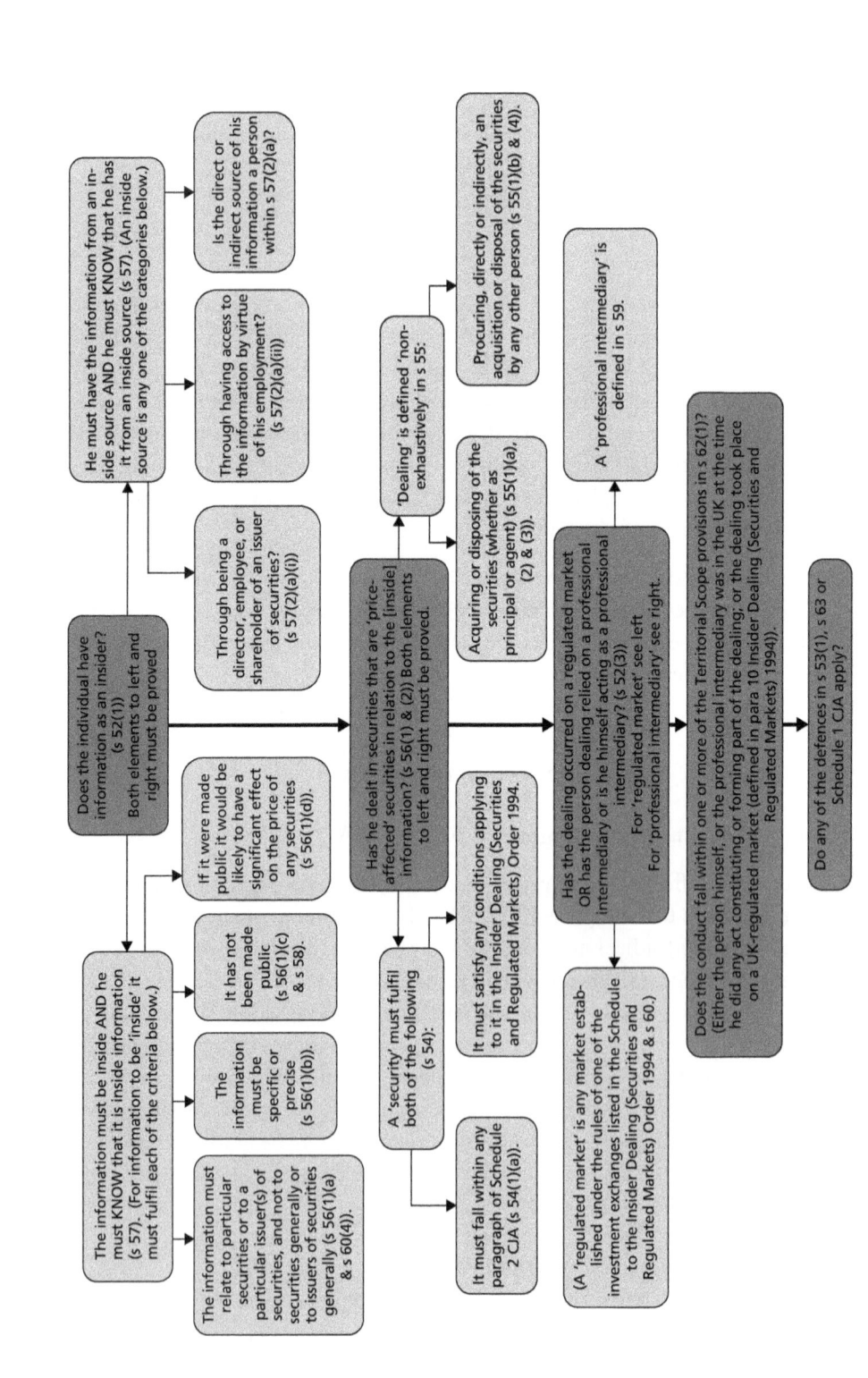

Figure 1. Flow chart for the s 52(1) 'Primary' offence

Particulars of Offence

XY between the ... day of ... 20 ... and the ... day of ... 20 ..., being an individual who had information as an insider which related to a proposed takeover of a particular issuer of securities, namely Z ltd, encouraged another person namely ..., to deal in securities that were price affected securities in relation to that information, knowing or having reasonable cause to believe that the dealing would take place.

5.23 The various specific elements that must be proved in for this offence are set out in Figure 2.

5.24 The offence of encouraging another person to deal does not have to involve the actual passing on of inside information. This is clear from the fact that s 52(2)(b) CJA creates a separate offence of improper disclosure of inside information. 'Encourage'[18] is not defined in the CJA and it must therefore be interpreted in accordance with the ordinary everyday meaning of that term. Whether the defendant's conduct amounts to encouragement is therefore a question of fact which must be determined by a jury on the basis of the evidence.

5.25 To date, there has been only one case in which offences of Encouraging Dealing have been prosecuted. This was the case of *R v Sanders and others*.[19] Here, it was alleged that James Sanders had encouraged the clients of his CFD brokerage Blue Index to deal in securities in respect of which he was an insider. This was achieved by encouraging certain clients to deal, and also by telling the Blue Index traders which stocks to encourage the clients to invest in. The clients and traders were not told the basis for these tips. James Sanders did not contest that it was appropriate to indict for Encouraging Dealing offences in respect of these allegations and eventually pleaded guilty to these counts.

Disclosing inside information ('Disclosing') (s 52(2)(b) CJA)

5.26 The essence of this offence is the disclosure of inside information by an insider in circumstances in which the disclosure itself is not within the proper performance of the functions of his employment, office, or profession.

---

[18] Part 2 of the SCA 2007 (into force 1 October 2008: SI 2008 No 2504 (ante)) introduced new offences relating to encouraging or assisting crime. For commentary on Part 2, see, in particular, J Spencer and G Virgo, 'Encouraging and Assisting Crime: Legislate in Haste, Repent at Leisure' (2008) 9 Archbold News 7; David Ibbetson, 'Encouraging or Assisting Attempt' (2009) 3 Archbold News 8; and David Ormerod and Rudi Fortson, 'Serious Crime Act 2007: The Part 2 Offences' (2009) Crim LR 389.

[19] *James Sanders and others* (n 13).

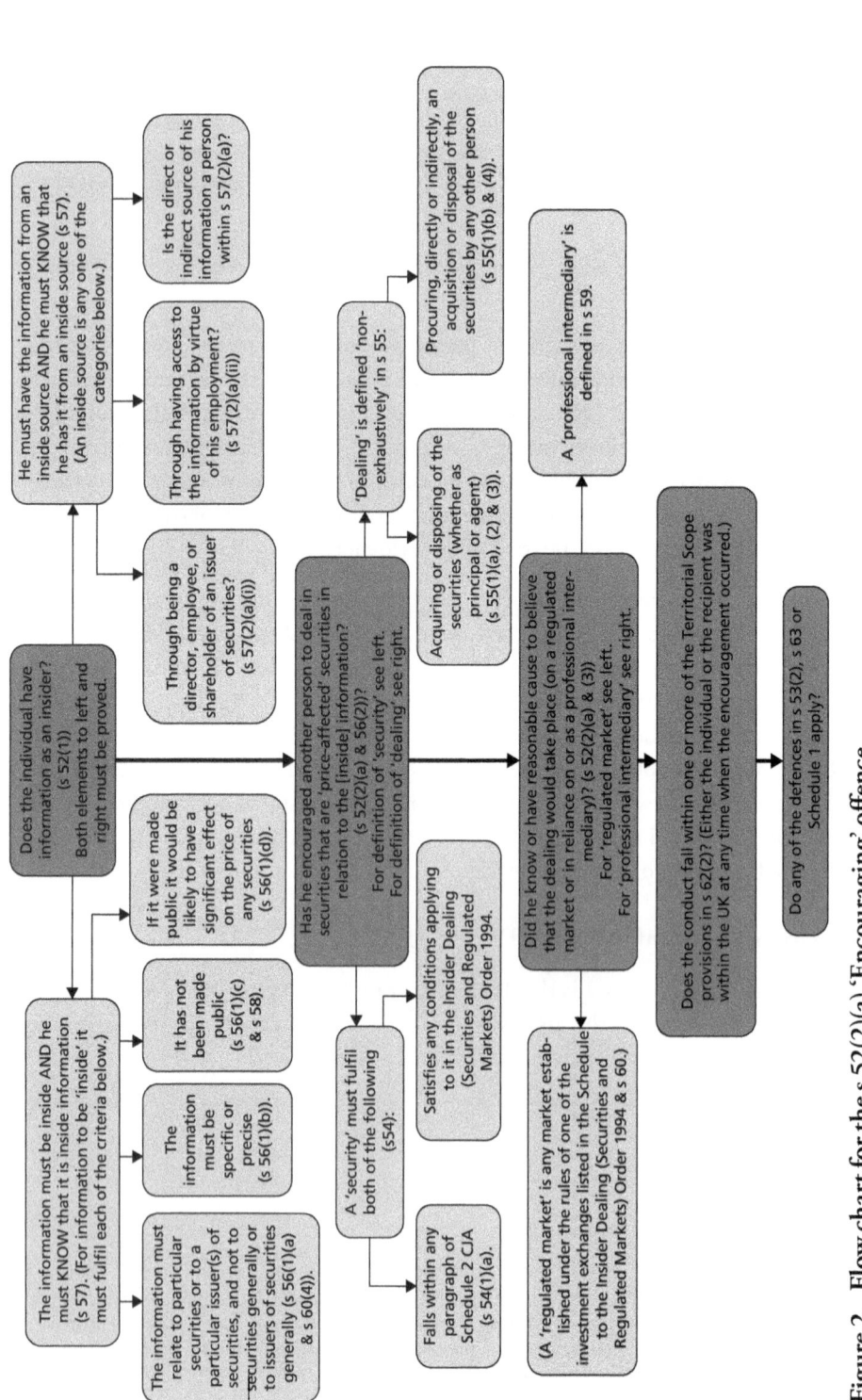

Figure 2. Flow chart for the s 52(2)(a) 'Encouraging' offence

Sample indictment: 5.27

Statement of Offence

Insider dealing, contrary to Section 52(2)(b) of the Criminal Justice Act 1993.

Particulars of Offence

XY between the ... day of ... 20 ... and the ... day of ... 20 ..., being an individual who had information as an insider which related to a proposed takeover of a particular issuer of securities, namely Z Ltd, disclosed the information to ... otherwise than in the proper performance of the functions of his employment, office or profession.

The various specific elements that must be proved in relation to this offence are set out in Figure 3. 5.28

As can be seen from the flowchart, the 'proper performance of the functions of his employment, office or profession' is not defined by any other provision of the CJA. This issue therefore falls to be determined as a question of fact on the basis of the evidence. In many cases, the real issue in a case will not be whether the information has been disclosed improperly, but whether it has been disclosed at all. However, it is not too difficult to envisage cases in which this element may be more central. An example might be a case in which a broker discloses to a shareholder inside information regarding a forthcoming equity issuance by his client, in circumstances in which he has not followed proper wall-crossing procedures. This situation arose in the civil market abuse context in the case of Andrew Osborne.[20] 5.29

Mr Osborne was a Managing Director in the Corporate Broking Department of Merrill Lynch International ('MLI') and led the corporate broking team at MLI in acting for Punch Taverns plc ('Punch') as joint book runner and co-sponsor in relation to a new equity issuance. His role included responsibility for wall crossing certain shareholders in Punch for which specific wall-crossing procedures had been put in place by MLI, requiring agreement to the terms of a written non-disclosure agreement ('NDA'). Mr Osborne nevertheless disclosed inside information relating to the equity issuance to one of the Punch shareholders (David Einhorn of Greenlight Capital Inc), in circumstances which were clearly in breach of these wall crossing procedures. The FSA found that this conduct amounted to the improper disclosure of inside information under s 118(3) of FSMA.[21] 5.30

If a case involving these facts is dealt with as a criminal case under s 52 CJA, it would be possible to assert that, despite the fact that the disclosure took place within the functions of the discloser's employment, the circumstances were such as to not amount to 'proper performance'. Whether this would in practice be an easy distinction for a jury to draw, has not thus far been tested. 5.31

---

[20] *Andrew Osborne*, Final Notice 15 Feb 2012.
[21] See Chapter 17, Section 2, para 17.7.

Flow chart for the s 52(2)(b) 'Disclosing' offence

Does the individual have information as an insider? (s 52(1)) Both elements to left and right must be proved.

The information must be inside AND he must KNOW that it is inside information (s 57). (For information to be 'inside' it must fulfil each of the criteria below.)

- The information must relate to particular securities or to particular issuer(s) of securities, and not to securities generally or to issuers of securities generally (s 56(1)(a) & s 60(4)).
- The information must be specific or precise (s 56(1)(b)).
- It has not been made public (s 56(1)(c) & s 58).
- If it were made public it would be likely to have a significant effect on the price of any securities (s 56(1)(d)).

He must have the information from an inside source AND he must KNOW that he has it from an inside source (s 57). (An inside source is any one of the categories below.)

- Through being a director, employee, or shareholder of an issuer of securities? (s 57(2)(a)(i))
- Through having access to the information by virtue of his employment? (s 57(2)(a)(iii))
- Is the direct or indirect source of his information a person within? (s 57(2)(a))

↓

Has he disclosed the information to another person? (s 52(2)(b)).

↓

Was this disclosure otherwise than in the proper performance of the functions of his employment, office, or profession? (s 52(2)(b)).

↓

Does the conduct fall within one or more of the Territorial Scope provisions in s 62(2)? (Either the individual or the recipient was within the UK at any time when the disclosure occurred.)

↓

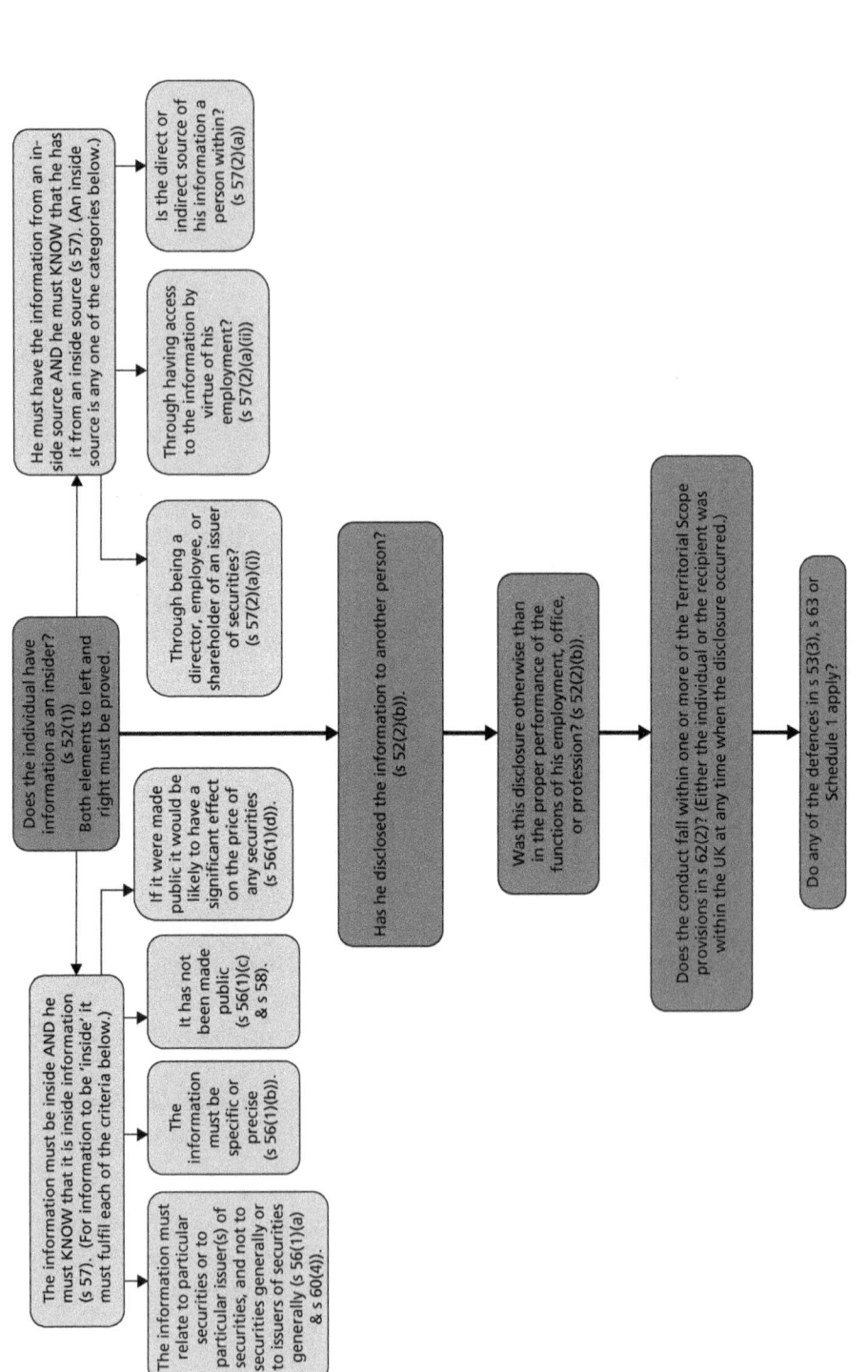

Do any of the defences in s 53(3), s 63 or Schedule 1 apply?

Figure 3. Flow chart for the s 52(2)(b) 'Disclosing' offence

5.32 In the case of *Grongaard and Bang*,[22] the ECJ considered the meaning of Article 3(a) of the IDD which required Member States to prohibit an insider from 'disclosing that inside information to any third party unless such disclosure is made in the normal course of the exercise of his employment, profession or duties'. The ECJ held that the purpose of the Directive was to protect investor confidence in the transferable securities market by prohibiting insider dealing, thereby ensuring that the market functioned properly. The exception contained in Article 3 applied where such disclosure was made by the person in the normal course of his employment. That exception was only justified by a close link between the disclosure and the exercise of the person's professional duties; therefore it had to be strictly necessary and proportionate. Whether the disclosure came within the exception depended on the national rules governing the employee's duties. The national court should apply the exception strictly and take account of the sensitivity of the information and the fact that each incidence of disclosure was liable to increase the risk of a breach of the IDD.

5.33 Another important matter is that neither the encouraging nor disclosing offences require actual dealing to result from the encouragement or disclosure. This is confirmed by a statement made by the then Economic Secretary to the Treasury, Anthony Nelson, when he introduced the Criminal Justice Bill to the House of Commons Standing Committee in June 1993:[23]

> The second and third forms of the offence are effectively anti-avoidance measures. They prohibit disclosure of information which could be used for insider dealing and for encouraging someone to deal in circumstances where he is not given inside information.

5.34 In respect of each of the secondary offences, the harm that the statute seeks to prohibit is the breach of the fiduciary duty owed by an insider as a result of being entrusted with inside information. This is consistent with the underlying rationale of the IDD and the CJA—that it is the abuse of this confidential relationship that undermines the integrity of markets and more importantly investor confidence in those markets, and therefore this conduct needs to be criminalised in its own right. In these respects, s 52 CJA covers, and is intended to cover, the full range of insider dealing behaviour.

---

[22] C-384/02 *Grongaard and Bang* [2005] ECR I-9939; [2006] 1 CMLR 30; [2006] CEC 241; [2006] IRLR 214.
[23] HC Deb (n 1) 134.

6

INSIDE INFORMATION (s 56 CJA)

1. Introduction	6.01	6. Information which has not been 'made public' (s 56(1)(c))	6.64
2. The statutory definition of inside information	6.02	Proving that information has not been 'made public'	6.67
3. Identifying the inside information	6.03	The meaning of 'made public'	6.70
4. Relating to particular securities or issuers (s 56(1)(a) CJA)	6.10	Information 'made public' (s 58 CJA)	6.72
Information which may affect a company's business prospects	6.17	Circumstances in which information is conclusively 'made public' (s 58(2)(a)–(d))	6.76
5. Specific or precise (s 56(1)(b) CJA)	6.22	Journalists	6.84
Legislative background to s 56(1)(b) CJA	6.23	Circumstances in which information may be treated as 'made public' (s 58(3))	6.87
The meaning of 'specific or precise'	6.25	7. The evidential practicalities of proving that information has not been 'made public'	6.95
Company directors and inside information	6.33		
Company analysts, fund managers, and inside information	6.36	8. Likely to have a 'significant effect' on price (s 56(1)(d) CJA)	6.111
Specific or precise information and alleged secondary insiders	6.39	The meaning of 'significant effect'	6.115
Cases in which there is direct evidence of the information communicated	6.42	9. Price-affected securities	6.129
Cases which depend on inference from circumstantial evidence	6.48		

1. Introduction

6.01 This Chapter deals with the statutory definition of 'inside information' in s 56 of the Criminal Justice Act 1993 ('CJA') and each of the required elements which must be proved for information to qualify as 'inside information' for the purposes of the CJA. It also deals with the evidential issues that may arise in respect of each of these elements.

2. The statutory definition of inside information

Section 56—'Inside information', etc

(1) For the purposes of this section and section 57, 'inside information' means information which
  (a) relates to particular securities or to a particular issuer of securities or to particular issuers of securities and not to securities generally or to issuers of securities generally;
  (b) is specific or precise;
  (c) has not been made public; and
  (d) if it were made public would be likely to have a significant effect on the price of any securities.
(2) For the purposes of this Part, securities are 'price-affected securities' in relation to inside information, and inside information is 'price-sensitive information' in relation to securities, if and only if the information would, if made public, be likely to have a significant effect on the price of the securities.
(3) For the purposes of this section 'price' includes value.

6.02 The wording of s 56 CJA largely mirrors the wording of Article 1(1) of the Insider Dealing Directive ('IDD'),[1] save for the requirement that the information be 'specific or precise', the relevance of which is discussed below.[2] The IDD required that:

> 'inside information' shall mean information which has not been made public of a precise nature relating to one or several issuers of transferable securities or to one or several transferable securities, which, if it were made public, would be likely to have a significant effect on the price of the transferable security or securities in question.

3. Identifying the inside information

6.03 Whether or not the information in question is 'inside' must be objectively assessed in accordance with the criteria set out in s 56(1) CJA and will always depend on the facts of each case. What is critical is that the prosecution must be able to identify what information it relies on as being capable of being 'inside'. For example:

> Company X's shares are trading at 20p. Upon the announcement that Company Y has made a recommended all-cash offer for Company X, the price dramatically and suddenly increases to 40p. No one outside the Boards of Companies X and Y and their advisers knew about the deal, and there have been no leaks. It is perhaps not difficult in such a case to demonstrate that the information that Company X was the subject of a recommended all-cash offer was inside information.

---

[1] Council Directive 89/592/EEC Article 1(1).
[2] See Chapter 6, Section 5.

6.04 However, situations are rarely this straightforward. For example, it does not necessarily follow that a rise in price upon an announcement of a takeover or other significant event, can be taken as evidence that the information contained within the announcement must have been information 'likely to have a significant effect on price'. The reason for this is that many factors can operate to affect the share price of companies. For example, there may have been leaks prior to the official announcement that have caused the share price of the target company to rise, or there may have been other news—such as a general improvement in the performance of the sector in which the company operates.

6.05 It may also be the case that the extent of the price rise also gives rise to doubts about the 'significance' of the price effect. Sometimes a share price does not rise at all upon an announcement, perhaps because the ultimate deal is not one that the market considers to be particularly attractive. Sometimes there is no announcement at all because the negotiations break down and the deal comes to nothing.

6.06 Inside information cannot be seen as a constant, ie, it comes into existence, remains the same throughout negotiations and then is extinguished upon the official announcement. The reality is that a confidential negotiation, for example of a potential takeover, is an organic and incremental process. In these circumstances, the inside information is bound to ebb and flow and change over time. The outcome of the negotiation may have a significant effect on the price of the target's shares when the official announcement is made, or it may not. The negotiations may fail altogether and no announcement is made, but this does not necessarily mean that information regarding the prior negotiations is not capable of being inside information at the time those negotiations are taking place.

6.07 Given these difficulties, it is common in insider dealing cases for the prosecution to obtain expert evidence in order to identify what information is capable of being 'inside' information at any given time, particularly in relation to the issue of price sensitivity of the information in question. But whether expert evidence is obtained or not, it remains the prosecution's duty to identify the inside information upon which it relies and which must be measured against the s 56(1) CJA criteria. So for example, in the case of *R v Malcolm Calvert*,[3] which concerned insider dealing on the basis of inside information originating from an unknown source in the Corporate Broking division of Cazenove and Co, the inside information related to forthcoming corporate takeovers, and the prosecution identified specifically the pieces of information known within Cazenove at the time of the defendant's dealing (such as the likely takeover price, timing of the announcement, etc) and upon which it relied as being 'inside information'. Each piece of information, once identified, must then be measured against the requirements of s 56 CJA.

---

[3] *R v Malcolm Calvert*, unreported, Southwark Crown Court, His Honour Judge Testar and a jury, 16 Feb to 11 Mar 2010. FSA/PN/041/2010.

In some cases, it is straightforward to identify precisely what information was in the defendant's possession. In *R v Mustafa and others*,[4] the insiders worked in the confidential print rooms at JP Morgan Cazenove and UBS. As a result, they had access to documents which related to forthcoming corporate takeovers on which those investment banks were advising. The inside information was disseminated by the insiders to the trading defendants using a variety of methods, including telephone contact, emails, documents saved onto USB memory sticks and documents uploaded onto web-based email accounts. It was therefore possible to identify the documents in question and assess whether the information contained in those documents met the test for inside information. 6.08

A similar position arose in *R v Richard Joseph*,[5] where the defendant dealt on the basis of inside information contained in documents he had received from one of the same insiders as in the *R v Mustafa* case. 6.09

4. Relating to particular securities or issuers (s 56(1)(a) CJA)

By s 56(1)(a) CJA, the information in question must relate to particular securities or to a particular issuer of securities, or to particular issuers of securities and not to securities generally or to issuers of securities generally. 6.10

'Issuer' is defined in s 60(2) CJA: 6.11

> (2) For the purposes of this Part an 'issuer', in relation to any securities, means any company, public sector body or individual by which or by whom the securities have been or are to be issued.

'Company' is defined in s 60(3)(a) CJA: 6.12

> (a) 'company' means any body (whether or not incorporated and wherever incorporated or constituted) which is not a public sector body.

'Public sector body' is defined in s 60(3)(b) CJA as: 6.13

> (i) the government of the United Kingdom, of Northern Ireland or of any country or territory outside the United Kingdom;
> (ii) a local authority in the United Kingdom or elsewhere;
> (iii) any international organisation the members of which include the United Kingdom or another member state;
> (iv) the Bank of England; or
> (v) the central bank of any sovereign State.

An example of information relating to particular securities or issuers would be a situation in which Company A is in takeover negotiations with Company B. 6.14

---

[4] *R v Mustafa and others* unreported, Southwark Crown Court, His Honour Judge Pegden QC and a jury, 5 March to 23 July 2012. FSA/PN/080/2012.
[5] *R v Richard Joseph*, unreported, Southwark Crown Court, His Honour Judge Pegden QC and a jury, 30 Jan to 11 Mar 2013. FSA/PN/023/2013.

Other examples are—that Company C's trading results are significantly better or worse than the market expected, or that Company D has won or lost an important contract.

6.15 In most of the insider dealing prosecutions brought by the FSA, the alleged inside information has concerned takeover negotiations. This is perhaps not surprising given that such events provide the greatest scope for significant price movements and at the same time are subject to more intensive market monitoring so that abnormal trading is more likely to be detected. In such cases, it is unlikely to be in issue that information that Company A is in takeover negotiations with Company B amounts to information which 'relates to particular issuers of securities'.

6.16 Other examples which would fall into this category include information regarding positive drilling results in relation to an oil and gas company,[6] and knowledge of an imminent announcement of negative trading results.[7] Recently in the US, concerns have been raised regarding the practice of providing high-frequency traders with market moving consumer survey results seconds before the information is given to other subscribers. The two-second advantage is more than enough time for such traders to take advantage of the information to execute large volumes of trades. The information in question, however, relates to surveys of consumer sentiment, and therefore it would be difficult to assert that the information relates to particular issuers / securities.[8]

Information which may affect a company's business prospects

6.17 By s 60(4) CJA:

> information shall be treated as relating to an issuer of securities[9] which is a company not only where it is about the company but also where it may affect the company's business prospects.

6.18 The Treasury commentary on the original draft of the Criminal Justice Bill (October 1992)[10] argued for this provision, stating that an insider dealing statute would not be effective if it did not apply to dealing on the basis of price-sensitive information about a company's business prospects that did not relate specifically to the companies themselves. The section attracted a fair amount of criticism in the

---

[6] *R v Neel and Matthew Uberoi*, unreported, Southwark Crown Court, His Honour Judge Testar and a jury, 28 Oct to 6 Nov 2009. FSA/PN/149/2009.
[7] *R v McQuoid and Melbourne*, unreported, Southwark Crown Court, His Honour Judge Testar J and a jury, 9 to 27 Mar 2009. FSA/PN/042/2009.
[8] See Peter Lattman, 'Thomson Reuters to Suspend Early Peeks at Key Index', *New York Times* (8 July 2013).
[9] 'Security' is defined in s 54(1) CJA as any security which falls within those listed in Schedule 2 CJA (which includes shares) and which satisfies any conditions applying to it in the Insider Dealing (Securities and Regulated Markets) Order 1994. See Chapter 8.
[10] Treasury commentary on the original draft of the Criminal Justice Bill (October 1992) para 15.

Parliamentary debates for its potential breadth and scope.[11] Of particular concern at the time was that this provision had the potential to capture investment analysts on the basis that any company briefing they attended would be likely to contain some information about a company's business prospects which may well also contain information relevant to the business prospects of other companies within the same sector.[12]

What is clear is that s 60(4) CJA is (and is intended to be), potentially very broad. It expands the potential scope of the s 52 CJA offences to include, for example, information that relates to Company A's key suppliers or clients which would be likely to have a significant knock-on effect on Company A's future business prospects. **6.19**

Section 60(4) CJA is also wide enough to cover information that affects entire market sectors. For example, it would include information that environmental requirements for the disposal of waste were to be significantly increased, which would thereby significantly increase the operating costs of Company A which operates in the waste disposal sector; decisions by regulators such as the Office of Communications ('OFCOM') would also potentially be included.[13] **6.20**

That said, despite the concerns expressed in Parliament about the position of the investment analyst, only one such analyst has ever been prosecuted for insider dealing on the basis of information of this type received during a company briefing. This was a Scottish case concerning an Edinburgh analyst named Mr Mackie.[14] Where information exists that may affect a company's business prospects, it is also invariably going to be information about the company itself and therefore caught by s 56(1)(a) CJA. Moreover, although this section has the potential to be wide ranging of itself, in reality its scope will be limited by the other requirements of s 56(1) CJA which also need to be satisfied. Probably for these reasons, s 60(4) CJA is not an issue that has troubled the criminal courts and perhaps could be viewed as unlikely to do so. **6.21**

5. Specific or precise (s 56(1)(b) CJA)

The requirement that the information be 'specific or precise' operates as a check on the potentially wide reach of the first element discussed above. It means that information will only be 'inside' if it is sufficiently definite to amount to more than rumour, supposition, innuendo or everyday knowledge. **6.22**

---

[11] HL Deb vol 540, 3 Dec 1992, col 1495, and see Brenda Hannigan, *Insider Dealing* (2nd edn, Longman 1994) 60–1.
[12] HC Deb, Session 1992–93, Standing Committee B, 10 June 1993, cols 196–7.
[13] Government Minister Anthony Nelson specifically referred to decisions by Regulators that would have an impact on the structure of an industry as falling within the ambit of this provision. See HC Deb (n 12).
[14] *Mackie (Thorold) v HM Advocate*, 1994 JC 132; 1995 SLT 110; 1994 SCCR 277; *The Times*, 7 Nov 1995; *The Independent*, 11 Dec 1995 (CS) CA and para 6.38 below.

Legislative background to s 56(1)(b) CJA

6.23 The legislative background demonstrates that this choice of wording in s 56(1)(b) CJA—'specific *or* precise' was deliberate. The term 'specific' had its roots (so far as the UK was concerned) in its predecessor legislation—s 10 of the Company Securities (Insider Dealing) Act 1985 ('CSA') which referred to information, 'which relates to specific matters relating or of concern to that company'.

6.24 The Proposal for the IDD[15] originally defined inside information as information 'of a specific nature'. However, by the time the final version of the IDD was published, this requirement was contained in Article 1(1) IDD and the wording had been changed to information 'of a precise nature'.[16] It is not clear why this change occurred. The Economic and Social Committee's Opinion on the Draft Directive[17] commented that the words 'of a specific nature' were not sufficiently clear for Member States to transpose into their national law, but this does not explain why the European legislators subsequently decided that 'of a precise nature' was any clearer. The UK Government quite deliberately hedged its position by using the term 'specific or precise', and in so doing, the CJA has deliberately exceeded the minimum requirement imposed by the IDD.

The meaning of 'specific or precise'

6.25 During the Parliamentary debates it was suggested that given the importance of these terms to the offence as a whole, a legislative definition of 'specific' and 'precise' should be included within the CJA. This option was not taken up on the basis that '[i]t is difficult, if not impossible, to give an exhaustive definition of all circumstances that would be covered by one word or the other'.[18]

6.26 What is clear, however, is that in s 56(1)(b) CJA, 'specific' or 'precise' are, and are intended to be, two distinct elements. The reason for adopting this approach was explained by the Economic Secretary to the Treasury during the Parliamentary debates.[19] He explained that the term 'precise' derived from the IDD but that the Government was concerned that using 'precise' alone might be interpreted narrowly by the courts. For that reason, the legislative draughtsman added the term 'specific' as an alternative.[20] In terms of the difference between the two terms he stated:

> In general, specific information might typically be that a bid was going to be made. Precise information would be the price at which that bid was going to be made.

---

[15] Proposal for a Council Directive coordinating regulations on insider trading COM(B 7) 111 final (25 May 1987) (87/C 153/09), Draft Article 6.
[16] Council Directive 89/592/EEC, 13 Nov 1989.
[17] Opinion on the proposal for a Council Directive co-ordinating regulations on insider trading (88/C 35/10), Comments on Draft Article 6.
[18] HC Deb (n 12) col 174.
[19] HC Deb (n 12) cols 174–75 (Anthony Nelson).
[20] HC Deb (n 12) col 173.

On that basis, precise information would be narrow, exact and definitive. Therefore its meaning could be construed extremely narrowly and would be a much narrower definition that in existing legislation. We believe that the addition of 'specific' would keep the integrity of what was required by the directive and what the existing legislation allows.[21]

6.27 The term 'specific' is therefore wider in scope than 'precise'. Specific information need not necessarily be precise, but precise information will always be specific. So, for example, the fact that negotiations are taking place for a takeover of Company A by Company B will be specific information, but it will not necessarily be precise information unless such details as the price and timing are additionally known. However, the term 'precise' is not limited to the price at which a bid is to be made, or the timing of the bid, but would also include, for example, a date, an event, or a fact.[22] What is clear is that the purpose of this provision was to exclude mere rumour and speculation from falling within the definition of inside information.[23]

6.28 The fact that both terms are undefined by statute means that whether information is specific or precise will be a question of fact and degree, based on all the surrounding circumstances. The construction of these terms is a matter of language not law. Ultimately, it will be a matter for the jury to decide on the evidence in any particular case whether there is information capable of satisfying either (or both) of these concepts.

6.29 If information is viewed on a scale, it would start at one end with innuendo, rumour, hint, and the like, rising to general information in the middle, and at the other end specific or precise information. However, it is important to recognise that 'specific' or 'precise' is not synonymous with 'certain'. For example, in the context of a bid negotiation, inside information prior to an announcement will be subject to the possibility that the bid does not proceed, or does not proceed at the expected price. A takeover negotiation is a stage process, and every fact to do with the process, as well as the totality of the process itself, is capable of amounting to specific or precise information. Likewise, contingencies relating to the actual occurrence of the final event do not mitigate the specific or precise nature of the information at the time at which the trading occurs.

6.30 There is also a distinction between information which is specific or precise and information which is detailed. For example, information that a named company is engaged in takeover negotiations is specific without being detailed. There is no need for the insider who passes on that information, to identify the names of those involved or the contractual terms. If those additional details are provided, they in turn amount to further pieces of specific or precise information. For example, in

---

[21] HC Deb (n 12) col 174.
[22] HC Deb (n 12) col 175.
[23] HC Deb (n 12) col 174.

the case of *R v Malcolm Calvert*,[24] the specific information in Mr Calvert's possession in relation to the stocks traded, was the fact of the takeover negotiations and the precise information included such matters as likely target price, timing, and number of bidders.

6.31 In *R v Neil Rollins*,[25] the specific information relied upon by the prosecution was that the trading results of the company whose shares were traded were going to be significantly worse than the market had expected, and the precise information was the timing of the announcement of those results to the market.

6.32 In *R v Mustafa and others*,[26] the specific information concerned the fact of forthcoming takeovers and the precise information was the timing and content of those announcements—which came from confidential documents which the defendants had obtained via the print room of UBS and JP Morgan Cazenove.

Company directors and inside information

6.33 Company directors are inevitably going to be far better informed than anyone else about their company's day-to-day activities. Does this mean that they are effectively prevented from ever using this advantage to inform their dealing in the shares of their own company? The answer to this is that company directors are required to assess whether the information they have, viewed objectively, fulfils the necessary criteria for inside information under s 56(1) CJA. Applying this test will help to distinguish the general information about a company that a director inevitably holds, from the specific or precise information that will from time to time be in his possession, which will amount to inside information if it also fulfils the other criteria set out in s 56(1) CJA.[27]

6.34 However, in recognition of the potential for company directors to abuse their special position, the FCA has published the 'Model Code.'[28] It imposes restrictions on the dealing in securities of a listed company beyond those imposed by the criminal law. The purpose of the Model Code is to ensure that persons discharging managerial responsibilities (referred to as 'restricted persons') and employee insiders, do not abuse, and do not place themselves under suspicion of abusing, inside information that they may be thought to have, especially in the period leading up to the announcement of a company's results.

---

[24] *R v Malcolm Calvert* (n 3).
[25] *R v Neil Rollins*, unreported, Southwark Crown Court, 16 to 26 Nov 2010. FSA/PN/168/2010.
[26] *R v Mustafa and others* (n 4).
[27] See *R v Neil Rollins* (n 25).
[28] FCA Handbook of Rules and Guidance, LR9 Annex 1 The Model Code (R).

6.35 The Model Code requires restricted persons to obtain clearance to deal in advance of dealing in the company's shares and also imposes bans on such persons dealing at all during 'prohibited periods'—which are specified periods of time prior to publication of the company's results (known as 'closed periods'). 'Restricted persons' are also prevented from dealing on a short-term basis (which is considered in the Model Code to be a period of 1twelve months or less). In addition, 'restricted persons' are required to take reasonable steps to prevent dealing by or on behalf of a 'connected person' in similar circumstances.

Company analysts, fund managers, and inside information

6.36 During the Parliamentary debates on the Criminal Justice Bill, the Government made it clear that it did not wish to impede the legitimate relationship of the investment analyst or the fund manager with the companies they cover, and that it viewed such relationships as being as much in the interests of investors in the financial markets as they are in the companies themselves.[29]

6.37 There is a difference, however, between information imparted by companies to analysts and fund managers as part of their ordinary business relationship—and from which analysts would then form their own independent views of the company in question and its prospects, and the imparting of specific or precise information, which would be capable of being 'inside' provided the other s 56 CJA criteria are satisfied. The CJA does not place analysts in receipt of inside information in any special category. They are subject to exactly the same restrictions on their ability to deal, encourage others to deal, or disclose that information as any other member of the public.[30]

6.38 Since 1993 there has been only one prosecution of an investment analyst for insider dealing. This was a Scottish case—*Mackie (Thorold) v HM Advocate*, which concerned an Edinburgh analyst named Mr Mackie,[31] whose conviction was subsequently quashed on appeal. Mr Mackie worked at the time for a firm of Edinburgh stockbrokers called Bell Lawrie Wright. In September 1991, Bell Lawrie clients sold two million shares in Shanks & McEwan, a waste-disposal and construction company. The sale followed advice from Mr Mackie after he had attended a meeting with a Peter Runciman who was then Chairman of Shanks & McEwan. The issue at trial was whether Mr Runciman had told Mr Mackie about the impending profit warning (which would have amounted to specific or precise information), or whether (as Mr Mackie contended), he had merely been informed in general terms that Shanks & McEwan had not had a particularly good year—which was neither

---

[29] HC Deb, Session 1992–93 Standing Committee B, 10 June 1993, col 175. See Donald C Langevoort, 'Investment Analysts and the Law of Insider Trading' (1990) 76 Virginia L Rev 1023 for a more circumspect view of this relationship.
[30] 'The Law on Insider Dealing, a Consultative Document' DTI, (Dec 1989) para 2.5.
[31] *Mackie (Thorold) v HM Advocate*, 1994 JC 132; 1995 SLT 110; 1994 SCCR 277; *The Times*, 7 Nov 1995, *Independent*, 11 Dec 1995 (CS) CA.

Specific or precise information and alleged secondary insiders

6.39 Ultimately, whether the information held by an alleged insider is specific or precise (or both) is always going to be fact-specific and therefore a matter to be determined by the courts in each given case. In each case, the court will need to look objectively at the information and make an assessment as to where it sits on the sliding scale rising from, at one end, innuendo, rumour, gossip, hint, through to specific or precise information at the other.

6.40 Sometimes the specificity or precision of the information will be glaringly obvious.[32] At other times, the position will be rather more complicated. In many instances, the nature and content of information regarding an event will change organically overtime (for example as a takeover negotiation proceeds) and will also be affected by what information is in the public domain at any given time.

6.41 A further complicating factor is the position of an alleged secondary insider—a person who the prosecution alleges is one or more steps removed from the source of the inside information. Even if the primary insider (A) is in receipt of specific or precise information is it likely that he will have communicated this in full to the alleged secondary insider (B) who goes on to deal? Perhaps sometimes it will have been, but is it not more likely that in most instances B will simply have been 'tipped' by A to 'buy some of these'? And what is the position if it is alleged that B has gone on to tip a third party (C)? In the vast majority of cases, there will be no direct evidence proving exactly what information was passed from A to B or C, or in what form. Insider dealers do not generally pass inside information to each other in circumstances where they are likely to be overheard—or worse, recorded.

Cases in which there is direct evidence of the information communicated

6.42 There are of course notable exceptions to the above, for example *R v Sanders and others*,[33] in which the FSA obtained tape recordings of the telephone lines at Blue Index and found telephone calls in which certain of the defendants were recorded openly discussing inside information relating to some of the stocks that were traded. Where there is direct evidence such as this, a court is able to make an assessment based on the actual information that is passed from A to B and decide whether that information passes the hurdles of specificity or precision.[34]

---

[32] *R v Rollins* (n 25); *R v Calvert* (n 3), and *R v Mustafa* (n 4) paras 6.30–6.32.
[33] *R v Sanders and others*, unreported, Southwark Crown Court, Mr Justice Simon, 20 June 2012. FSA/PN/060/2012 & FSA/PN/067/2012.
[34] In the *Sanders* case, this was not necessary as the defendants in question subsequently pleaded guilty.

Specific or precise (s 56(1)(b) CJA)

6.43 In the case of *R v Staines and Morrissey*,[35] the Court of Appeal was concerned with a case of insider dealing under the CSA and determined that information was perfectly capable of being specific even if it is incomplete or vague in certain details. Whether it is specific or not would depend on an assessment of all the surrounding facts and circumstances.

6.44 The appellants in *R v Staines and Morrissey* were convicted of counselling or procuring another to deal in securities whilst being insiders (referred to as 'prohibited persons'). The facts which gave rise to this case were interesting. Mr Martin Priddle was a chartered accountant, who as a result of his employment, became aware that one of his firm's clients was considering a takeover of a company called Aaronson's at a large premium. Shortly after this, Mr Priddle met the appellants for a social evening, during the course of which he mentioned that he was working on a bid that one of his firm's clients was proposing to make for the publicly quoted capital of a target company. He did not give the company's name. There then followed a guessing game during which Mr Priddle gave certain details, such as the target's business, its price / earnings ratio, the current share price, and the likely offer price. He also stated that the announcement was likely to be in two to three weeks' time.

6.45 In the days following these disclosures, the defendants, having guessed correctly that the company Mr Priddle was referring to was Aaronson's, persuaded others to buy shares in Aaronson's on their behalves. The prosecution case was that, because it was easy for the company to be identified by looking in the newspapers and making some telephone calls, the information which Mr Priddle had given was 'specific' within the meaning of the CSA. The jury convicted. The appellants appealed, contending that the information provided by Mr Priddle did not contain sufficient detail to be specific.

6.46 The Court of Appeal rejected this argument. The Lord Chief Justice, Lord Bingham CJ gave the judgment of the Court in which he said:

> The most obvious case of insider dealing plainly occurs where a connected person tells a friend that he is advising a client who is prepared to make a bid for the share capital of named Company B. But there will doubtless occur less obvious cases where a connected person supplies a friend with information which enables the friend to identify Company B. It all depends upon what is said and to whom. Material which may be meaningless to a hearer ignorant of the operation of the securities market may be of great significance to a sophisticated city analyst. Provided there is material fit for a jury to consider, it is very much a matter for the jury.[36]

6.47 The Lord Chief Justice also specifically approved the reasoning of the trial Judge who had held that it was not a requirement of s 10 of the CSA that the company in

---

[35] *R v Staines and Morrissey* [1997] 2 Cr App R 426.
[36] *R v Staines and Morrissey* (n 35) 436e–f.

question be specifically named by the tipster in order to make the information he imparts regarding a company's securities price-sensitive.[37]

Cases which depend on inference from allegedly circumstantial evidence

6.48 In many cases, the prosecution will need to prove the passage of inside information from the primary insider (A) to the alleged secondary insider (B), by way of inference from strands of circumstantial evidence. This may include, for example, the timing of telephone calls and / or meetings, timeliness of trading, substantial trading outside the trader's usual pattern, etc. In such circumstances, there may be no direct evidence of the alleged tip at all, or at least none unless and until the defendant himself gives evidence at trial.

6.49 It follows therefore that information must be capable of being specific or precise even if it is not articulated in full. This was the view of the Court of Appeal in *R v Staines and Morrissey*.[38] It must also follow from this that communication of inside information does not have to be explicit and may be made by inference as well as by express words. For example, a person who is known to work as an accountant dealing with mergers and acquisitions, who tips a friend to buy securities in Company X, is giving that person specific and precise information without giving the detail he possesses.

6.50 When a person is known to the recipient to be in possession of inside information, in some cases the emphasis placed on the recommendation, or the manner in which it is delivered, can itself convey the requisite degree of precision or specificity. In effect, the information has been conveyed in such a manner that the recipient knows what he is really being told. In such circumstances, it is perfectly possible to impart inside information by way of little more than a 'nudge and a wink'.

6.51 Were this not the case, it would be a complete defence to all offences under s 52(1) and 52(2) of the CJA to simply ensure that the information was passed from A to B, merely by saying, for example, 'I would buy company X's shares if I were you', even when B knows that the person making this statement is engaged in a capacity that gives him legitimate or illegitimate access to inside information.

6.52 Ultimately, the issue will depend on the facts of each case and the relationship between the individuals concerned and should, in most cases, be left to the jury to decide in accordance with Lord Bingham's judgment in *R v Staines and Morrissey*.[39] That said, the issue still causes difficulties for the Courts as demonstrated by a subsequent case in which this issue arose.

---

[37] *R v Staines and Morrissey* (n 35) 434–35.
[38] *R v Staines and Morrissey* (n 35).
[39] *R v Staines and Morrissey* (n 35).

Specific or precise (s 56(1)(b) CJA)

6.53 *R v Power and Carlisle*[40] was a Department of Trade and Industry ('DTI') insider dealing prosecution under the CJA. The prosecution alleged that in 1997 and 1998, Power, who was employed in a senior position at a company named Belgo's, passed on inside information regarding Belgo's to his friend Mr Carlisle which Carlisle then traded on, making approximately £90,000 in profits.

6.54 At the commencement of the trial, Mr Power (the insider) pleaded guilty. The trial therefore proceeded against Carlisle alone. The prosecution did not adduce evidence of Mr Power's guilty plea at the trial, and Mr Carlisle's case was that he had bought shares in Belgo's for his own legitimate reasons and not because he had received any inside information from Power.

6.55 At the close of the prosecution case, the defence on behalf of Mr Carlisle made a successful half time submission of no case to answer on a number of grounds.[41] One of the grounds for that application was that there was no evidence that specific or precise information regarding Belgo's had been passed from Power to Carlisle.

6.56 During legal argument there was some discussion of what the terms 'specific or precise' meant in this context. The arguments on this issue are summarised in the trial judge's subsequent explanation to the jury when directing a not guilty verdict in respect of Mr Carlisle:[42]

> I asked prosecuting counsel, 'If somebody I know is an insider, operations director or whatever Power's title was, says to me, "Buy shares in X because they are about to take our company over", that is information that a the jury could safely say was specific or precise ... Supposing the director of operations says to me, "Cannot tell you why, but if I were you, I would buy shares in Goggins Ltd next week", and I do that because I trust him, he is a good friend, the jury could not say that I had been given precise and specific information about price-sensitive movement. I have just been given what we have been calling in argument a "bare tip" and I am relying then not on knowledge that I have been given, but really on the trust I have in a friend.'
>
> Parliament has said that is not insider dealing. It is a fairly narrow line, but after hearing a lot of very helpful submissions from counsel and thinking carefully about it, I have come to the view that if I gave you those instructions, you could not safely and confidently be sure of guilt.

6.57 It is not clear from the transcript whether the trial judge was referred to the Court of Appeal's judgment in *R v Staines and Morrissey*.[43] In any event, he appears to have taken a more restrictive view than the judgment in *R v Staines and Morrissey*

---

[40] *R v Power and Carlisle*, unreported, transcript of ruling of His Honour Judge Wadsworth QC, 24 Feb 2009 (Merrills Corp).
[41] These grounds included that Carlisle traded on the basis of information that was already in the public domain and that there was no evidence to suggest that Power had said anything at all to Carlisle, let alone passed him inside information.
[42] *R v Power and Carlisle* (n 40).
[43] *R v Staines and Morrissey* (n 35).

would necessarily require. Leaving aside the facts in the *Power and Carlisle* case, there appears to be no reason why the 'heavy tip' imparted in circumstances where a recipient knows that a provider is in a position of knowledge as regards the company in question, should not be sufficient to constitute inside information. This would clearly be within the contemplation of the ruling in *R v Staines and Morrissey* and would also appeal to common sense, given that this is invariably likely to be the way that information is passed along a chain of alleged insiders.

6.58 A further first instance legal ruling was given on this issue by Mr Justice Simon, the trial judge in the case of *R v Adam Buck*.[44] This ruling follows the rationale in *R v Staines and Morrissey*. The case arose out of the *R v Sanders and others*[45] case. The prosecution alleged that James Sanders[46] had provided specific and precise inside information about one stock (Getty Images Inc ('Getty')) to Mr Buck, who had then traded on the basis of this information. There was no direct evidence on this issue, and the prosecution therefore relied on inferences to be drawn from allegedly circumstantial evidence. Mr Buck successfully defended this allegation at trial. His case (which the jury accepted by its not guilty verdict) relied on a number of matters in his defence, including that he did not know and had no reason to believe that anything said to him by James Sanders about Getty was based on inside information. He also pointed to a number of public announcements about the fact that Getty had put itself up for auction, which caused a good deal of public speculation about a forthcoming takeover and a corresponding increase in the share price indicating a good deal of market support and therefore a reasonable and rational basis for buying Getty. He also relied on the fact that his trading pattern was inconsistent with him having traded on the basis of inside information. In addition, he submitted that there was no evidence that any specific or precise information had been passed to him by James Sanders.

6.59 Mr Justice Simon's ruling on the 'specific or precise' issue followed a half time submission made on Mr Buck's behalf on a number of grounds, which included the matters above. One of the grounds for the submission was that there was no evidence that specific or precise information had been passed to him from the known insider (James Sanders). The trial judge on this issue held that:

> Apart from the fact that vague or imprecise information will not be sufficient, the [CJA] does not set out the degree to which the information must be specific or precise. However I accept the prosecution submission that the information can be specific or precise without being detailed (for example on terms as to price and timing). Nor need the information be fully articulated. Thus, if a lawyer, banker or accountant who is known to be involved in takeovers or mergers, tips a friend

---

[44] *R v Adam Buck*, Southwark Crown Court, Approved ruling of Mr Justice Simon, 9 May 2012.
[45] *R v Sanders and others* (n 33).
[46] James Sanders had by this stage pleaded guilty to insider dealing in Getty shares and there was therefore no issue that he was an insider.

to buy shares in a particular company it may, depending on the circumstances, amount to giving specific information, although there may be no further detail.

6.60 The judge specifically referred to Lord Bingham's judgment in *R v Staines and Morrissey*[47] and observed that the Lord Chief Justice was stressing the importance in this type of case of the particular facts and the importance of the jury's function in assessing the facts.

6.61 Therefore *R v Staines and Morrissey*[48] provides a useful starting point regarding the approach to be taken in cases where it is a matter in issue as to whether 'specific or precise' information has been passed from A to B. The ruling in *R v Adam Buck*[49] strongly suggests that the Judge's interpretation of those words in *R v Carlisle*[50] should not be considered a suitable template for future cases. It also takes the *R v Staines and Morrissey*[51] rationale a stage further as it deals with the current legislation (the CJA), concerns a case which relied (ultimately unsuccessfully) wholly on inference to be drawn from allegedly circumstantial evidence, and underlines the fact that, in the end, this is an issue of fact, not law, and therefore falls to be determined by the jury.

6.62 The effect of these authorities is to underline that information that satisfies s 56 CJA need not be articulated in full. Communication does not have to be explicit. Communication can be by inference as well as by express words. In some cases, the emphasis placed on the recommendation, or the manner in which it is delivered, can itself convey that degree of precision or specificity required for inside information. This is so if it conveys some information not publicly known that enables the recipient of the information to take advantage of it in circumstances contrary to the purpose of the IDD and FSMA. In effect, the information has been conveyed in such a manner that the recipient knows what he is really being told.

6.63 Were this not the case, it would be a complete defence (to all offences under s 52(1) and (2)) to ensure that the information was passed merely by saying, for example, 'I would buy X company shares if I were you', when the recipient knows that the person saying that is engaged in a capacity that gives him legitimate or illegitimate access to inside information.

6. Information which has not been 'made public' (s 56(1)(c) CJA)

6.64 A further requirement for information to qualify as 'inside' is that the information must not have been made public. It is for the prosecution to prove this negative. Information that has been made public is not inside information and, obviously, it

---

[47] *R v Staines and Morrissey* (n 35).
[48] *R v Staines and Morrissey* (n 35).
[49] *R v Adam Buck* (n 44).
[50] *R v Carlisle* (n 40).
[51] *R v Staines and Morrissey* (n 35).

is not an offence to trade using any information that has been made public. If information is 'made public' within the meaning of the CJA, it is irrelevant whether or not the defendant knew that it had been made public. Whether information has or has not been 'made public' is an issue of fact not knowledge. During the Parliamentary debates, it was said that:

> When information has and has not been made public is the single issue that has caused most concern to the organisations with which the Government has been discussing the Bill.[52]

6.65 In an insider dealing case, a defendant commonly asserts either that the inside information in question was wholly or partly in the public domain prior to his trading, or that other information was in the public domain and it was this which prompted his trading. Put colloquially, it may be suggested that the inside information was already 'out there'.

6.66 Sometimes, the prosecution will allege that a defendant has sought to justify his trading after the event, by reference to information that was publicly available at the time, and which, he asserts, would provide an investor with reasons for trading. This was the case in *R v Neel and Matthew Uberoi*,[53] in which Neel Uberoi produced printouts from the share information website ADVFN which related to one of the stocks with which he was indicted (Neutec Pharma plc), which he claimed supported his belief that the company was a good investment prospect and a possible takeover target.

Proving that information has not been 'made public'

6.67 Taken in isolation, the requirement in s 56(1)(c) CJA, to prove that information has not been made public, is potentially onerous. Plainly, the prosecution must adduce sufficient evidence to make the jury sure that the information in question had not been made public but does this mean that the burden on the prosecution to prove a negative is in effect limitless? How far does the prosecution have to go to prove a negative?

6.68 The extent of the potential problem is a useful starting point. Parliament surely could not have intended to create an offence that it is in the public interest to prohibit, but then make it impossible to successfully prosecute the offence. Simple principles of statutory interpretation would suggest that Parliament did not intend to set so high a barrier that it would in effect frustrate Part V of the CJA altogether.

6.69 The words of s 56(1)(c) CJA should be construed in the context of s 56(1) CJA as a whole. The remaining paragraphs of s 56(1) qualify the nature of what information has to be in the public domain to activate paragraph (c). Thus the information

---

[52] HC Deb (n 12) col 182.
[53] *R v Neel and Matthew Uberoi* (n 6).

in the public domain must relate to 'particular securities' or a 'particular issuer of securities' and must be 'specific or precise'. In addition, it must be information which, if it were made public, would be likely to have a significant effect on the price of the securities in question—in effect neutralising the price-sensitive effect of the inside information, even if it does not replicate it precisely. Plainly, the information would cease to be price-sensitive, and therefore no longer inside information, if it was public knowledge. However, mere general information or speculative chatter about a company will not be sufficient when set against the requirements of s 56(1) CJA as a whole.

The meaning of 'made public'

6.70 Article 1(1) of the IDD provided only that 'inside information shall mean information which has not been made public'.[54] What this meant was not further defined. The UK's previous domestic law, the CSA, provided no assistance either. The s 10(b) CSA provided only that the inside information must 'not be generally known to those persons who are accustomed or would be likely to deal in those securities'. This was rightly criticised for its lamentable lack of clarity.

6.71 The original draft of the Criminal Justice Bill, following this previous pattern, did not provide any definition of the 'made public' concept at all. The Treasury Commentary noted that it would not be helpful to provide a detailed definition because of 'the risk of causing difficulties for legitimate activities or seriously undermining the effectiveness of the legislation.'[55] Ultimately, this view did not prevail, largely due, it seems, to criticism that definition of such a crucial element could not be left to jury (or judicial) interpretation that would be bound to produce inconsistent results.

Information 'made public' (s 58 CJA)

> Section 58—Information 'made public'
>
> (1) For the purposes of section 56, 'made public', in relation to information, shall be construed in accordance with the following provisions of this section; but those provisions are not exhaustive as to the meaning of that expression.
> (2) Information is made public if
> (a) it is published in accordance with the rules of a regulated market for the purpose of informing investors and their professional advisers;
> (b) it is contained in records which by virtue of any enactment are open to inspection by the public;
> (c) it can be readily acquired by those likely to deal in any securities
>   (i) to which the information relates, or
>   (ii) of an issuer to which the information relates; or

---

[54] Council Directive (n 1).
[55] Treasury commentary (n 10) para 23.

(d) it is derived from information which has been made public.
(3) Information may be treated as made public even though
  (a) it can be acquired only by persons exercising diligence or expertise;
  (b) it is communicated to a section of the public and not to the public at large;
  (c) it can be acquired only by observation;
  (d) it is communicated only on payment of a fee; or
  (e) it is published only outside the United Kingdom.

6.72 During the Parliamentary debates, the Economic Secretary to the Treasury stated that the purpose of this section was:

> to bring a good deal more clarity and a good deal more understanding on the part of those who will have to operate within the law about what it does and does not mean. As for what is made public, it is a matter of fact—I hope this does not sound too much of a truism—as to whether something is made public. In the last resort, the courts may have to determine whether a piece of information had or had not been made public.[56]

6.73 Section 58 CJA is expressly stated to be a non-exhaustive definition and the ways in which information may be made public are disjunctive and not conjunctive. This turned out to be a wise decision on the part of the Government and the legislative draughtsmen, given that in 1993 it would have been scarcely possible to contemplate the explosion of the internet as a means of creation and dissemination of information. At the time of this drafting, financial websites such as ADVFN and 'Motley Fool', blogging, tweeting, and all manner of other social media which bring a torrent of information to the public, could scarcely have been imagined. But such media are now routinely used and inevitably form a part of any insider dealing case.

6.74 Section 58 CJA is divided into two distinct parts.[57] The first—s 58(2)(a)–(d)—describe the circumstances in which information is to be conclusively regarded as having been made public. If the information conforms with one of the requirements set out in (a)–(d), then it has been made public and it is not therefore 'inside' information. This issue is a question of fact and can be proved or disproved by appropriate evidence.

6.75 The second part (s 58(3)(a)–(e))—describes circumstances in which information *may* be treated as made public. There is therefore an element of discretion here. The fact that the information has (or has not) been dealt with in accordance with these sections, *may* (or may not) mean that it has been made public. Whether it has or not will depend on the facts of each individual case.

---

[56] HC Deb (n 12) col 186 (Anthony Nelson).
[57] This was precisely the intention of the Government—see HC Deb (n 12) col 182.

Circumstances in which information is conclusively 'made public' (s 58(2)(a)–(d))

Information is 'made public' when it is: **6.76**

- Section 58(2)(a)—published in accordance with the rules of a regulated market for the purpose of informing investors and their professional advisers.[58] This of course includes the Stock Exchange's Regulatory News Service and the equivalents in relation to other regulated markets.
- Section 58(2)(b)—contained in records which by virtue of any enactment are open to inspection by the public. This would of course include information at Companies House or the Patents Registry, or Public Records held at the National Archives. The essential requirement is that the public is entitled to inspect the record 'by virtue of any enactment'—therefore there must be some statutory basis for the right to inspect. Mere convention or practice will not suffice. In the Parliamentary debates it was made clear that this provision was deliberately drafted in order to prevent an insider from relying on publication in an obscure and unread publication such as a parish record.[59]
- Section 58(2)(c)—it can be readily acquired by those likely to deal. The predecessor to this section under the CSA was that the information had to be 'generally known to those accustomed or likely to deal'. This requirement was loosened in the CJA so that it is now sufficient if it can be 'readily acquired', even if it is not actually known.

The CJA does not further define 'readily acquired'. If information can be obtained **6.77**
via a subscription service does this mean that it can be 'readily acquired' albeit on payment of a fee? The answer is probably 'yes'—but will be a question of fact and degree in all cases. The Parliamentary debates made clear that this provision was also intended to cover situations in which the information has been made public by other means than written publication—perhaps by oral announcement or an obvious course of action being undertaken by a company.[60]

What about publication in an obscure journal in a remote location (for exam- **6.78**
ple information regarding a UK listed company, published in Kyrgyzstan)? Does this mean the information has been 'made public'? The answer is to refer back to the definition in s 58(2)(c) CJA and ask whether this publication can be 'readily

---

[58] The Traded Securities (Disclosure) Regulations 1994 (SI 1994 no 188) gives effect to Art 7 of the European Community Directive 89/592 [1989] OJ L334/30 which requires all companies and undertakings whose shares are admitted to trading on any investment exchange to inform the public as soon as possible of any major new developments in the companies' sphere of activity which are not publicly known, and if known would lead to substantial movements in the share price. There is provision for exemption where disclosure would prejudice the company concerned.
[59] HC Deb (n 12) col 183.
[60] HC Deb (n 12) col 183.

acquired' by those likely to deal. The Government in fact made it clear during debates that it did not consider that a publication in an obscure journal would be readily acquirable by those likely to deal in securities.[61] However, this may have been an easier question to determine at the time this legislation was enacted and before the massive development of the internet as a research tool, which brings all manner of obscure information sources to all manner of people at pretty much the touch of a button.

6.79 Information is not in the public domain unless it is 'public'. Whether an article in an obscure journal, a remote location, or even a Facebook entry, would qualify as 'public' would depend on the facts and circumstances of the case in question. Furthermore, the publicly available information in question must be 'likely to have a significant effect on the price of the securities'. It is not going to have that effect unless the information is sufficiently prominent—at least among those likely to deal in the securities in question—so as to have an effect on the price.

6.80 An example, albeit wholly unrelated to insider dealing and the CJA, of how material is made public so as to remove the confidentiality of that information is the *Spycatcher* case.[62] In that case, widespread publication overseas deprived the contents of the book of the confidentiality that would have justified an injunction against publication in the UK. As the *Spycatcher* case indicates, sometimes overseas publication may be material—but in an insider dealing / CJA context, this will only be when it is accessible to those who are likely to deal in the securities and/or has an effect on the price.

- Section 58(2)(d)—derived from information which has been made public.

6.81 It is clear from the Treasury Commentary and Parliamentary debates that this was intended to cover information (such as research recommendations) derived by analysts from information that has been made public.[63] Therefore, assuming that the sources from which the analyst has derived his opinion are wholly publicly available, then his report will be deemed to be 'made public' and therefore not inside information.

6.82 Therefore, in a case alleging dealing on the basis of information contained in an analyst's report (prior to any publication), it is not going to be sufficient of itself that such a report may be the proprietary material of the analyst's employer, and therefore confidential to the employer, or that the report has been written by an analyst who is regarded by the market as sufficiently influential that his views are capable of significantly affecting the share price of the stocks concerned. It will be necessary to look behind the report and establish the source of the material

---

[61] HC Deb (n 12) col 187.
[62] *Observer and Guardian v UK*, Application no 13585/88, 26 Nov 1991, paras 66–69.
[63] Treasury commentary (n 10) para 27.

contained within it. If the content of the report is derived from publicly available information, then the report itself is to be treated as 'made public' and is not therefore inside information.[64]

6.83 However, in such circumstances it may be possible to draw a distinction between the content of the analyst's report itself and knowledge of the fact that a recommendation was about to be made by such an influential analyst. Let us assume that the allegation is that an employee (A) of a large investment firm has got wind of the fact that the firm's top ranked analyst is about to publish a 'strong buy' recommendation on Company X. A buys shares in Company X in advance of publication of this report, because he knows that the analyst is sufficiently influential in the market that his recommendations are likely to have a significant effect on Company X's share price. In such a case, the argument would have to be that knowledge of the very fact that a recommendation is about to be made by a highly regarded analyst is of itself inside information, assuming all the other necessary elements are present.[65]

Journalists

6.84 A journalist who is given inside information by a source and who trades on that information is in exactly the same position as regards s 52 CJA as anyone else. It is common for certain financial journalists to be provided with such information about forthcoming large corporate announcements on an 'embargoed' basis—meaning that they agree not to publish the information until an agreed time and date. In general terms, there is nothing wrong with this. It might be said to be beneficial in that it gives the journalist time to absorb the information and its implications and prepare for it, which ought to lead to more balanced and considered reporting. However, while the information in his possession is embargoed, he holds it on the same confidential basis as any other insider and is therefore subject to the same restrictions on his ability to deal or disclose the information improperly.

6.85 What of the journalist who tips a stock and then trades in that same stock prior to publication, in anticipation of a price rise on the back of his tip? Is the journalist an insider and is the information about his tip inside information? This practice is known as 'share ramping'—and is precisely what occurred in the '*City Slickers*' case.[66] This was a prosecution brought by the DTI in respect of two financial journalists on the Daily Mirror—James Hipwell and Anil Bhoyrul and a private

---

[64] See the discussion regarding 'Star Analysts' in Michael Blair QC, George Walker, and Robert Purves, *Financial Services Law* (2nd edn, OUP 2009) 457, para 9.21.
[65] See Hannigan (n 11) 68–9. See also Blair et al (n 64).
[66] *R v Hipwell, Bhoyrul and Shepherd*, Southwark Crown Court, see press reports, BBC News 7 Dec 2005; 21 Jan 2006; *Guardian* 21 Jan and 10 Feb 2006. See also the '*Heard on the Street*' case *US v Winans* 612 F supp 827 (1985), relevant part affirmed in *US v Carpenter* 791 F 2d 1024 (2nd Cir 1986). See also R Foster Winans, *Trading Secrets* (St Martin's Press 1987).

investor Terry Shepherd. The three were charged with conspiracy to breach s 47 of the (then) Financial Services Act 1986.[67] Mr Hipwell and co-columnist Anil Bhoyrul would first buy significant quantities of a stock and then 'ramp' the price of the share—by highlighting it as 'tip of the day' in their column in the *Daily Mirror*, some twenty-four hours later. They would then sell their holdings at a profit as the price rose.[68]

6.86 It is difficult to see that such a practice would also incur liability under the CJA. It is technically possible that knowledge of the fact that a share was about to be tipped as 'tip of the day' by a publication which is sufficiently influential to significantly move the share price of the subject of the tip, could be considered to be inside information, provided all the other relevant criteria under the CJA are satisfied, however the journalist in question would also have to fulfil the criteria of an 'inside source.'[69] Although such scenarios present interesting theoretical arguments, in practice it is unlikely that a s 52 CJA insider dealing offence would be considered to be the most appropriate charge.[70]

Circumstances in which information may be treated as 'made public' (s 58(3) CJA)

6.87 Section 58(3) CJA makes clear that the question of whether information has been made public in any given case will be fact-specific and therefore dependent on all relevant circumstances.

- Section 58(3)(a)—Information that can be acquired only by persons exercising diligence or expertise. This would include information published in scientific journals which require some specialist knowledge to understand. It would also cover obscure foreign journals. However, it will always be a question of fact and degree dependent upon the facts of each case as to whether the circumstances of publication are such as to bring it within the ambit of the subsection.[71]
- Section 58(3)(b)—Information that is communicated to a section of the public and not to the public at large. This would plainly cover subscription only services, or services which are so prohibitively expensive as to be beyond the means of the public at large.[72]

---

[67] Misleading statements and practices.
[68] The 'share-ramping' scheme involved 44 separate incidents between 1 Aug 1999 and 29 Feb 2000. Shepherd was recruited by Hipwell and Bhoyrul to take part in the dealing, after contacting them through a message board. Hipwell made £41,000 in profits, Bhoyrul £15,000, and Shepherd £17,000. Bhoyrul pleaded guilty and received a Community Order. Shepherd was sentenced to three months' imprisonment and Hipwell six months' imprisonment with three months suspended.
[69] CJA, s 57.
[70] For a slightly more positive outlook on this scenario, see Hannigan (n 11).
[71] The 'highly regarded analyst' whose recommendation is based on his own superior diligence and expertise would also be covered under s 58(3)(a) CJA.
[72] See Hannigan (n 11) 71, in which it is suggested that if information is provided to newspapers and television stations on an embargoed basis, prior to a formal Regulatory News Service ('RNS')

- Section 58(3)(c)—the Information can be acquired only by observation. In the Parliamentary debates,[73] the Minister gave the example of a smoking factory chimney:

> The point to consider is whether a factory chimney smoking at night could be regarded as public information, since everybody could go and see a smoking chimney and take the view that the factory was working overtime, or whether it would be regarded as information that had not been promulgated or made public. The point is that the court can decide the matter in question, taking into account all of the circumstances.

6.88 The difficulty with this example is that it is not realistic, for no one would seriously claim that the observation of a smoking factory chimney, albeit at night, would be sufficient to amount to 'specific or precise' information and therefore a case based on something as nefarious as this would be likely to fail.

6.89 Another example might be an observation that a company's main factory is on fire and is being burned to the ground. A court in looking at such a scenario would be likely to take the view that such information is potentially available to anyone in the vicinity without restriction and that therefore this is information that has been 'made public' within the meaning of s 58.

- Section 58(3)(d)—the information is communicated only on payment of a fee. The purpose of this section was to make clear that 'payment clearly cannot have the effect of preventing information from having been made public but payment itself cannot be sufficient to make information public'.[74] Payment of a fee is simply one of the factors that a court will consider in deciding whether or not the information in question has been 'made public'. In the US, data companies routinely provide market moving consumer survey information to subscribers who pay a higher fee, some five minutes before the information is released to ordinary subscribers. In addition, for an even higher fee, high frequency traders are able to obtain the information a few seconds earlier enabling them to place high volume trades a few seconds prior to the information being given to other paying subscribers. Whether this amounts to the information having been 'made public' would probably depend on such considerations as the manner and circumstances of its provision, as well as the number of recipients.[75]
- Section 58(3)(e)—the Information is published only outside the United Kingdom. During the House of Commons Parliamentary debates, the Minister stated that information might fall into this category if it was published in a major overseas newspaper. If, however, it was published in the '*Tonga Evening News*', it

---

announcement, then it is unlikely that the information has been 'made public'. However, in all cases, it will be necessary to examine the surrounding circumstances with particular care.

[73] HC Deb (n 12) col 184.
[74] HC Deb (n 12) col 182.
[75] Lattman (n 8).

would be extremely unlikely to be considered to have been made public, unless the information related to a Tonga mining company, for example, or another local company. The information would be unlikely to be treated as having been made public. But it might be made public if it was published in *Handelsblatt*, or one of the major overseas newspapers. If it had been promulgated, but not in the United Kingdom, that might well mean that it had been made public.[76]

6.90 The House of Lords Debates expressed a slightly more modern view, and considered that, given the speed and ease of communication in the modern world (even in 1993), it would be difficult to conceive of situations in which price-sensitive information is available abroad but could not be obtained in the UK.[77] In the twenty-first century, this would be almost impossible to conceive.

6.91 Critics have posed the question whether in fact s 58(3) CJA serves only to raise more issues than it answers and therefore whether it should have been included in the CJA at all, particularly given that s 58(1) CJA specifically states that its provisions are 'non-exhaustive' as to the meaning of 'made public'.[78]

6.92 In the Parliamentary debates, the Minister was asked whether this subsection was designed to enable the court to take a broad, common sense view as to whether the information is public having regard to all the circumstances.[79] The Minister's response was that:[80]

> It was important to insert these examples of information which may be treated as made public, because many people felt that unless such examples were included, information might well be considered not to have been made public. A great deal of comfort and reassurance has been derived from the fact that it may indeed be made public. However a precise definition would be a matter for the courts, and they would have to take into account all the circumstances when in fact the opposite should be the case.

6.93 Picking through this rather convoluted language, it appears therefore that the concern which gave rise to s 58(3) CJA was not that insider dealers could escape liability by relying on an obscure publication in, for example, Tonga, but that they should be entitled to do so! The Minister stated, however:[81]

> It will be a matter for the court, in its wisdom, to decide in all the circumstances whether the information had been made public.

6.94 Despite its critics, what s 58(3) CJA does achieve is to provide some sort of framework for the court to work with when determining the issue of whether information has been 'made public' for the purposes of the CJA, and similarly it provides

---

[76] HC Deb (n 12) col 183–4.
[77] HL Deb, vol 540, 3 Dec 1992, col 1503.
[78] See Hannigan (n 11) 72.
[79] See question from Alistair Darling: HC Deb (n 12) col 184.
[80] HC Deb (n 12) col 184.
[81] HC Deb (n 12) col 184.

a framework for the prosecution and defence when considering this aspect of their respective cases. To that extent, it is helpful.

7. The evidential practicalities of proving that information has not been 'made public'

6.95 The burden of proof is on the prosecution to demonstrate that the inside information upon which it relies had not been 'made public'. In order to discharge this burden, it is necessary for the prosecution to conduct appropriate searches of publicly available material and to be able to demonstrate to the defence and the court that it has done so. This duty encompasses the prosecution's responsibility in any criminal case, to comply with its duties and requirements in relation to the obtaining, retention, and disclosure of relevant and 'unused' material, contained in the Criminal Procedures and Investigations Act 1996 ('CPIA')[82] and Code of Practice[83] made under Part II of the CPIA. In carrying out these duties a prosecutor must also comply with the Attorney-General's Guidelines on Disclosure.[84]

6.96 The Code of Practice,[85] imposes a duty on an investigator to pursue all reasonable lines of enquiry, whether these point towards or away from a suspect. What is reasonable will depend upon the circumstances of a particular case. What is clear, is that the prosecution must be able to demonstrate that it has made reasonable enquiries to establish whether such material exists and, if so, whether it may be relevant and that this must of necessity include enquiries as to the existence of relevant material in the possession of a third party. The Code of Practice requires that material of any kind, including information and objects, which is obtained in the course of a criminal investigation as defined by the CPIA 1996 and which may be relevant to the investigation must be retained.[86]

6.97 In the context of proving that information has 'not been made public', these duties create at times an uneasy tension. Section 56(1)(c) CJA plainly does not require the prosecution to conduct disproportionate searches in order to capture every reported article or news item regarding the relevant company. What is in issue is whether the particular information that is said by the prosecution to constitute specific or precise 'inside information' was in the public domain prior to the alleged insider dealing. However, the prosecution's disclosure duties appear to require that a broad

---

[82] As amended by the CJA 2003.
[83] CPIA Code of Practice Under Part II, 4 April 2005.
[84] Attorney-General's Guidelines on Disclosure, Apr 2005. See also supplementary guidelines on disclosure of digitally stored material. See also the Review of disclosure in criminal proceedings—September 2011 (Gross LJ) and Further review—sanctions for disclosure failure—November 2012 (Gross LJ).
[85] CPIA Code of Practice (n 83) paras 3.5–3.6.
[86] CPIA Code of Practice (n 83) paras 4.1–5.10.

6.98 Thereafter, the CPIA requires the prosecution to apply the test for disclosure of material to the defence. Section 3(1)(a) CPIA deals with the 'initial duty' of the prosecutor to disclose to the accused: ' ... any prosecution material which has not previously been disclosed to the accused and which might reasonably be considered capable of undermining the case for the prosecution against the accused or of assisting the case for the accused ... ' This initial disclosure on the part of the prosecutor will be followed by the accused giving a 'defence statement' to the prosecutor and the court.[88] The CPIA now requires defence statements to set out particular information including particular matters of fact on which he intends to rely for the purposes of his defence.[89]

approach must be taken to this determination in order to ensure that material satisfying the broad test of 'relevance' is obtained and properly considered.[87]

6.99 Therefore where a defendant has raised an issue in interview or in his defence statement that the information upon which he traded was not in fact price-sensitive because it was in the public domain; the prosecution would be entitled to request further particulars of what information is relied upon and where it is to be found (assuming that these have not already been provided). The Prosecution must then make reasonable enquiries based on the defendant's assertions. Plainly, this will include reviewing any specific publications or internet sites to which the Defendant has referred.

6.100 However, the Prosecution also has a 'continuing duty' in relation to disclosure. Pursuant to s 7A CPIA,

> The prosecutor must keep under review the question whether at any given time (and, in particular, following the giving of a defence statement) there is prosecution material which might reasonably be considered capable of undermining the case for the prosecution against the accused or of assisting the case for the accused, and has not been disclosed to the accused.[90]

This continuing duty is applicable whether or not the defendant has produced a defence statement in accordance with the requirements. It will not be sufficient therefore for a prosecutor to simply say, 'well, the defence have declined to name the sources of the information they claim was publicly available, therefore there is nothing further to be done'.

6.101 In practical terms, however, publicly available information searches are not like searching for the proverbial needle in a haystack as there will always be some fairly large clues as to whether and if so where, the information can be found. For example, in all likelihood, information in the public domain that is of sufficient

---

[87] See Attorney-General's Guidelines on Disclosure, Apr 2005, paras 1–7.
[88] CPIA ss 5, 6 and 6B.
[89] CPIA s 6A(1).
[90] CPIA s 7A.

quality to be specific or precise is going to cause more than a few people to trade. Therefore the volume of trading at the relevant time will provide an indication as to whether there really was such information in the public domain. The timing of the defendant's alleged insider trading as against the publication of information will also be important. If the defendant's trading takes place shortly before a RIS announcement of a takeover, but he points to publicly available information published some months earlier as justifying his reason for trading, then it will be a question of fact for the jury to decide as to what the real basis for his trading was.

In many cases, the computers used by the defendants will have been seized or imaged during the investigation phase. These will then be interrogated and it may be possible to see what sites a defendant has actually used for research purposes. **6.102**

In addition, companies and their advisers, when involved in price-sensitive activities such as takeover negotiations, will need to actively monitor what information is in the public domain in order to ensure that there is no 'leak' and in order to comply with obligations under the Takeover Code.[91] Evidence of this may be relied upon by the prosecution as evidence that no information had been made public. **6.103**

Whatever searches are conducted, the prosecution will need to be able to demonstrate a sound methodology.[92] In most cases, this will mean using search engines which are sophisticated enough to cover all the most likely forms of international print and internet media, including blogs, journals, and chat rooms, in which inside information could properly be said to have been 'made public'. It will also mean demonstrating that the time periods, within which the searches are conducted, are wide enough to encompass the defendant's trading and the eventual formal RIS announcement, and also a sufficient period in advance of these events to demonstrate that there was no information in the public domain to justify the trading. **6.104**

In most cases, it is likely that a basic methodology would incorporate the sources that are generally regarded as providing comprehensive capturing and coverage of information, such as *The Financial Times, Factiva*,[93] and *ADVFN* [94] and *Interactive Investor*[95] bulletin boards. It will also need to be tailored to the relevant stock in question, incorporating further sources, where appropriate. It is possible to simplify the searching task by the use of appropriate search strings. The particular search string used will be dependent upon the source being searched, the particular stock, and the background to the deal in question. **6.105**

---

[91] Panel on Takeovers and Mergers, Takeover Code (10th edn, Sept 2011).
[92] Review of Disclosure in Criminal Proceedings, Lord Justice Gross Sept 2011.
[93] *Factiva* is a business information and research tool which aggregates content from both licensed and free sources and provides searching, alerting, dissemination, and other information management resources.
[94] *ADVFN* is a financial market website that provides online data and services regarding stocks and trading information to private investors.
[95] *Interactive Investor* is a UK-based commercial online financial services provider providing stock and trading information.

6.106 In two recent insider dealing prosecutions (*R v Sanders and others*[96] and *R v Mustafa and others*[97]) there were a large number of indicted stocks and period ranges for the indicted dealing. The FSA therefore instructed an external expert to conduct the publicly available information searches—a company that specialises in the monitoring and provision of information about major corporate events. This company devised and carried out a research programme that was intended to identify and analyse certain publicly available information about the companies in question during specified periods (which in the *R v Sanders* case were date ranges of several months before and after the dealing by the defendants and the public announcements by the companies).

6.107 In an appropriate case there are many advantages for both the prosecution and the defence, in using an expert in this field. First, such companies are experienced in tasks of this nature and therefore have established and tested methodologies. Second, such a company has access to most relevant sources of information. It will be important to set out clearly the date ranges that have been employed, the purpose of the searches, and the search tools employed. It would probably also be appropriate for the defence to be provided with these in advance and for their views to be sought, so that (if necessary) the searches can be widened to encompass other matters relevant to the defence case.

6.108 In both cases, this evidence was largely agreed by the parties. This ought invariably to be the position, provided the task has been undertaken appropriately, responsibly, and with a sound methodology and where the defence have been engaged at an appropriate stage in the process. This approach also has the added advantage of avoiding generating considerable quantities of irrelevant unused material, which is subject to the requirements set out in the CPIA. The material will therefore have to be assessed carefully in accordance with the prosecution's disclosure requirements to establish whether any of it undermines the prosecution's case and/or assists the defence case.

6.109 In *R v Mustafa and others*,[98] the expert was asked to confront the difficulty that it is impossible in the internet era to reconstruct precisely what was available at the relevant time. His answer, which was not challenged the defence, was that while, several years after the event, one cannot know precisely what information might have been available immediately before the trading period in question, the range of sources and time periods searched would have revealed any significant rumours during these periods.

6.110 This demonstrates that, provided these steps have been undertaken properly it ought to be possible to deal with the requirement in s 56(1)(c) CJA in a manner which is proportionate, fair to the defence, and in accordance with the prosecution's duties but which avoids the prosecution having to prove an impossible negative.

---

[96] *R v Sanders and others* (n 33).
[97] *R v Mustafa and others* (n 4).
[98] *R v Mustafa and others* (n 4).

8. Likely to have a 'significant effect' on price (s 56(1)(d) CJA)

6.111 In addition to the other criteria, for information to qualify as inside information it must be of a type which if made public, would be likely to have a significant effect on the price of *any* securities. Section 56(3) CJA states that for the purposes of this section 'price' includes value.

6.112 In the Parliamentary debates it had been suggested that the legislation should cover information which had any effect at all on the price of any securities. The Minister noted (in relation to the 'significant' requirement):

> That requirement serves to ensure that prohibitions on insider dealing apply to major matters such as impending takeover bids, forthcoming profits and dividend announcements which are out of line with expectations. Those are the stuff of insider dealing as commonly understood. Those are the stuff to which the prohibitions should apply.[99]

6.113 This underlines the fact that the purpose of the CJA, and therefore the purpose to which s 56(1)(d) CJA is directed, is not to capture dealing on the basis of knowledge of a company's day-to-day affairs but dealing on the basis of information regarding significant events which would be likely to have a correspondingly significant effect on a company's share price.

6.114 The Minister went on to point out that any removal of the 'significant effect' requirement would

> bring within the ambit of the legislation a dealing where someone possessed information which was likely to have any effect—not just a significant effect—on the price of securities. One possible consequence of adopting such an approach would be that there were many technical breaches of the law because of dealings by people who possessed information likely to have only a trivial effect on the price of securities. That would not be satisfactory; it would either lead to a host of prosecutions where there is no real mischief or the law would fall into disrepute.[100]

The meaning of 'significant effect'

6.115 Neither the CJA, nor the IDD provide any definition of 'significant effect'. The Treasury Commentary to the Criminal Justice Bill, noted that the range of securities which is covered by the legislation are such that it would not be practicable to indicate what effect would be significant as this will depend on the facts of each case.[101]

---

[99] HC Deb (n 12) col 177.
[100] HC Deb (n 12) col 177.
[101] Treasury commentary (n 10) para 25.

6.116 This was also the view of the London Stock Exchange ('LSE') which at the time was also the UK Listing Authority. Its Guidance on the Dissemination of Price Sensitive Information, which was in force in 1996,[102] stated

> It is not feasible to define any theoretical percentage movement in a share price which will make a piece of information price sensitive. Attempts at a precise definition of 'price sensitive' are not possible, since it is generally necessary to take into account a number of factors specific to the particular case.

6.117 The Oxford English Dictionary[103] provides a definition of 'significant' as 'important or large enough to be noticed' or 'meaningful'. But what does this mean in the context of a potential share price movement? The first thing to have in mind is that this is not a prospective test. Therefore the issue is not whether the information (when made public) *did* have a significant effect on the price of the securities concerned, but whether at the time the defendant's dealing occurred, the information would have been *likely* to do so.

6.118 By the time of an investigation or prosecution there is always an element of hindsight and prosecutors and defence often claim that the actual movement in the share price following an announcement does or does not mean that the information itself was 'likely to have a significant effect' on the price of the securities in question.

6.119 In many cases, this may be a safe assumption, but not always. For example, in a takeover negotiation where there have been a number of leaks prior to the announcement, it is possible that the share price may already have moved near to or at the price it achieves post announcement. This does not mean, however, that the specific or precise information known to the defendant at the time he dealt is not capable of being inside information. Similarly, where a defendant deals on inside information regarding a takeover negotiation that ultimately comes to nothing. This occurred in the *Sanders* case,[104] in which some of the defendants traded in a stock named ChoicePoint Inc which at the time they traded, and to their knowledge, was in takeover talks with another entity. However, these negotiations ultimately broke down and no takeover actually occurred. The defendants therefore variously made a very small profit or in one case a loss on this trading.

6.120 It is necessary therefore to make a 'real-time' judgement on the basis of the information available to the defendant at the time he dealt, rather than further down the line at the time of the public announcement. This puts the issue squarely as a question of fact to be determined by the jury in the context of all the available evidence. It is common for the prosecution to obtain and call expert evidence to assist the Jury with this task.

---

[102] Guidance on the Dissemination of Price Sensitive Information, Stock Exchange. London, 1996.
[103] 2007 edn.
[104] *R v Sanders and others* (n 33).

6.121 In *R v Gray*,[105] the prosecution called evidence on this point from a Mr Crowley who was a market analyst with a well-known firm of Stockbrokers specialising in the types of securities with which the trial was concerned. He was called as someone unconnected with the facts of the particular transactions in the case, who could give evidence about the general perception of the market and the price sensitivity of the alleged inside information. Although Mr Crowley was cross-examined as to his conclusions, no issue was taken (rightly) with either his competence as an expert or whether he was entitled to give evidence about these matters.

6.122 In *R v Neel and Matthew Uberoi*,[106] Matthew Uberoi worked as an intern in the corporate broking department of Hoare Govett and passed inside information regarding deals his team were working on, to his father who traded in the securities concerned. In addition to the employees of Hoare Govett who gave evidence of their perception of the price sensitivity of the information they held, the FSA also obtained independent evidence to this effect from a market expert. One of the stocks in question was an oil and gas company named Gulf Keystone Petroleum ('GKP') who had signed an advantageous 'farm out' agreement with the Algerian State oil company Sonatrach. The prosecution therefore also obtained evidence from an oil and gas expert as to whether knowledge of this partnership agreement would have been price-sensitive at the time Neel Uberoi dealt in GKP shares.

6.123 In *R v Calvert*,[107] the defendant was a former partner of the well-known Stockbroking firm Cazenove and Co. The prosecution case was that he had obtained inside information from an unknown source at Cazenove, regarding forthcoming takeover negotiations and announcements. The prosecution called an expert who was a former head of corporate broking at Dresdner Kleinwort Wasserstein, who was unconnected with the transactions that were the subject of the case. He examined the information in the possession of Cazenove at the time of the dealing and expressed an opinion on whether this information was (at the time of the dealing) price-sensitive in the context of the stocks in question.

6.124 In *R v Sanders and others*,[108] the prosecution again obtained evidence from an independent expert on the issue of price sensitivity. This expert took the view that it was necessary to attempt to define what 'significant' meant in this context. He therefore adopted the definition used by the Takeover Panel[109] in considering whether a share price movement over a period has been 'untoward' for the purposes of requiring an announcement—and thereby considered a price increase of approximately 10 per cent to be an appropriate measure of price sensitivity.

---

[105] *R v Gray* [1995] 2 Cr App R 100, CA.
[106] *R v Neel and Matthew Uberoi* (n 6).
[107] *R v Malcolm Calvert* (n 3).
[108] *R v Sanders and others* (n 33).
[109] Rule 2.2 of the City Code on Takeovers and Mergers.

6.125 This expert's approach has some support in Europe. Sweden sets a 10 per cent threshold in its insider trading legislation. This threshold specifies that 10 per cent is relevant only to the likely effect of the information in question. It is irrelevant therefore if the actual effect of the information is less. Denmark also uses the 10 per cent threshold as a matter of prosecution practice.[110]

6.126 However, it should not be assumed that this is a definition that should be applied in every case. In some circumstances, it may be appropriate—in others it may not. For example, can it be said that a price movement of 9.5 per cent is not significant but a movement of 10.00 per cent is? Also, what of a stock whose price has been effectively static for a significant period? In such a case, it could be argued that any movement is capable of being significant.

6.127 In *R v Mustafa and others*,[111] the prosecution expert proposed a definition of 'significant effect' which in the light of the above, it is suggested is to be preferred:

> a movement in the price of a security which, in my opinion, is not accounted for by normal market movements.[112]

6.128 This definition was not challenged by the defence. The same expert subsequently gave evidence in another insider dealing prosecution, *R v Richard Joseph*.[113] He adopted the same definition, which again went unchallenged by the defence. This definition has the advantage of simplicity and also does not attempt to import words or definitions into the statute that were deliberately not inserted by Parliament. It also has the advantage clearly intended by Parliament that what is 'significant' in any given case will depend on the facts and circumstances of that case and should therefore be approached on a case by case basis.

9. Price-affected securities

6.129 Both the primary insider dealing offence and the secondary 'encouraging' offence, relate to dealing in 'price-affected securities'.[114] Section 56(2) makes clear that 'price-affected securities' are those that are affected by price-sensitive information. Therefore, there must be a direct causal link between the inside information and its likely effect on the share price of the securities in which the insider dealt or encouraged others to deal.

---

[110] See R C H Alexander, *Insider Dealing and Money Laundering in the EU: Law and Regulation* (Ashgate 2007) for an interesting comparative study of the various insider dealing regimes in operation in Europe's member states.
[111] *R v Mustafa and others* (n 4).
[112] Report of Christopher Airey. *R v Mustafa and others* (n 4).
[113] *R v Richard Joseph* (n 5) Mar 2013.
[114] CJA, ss 52(1) and 52(2)(a).

7

INSIDERS (s 57 CJA)

1. Introduction	7.01	5. An inside source	7.16
2. Meaning of 'insider'	7.02	6. Categories of insider	7.19
3. The elements of knowledge	7.03	The inner circle (s 57(2)(a)(i) CJA)	7.21
4. Inside information at the time of dealing	7.10	The middle circle (s 57(2)(a)(ii) CJA)	7.25
		The outer circle (s 57(2)(b) CJA)	7.33

1. Introduction

This Chapter deals with the elements that must be proved in order to establish that a person has information as an 'insider'. **7.01**

2. Meaning of 'insider'

Section 57—'Insiders'

(1) For the purposes of this Part, a person has information as an insider if and only if
    (a) it is, and he knows that it is, inside information, and
    (b) he has it, and knows that he has it, from an inside source.
(2) For the purposes of subsection (1), a person has information from an inside source if and only if
    (a) he has it through
        (i) being a director, employee or shareholder of an issuer of securities; or
        (ii) having access to the information by virtue of his employment, office or profession; or
    (b) the direct or indirect source of his information is a person within paragraph (a).

Breaking s 57 down, the requirements are that the person in question: **7.02**

1. has inside information (this is a question of fact which is determined in accordance with the criteria set out in s 56 CJA);

2. knows that it is inside information;
3. has the inside information from an inside source; and
4. knows that he has it from an inside source (inside source is defined in s 57(2) CJA).

3. The elements of knowledge

7.03 Section 57 CJA demonstrably requires actual knowledge on the part of the defendant. Belief will not suffice.[1] In imposing this requirement the CJA is consistent with the Insider Dealing Directive ('IDD')[2] which required that persons be prohibited from 'taking advantage of [inside] information with *full knowledge of the facts*'.[3]

7.04 There is some authority for the proposition that 'knowledge' in the criminal law includes 'wilfully shutting one's eyes to the truth'.[4] However, this proposition should probably be approached with caution, particularly in the context of an insider dealing case.[5] The preferred view is that nothing short of actual knowledge will suffice, and whether actual knowledge has been established will depend on the evidence in any given case.[6]

7.05 This requirement of actual knowledge can be difficult to prove in insider dealing cases which tend to be based, for the most part, on circumstantial evidence. The jury is therefore being asked to infer actual knowledge from the surrounding facts and circumstances.

7.06 In *R v Holyoak, Hill and Morl*,[7] the Defendants were employees of Touche Ross, a firm of accountants that was advising the bidders in a takeover deal. They dealt in the takeover target's shares seven minutes prior to the announcement of the takeover deal. They sold the shares the next day making £13,000 profit. The defendants'

---

[1] In 'The Law on Insider Dealing, a Consultative Document' (para 2.3), produced by the DTI in December 1989, the point was made that it would be inappropriate to criminalise an individual who did not realise that the information he had was inside information.
[2] Council Directive 89/552/EEC, 13 Nov 1989.
[3] IDD (n 2) Article 2(1). Emphasis added.
[4] For example, per Lord Reid in *Warner v Commissioner of Police of the Metropolis* [1969] 2 AC 256 at 279, HL; *Atwal v Massey*, 56 Cr App R 6, DC; and *Flintshire CC v Reynolds*, 170 JP 73, DC. Atwal dealt with constructive knowledge—where a person has the means of acquiring knowledge but chooses not to. The case decided that constructive knowledge is insufficient where actual knowledge is required.
[5] For a more robust view see Neha Jain, 'Significance of Mens Rea in Insider Trading' (2004) 25(5) Comp Law 132, 136.
[6] In *Westminster City Council v Croyalgrange Ltd*, 83 Cr App R 155, 164, HL, Lord Bridge stated that it was always open to the tribunal of fact 'to base a finding of knowledge on evidence that the defendant had deliberately shut his eyes to the obvious or refrained from inquiry because he suspected the truth but did not wish to have his suspicion confirmed'. See also *R v Sherif and Others*, *The Times* (11 Feb 2009), CA.
[7] *R v Holyoak, Hill and Morl*, FT (London, 28 Oct 1989).

case was that they thought that the takeover was public knowledge when they dealt. The jury acquitted the defendants and, although it is not possible to know the basis for the acquittal, one ground may well have been that the prosecution had failed to prove that the defendants knew that the information upon which they were dealing was unpublished and therefore 'inside'.

7.07 The requirement to prove actual knowledge received some criticism at the time the CJA was enacted and it was even suggested that the test should be altered to place a burden on the defendant to prove that he did not know the information was 'inside'.[8]

7.08 However, such a view must be set against the backdrop of the (largely) unsuccessful attempts at prosecution under the predecessor legislation.[9] The prosecutions brought by the Financial Services Authority ('FSA') in the last few years have demonstrated that it is perfectly possible for the prosecution to prove actual knowledge on the part of a defendant even where the evidence is purely circumstantial. One example of this is the case of

7.09 *R v Rupinder Sidhu*,[10] Mr Sidhu obtained inside information from his friend Anjam Ahmad who was employed as a trader at a Hedge Fund named AKO Capital ('AKO'). Mr Ahmad tipped Mr Sidhu to buy shares in European stocks in advance of large positions being taken by AKO—and thereby profit from the significant price movement caused by the size of these positions. Mr Ahmad pleaded guilty to insider dealing and was not called as a witness in Mr Sidhu's trial, and the jury was not told that Mr Ahmad had pleaded guilty or of the admissions he had made to participating in a joint enterprise with Mr Sidhu. The trial was therefore conducted purely on the basis of circumstantial evidence, and the jury ultimately convicted Mr Sidhu of all counts.

4. Inside information at the time of dealing

7.10 The insider must be in possession of the inside information *at the time* he either dealt, encouraged another to deal, or improperly disclosed inside information.[11]

7.11 This requirement is demonstrated by the case of *R v Coren and Greenwood*.[12] The prosecution was forced to abandon its case because it had not produced evidence

---

[8] Brenda Hannigan, *Insider Dealing* (2nd edn, Longmans 1994) 76.
[9] See 'A case of frustration for the DTI—Raymond Hughes on recent hearings of insider dealing charges', *FT* (28 Nov 1989).
[10] *R v Rupinder Sidhu*, unreported, Southwark Crown Court, His Honour Judge Gledhill QC and a jury, 28 Nov 2011 to 15 Dec 2011. FSA/PN/114/2011.
[11] Within the meaning of s 52(1) or (2) CJA.
[12] *R v Coren and Greenwood*, unreported, but see *FT* (London, 24 Jan 1990).

demonstrating that the defendants were in possession of inside information at the time of dealing. The defendants were a secretary at the Office of Fair Trading ('OFT') and her brother. It was alleged that they dealt on the basis of information concerning company merger referrals that the secretary was able to obtain as a result of her employment. The OFT did not produce evidence to prove when it was that the secretary obtained her information, nor that the information was inside information at the time of the dealing.

7.12 In *R v Sanders and others*,[13] one of the stocks with which James and Miranda Sanders were charged was Adesa Inc ('Adesa'). Adesa was a public company, listed on the New York Stock Exchange ('NYSE'). On 26 July 2006, the board of Adesa resolved to put the company up for sale and a number of private equity firms were invited to bid. One of these was a company for whom Deloitte, San Francisco acted and where the Sanders' brother-in-law (A) was employed. The prosecution evidence was that one of the pieces of inside information that Deloitte knew was that 'the deal size would be somewhere around $2.2–2.5 billion'. It was the prosecution's case that inside information about this deal was passed to the Sanders by A's wife (Miranda Sanders' sister) and that the Sanders dealt in Adesa on the basis of this information by placing a £5 per point spread bet at $25.05.

7.13 The defence made representations[14] that at the time James Sanders dealt, the information that A had (that 'the deal size would be somewhere around $2.2–2.5 billion') was not inside information because it was not information which if it were made public would be likely to have a significant effect on the price of any securities (s 56(1)(d)).

7.14 The thrust of the defence submission was that as there were 90.2 million Adesa shares in issue at the relevant time, a deal of $2.2 billion would value each share at $24.39 or at $27.72 if the deal was at $2.5 billion. James Sanders' trade was therefore made at a price that was *above* the lower end of the potential bid range. Therefore, had the information of Deloitte's assessment of the likely bid range been made public at the time James Sanders dealt, it would not have had a significant effect on the Adesa share price.

7.15 In the event, this issue was not litigated because the prosecution decided not to proceed with the Adesa Count given the acceptable pleas that had been entered in respect of all other counts on the indictment. What it does do however is demonstrate the need to prove that the information in the defendant's possession is inside information at the actual time of his dealing.

---

[13] *R v Sanders and others*, unreported, Southwark Crown Court, Mr Justice Simon, 20 June 2012, FSA/PN/060/2012 and FSA/PN/067/2012.
[14] *R v Sanders and others*, unreported, pre-trial hearing, 12 Mar 2012.

5. An inside source

Section 57

(2) For the purposes of subsection (1), a person has information from an inside source if and only if
(a) he has it through
    (i) being a director, employee or shareholder of an issuer of securities; or
    (ii) having access to the information by virtue of his employment, office or profession; or
(b) the direct or indirect source of his information is a person within paragraph (a).

7.16 Section 57(2) CJA broadly mirrors the minimum categories of persons whom the IDD required should qualify as insiders under domestic law.[15]

7.17 Section 57(2)(a) CJA is significantly wider than its predecessor under the Company Securities (Insider Dealing) Act ('CSA'). Section 9 CSA provided that an insider was an individual connected with a company who was a director, an officer or employee, or those in a professional or business relationship with the company. The provision was further restricted by the fact that the officer or employee or person in a professional or business relationship with the company had to occupy a position which may reasonably be expected to give him access to information which was unpublished, price-sensitive information.

7.18 All that s 57(2)(a) CJA requires is that the person has inside information *through* being a director, employee, or shareholder. This was deliberately widely drafted. The Government had recognised the problems with the definition in the CSA which:

> has on occasion meant that there has been no breach of the law, even though there was evidence of what would generally be regarded as improper conduct. That is an important and desirable change which reflects the insider dealing directive, because it is quite possible for someone to have direct access to price-sensitive information without being connected to a company.[16]

6. Categories of insider

7.19 The drafting of s 57(2) CJA, in effect layers the categories of insider:

1. The inner circle who have inside information 'through being a director, employee or shareholder of an issuer of securities' (s 57(2)(a)(i) CJA).
2. The middle circle who have access to inside information by virtue of their employment, office or profession (s 57(2)(a)(ii) CJA).
3. The outer circle—whose direct or indirect sources of inside information is someone in either the inner circle or middle circle (s 57(2)(b) CJA).

---

[15] Dir 89/592/EEC, Arts 2(1) and 4.
[16] HC Deb, Session 1992–93, Standing Committee B, 10 June 1993, cols 189–90.

7.20 This layering ensures that, by one means or another, all potential categories of insider are caught by the legislation. It also forestalls any technical arguments as to the basis upon which the information was acquired because provided the prosecution can prove how a person came by inside information, the manner in which he has acquired it will inevitably be caught by one of the means set out in s 57(2) CJA.

The inner circle (s 57(2)(a)(i) CJA)

Company directors

7.21 A director of an issuer of securities is an inside source by virtue of s 57(2)(a)(i) CJA if he has obtained the information 'through being a director' of an issuer of securities. The provision is deliberately widely drawn to include both executive and non-executive directors. This category of insider is not controversial, and there are numerous examples of cases of insider dealing involving company directors.[17] Directors are plainly the persons most likely to have access to inside information by virtue of the positions they occupy within a company. An issue arises as to whether shadow directors[18] are included within this category. However, a shadow director who deals on inside information will certainly fall under either s 57(2)(a)(ii) or s 57(2)(b) CJA.

7.22 It should be noted that provided the inside source is a director, employee, or shareholder of *an* issuer of securities, it is not necessary for it to be the same securities that are traded. For example, in a takeover situation, a director of the acquiring company, who is aware of the forthcoming takeover would be caught by this provision if he deals in the shares of the target company, provided that the company of which he is a director is also an issuer of securities.

Employees

7.23 There is no restriction on the types of employee caught by this section. Any employee is caught, provided that he is employed by 'an issuer of securities'. This will include, for example, a secretary who word processes documents containing inside information.[19]

---

[17] *R v Dickinson*, unreported but noted (1982) 3 Co Law 185; *R v Naerger*, unreported but see the *Guardian* 29 & 30 Apr 1986; *R v John Morris Cross*, Court of Appeal, 25 Jan 1990, [1990] 91 Cr App R 115; *R v Rollins*, unreported, Southwark Crown Court, 16 to 26 Nov 2010, FSA/PN/168/2010; 21 Jan 2011, FSA/PN/010/2011.
[18] A shadow director is defined in s 251(1) of the Companies Act 2006 as 'a person in accordance with whose directions or instructions the directors of the company are accustomed to act'. An identical definition appeared in s 741(2) of the Companies Act 1985.
[19] See *R v Jenkins*, unreported but see *FT* (London, 18 July 1987).

Shareholders

Shareholders are included as specific insiders in order to give effect to Article 2(1) of the IDD.[20] If a person has inside information 'through being' a shareholder, then he is within the ambit of the legislation, regardless of the size or nature of his holding. **7.24**

The middle circle (s 57(2)(a)(ii) CJA)

In the Parliamentary debates, the Economic Secretary to the Treasury described this provision as 'both necessary and unexceptional'.[21] The persons who have access to inside information by virtue of their employment, office or profession are potentially extremely broad. **7.25**

For example, in a takeover negotiation, each side will in all likelihood employ (as a minimum) corporate brokers, solicitors, and accountants to advise them on various aspects of the deal. In turn, such advisers will have employees who work directly on the deal and other staff who, while not being directly involved, still have access to information about the takeover—for example, administrative staff. It is quite clear that this provision is intended to cast the net wide enough to catch all such persons without having to envisage and define all potential categories of insider.[22] **7.26**

This category is also plainly wide enough to cover investment analysts who receive inside information as a result of discussions with a company that they cover. It will also cover public employees who have access to inside information such as officers and employees of the Takeover Panel, the Financial Conduct Authority ('FCA'), other regulatory bodies, and Government employees. In addition, this category would cover journalists who acquire inside information and trade upon it in advance of publication. **7.27**

The only limitation on this category is that the person concerned must have access to the inside information 'by virtue of' their employment, office or profession. This plainly requires some causal connection between the person's employment, office or profession and their access to the inside information in question. **7.28**

In *R v Kean and Floydd*,[23] the defendants were market makers at County NatWest Securities who were the brokers to a hotel chain named Grand Metropolitan. The prosecution alleged that these two overheard a junior analyst talking about an imminent takeover announcement concerning Grand Metropolitan. The prosecution brought under the CSA failed, partly[24] due to doubts as to whether the junior **7.29**

---

[20] IDD (n 2).
[21] HC Debs (n 16) col 190.
[22] This is confirmed in the Treasury commentary on the original draft of the Criminal Justice Bill (Oct 1992) para 30.
[23] *R v Kean and Floydd*, unreported but see *FT* (London, 7 June 1991).
[24] It appears from the *FT* report that the prosecution was also unable to prove that the dealing took place prior to the announcement being made.

analyst could be regarded as a person occupying a position which may reasonably be expected to give her access to unpublished, price-sensitive information (she had only been told because her boss was unavailable). This was a necessary requirement under the CSA. There would, however, have been no such difficulty under the CJA, because it would have been possible to assert that the junior analyst and the defendants had the information 'by virtue of' their employment which would have brought them within s 57(2)(a)(ii) CJA.

7.30 In *R v Geoffrey Collier*,[25] Mr Collier was the head of securities at Morgan Grenfell. He was instructed to advise a client of Morgan Grenfell's which was intending to launch a takeover bid the following day for an engineering company named AE. Mr Collier dealt in AE shares on his own behalf shortly prior to the announcement of the bid.

7.31 In *R v Littlewood and others*,[26] in addition to takeover deals with which he was directly involved, Christian Littlewood also had little difficulty obtaining access to information regarding takeovers that he was not himself working on but which were being handled by the departments in which he worked. He also passed information regarding these to his co-defendants, who traded on the basis of this information.

7.32 In *R v Mustafa and others*[27] and *R v Richard Joseph*,[28] the insiders were two employees in the confidential print rooms at JP Morgan Cazenove and UBS respectively. As a result of their employment, they had access to inside information concerning forthcoming takeovers which was contained in the documents sent to the print room for printing. The inside information was disseminated by the insiders to the trading defendants using a variety of methods, including telephone contact, emails, documents saved onto USB memory sticks, and documents uploaded onto web-based email accounts.

The outer circle (s 57(2)(b) CJA)

7.33 Many insider dealing cases will involve persons in this category. This is not surprising as in most instances the primary insider will want to 'layer' the trading by putting another person between himself and the trading, in order to lessen suspicion. This will also be the case in any insider dealing 'ring' or 'network'—therefore any of the more sophisticated insider dealing enterprises.

---

[25] *R v Geoffrey Collier*, unreported but see 'Bang Goes a Scandal', *Sunday Times* (London, 16 Nov 1986); 'Collier's Rise and Fall', *Independent* (London, 2 July 1987); 'Mischief that may stop the Market's Heart' *Financial Times* (London, 2 July 1987).

[26] *R v Littlewood and others*, unreported, Southwark Crown Court, His Honour Judge Anthony Leonard QC, 10 Jan 2011, FSA/PN/062/2011; 2 Feb 2011, FSA/PN/018/2011. See Chapter 7, para 7.36.

[27] *R v Mustafa and others*, unreported, Southwark Crown Court, His Honour Judge Pegden QC and a jury, 5 Mar to 23 July 2012; 27 July 2012, FSA/PN/080/2012.

[28] *R v Richard Joseph*, unreported, Southwark Crown Court, His Honour Judge Pegden QC and a jury, 30 Jan to 11 Mar 2013, FSA/PN/023/2013.

Categories of insider

7.34 Provided the defendant can be proved to have obtained the information directly or indirectly from someone within the inner or middle circles, he will be caught by this section. It does not matter in these circumstances whether he is a passive recipient or has deliberately procured the information. This is in contrast to the CSA which required the 'tippee' to have *obtained* inside information directly or indirectly from a primary insider.[29] This wording caused difficulty for the prosecution in the case of *R v Fisher*[30] in which the defendant was acquitted following a successful submission that he had not 'obtained' inside information because he was (in effect) a passive recipient. Subsequently, the Attorney-General referred the issue of whether 'obtained' had a wider meaning than that found by the trial judge. The Court of Appeal held that 'obtained' meant no more than 'received' and therefore had a wider meaning than had been found at trial. The matter reached the House of Lords which affirmed the Court of Appeal's decision.

7.35 There are numerous examples of cases in the 'outer circle' category:

R v Malcolm Calvert:[31] the defendant acquired inside information on forthcoming takeovers from an unknown source in the corporate broking department at Cazenove and Co. He tipped his friend Bertie Hatcher to buy shares in the target companies on their joint behalf and they split the profits. Mr Calvert was therefore within s 57(2)(b) CJA on the basis that the direct or indirect source of his inside information must have been someone within s 57(1)(a) CJA. Mr Hatcher was also a secondary insider because he had received the information indirectly from someone within s 57(1)(a) CJA.

R v Rupinder Sidhu:[32] Mr Sidhu was brought within s 57(2)(b) CJA on the basis that he had received inside information about forthcoming large trades by a hedge fund named AKO Capital, from his friend Anjam Ahmad who was employed as a trader at AKO.

R v Littlewood and others:[33] the insider Christian Littlewood worked at Dresdner Kleinwort Wasserstein ('DKW') as a manager in the Corporate Finance department. He left DKW in March 2008, and between August 2008 and March 2009 he was employed in a similar role at Shore Capital and Corporate Ltd. Much of Christian Littlewood's work in these institutions involved corporate takeovers and therefore as a result of his employment he had access to price-sensitive information on a continuous basis. He passed this information to his co-defendants—his wife Angie Littlewood and Helmy Omar Sa'aid

---

[29] CSA, s 1(3). See *R v Fisher,* Southwark Crown Court, 14 Apr 1988, 4 BCC 360, Judge Gerald Butler QC, and Attorney-General's Reference (no 1 1988) [1989] 2 WLR 729; [1989] AC 971.
[30] *R v Fisher* (n 29).
[31] *R v Calvert*, unreported, Southwark Crown Court, His Honour Judge Testar and a jury, 16 Feb to 10 Mar 2010. FSA/PN/041/2010; 11 Mar 2010, FSA/PN/043/2010.
[32] *R v Sidhu* (n 10).
[33] *R v Littlewood and others* (n 26).

who traded on the basis of this information. Both Angie Littlewood and Said were therefore brought within the ambit of s 57(2)(b) CJA.

R v Mustafa and others:[34] the two insiders passed on inside information to a network of friends and family who traded upon it. These traders therefore fell within s 57(2)(b) CJA as secondary insiders.

Proving liability under s 57(2)(b) CJA

7.36 The above cases demonstrate the breadth of the provision, but it must be remembered that it is still necessary to establish that the source of the information was an insider and that the defendant knew this to be the case. Some critics of the CJA took the view that this hurdle was impossible to overcome in certain circumstances.[35] However, the above cases demonstrate that it is perfectly possible (but by no means straightforward) to successfully bring cases based on just such a scenario.

7.37 Where the prosecution asserts that a particular person is the inside source ('primary insider') from which the alleged secondary insider derived his information, and both are prosecuted, it is important to recognise that the legislation does not require the prosecution to essentially prove a negative, ie, that no one other than the primary insider could have passed the inside information to the alleged secondary insider. In such circumstances, the proper question is whether a reasonable jury, properly directed, can be sure that the primary insider did provide the inside information to the alleged secondary insider. This was confirmed in the case of *The Queen on the Application of the FSA v MM, AR and AK*[36] in which the FSA applied for leave to appeal pursuant to s 58 of the CJA 2003 against a terminating ruling made by the trial judge. The terminating ruling in question had allowed the defendants' half time submission of no case to answer.

7.38 The case concerned allegations of insider dealing and disclosing inside information. The defendant AK was the finance director of a company (NT). It was alleged that he disclosed the fact that NT was involved in takeover discussions to his friend and co-defendant MM, who in turn disclosed it to AR. Both MM and AR then traded. It was common ground that, for the prosecution to prove its case, the jury had to be sure that MM obtained inside information from AK. Therefore the issue on the half time submission was: could a reasonable jury properly directed be sure on the evidence as it then stood, that MM had obtained inside information from AK?

---

[34] *R v Mustafa and others* (n 27). See Chapter 7, para 7.36.
[35] Brenda Hannigan (then the Senior Lecturer in Law at the University of Southampton), wrote in 1994: 'It may be possible to show that an individual has dealt in particular securities suspiciously prior to some change in the company's fortunes. It may also be possible to establish business/personal/family links between the person who dealt and an insider. But the connection between these two possibly coincidental facts still has to be established. In practice, if both parties choose to deny their respective roles it is impossible to establish that A, the insider was the source of B's (the tippee) information.' Hannigan (n 8) 88.
[36] *The Queen on the Application of the FSA v MM, AR and AK* [2010] EWCA Crim 1151.

7.39 In the view of the Court of Appeal, the trial judge had erred by putting this essential question in rather wider terms and asking instead whether it would be safe for the jury to conclude, on the basis of the evidence that they had, that *nobody other than* AK could have passed inside information to MM. The trial judge then having asked the question in this way, went on to decide that it would not be safe. In the view of the Court of Appeal, the judge misdirected himself in this regard and as a result, arrived at a ruling that it was not reasonable for the judge to have made.[37]

7.40 The Court of Appeal held that the proper question for the judge on the facts of this case was whether a reasonable jury properly directed could be sure that MM had inside information from AK and not the more general question as framed by the trial judge. In the Court's view, once the right question was asked, the only reasonable answer was that a reasonable jury properly directed could be sure that AK provided inside information to MM. The Court therefore allowed the prosecution's appeal, reversed the trial judge's ruling and directed that the trial proceed.[38]

7.41 Where the prosecution does not allege (or does not know) the identity of inside source, it is suggested that all that is necessary for the purposes of s 57(2)(b) CJA is to prove that the alleged secondary insider knows that the information is from an inside source of some sort. It is not necessary to prove that the alleged secondary insider knows exactly which primary insider was the source. It is sufficient to prove simply that he knew that it did come from an inside source of some sort.

---

[37] CJA 2003, s 67(c) and *The Queen on the Application of the FSA* (n 36) para 61.
[38] *The Queen on the Application of the FSA* (n 36) paras 62–6. The trial did proceed and all three defendants were subsequently acquitted by the jury of all counts on the indictment. This demonstrates that the jury did not in fact consider the prosecution case to have been proved against any of the defendants in the case.

8

SECURITIES AND REGULATED MARKETS

1. Introduction	8.01	The Insider Dealing (Securities and Regulated Markets) Order 1994	8.25
2. The correct analysis	8.02	4. Regulated markets	8.29
3. Securities	8.03	5. Securities other than shares	8.37
Securities listed in Schedule 2 CJA	8.04	Contracts for difference	8.38
Do spread bets fall within Schedule 2 CJA?	8.15		

1. Introduction

8.01 This Chapter explains how a 'security' and a 'regulated market' are defined for the purposes of the CJA. It describes the different types of securities listed in the Insider Dealing (Securities and Regulated Markets) Order 1994 (as amended) ('IDO') and deals with the issue of whether spread bets fall within the CJA regime.

2. The correct analysis

8.02 The correct analysis in an insider dealing case is to approach the topic of securities and regulated markets in two stages:

1. First, to establish that the asset in question falls within the requirements for the definition of 'security' as contained in Part V CJA, s 54, Schedule 2 CJA, and the IDO.
2. Second, to establish that the conduct carried out in relation to those securities falls within the ambit of Part V CJA. This is dealt with in the next Chapter.

3. Securities

Section 54—Securities to which Part V applies

(1) This Part applies to any security which—
 (a) falls within any paragraph of Schedule 2; and
 (b) satisfies any conditions applying to it under an order made by the Treasury for the purposes of this subsection;
 and in the provisions of this Part (other than that Schedule) any reference to a security is a reference to a security to which this Part applies.
(2) The Treasury may by order amend Schedule 2.

8.03 The CJA approaches the definition of securities in two ways. Firstly, by listing in Schedule 2 CJA, those securities to which the CJA applies, and secondly specifying by way of Statutory Instrument (the IDO), the conditions which a security must satisfy before it can fall within the ambit of the legislation. The purpose of this approach was explained by the Minister during the Parliamentary debates:[1]

> [The] approach has been adopted because it is not the intention to catch transactions in all Schedule 1 [now Schedule 2] securities—for example, in respect of all shares even those in private companies. The purpose of the legislation is to ensure confidence in the market in its broadest sense. So only transactions in securities that are market related are to be caught. But, because the terms on which securities are admitted to formal markets differ widely, and because of the need to ensure that it is possible to apply the legislation to situations where there is a ready trade in securities related to those traded on formal markets, the clause includes a power to describe the securities by order.

Securities listed in Schedule 2 CJA

8.04 Schedule 2[2] to the CJA therefore provides a list of securities that fall within the ambit of Part V. Securities are dealt with by paragraphs which comprise a heading followed by a description of the security in question:

Shares[3]

1. Shares and stock in the share capital of a company ('shares').

Debt securities

2. Any instrument creating or acknowledging indebtedness which is issued by a company or public sector body, including, in particular, debentures, debenture stock, loan stock, bonds and certificates of deposit ('debt securities').

---

[1] HC Deb, Standing Committees A & B, Official Report, Session 1992–93, vol II, col 166.
[2] See Appendix 2c.
[3] See Chapter 2, Section 2.

8.05 The accepted generic name for all types of debt securities is 'bonds'. Bonds are a form of debt and they are normally issued by companies, governments, or public bodies. Bonds are normally issued with a fixed coupon and a fixed life although there are variations such as undated debt, debt with floating or variable rate coupons and index-linked debt. In the last decade, debt instruments have been created by packaging Bonds or by securitising a stream of income, for example mortgages, credit card payments, etc. It is these latter products that are widely regarded as being at the root of the current economic crisis.

8.06 Warrants

> 3. Any right (whether conferred by warrant or otherwise) to subscribe for shares or debt securities

A warrant gives the holder the right to purchase securities (usually equities) from the issuer at a specific price within a certain time frame. Warrants are often included in a new debt issue in order to attract investors. Warrants are issued and guaranteed by the issuer, and the life span of a warrant can typically be measured in years.

8.07 Depositary receipts

> 4. (1) The rights under any depositary receipt.
> (2) For the purposes of sub-paragraph (1) a 'depositary receipt' means a certificate or other record (whether or not in the form of a document)—
>   (a) which is issued by or on behalf of a person who holds any relevant securities of a particular issuer; and
>   (b) which acknowledges that another person is entitled to rights in relation to the relevant securities or relevant securities of the same kind.
> (3) In sub-paragraph (2) 'relevant securities' means shares, debt securities and warrants.

A Depository Receipt is a negotiable financial instrument issued by a bank to represent a foreign company's publicly traded securities. It is traded on a local financial market. The purpose of a Depository Receipt is to enable an issuer to raise capital in markets outside the home State, without the shares themselves having to leave the home State.

8.08 Options

> 5. Any option to acquire or dispose of any security falling within any other paragraph of this Schedule.

An option is a derivative financial instrument that specifies a contract between two parties for a future transaction of an asset at a reference price (known as the 'strike' or 'exercise' price). The underlying asset is commonly a stock, a bond, a currency, or a futures contract. The buyer of the option gains the right (but not the obligation) to engage in that transaction, while the seller incurs the corresponding obligation to fulfil the transaction (known as 'writing' the option).

An option which conveys the right to buy something at a specific price is called **8.09**
a 'call option' and an option which conveys the right to sell something at a specific price is called a 'put option'. In return for writing the option, the writer collects a payment (the 'premium') from the buyer. If the option is exercised, the writer must make good on delivering (or receiving) the underlying asset or the cash equivalent. Most options have an expiry date by which the option must be exercised.

An option can usually be sold by its original buyer to another party. The price of **8.10**
an option derives from the difference between the strike price and the value of the underlying asset plus a premium based on the time remaining until the expiry of the option.

Futures **8.11**

6. (1) Rights under a contract for the acquisition or disposal of relevant securities under which delivery is to be made at a future date and at a price agreed when the contract is made.
   (2) In sub-paragraph (1)
      (a) the references to a future date and to a price agreed when the contract is made include references to a date and a price determined in accordance with terms of the contract; and
      (b) 'relevant securities' means any security falling within any other paragraph of this Schedule.

A futures contract is a standardised contract between two parties to buy or sell a specified asset of standardised quantity and quality for a price agreed today (the 'futures price' or 'strike price') with delivery and payment occurring at a specified future date ('the delivery date'). The buyer of the contract (the party who agrees to buy the underlying asset in the future) is said to be 'long', whereas the seller (the party agreeing to sell the asset in the future) is said to be 'short'.

Futures contracts are negotiated at a futures exchange, which acts as an intermediary **8.12**
between the two parties. The exchange requires both parties to put up an initial amount of cash (called 'margin'), and the difference in the delivery date price and the daily futures price (called 'variation margin') is settled daily (known as 'marking to market'). Therefore since any gain or loss has already been settled by the marking to market process, on the delivery date, the amount exchanged is not the specified price on the contract but the 'spot value'.

Unlike an option, both parties to a futures contract must fulfil the contract on **8.13**
the delivery date. To exit the commitment prior to the delivery date, the holder of a futures position can close out his position by taking the opposite position on another futures contract on the same asset and delivery date.

8.14 Contracts for differences[4]

> 7. (1) Rights under a contract which does not provide for the delivery of securities but whose purpose or pretended purpose is to secure a profit or avoid a loss by reference to fluctuations in
> (a) a share index or other similar factor connected with relevant securities;
> (b) the price of particular relevant securities; or
> (c) the interest rate offered on money placed on deposit.[5]
> (2) In sub-paragraph (1) 'relevant securities' means any security falling within any other paragraph of this Schedule.

Contracts for difference were not included within the minimum requirements of Article 1(2) of the Insider Dealing Directive ('IDD').[6] By including these, the CJA has implemented measures which are more onerous than those required by Europe.

Do spread bets fall within Schedule 2 CJA?

8.15 Spread bets are not specifically listed in the categories of securities contained in Schedule 2 of the CJA. This is not surprising given that at the time the CJA was enacted, no-one could have conceived of the role that spread betting would come to play in relation to the financial markets.[7] Despite this, it has come to be accepted by the Courts that spread bets do nevertheless fall within Schedule 2 and are therefore 'securities' for the purposes of the CJA.

8.16 The point was first argued in *R v Beale, Judson, Masters, Butt and Coleman* ('*R v Butt and others*'),[8] in which the defendants were charged with conspiracy to commit insider dealing where the trading took place by placing spread bets on the price movements of the companies about which the defendants were in possession of inside information.

8.17 Following transfer to the Crown Court, the defendants applied to the trial judge, His Honour Judge Elwen, for dismissal of the charges on the primary ground that spread bets were not 'securities' because they were not listed in Schedule 2 CJA.

---

[4] See Chapter 2, Section 7.
[5] This appears to have been added at the insistence of LIFFE in order to cover short-term interest rate contracts, even though there is no underlying security. See HC Deb, Session 1992–93, Standing Committee B, col 218, 15 June 1993.
[6] Dir 89/592/EEC.
[7] Spread betting is said to have been invented in the 1940s by Charles K McNeil, a bookmaker from Chicago who used it in relation to sporting events. It did not become popular in the UK until the 1980s—when it was still predominantly used in relation to wagering on sporting events. Spread betting is not therefore referred to in the Parliamentary debates. It was not until the second half of the 1990s, with the advent of the technology boom that investors began looking at spread betting as a versatile tool for taking advantage of short-term price movements in individual companies and indices.
[8] *R v Butt and others*, unreported, Southwark Crown Court, His Honour Judge Elwen, 17 Mar 2004.

It was argued that the heading to paragraph 7 of Schedule 2 CJA meant that this limited the scope of that paragraph to CFDs only and that spread bets were a different form of financial instrument.

8.18 The trial judge held that it was plain that spread bets do fall within Schedule 2, paragraph 7 CJA given that, with a spread bet, profit or loss is *prima facie* referenced to fluctuations in the price of the underlying share. Even though the spreads used by the spread betting companies may have such things as commission and financing charges factored into the size of the spread, the spreads were still calculated by reference to the underlying share to which the spread bet related. He observed that, were this not the case, then spread bets would have no underlying rationale. This must be correct as without the spreads being referenced to the price of the underlying share, the investor has no frame of reference upon which to base his bet.

8.19 He further held that the wording of Schedule 2, paragraph 7 CJA plainly did not make it necessary for the profit or loss to be determined wholly or exclusively by reference to the price of the underlying security,[9] provided that it could be said that the profit is secured or loss avoided 'by reference to fluctuations in' the price of the underlying security.

8.20 Spread bets have been the topic of several high court and Court of Appeal decisions,[10] which while being concerned with the Market Abuse regime under the FSMA and its predecessor the Financial Services Act 1986, provide support for Judge Elwen's view that spread bets are in a real and practical sense referenced to fluctuations in the price of the underlying security.

8.21 The judgment of Rix LJ in *Spreadex v Battu*[11] provides a thorough description of spread betting on financial instruments which is entirely consistent with the analysis above.

8.22 Finally, should there remain any room for doubt, the value of side notes and headings in construing a statutory provision was determined by the House of Lords in *R v Montila and others*.[12] In summary, this case decided that headings and side notes in a statute may be taken into account, although the weight that is to be attached to them is limited by the fact that they are not subject to debate or capable of amendment during the Parliamentary process. Applying this rationale to the heading 'Contracts for Differences' in respect of Schedule 2, paragraph 7 CJA means that an argument that the heading itself restricts that paragraph only to CFDs is unlikely to succeed.

---

[9] *R v Butt and others* (n 8).
[10] The Court of Appeal case of *City Index Ltd v Leslie* was referred to by both sides in the legal argument in *R v Butt and others* (n 8). See also *Spreadex Ltd v Battu* [2005] EWCA Civ 855; *Spreadex Ltd v Sekhon* [2008] All ER (D) 329 (May); *City Index Ltd (t/as FinSpreads) v Balducci* [2011] EWHC 2562.
[11] *Spreadex v Battu* (n 10) pp 2–4.
[12] *R v Montila and others* [2004] UKHL 50, in particular paras 31–6; [2005] 1 Cr App R 26.

8.23 In several recent insider dealing prosecutions, the alleged insider trading was conducted by way of spread-betting. Although the issue of whether spread bets fall within paragraph 7 of Schedule 2 CJA was initially raised by the defendants in these cases, the point was ultimately not pursued.[13]

8.24 On one view, it might have been easier had the Treasury simply exercised its power to amend Schedule 2 CJA to include spread bets. For reasons unknown, this has not happened and given the various decisions outlined above, it is now unlikely to be considered necessary.

The Insider Dealing (Securities and Regulated Markets) Order 1994

8.25 In addition to falling within Schedule 2 CJA, the security in question must also satisfy 'any conditions applying to it under an order made by the Treasury for the purposes of this subsection' (s 54(1)(b) CJA).

8.26 The relevant 'order made by the Treasury' is the IDO,[14] the original version of which came into force on 1 March 1994.

8.27 The Treasury Commentary confirmed the intention behind the IDO:[15]

> The intention is to use the order making power in a way which ensures that all securities markets which operate in the UK are within the ambit of the legislation ... The power will also be used to catch other EC securities markets, both official lists and junior stocks; and it will include over the counter as well as exchange traded derivative products.

8.28 As the Minister confirmed during the Parliamentary debates,[16] the IDO therefore restricts the ambit of the CJA to market based securities. Article 4 of the IDO set out the condition that a security must satisfy for the purpose of s 54(1) CJA:

Article 4 IDO

> It is officially listed in a State within the European Economic Area[17] or that it is admitted to dealing on, or has its price quoted on or under the rules of, a regulated market.

---

[13] *R v Sanders and others*, unreported, Southwark Crown Court, Mr Justice Simon, 20 June 2012. FSA/PN/060/2012 & FSA/PN/067/2012; *R v Mustafa and others*, unreported, Southwark Crown Court, His Honour Judge Pegden QC and a jury, 5 Mar to 23 July 2012; 27 July 2012. FSA/PN/080/2012; *R v Rupinder Sidhu*, unreported, Southwark Crown Court, His Honour Judge Gledhill QC and a jury, 28 Nov 2011 to 15 Dec 2011. FSA/PN/114/2011.

[14] SI No 1994/187. The order was subsequently amended by: the Insider Dealing (Securities and Regulated Markets) (Amendment) Order 1996, SI 1996/1561; the Insider Dealing (Securities and Regulated Markets) (Amendment) Order 2000, SI 2000/1923; Insider Dealing (Securities and Regulated Markets) (Amendment) Order 2002, SI 2002/1874. The fully amended version is contained in Appendix 2.

[15] Treasury Commentary on the original draft of the Criminal Justice Bill, October 1992, paras 6 and 7.

[16] HC Deb (n 1) col 166.

[17] Article 2 states: 'In this Order a "State within the European Economic Area" means a State which is a member of the European Communities and the Republics of Austria, Finland and

4. Regulated markets

Section 60 CJA states: **8.29**

> **60. Other interpretation provisions**
>
> (1) For the purposes of this Part, 'regulated market' means any market, however operated, which, by an order made by the Treasury, is identified (whether by name or by reference to criteria prescribed by the order) as a regulated market for the purposes of this Part.

A regulated market is described in Article 9 IDO as any market which is established under the rules of an investment exchange specified in the Schedule to the IDO, and the market known as OFEX.[18] **8.30**

OFEX subsequently became the PLUS Derivatives Exchange ('PLUS-DX'), which was recently acquired by ICAP and is now known as the ICAP Securities and Derivatives Exchange ('ISDX'). **8.31**

Schedule 2 to the IDO sets out a long list of investment exchanges. There have been various amendments to this list over the years as new markets have been created or old ones cease to exist.[19] **8.32**

It is important to note that this list includes '[a]ny market which is established under the rules of', one of the investment exchanges contained in this list. 'Established under the rules of' is not a legal concept, it is not further defined and has no special meaning. Therefore it will be a question of fact in each case as to whether a particular market is 'established under the rules of' one of the listed investment exchanges. As we shall see, this issue was directly relevant in *R v Sanders and others*.[20] **8.33**

The main problem with Schedule 2 to the IDO is that it was last updated in July 2002[21] and is therefore out of date. For example: **8.34**

- virt-x Exchange Limited appears on the list. However, virt-x was purchased by SWX Swiss Exchange in 2002 and was later renamed SWX Europe. As of

---

Iceland, the Kingdoms of Norway and Sweden and the Principality of Liechtenstein.' The Treaty of Lisbon (Changes in Terminology) Order 2011 SI 2011/1043 provides that as from 22 Apr 2011, references to the European Communities should be substituted by references to the European Union.

[18] Paragraph (a) designated as such and para (b) added by the Insider Dealing (Securities and Regulated Markets) (Amendment) Order 2000/1923 art 2(2) (20 July 2000). Words at para (b) repealed by the Insider Dealing (Securities and Regulated Markets) (Amendment) Order 2002/1874 art 2(2) (19 July 2002).

[19] The current version of the list is contained in Appendix 2.

[20] *R v Sanders and others* (n 13) and see Chapter 8, paras 8.39ff; Chapter 9, Section 5, paras 9.22—Simon J, Ruling on Preparatory Hearing held pursuant to ss 7 and 9 of the CJA 1987 to determine a point of law that arises under Part V of the CJA 1993.

[21] Insider Dealing (Securities and Regulated Markets) (Amendment) Order 2002 SI 2002/1874.

30 April 2009, SWX Europe ceased trading and all business was transferred to SIX Swiss Exchange, Switzerland's principal stock exchange.
- CoredealMTS also appears on the list but was in fact de-recognised as an investment exchange on 29 November 2002 when it was absorbed by EuroMTS.
- OMLX, the London Securities and Derivatives Exchange appears on the list but in fact transferred its markets in 2003 to EDX London.
- ICE Futures Europe is not included on the list despite the fact that this is the London-based regulated futures exchange for global energy markets operated by the Intercontinental Exchange ('ICE').

8.35 The only non-European investment exchange listed in the Schedule is NASDAQ.[22] The reason for NASDAQ's inclusion appears to have been that, at the time the original list was created, NASDAQ had physical trading screens in the UK and so it was possible for trading on NASDAQ to take place in the UK. In the twenty-first century era of global markets, cross-border trading is increasingly common and the opportunities to access overseas markets from the UK are effectively unlimited, yet NASDAQ remains the only non-European investment exchange to be included. In particular, the NYSE[23] is a market that is readily accessible and is commonly traded from the UK, and yet it has never been included in the Schedule. This makes for the anomalous situation that trading in shares which are listed on NASDAQ would be caught by Part V of the CJA (provided all the other required elements are present), whereas trading in shares which are listed on NYSE would not.

8.36 However, one of the consequences of a global market is that it is possible for a company's shares to be listed on more than one investment exchange in more than one country. It is also of course perfectly possible for a company to be admitted to dealing on, or have its price quoted on, or under the rules of, more than one exchange. If any one of these events has occurred in relation to a regulated market as defined in Article 4 and Schedule 2 of the IDO, or (in accordance with Article 4 of the IDO) the stock appears on the Official List[24] of a State within the European Union, then this is sufficient to bring the security within the ambit of the CJA.

5. Securities other than shares

8.37 What, however, is the position where it is not shares that have been traded but some other product? In such circumstances, it is necessary to look at Articles 5 to 8 of the IDO. These articles provide that in the case of a warrant, depositary receipt,

---

[22] National Association of Securities Dealers Automated Quotations, a US computerised system for trading in securities.
[23] New York Stock Exchange.
[24] In the UK, this is a list kept by the FCA of all securities traded on the main market of the London Stock Exchange.

option, or future, the product must relate to a share or debt security of the same class as one which is officially listed in a State within the European Union, or that is admitted to dealing on, or has its price quoted on or under the rules of, a regulated market listed in the Schedule to the IDO.

Contracts for difference

These are covered by Article 8 of the IDO: 8.38

> The following alternative condition applies in relation to a contract for differences, that is, that the purpose or pretended purpose of the contract is to secure a profit or avoid a loss by reference to fluctuations in
> (a) the price of any shares or debt securities which satisfy the condition in article 4, or
> (b) an index of the price of such shares or debt securities.

In each case, therefore, the underlying share or debt security must satisfy one or the other of the conditions in Article 4. If it does so then it will be caught by the CJA as a 'security'.[25] Given the tortuousness of the legislation and the anomalies it contains, navigating these provisions requires a certain amount of legal gymnastics. It is not surprising therefore that there is the potential for legal argument. An example of this occurred in the *Sanders* case.[26] 8.39

In *R v Sanders and others*, the defendants placed spread bets relating to three stocks[27] that each had their primary listing on the NYSE which (as we have established) is not a regulated market under the IDO. The spread bets which the defendants made were referenced to the price of the underlying shares traded on the NYSE. That would have been the end of the case as far as these three stocks were concerned had it not been for the fact that all three stocks (at the relevant times), were also admitted for dealing on the Open Market ('Freiverkehr') of the Berlin Stock Exchange ('Boerse Berlin'). 8.40

The prosecution therefore had to prove that the Berlin Open Market is (and was at the time of the trading) a market 'established under the rules of' the Boerse Berlin, which would make it a 'regulated market' pursuant to the Schedule to the IDO. This necessitated the prosecution obtaining a witness statement from the Legal Counsel for Boerse Berlin and the Head of the Boerse Berlin Listing Department confirming this. 8.41

In addition, to meet the requirements of Articles 4 and 8 IDO, it had to be established that the shares listed on NYSE—to which the defendants' spread bets were referenced, and the shares admitted to dealing on the Berlin Open Market—were one and the same. 8.42

---

[25] Provided that the underlying product is also listed in Schedule 2 CJA.
[26] *R v Sanders and others* (n 13).
[27] Adesa Inc ('Adesa'), ChoicePoint Inc ('ChoicePoint'), and Getty Images Inc ('Getty').

8.43 Quite often a company will issue different types of shares. In the US, these are usually referred to as Common Stock[28] or Preferred Stock.[29] There is also a type of share known as a 'Regulation S' share or 'Reg S'.[30] In the UK, as explained in Chapter 2,[31] types of shares include ordinary shares and preference shares.

8.44 Therefore, to take an example: If a defendant trades Adesa Common Stock on the NYSE but only Adesa Regulation S shares are admitted to dealing on a Regulated Market (such as the Boerse Berlin), then the securities the defendant actually traded would not meet the requirements of Article 4 of the IDO. Fortunately in all cases, the shares in question were 'common ctock'.

8.45 At a preparatory hearing[32] on this issue, the trial Judge, Mr Justice Simon held that:

> On an ordinary reading of the words of Articles 8 and 4 [IDO], it is sufficient if the share is admitted to dealing or has its price quoted on a regulated market. In the light of the wording and the broad purpose of the Part V legislation, it does not matter that the transactions were conducted by reference to the price on an unregulated market, if the share was admitted to dealing or had its correlated price quoted on a regulated market.

8.46 This demonstrates the legal gymnastics that at times need to be performed in order to determine whether the security in question falls within the CJA regime. It also shows that approaching this issue in two stages, in the way suggested at the outset of this chapter, will ensure that the correct analysis is applied. Once it has been established that the asset in question does fall within the requirements for the definition of 'security' as contained in Part V CJA, s 54, Schedule 2 CJA and the IDO, the next step is to establish whether the conduct carried out in relation to those spread bets falls within the ambit of Part V CJA. This is dealt with in the next Chapter.

---

[28] Common stock is the most 'common' share issued by a US Company. Common shares represent ownership in a company and a claim (dividends) on a portion of profits.

[29] Preferred stock represents some degree of ownership in a company but usually doesn't come with the same voting rights. Investors are usually guaranteed a fixed dividend.

[30] Regulation S provides an exclusion from the s 5 registration requirements of the Securities Act of 1933, as amended (the 'Securities Act'), for offerings made outside the United States by both US and foreign issuers. A securities offering, whether private or public, made by an issuer outside of the United States in reliance on Regulation S need not be registered under the Securities Act.

[31] Chapter 2, Section 2.

[32] The Hon Mr Justice Simon, Ruling on Preparatory Hearing held pursuant to ss 7 and 9 of the CJA 1987 to determine a point of law that arises under Part V of the CJA 1993.

9

DEALING

1. Introduction — 9.01
2. Dealing (s 52(3) CJA) — 9.02
3. Acquisitions and disposals (s 55(1)–(3) CJA) — 9.06
4. Procuring an acquisition or disposal (s 55(4) CJA) — 9.11
5. Professional intermediaries — 9.20

1. Introduction

Once it has been established that the asset in question qualifies as a 'security', it is necessary to consider whether dealing has taken place with respect to that security. This Chapter deals with the provisions of Part V of the CJA which inform what 'dealing' means and the ways in which it can occur in order to come within the CJA's ambit. **9.01**

2. Dealing (s 52(3) CJA)

The Insider Dealing Directive[1] ('IDD') required Member States to prohibit those who possess inside information from dealing either on their own account, or through a professional intermediary such as a stock broker.[2] **9.02**

Therefore, under s 52(3) CJA, in order to be guilty of the primary offence of insider dealing (contrary to s 52(1) CJA), an individual must deal in price affected securities in the following circumstances: **9.03**

> The circumstances referred to above are that the acquisition or disposal in question occurs on a regulated market, or that the person dealing relies on a professional intermediary or is himself acting as a professional intermediary.

---

[1] Council Directive 89/552/EEC, 13 Nov 1989.
[2] Article 2(1) and (3) Dir 89/592/EC.

9.04 Section 52(3) CJA also applies to the secondary 'encouraging' offence (s 52(2)(a) CJA) to the extent that when an individual encourages another to deal, he must know or have reasonable cause to believe that the dealing would take place in the circumstances mentioned in s 52(3) CJA.

9.05 The effect of s 52(3) CJA was summed up by the Minister during the Parliamentary debates as follows: 'The provision applies to deals on regulated markets. If they are off market, they are not covered, but if they take place through a professional intermediary they are.'[3]

3. Acquisitions and disposals (s 55(1)–(3) CJA)

Section 55—'Dealing' in securities

(1) For the purposes of this Part, a person deals in securities if
   (a) he acquires or disposes of the securities (whether as principal or agent); or
   (b) he procures, directly or indirectly, an acquisition or disposal of the securities by any other person.
(2) For the purposes of this Part, 'acquire', in relation to a security, includes
   (a) agreeing to acquire the security; and
   (b) entering into a contract which creates the security
(3) For the purposes of this Part, 'dispose', in relation to a security, includes
   (a) agreeing to dispose of the security; and
   (b) bringing to an end a contract which created the security.

9.06 The purpose behind s 55 CJA was to ensure that 'dealing' for the purposes of Part V of the CJA was broadly defined, in order to encompass the full range of potential activities which ought to be prohibited if the legislation was to have thorough and meaningful effect in preserving the integrity of financial markets. As the Minister put it during the Parliamentary debates:[4]

> [the section] defines 'dealing' in a way which catches a wide range of transactions to prevent creating loopholes which could be readily exploited by a determined insider.

9.07 Acquiring and disposing are therefore broadly defined by s 55(2) and (3) CJA to cover not only situations in which legal title to the securities is actually acquired or disposed of by the person concerned as principal, but also where the person acquires or disposes of securities as an agent—for example by dealing in securities on behalf of another. The Minister explained:

> That ensures that, for example, the prohibitions on using inside information to make a profit or avoid a loss apply as much to a person or agent who deals in order to

---

[3] HC Deb 10 June 1993, Standing Committee B, col 192.
[4] HC Deb (n 3) col 168.

get a benefit for his principal and for himself as they do to a person's own private dealings.[5]

9.08 The definition also extends to situations in which a person agrees to acquire or dispose of securities. 'That ensures that, for example, someone does not escape the legislation if he agrees to buy shares and also sells them during the same account and thereby makes a profit without having taken legal title to them.'[6]

9.09 Section 55(2)(b) and s 55(3)(b) CJA also include entering into a contract which creates a security or bringing to an end a contract which created a security. This was specifically enacted to cover:

> dealing in derivates such as options. ... The reference to bringing to an end a contract which created a security ensures that where a person terminates a contract he is to be regarded as disposing of the security. That is particularly important for index contracts and other contracts for differences.[7]

9.10 This provision is particularly important today given the explosion in the ready availability of derivative products such as contracts for difference ('CFDs') and spread bets. These are particularly attractive products for an insider dealer given their inherent leverage and therefore their potential to realise large profits without the need to purchase the underlying share.

4. Procuring an acquisition or disposal (s 55(4) CJA)

Section 55(4)

For the purposes of subsection (1), a person procures an acquisition or disposal of a security if the security is acquired or disposed of by a person who is

(a) his agent,
(b) his nominee, or
(c) a person who is acting at his direction, in relation to the acquisition or disposal.

(5) Subsection (4) is not exhaustive as to the circumstances in which one person may be regarded as procuring an acquisition or disposal of securities by another.

9.11 Section 55(4) CJA was intended to cover the common scenario in which the insider does not deal himself but procures another to deal on his behalf—perhaps to 'layer' the trading in order to disguise his involvement in it.

9.12 This occurred in *R v Goodman*[8] in which the insider was a company chairman who was aware that his company was about to announce significant losses. He therefore

---

[5] HC Deb (n 3) col 168.
[6] HC Deb (n 3) col 168.
[7] HC Deb (n 3) col 168.
[8] *R v Goodman*, unreported but see *FT* (London, 1 May 1991 and 16 June 1992). See also *Chase Manhattan Equities Ltd v Goodman* [1991] BCLC 897 in which Chase Manhattan which had bought the shares in its capacity as Market Maker sued Goodman over the validity and enforceability of the sale.

gave his entire holding in the company's shares to his girlfriend who sold them in advance of this announcement. He was apparently treated as having procured the disposal.

9.13 Section 55(4) CJA is not intended to be a straight jacket—to restrict the ways in which dealing can occur. The purpose of s 55(4) is to widen the ambit of persons whose conduct would be caught by the insider dealing provisions, not to narrow it. This was confirmed during the Parliamentary debates in which the Minister used an example of a sole shareholder in a company:

> As sole shareholder, one uses one's influence over the company to get it to deal in the shares. Any profit made or loss avoided would accrue to the company, but, as sole shareholder, one would benefit from the company's increased profitability. It is to that type of case that the reference to a person acting at another person's direction is targeted. A company is included in the definition of a person. The clause [now s 55] expressly says that the list of circumstances is not exhaustive. There may be other ways in which one person could procure another person to deal.[9]

9.14 This was demonstrated in *R v Neel and Matthew Uberoi*.[10] Matthew Uberoi provided inside information to his father who then dealt on the basis of the information, with Matthew's full knowledge and agreement. However there was no evidence that Matthew benefitted personally from his father's trading. At trial the prosecution put its case on the basis that Matthew had aided and abetted his father's dealing and was therefore liable as a joint principal on the basis of joint enterprise.

9.15 The defence in the Uberoi case submitted that s 55(4) CJA in effect ring-fenced the manner in which a person could 'deal' in securities for the purposes of Part V of the CJA and that the prosecution was therefore required to demonstrate that Matthew Uberoi fell within one of the provisions of s 55 CJA, in particular s 55(4) CJA.

9.16 The prosecution submitted (and the trial judge agreed), that the provisions contained in s 55(4) CJA were designed for circumstances in which a person procured another to deal on their behalf in circumstances where the dealer does not know that the dealing is taking place on the basis of inside information. It was not intended to prevent ordinary principles of criminal law such as joint enterprise and accessory liability from being applicable in insider dealing cases as they are in any other criminal case. In any event s 55(5) CJA specifically provides that s 55(4) CJA is not exhaustive as to the circumstances in which one person may be regarded as procuring an acquisition or disposal of securities by another.

---

[9] HC Deb (n 3) cols 171–2.
[10] *R v Neel and Matthew Uberoi*, unreported, Southwark Crown Court, His Honour Judge Testar and a jury, 28 Oct to 6 Nov 2009. FSA/PN/149/2009; 10 Dec 2009, FSA/PN/170/2009.

9.17 This is plainly correct. This approach is also consistent with common law principles. In the leading case of Attorney-General's Reference (No 1 of 1975),[11] 'to procure' was described as follows:

> To procure means to produce by endeavour. You procure a thing by setting out to see that it happens and taking the appropriate steps to produce that happening. We think that there are plenty of instances in which a person may be said to procure the commission of a crime by another even though there is no sort of conspiracy between the two, even though there is no attempt at agreement or discussion as to the form which the offence should take.[12]

9.18 On that basis, Matthew Uberoi would in all likelihood have come within the definition of 'procuring' given that his father's dealing was brought about by Matthew's deliberate and knowing endeavour.

9.19 In the Parliamentary debates, concern was expressed about the position of an individual whose trading is conducted by a discretionary account manager. If the individual becomes an insider in relation to a particular stock, but has no contact with the investment manager, who then proceeds to trade in the same stock?; has he or the account manager committed an offence? The Minister thought not[13]—and he is almost certainly right. The account manager has committed no offence because he is not in possession of any inside information. The individual has also not committed any offence because he has not procured the dealing in these shares other than in the very general sense of granting discretion to the account manager, which would not be nearly sufficient to fix the individual with any criminal liability. The position would of course be different if the individual telephones his account manager and tips him to buy shares in the company in respect of which he has inside information.

5. Professional intermediaries

9.20 By s 52(3) CJA, if the dealing does not occur on a regulated market, it will still be caught by Part V of the CJA if the person dealing relies on a professional intermediary or is himself acting as a professional intermediary.

9.21 So if two private clients deal off market, that transaction would not be caught by the legislation. Similarly, if two parties deal on an unregulated market without the involvement of a professional intermediary on either side of the transaction (if this is conceptually possible), this would not be caught. However, both transactions are brought within the ambit of Part V of the CJA if either party relies

---

[11] [1975] 61 Cr App R 118, CA.
[12] [1975] 61 Cr App R 118, CA, 121.
[13] HC Deb (n 3) cols 172–73.

on a professional intermediary or is itself acting as a professional intermediary in relation to the transaction. In Parliamentary debates, the example used was the Eurobond market:

> Although London is an important centre for listed Eurobonds, many are listed in Luxembourg. Those bonds are securities to which the legislation will apply. However they are not traded on a regulated market. Trading, which is predominantly based in London, generally involves market makers who act as principals in the transactions.[14]

9.22 This point was argued as part of the preparatory hearing in the *Sanders* case. Counsel for James Sanders argued that s 53(3) should be interpreted as requiring the dealing to occur on a regulated market whether or not a professional intermediary is relied on. The trial judge (Simon J), rejected this submission, ruling that:[15]

> The requirements of s 52(3) are disjunctive: it is sufficient for the Prosecution to rely either on acquisitions or disposals which 'occur on a regulated market *or* that the person dealing relies on a professional intermediary.' In other words, if the prosecution can show that the person dealing relied on a professional intermediary, it does not matter whether or not the dealing occurred on a regulated market.

9.23 The term 'Professional Intermediary' is specifically defined in s 59 CJA:

Section 59—'Professional intermediary'

(1) For the purposes of this Part, a 'professional intermediary' is a person—
   (a) who carries on a business consisting of an activity mentioned in subsection (2) and who holds himself out to the public or any section of the public (including a section of the public constituted by persons such as himself) as willing to engage in any such business; or
   (b) who is employed by a person falling within paragraph (a) to carry out any such activity.
(2) The activities referred to in subsection (1) are—
   (a) acquiring or disposing of securities (whether as principal or agent); or
   (b) acting as an intermediary between persons taking part in any dealing in securities.
(3) A person is not to be treated as carrying on a business consisting of an activity mentioned in subsection (2)
   (a) if the activity in question is merely incidental to some other activity not falling within subsection (2); or
   (b) merely because he occasionally conducts one of those activities.
(4) For the purposes of section 52, a person dealing in securities relies on a professional intermediary if and only if a person who is acting as a professional intermediary carries out an activity mentioned in subsection (2) in relation to that dealing.

---

[14] HC Deb (n 3) col 192.
[15] The Hon Mr Justice Simon, Ruling on Preparatory Hearing held pursuant to ss 7 and 9 of the CJA 1987 to determine a point of law that arises under Part V, para 45 CJA 1993.

Under s 59(2) CJA, for someone to qualify as a professional intermediary his business must be acquiring or disposing of securities (for example as a market maker), or acting as an intermediary between market participants (for example as a stockbroker). **9.24**

If the transaction in question involves such a person, then it will be caught by the CJA provided that in relation to the dealing: **9.25**

1. The professional intermediary carries on a business consisting of one of the activities set out in s 59(2) CJA.
2. These activities are not merely incidental to other activities which do not fall within s 59(2) CJA (for example a solicitor or accountant providing investment advice as part of his advice to the client) (s 59(3)(a) CJA).
3. These activities are not conducted by the professional intermediary on an occasional basis (s 59(3)(b) CJA).
4. At least one of the activities mentioned in s 59(2) CJA is carried out by the professional intermediary in relation to the dealing in question (s 59(4) CJA).

Whether or not a professional intermediary has been 'relied on' is therefore a question of fact to be determined in accordance with the s 59 CJA criteria. In this sense, the term 'professional intermediary' is a description of an identity as well as of function or role in a particular transaction. The professional intermediary criterion is of particular importance in cases in which the trading is in derivative products such as CFDs and spread bets which are not themselves traded on regulated markets. Brokers such as City Index, IG Index, and CMC Markets who offer these products, carry on the business of acquiring or disposing of securities whether as principal or agent; and this includes entering into contracts which create the securities (CFDs or spread bets), and holding themselves out as willing to engage in this business. They therefore fall within the definition of professional intermediary for the purposes of the CJA regime.[16] **9.26**

---

[16] See n 15.

10

TERRITORIAL SCOPE (s 62 CJA)

1. Introduction	10.01	3. Secondary 'Encouraging' and 'Disclosing' offences (s 62(2) CJA)	10.05
2. Primary insider dealing offence (s 62(1) CJA)	10.02	4. The scope of s 62 CJA	10.06

1. Introduction

10.01 This Chapter deals with the territorial scope provisions in relation to the primary and secondary insider dealing offences. Even if conduct would otherwise fall within the CJA regime, it will not be caught unless it falls within one of the specific territorial scope provisions contained in s 62 CJA.

2. Primary insider dealing offence (s 62(1) CJA)

10.02 Section 62(1) CJA sets out the territorial scope provisions for the primary insider dealing offence (s 62(1) CJA).

Section 62—Territorial scope of offence of insider dealing

(1) An individual is not guilty of an offence falling within subsection (1) of section 52 unless
   (a) he was within the United Kingdom at the time when he is alleged to have done any act constituting or forming part of the alleged dealing;
   (b) the regulated market on which the dealing is alleged to have occurred is one which, by an order made by the Treasury, is identified (whether by name or by reference to criteria prescribed by the order) as being, for the purposes of this Part, regulated in the United Kingdom; or
   (c) the professional intermediary was within the United Kingdom at the time when he is alleged to have done anything by means of which the offence is alleged to have been committed.

Secondary 'Encouraging' and 'Disclosing' offences (s 62(2) CJA)

10.03 In summary, s 62(1) requires that the insider dealer must be either:

- within the UK at the time of dealing; or
- the dealing must have taken place on a UK regulated market; or
- the dealing must take place relying on a professional intermediary who is within the UK.

10.04 Article 10 of the Insider Dealing (Securities and Regulated Markets) Order 1994 ('IDO') defines UK Regulated Markets for the purposes of s 62(1):

United Kingdom Regulated Markets

Article 10[1]

The regulated markets which are regulated in the United Kingdom for the purposes of Part V of the Act of 1993 are any market which is established under the rules of

(a) the London Stock Exchange Limited;
(b) LIFFE Administration & Management;
(c) OMLX, the London Securities and Derivatives Exchange Limited;
(d) virt-x Exchange Limited;
(e) the exchange known as CoredealMTS

together with the market known as OFEX.

3. Secondary 'Encouraging' and 'Disclosing' offences (s 62(2) CJA)

Section 62(2)

An individual is not guilty of an offence falling within subsection (2) of section 52 unless

(a) he was within the United Kingdom at the time when he is alleged to have disclosed the information or encouraged the dealing; or
(b) the alleged recipient of the information or encouragement was within the United Kingdom at the time when he is alleged to have received the information or encouragement.

---

[1] As amended by Insider Dealing (Securities and Regulated Markets) (Amendment) Order 1996 SI 1996/1561 art 3; Insider Dealing (Securities and Regulated Markets) (Amendment) Order 2000, SI 2000/1923 art 2(1) and (3); Insider Dealing (Securities and Regulated Markets) (Amendment) Order 2002, SI 2002/1874 art 2(1) and (3). Virt-x was purchased by SWX Swiss Exchange in 2002 and was later renamed SWX Europe. As of 30 April 2009, SWX Europe ceased trading and all business was transferred to SIX Swiss Exchange, Switzerland's principal stock exchange. CoredealMTS was in fact de-recognised as an investment exchange on 29 Nov 2002 when it was absorbed by EuroMTS. OMLX, the London Securities, and Derivatives Exchange transferred its markets in 2003 to EDX London. OFEX subsequently became the PLUS Derivatives Exchange ('PLUS-DX'), which was recently acquired by ICAP and is now known as the ICAP Securities and Derivatives Exchange ('ISDX').

10.05 For each of the secondary offences under s 52(2) CJA, either the insider or the recipient (or both) must be within the United Kingdom at the time the encouragement or improper disclosure takes place.

4. The scope of s 62 CJA

10.06 The territorial scope provisions as set out in s 62 CJA give effect to Article 5 of the Insider Dealing Directive ('IDD')[2] which required each Member State to apply the insider dealing prohibitions at least to actions undertaken within its territory to the extent that the transferable securities concerned are admitted to trading on a market of a Member State or a market situated or operating within its territory.

10.07 The intention behind the IDD and the UK's domestic legislation is plain. Each State deals with insider dealing most directly connected with its territory. In giving effect to this, s 62 CJA seems to be clear and explicit. However, the issue was the subject of legal argument in the case of *R v Ammann, Weckewerth and Mang*.[3]

10.08 The defendants were charged with the primary offence of insider dealing (s 52(1) CJA). Mr Amman worked for Mizuho in its London-based Mergers and Acquisitions advisory team which was advising Canon in its takeover bid for Oce NV ('Oce'), a Dutch company. It was alleged that he used inside information about this deal to trade in Oce shares by getting his two co-defendants to trade on his behalf. Some of the trading in this stock was conducted by Ms Weckewerth who was situated in Germany at the time of the trading. Her trading was conducted through German professional intermediaries and the transactions took place on the NYSE Euronext Exchange which is based in Amsterdam.[4]

10.09 The defence for Ms Weckewerth took a preliminary legal point[5] that the territorial scope of s 52(1) CJA is governed by s 62(1) CJA which required Ms Weckewerth to be within the United Kingdom when any act is performed, constituting or forming part of the alleged dealing. Plainly, Ms Weckewerth was not within the UK at the relevant time, and for that matter, nor was her dealing conducted on a UK Regulated Market or in reliance on a professional intermediary situated within the UK. The defence therefore argued that Ms Weckewerth did not fall within the territorial requirements of s 62(1) CJA.

---

[2] Dir 89/592.

[3] *R v Ammann, Weckewerth and Mang*, unreported, Southwark Crown Court, approved ruling of His Honour Judge Anthony Leonard QC, 24 May 2012.

[4] Note that at the subsequent trial, Weckeworth and Mang were both acquitted by the jury of all offences they faced and therefore the prosecution's case against them was plainly not proved. *R v Weckewerth and Mang*, unreported, Southwark Crown Court, His Honour Judge Leonard QC, 15 Oct to 14 Nov 2012. Ammann had pleaded guilty on an earlier occasion, *R v Thomas Ammann*, unreported, Southwark Crown Court, His Honour Judge Leonard QC, 15 Nov 2012. FSA/PN/103/2012; 13 Dec 2012. FSA/PN/113/2012.

[5] *R v Ammann* (n 3).

10.10 The prosecution argued that the common law principle of joint enterprise overrode s 62(1) CJA. This was rejected by the trial judge who held[6] that the requirements of s 62(1) CJA are clear and unambiguous. The prosecution must prove either that the defendant who did the dealing was within the United Kingdom when he did any act constituting or forming part of the alleged dealing, or that the trading took place on a UK Regulated Market, or that the defendant has relied on a professional intermediary who is within the UK at the relevant time. In the absence of any of these factors, a prosecution under s 52(1) CJA was not possible and the common law principles of joint enterprise could not be engaged to overcome the territorial scope established by s 62(1) CJA. He therefore dismissed this count of insider dealing against Ms Weckewerth.

10.11 This ruling reinforces the central importance of s 62 CJA and the need to ensure that at least one of its provisions applies in relation to the s 52 CJA offence(s) alleged.

---

[6] *R v Ammann* (n 3).

11

STATUTORY DEFENCES

1. Introduction		11.01	4. Statutory defences to the secondary 'Disclosing' offence (s 53(3) CJA)	11.19
2. Statutory defences to the primary insider dealing offence (s 53(1) CJA)		11.02	5. Special defences	11.24
Did not expect the dealing to result in a profit (s 53(1)(a) CJA)		11.03	Market makers (Schedule 1(1) CJA)	11.26
Believed on reasonable grounds that the information had been disclosed widely enough (s 53(1)(b) CJA)		11.07	Persons in possession of market information (Schedule 1(2) CJA)	11.29
			Dealings to facilitate the accomplishment of an acquisition or disposal (Schedule 1(3) CJA)	11.34
He would have done what he did even if he had not had the information (s 53(1)(c) CJA)		11.12	Price stabilisation (Schedule 1(5) CJA)	11.36
3. Statutory defences to the secondary 'Encouraging' offence (s 53(2) CJA)		11.17	Dealings in pursuit of monetary policies (s 63 CJA)	11.40
			6. Statutory defences—legal and evidential burden on the defence	11.43

1. Introduction

11.01 This Chapter deals with the various statutory defences which are set out in s 53 and Schedule 1 CJA. It also deals with the issue of whether these defences impose a legal 'reverse' burden on a defendant in addition to an evidential burden.

2. Statutory defences to the primary insider dealing offence (s 53(1) CJA)

11.02 Section 53(1) provides three potential defences for the primary insider dealing offence:

> (1) An individual is not guilty of insider dealing by virtue of dealing in securities if he shows
> (a) that he did not at the time expect the dealing to result in a profit attributable to the fact that the information in question was price-sensitive information in relation to the securities; or

(b) that at the time he believed on reasonable grounds that the information had been disclosed widely enough to ensure that none of those taking part in the dealing would be prejudiced by not having the information; or
(c) that he would have done what he did even if he had not had the information.

Did not expect the dealing to result in a profit (s 53(1)(a) CJA)

11.03 Section 53(6) CJA provides that references to a profit include references to the avoidance of a loss.

11.04 The Law Society's Company Law Committee regarded this defence as 'particularly obscure'.[1] In practice, it is difficult to see how dealing in shares, in respect of which the dealer has inside information, which of its very nature is price-sensitive, could be for any reason other than one connected to that inside information and therefore in the expectation of a profit to be gained.

11.05 In the Parliamentary debates, the Minister gave as an example, someone who sold shares while in possession of information which he expected to receive a favourable reaction from the market.[2] The Treasury Commentary suggested another scenario: A person deals but does so at a price which allows for the likely effect that the information would have on the price of the security if it were made public.[3] It is difficult to see how in reality, either of these two scenarios would ever actually arise.

11.06 One possible example is *R v Gooding*[4] in which the defendant purchased shares in a company that he knew was in the midst of takeover negotiations. He stated that he believed that the takeover bid would not be agreed and that he in fact bought the shares as a long-term investment. His intention therefore was not to make a profit based on his inside information about the takeover, although in fact as things turned out, he did exactly that, because his company's compliance officer instructed him to sell the shares after the takeover was announced.

Believed on reasonable grounds that the information had been disclosed widely enough (s 53(1)(b) CJA)

11.07 In the Parliamentary debates, it was said that this defence was intended to deal with the particular circumstances of underwriters and other professionals who

---

[1] Law Society Company Law Committee, 'The Law on Insider Dealing' (Dec 1992) memo 281, para 9.2.
[2] HC Deb, Standing Committees A and B, Session 1992–93, col 157.
[3] See Treasury Commentary on the original draft of the Criminal Justice Bill, Oct 1992, para 50.
[4] *R v Gooding*, unreported but see *FT* (London, 2 Mar 1990).

are in possession of information which is not generally or publicly known and on the basis of which they undertake a transaction, who might otherwise fall within s 52(1) CJA.[5]

11.08 The Minister explained:

> The point to be grasped is that we are concerned with closed circles, with a circumstance in which both counterparties to, let us say, an underwriting transaction know the information on which they are agreeing the transaction, and it is not more widely known outside. In such cases, in which otherwise the information might be insider information on which they would be prohibited from entering into a transaction, the new clause makes specific the defence, allowing them to continue comfortably to enter into such transactions, both side knowing the relevant information. The measure does not go beyond that.[6]

11.09 This defence is therefore extremely limited. A defendant would need to demonstrate that the actual counterparty to the deal in question was not prejudiced—in effect, that there was a 'level playing field' on both sides of the transaction.

11.10 This interpretation is supported by the European Court of Justice ('ECJ') in the case of *Ipourgos Ikonomikon v Georgakis*.[7] Here, the main shareholders and directors of a Greek company agreed to effect between themselves stock market transactions in the transferable securities of their company, the purpose of which was to artificially increase the Company's share price. The issue for the ECJ was whether the participants in this scheme were in breach of Article 2(1) of the Insider Dealing Directive ('IDD') by 'taking advantage of [inside information] with full knowledge of the facts'.[8]

11.11 The ECJ decided that the participants were in possession of inside information (on the ground that knowledge of the common decision to effect the transactions in order to increase the price of the Company's shares was information which had not been made public and was likely, if made public, to have a significant effect on the price). However, given that all the parties were on an equal footing, they did not take advantage of that information with full knowledge of the facts when carrying out those transactions.[9]

---

[5] HC Deb (n 2) col 159; see also 'The Law on Insider Dealing' (n 1) memo281, paras 5.1–5.5 on underwriting problems arising from the legislation.
[6] HC Deb (n 2) col 158.
[7] C-391/04, *Ipourgos Ikonomikon v Georgakis* European Court of Justice (Third Chamber), 10 May 2007. Case Analysis [2007] All ER (EC) 1106; [2007] ECR I-3741; [2007] 2 BCLC 692; [2007] 3 CMLR 4; [2007] CEC 891.
[8] Article 2(1) IDD – Com 89/592/EC.
[9] See also David Moalem and Jesper Lau Hansen, 'Insider dealing and parity of information—is Georgakis still valid?' 2008 19(5) EBL Rev 949 which discusses this decision in the context of the Market Abuse Directive 2003.

He would have done what he did even if he had not had the information (s 53(1)(c) CJA)

11.12 This defence also reflects Article 2(1) of the IDD—that it is only those who *take advantage* of inside information in order to deal that should be penalised.[10] An example of where the defence would be available is a defendant who is a professional trader and who claims that the dealing in question forms part of a pre-determined trading strategy. The defence would also cover, for example, a pre-determined plan to sell shares to pay off debts.

11.13 The defence will be particularly relevant to liquidators, receivers, or trustees whose work may mean that they have inside information in a wide variety of situations.[11] That said, this defence is potentially open to anyone who can bring themselves within it.

11.14 In *R v Cross*,[12] the managing director of a computer company sold his stake in the company ahead of a new share issue which, when it was announced, caused the company's share price to fall significantly. He claimed that he was about to resign from the company and he had been told (wrongly as it turned out) that he must sell his shares within thirty days of his resignation. His conviction was quashed on appeal, one of the grounds being that the trial judge had failed to leave this defence adequately to the jury.

11.15 In *R v Stebbing*,[13] a retired accountant bought 1000 shares in a company for his godchild's new baby. It so happened that at the time he dealt, he had inside information about the company's expansion plans. He stated that the purchase of these shares was something he had intended to do months earlier as a long term investment for the child, but he had forgotten to do so. The purchase was therefore unconnected with the inside information in his possession and there was no intention to profit from that information.

11.16 In *R v Mustafa and others*,[14] one defendant sought to rely on this defence. The trial judge directed the jury that the CJA does not require the defendant who raises this defence to show that he put the inside information in his possession completely out of his mind before he traded, but the legislation does require him to prove that it was more likely than not that he had a settled intention to trade and would have traded in the way he did, even if he had not had the information. This underlines the fact that this defence will always turn on the jury's assessment of the evidence. In this case, the jury convicted the particular defendant of the six counts of insider

---

[10] Article 2(1) (n 8) states that insiders should be prohibited from *taking advantage of* [inside] information with full knowledge of the facts.
[11] See Brenda Hannigan, *Insider Dealing* (2nd edn, Longman 1994) 109 for a discussion of the background to this defence.
[12] *R v Cross* [1990] 1 Cr App R 115.
[13] *R v Stebbing*, unreported but see *Accountancy*, Sept 1991, 12.
[14] *R v Mustafa and others*, unreported, Southwark Crown Court, His Honour Judge Pegden QC and a jury, 5 Mar to 23 July 2012 & 27 July 2012. FSA/PN/080/2012.

dealing he faced which covered trading in six different stocks. This demonstrates that the jury did not find this defence proved.

3. Statutory defences to the secondary 'Encouraging' offence (s 53(2) CJA)

11.17 The statutory defences available in respect of this offence are contained in s 53(2) CJA:

Section 53(2)

An individual is not guilty of insider dealing by virtue of encouraging another person to deal in securities if he shows

(a) that he did not at the time expect the dealing to result in a profit attributable to the fact that the information in question was price-sensitive information in relation to the securities, or
(b) that at the time he believed on reasonable grounds that the information had been or would be disclosed widely enough to ensure that none of those taking part in the dealing would be prejudiced by not having the information, or
(c) that he would have done what he did even if he had not had the information.

11.18 This wording is practically identical to the defences discussed above in relation to the primary insider dealing offence. There is a slight difference in s 53(2)(b) CJA to the effect that the insider believed on reasonable grounds that the information had been or *would be* disclosed widely enough to ensure that none of those taking part in the dealing would be prejudiced by not having the information. This allows for the fact that the 'encouraging' in question may occur at a stage prior to the inside information being disclosed to the counterparty to the transaction.

4. Statutory defences to the secondary 'Disclosing' offence (s 53(3) CJA)

11.19 The statutory defences available in respect of this offence are contained in s 53(3) CJA:

Section 53(3)

An individual is not guilty of insider dealing by virtue of a disclosure of information if he shows

(a) that he did not at the time expect any person, because of the disclosure, to deal in securities in the circumstances mentioned in subsection (3) of section 52; or
(b) that, although he had such an expectation at the time, he did not expect the dealing to result in a profit attributable to the fact that the information was price-sensitive information in relation to the securities.

11.20 Section 53(3)(a) CJA would cover a situation in which an insider discloses inside information to another in circumstances other than in the proper performance of his employment, office, or profession, but in circumstances in which he genuinely did not expect the person, to whom he has made the disclosure, to deal in the securities in question. This would cover, for example, a husband confiding in his wife, or the reverse. It would also potentially cover the situation in *R v Staines and Morrissey*[15] in which disclosures were made by a company's accountant to friends during an evening of drinking, in circumstances where he plainly did not expect his friends to take advantage of the information.

Leaving aside the facts of this case, in a similar scenario, this defence would be open to a company director whose case is that he had made a disclosure but did so not expecting the recipient (given his position), to take advantage of the information.

11.21 In *R v Mustafa and others*,[16] two of the defendants were charged with improperly disclosing the inside information that had been illicitly removed from the print rooms at JP Morgan Cazenove and UBS to the co-defendants who dealt on the information. These defendants raised the s 53(3)(a) CJA defence—namely that they did not at the time they disclosed the information, expect their co-defendants to deal in the securities to which the information related.

11.22 Section 53(3)(b) CJA might cover a situation in which the person making the improper disclosure believed that the person to whom he made the disclosure was intending to buy the shares in question with a view to holding them for the long term rather than to profit from the inside information.

5. Special defences

11.23 In addition to the defences available in respect of specific offences, s 53(4) CJA also provides for further 'special defences':

Section 53(4) Schedule 1 (special defences) shall have effect.

(5) The Treasury may by order amend Schedule 1.

11.24 Schedule 1 to the CJA provides that the three defences set out within it apply to the primary insider dealing offence and the secondary 'encouraging' offence.

---

[15] *R v Staines and Morrissey* [1997] 2 Cr App R 426.
[16] *R v Mustafa and others* (n 14).

Statutory Defences

Market makers (Schedule 1(1) CJA)

11.25 Schedule 1(1) CJA states:

> (1) An individual is not guilty of insider dealing by virtue of dealing in securities or encouraging another person to deal if he shows that he acted in good faith in the course of
> (a) his business as a market maker, or
> (b) his employment in the business of a market maker.
> (2) A market maker is a person who
> (a) holds himself out at all normal times in compliance with the rules of a regulated market or an approved organisation as willing to acquire or dispose of securities; and
> (b) is recognised as doing so under those rules.
> (3) In this paragraph 'approved organisation' means an international securities self-regulating organisation approved by the Treasury under any relevant order under section 22 of the FSMA.

11.26 The role of a market maker is to 'make a market' in a particular stock by constantly quoting bid and offer prices in minimum quantities.[17] However, such persons may frequently be in possession of inside information. Without any exemption, market makers would be required to abstain from dealing in particular shares at particular times and this would be to the detriment of the market in those shares.

11.27 This defence is available only to a person who holds himself out as a market maker and is recognised as such by the rules of a regulated market or proved organisation. The market maker must also demonstrate that the conduct occurred in the course of his business/employment as a market maker, and that he has acted in good faith.

Persons in possession of market information (Schedule 1(2) CJA)

11.28 This defence is contained within Schedule 1(2) CJA:

> (1) An individual is not guilty of insider dealing by virtue of dealing in securities or encouraging another person to deal if he shows that
> (a) the information which he had as an insider was market information; and
> (b) it was reasonable for an individual in his position to have acted as he did despite having that information as an insider at the time.
> (2) In determining whether it is reasonable for an individual to do any act despite having market information at the time, there shall, in particular, be taken into account
> (a) the content of the information;
> (b) the circumstances in which he first had the information and in what capacity; and
> (c) the capacity in which he now acts.

---

[17] See Chapter 2, Section 5, paras 2.23–2.24.

The first issue therefore is whether the information in question is 'market information'. This is defined in Schedule 1 paragraph 4: **11.29**

> 4. For the purposes of paragraphs 2 and 3 market information is information consisting of one or more of the following facts
>
> (a) that securities of a particular kind have been or are to be acquired or disposed of, or that their acquisition or disposal is under consideration or the subject of negotiation;
> (b) that securities of a particular kind have not been or are not to be acquired or disposed of;
> (c) the number of securities acquired or disposed of or to be acquired or disposed of or whose acquisition or disposal is under consideration or the subject of negotiation;
> (d) the price (or range of prices) at which securities have been or are to be acquired or disposed of or the price (or range of prices) at which securities whose acquisition or disposal is under consideration or the subject of negotiation may be acquired or disposed of;
> (e) the identity of the persons involved or likely to be involved in any capacity in an acquisition or disposal.

'Market information' in this context is intended to cover a variety of situations that routinely occur in a City context. For example, an underwriter is required to place the remaining shares in a rights issue (known as the 'rump'), even where knowledge of the size of the rump is itself inside information. Another example is where the corporate broking department of a merchant bank is advising a potential acquirer on a possible takeover. The merchant bank must be able to advise (encourage) the client to build a stake in the target company, despite the fact that the knowledge of the potential takeover amounts to inside information. **11.30**

In each case, the second requirement must also be satisfied—that it was reasonable for the insider to have acted in the way that he did despite having information as an insider at the time. This test of reasonableness attracted some complaint by commentators.[18] In Parliamentary debates, the Minister stated: **11.31**

> The requirement that people must act in a reasonable manner, particularly in relation to the criminal law, is an objective assessment and is probably not susceptible to further or more precise definition. In deciding whether it would be reasonable to use market information in specific circumstances, a practitioner would do well to consult the regulations of the body under which he is authorised to conduct investment business or the rules of the market in which he is dealing.[19]

The rules of the market on which the dealing took place will plainly be one factor that a Court would consider in the event that this defence is raised, other factors would be the circumstances in existence at the time, the reasons for the trading, the size and timing of the trading, and what factors were known or should have **11.32**

---

[18] The Law Society's Company Law Committee (n 1) para 9.2 stated: 'The concept of reasonableness is not applicable in this context where there is no generally accepted concept of reasonable behaviour.'
[19] HC Deb (n 2) col 217.

been known to the trader at the time. At the time of writing, I am not aware of this defence having been raised in a criminal prosecution.

Dealings to facilitate the accomplishment of an acquisition or disposal (Schedule 1(3) CJA)

11.33 Schedule 1(3) CJA provides for a further circumstance in which the 'Persons in Possession of Market Information' defence may be relied upon:

> 3. An individual is not guilty of insider dealing by virtue of dealing in securities or encouraging another person to deal if he shows
>
> (a) that he acted
> (i) in connection with an acquisition or disposal which was under consideration or the subject of negotiation, or in the course of a series of such acquisitions or disposals; and
> (ii) with a view to facilitating the accomplishment of the acquisition or disposal or the series of acquisitions or disposals; and
> (b) that the information which he had as an insider was market information arising directly out of his involvement in the acquisition or disposal or series of acquisitions or disposals.

11.34 This defence makes it permissible to use market information when acting in connection with the acquisition or disposal (or a series of acquisitions or disposals) which are under consideration/the subject of negotiation. The defence is available in circumstances where the trader is acting with a view to facilitating the accomplishment of the acquisition or disposal in question. This enables, for example, a potential bidder to buy shares in a target company in order to build the stake required for a successful takeover of that company. There is an obvious overlap between this defence and the defence contained in Schedule 1(2) CJA.

Price stabilisation (Schedule 1(5) CJA)

11.35 Schedule 1 paragraph 5 provides that:

> (1) An individual is not guilty of insider dealing by virtue of dealing in securities or encouraging another person to deal if he shows that he acted in conformity with the price stabilisation rules or with the relevant provisions of Commission Regulation (EC) No 2273/2003 of 22 December 2003 implementing Directive 2003/6/EC of the European Parliament and of the Council as regards exemptions for buy-back programmes and stabilisation of financial instruments.[20]
> (2) 'Price stabilisation rules' means rules made under section 144(1) of the FSMA.

---

[20] As amended by the FSMA (Market Abuse) Regulations 2005 SI 2005/381, reg 3.

Price stabilisation is a process by which the market price of a security is fixed during **11.36**
the period in which a new issue of shares is sold to the public. Its purpose is to deal
with a situation in which the price of a security is forced downwards by the effect
of the newly issued shares coming onto the market—prior to those shares being
acquired.

Subject to strict rules set down by the FCA,[21] the stabilising manager is permitted **11.37**
to buy back securities in the market that he has previously sold. The effect of this
will invariably be to keep the price of the securities at a higher level than would
otherwise be the position. Clearly, the stabilising manager, when he does this, is
dealing in securities at a time when he has inside information—to the effect that
stabilisation is taking place and the circumstances that require it. In order to establish this defence, it is necessary for the individual to show that he acted in conformity with price stabilisation rules as defined in paragraph 5(2).

The practice was employed to good effect in the privatisation of British Telecom **11.38**
where the Government's lead adviser spent £115 million on buying back BT
shares in the market thereby achieving a successful privatisation. At the time,
the *Financial Times* quoted an anonymous lawyer as saying: 'Market rigging is
what you call it when someone else does it, stabilisation is what you call it when
it's your own activity.'[22] However the practice is commonly used and is equally
considered to benefit investors by ensuring a smooth and orderly market.

Dealings in pursuit of monetary policies (s 63 CJA)

Section 63(1) CJA provides that: **11.39**

Section 63—Limits on section 52

(1) Section 52 does not apply to anything done by an individual acting on behalf of a public sector body in pursuit of monetary policies or policies with respect to exchange rates or the management of public debt or foreign exchange reserves.

This defence reflects Article 2(4) of the IDD[23] which required that such activities **11.40**
be excluded from the insider dealing prohibitions. It is necessary because individuals conducting these activities are invariably in possession of inside information
when they undertake the activities described in s 63(1) CJA.

The defence is specifically limited in its terms to the conduct specified and would **11.41**
not therefore include private dealings carried out by a public servant or public dealings which are not carried out in pursuit of monetary policy.[24]

---

[21] Price Stabilising Rules, MAR 2, FCA Handbook.
[22] *FT* (London, 14 November 1991).
[23] IDD (n 8).
[24] See Treasury Commentary (n 3) para 66.

6. Statutory defences—legal and evidential burden on the defence

11.42 The wording of s 53 and Schedule 1 CJA make clear that once the prosecution has proved the requisite elements for an offence of insider dealing, the burden shifts to the defence to raise one or other of the available statutory defences and prove it on the balance of probabilities. *R v Cross*[25] established (in relation to the CSA) that this reverse burden imposes on the defence a legal as well as an evidential burden.

11.43 *R v Cross* concerned an insider dealing prosecution brought under the Company Securities (Insider Dealing) Act 1985 ('CSA'). The Court of Appeal held that once the prosecution had proved the essential elements of the offence, the burden then shifted to the defence to prove any available statutory defence on the balance of probabilities. The Court observed that this would seem appropriate since the matters in issue are likely to be peculiarly within the defendant's own knowledge.[26]

11.44 In *Sheldrake v DPP*,[27] the House of Lords set out the guiding principles on the issue of whether a legal burden on a defendant is compatible with the presumption of innocence contained in Article 6(2)[28] of the European Convention on Human Rights ('ECHR'). These principles may be summarised as follows:

11.45 A reverse burden does not (per se) unjustifiably infringe the presumption of innocence. Whether it does so (or not) requires an examination of the following:

1. There must be a compelling reason why it is fair and reasonable to deny the accused person the protection normally guaranteed to everyone by the presumption of innocence.
2. It must be shown that, if a reverse burden is not imposed, the public interest will be prejudiced to an extent that justifies placing a reverse burden on the accused.
3. The more serious the punishment which may flow from conviction, the more compelling must be the reasons for imposing a reverse burden.
4. The extent and nature of the factual matters to be proved by the accused, and their importance relative to the matters required to be proved by the prosecution, must be considered as must the extent to which the burden on

---

[25] *R v Cross* [1990] 91 Cr App R 115.
[26] *R v Cross* (n 26) 120.
[27] *Sheldrake v DPP* [2004] UKHL 43, [2005] 1 AC 264, [2005] 1 All ER 237, [2004] 3 WLR 976 (14 Oct 2004), House of Lords.
[28] Article 6(2) of the ECHR states: '(2) Everyone charged with a criminal offence shall be presumed innocent until proved guilty according to law'. Section 3(1) of the Human Rights Act 1998 states: '(1) So far as it is possible to do so, primary legislation and subordinate legislation must be read and given effect in a way which is compatible with the Convention rights.'

the accused relates to facts which, if they exist, are readily provable by him as matters within his own knowledge or to which he has ready access.

Having considered all the above, the court should then stand back and ask itself whether a burden enacted by Parliament unjustifiably infringes the presumption of innocence.

11.46 Applying these principles to the statutory defences contained in s 53 and Schedule 1 CJA, it is suggested leads to the conclusion that imposing a reverse legal burden in respect of these defences would not infringe Article 6(2) ECHR:[29]

1. The IDD made clear that the mischief of insider dealing is that it undermines confidence in the integrity of the markets, which is essential to their effective operation. Insider dealing is therefore a serious crime, which may have substantial effects on the economic well-being of the United Kingdom and accordingly, it is punishable with a maximum sentence of seven years, imprisonment.
2. Before the reverse legal burden in s 53 CJA even arises, the prosecution must prove all the elements of the offence contained in Part V of the CJA.
3. The defences set out in s 53 CJA relate to facts which, if they exist, are readily provable by the defendant as matters within his own knowledge. Conversely, once a s 53 defence has been raised, it would be exceptionally difficult for the prosecution to disprove it (by in effect having to prove a negative). This would have a prejudicial effect on the ability to effectively prosecute the offence—a situation which would be contrary to the public interest. Put simply, a defendant is best placed to put forward his reasons for doing what he did.
4. The placing of a legal reverse burden on the defendant to prove a specific defence under s 53 CJA is therefore justified and does not therefore unjustifiably infringe the presumption of innocence.

11.47 This rationale was adopted in *R v Mustafa and others*.[30] In this case, the two Defendants who were charged with improper disclosure of inside information, raised the s 53(3)(a) CJA defence—namely that they did not at the time expect any person, because of the disclosure, to deal in securities. One of the trading defendants, raised the s 53(1)(c) CJA defence, namely that he would have traded in the stocks with which he was indicted, even if he had not had the inside information in question. Following legal argument, the trial judge ruled and in due course directed the jury that if and only if the prosecution had proved beyond reasonable

---

[29] It is only right to point out that in the case of *R v Neil Rollins*, unreported, Southwark Crown Court, 16 to 26 Nov 2010, FSA/PN/168/2010. The FSA submitted precisely the opposite—that the reverse burden was incompatible with the presumption of innocence and that the court ought to 'read down' the provisions of s 53(1)(c) CJA so as to impose only an evidential burden on the defendant. For the reasons set out above, it is submitted that this is not the approach to be preferred.

[30] *R v Mustafa and others* (n 14).

doubt all the elements of the offence against the defendant concerned, then it was for the defendant to establish the defence on a balance of probabilities.

11.48 The jury were directed that in order to determine this issue they should examine the defendant's state of mind and expectations at the time he made the disclosures in question. They should also take into account all the surrounding circumstances and draw common sense conclusions from these. The jury convicted.

11.49 However in the case of *R v Rollins*,[31] the prosecution appears to have submitted precisely the opposite, namely that the reverse burden was incompatible with the presumption of innocence and that the court ought to 'read down' the provisions of s 53(1)(c) CJA so as to impose only an evidential burden on the defendant. This decision appears to have been taken on the particular facts and circumstances of that case and, for the reasons set out above, it is suggested that the approach taken in *R v Mustafa and others*[32] is to be preferred.

---

[31] *R v Neil Rollins* (n 30).
[32] *R v Mustafa and others* (n 14).

12

PROSECUTION OF INSIDER DEALING OFFENCES

1. Introduction	12.01	5. Conspiracy or substantive counts	12.13
2. Prosecuting bodies	12.02		
3. Consent for prosecution	12.05	6. Summary proceedings: venue and time limit	12.21
4. Prosecution of other offences connected to insider dealing	12.09		

1. Introduction

12.01 This Chapter deals with the prosecution of insider dealing offences: who may prosecute, whether consent is required, whether the FCA can prosecute for other offences associated with insider dealing, and the time limit for instituting summary proceedings.

2. Prosecuting bodies

12.02 The Financial Services and Markets Act 2000 ('FSMA'), designated the Financial Services Authority ('FSA') as the Body responsible for market misconduct investigation and Enforcement, including the investigation and prosecution of insider dealing offences. As of 1 April 2013, the FSA ceased to exist and this responsibility therefore passed to its successor the FCA.

12.03 Section 402(1)(a) of FSMA provides that:

Section 402(1)

Except in Scotland, the Authority may institute proceedings for an offence under

(a) Part V of the CJA (insider dealing)

12.04 Section 402(1)(a) of FSMA was intended to give effect to the requirement contained in Article 8 of the Insider Dealing Directive ('IDD')[1] which required each Member State to designate the competent administrative authority responsible for ensuring that the provisions adopted pursuant to the IDD are applied.

3. Consent for prosecution

12.05 Section 61 CJA provides that:

> (2) Proceedings for offences under this Part shall not be instituted in England and Wales except by or with the consent of
> (a) the Secretary of State; or
> (b) the Director of Public Prosecutions.
> (3) In relation to proceedings in Northern Ireland for offences under this Part, subsection (2) shall have effect as if the reference to the Director of Public Prosecutions were a reference to the Director of Public Prosecutions for Northern Ireland.

12.06 In *R v Neel and Matthew Uberoi*,[2] the defendants applied for judicial review of the FSA's decision to commence an insider dealing prosecution against them on the ground that s 61(2) CJA required the FSA to obtain the consent of the DPP to bring a prosecution for insider dealing.

12.07 The Administrative Court held that the FSA had concurrent powers with the Secretary of State, the Director of Public Prosecutions ('DPP'), and the Director of the Serious Fraud Office ('SFO') in respect of insider dealing prosecutions, and that the FSA was not required to obtain the consent of the DPP to prosecute such conduct. The Court held that this power was specifically provided for by s 402(1)(a) of FSMA, and that the structure and content of FSMA amply demonstrated that it must have been Parliament's intention that the FSA would be able to institute proceedings under Part V of the CJA without needing to obtain the consent of another Body.

12.08 Although not specifically referred to in the judgment, this view is consistent with the requirement in Article 8 of the IDD.[3] Parliament could not have intended to give effect to this provision by designating the FSA as the lead body with respect to market misconduct (including insider dealing), but fail to empower it to prosecute insider dealing offences without specific consent from outside.

---

[1] Directive 89/592/EEC.
[2] *The Queen on the application of Matthew Francis Uberoi, Neel Akash Uberoi v City of Westminster Magistrates' Court*, Administrative Court, 2 Dec 2008, [2008] EWHC 3191 (Admin), 2008 WL 5044304.
[3] IDD (n 1).

4. Prosecution of other offences connected to insider dealing

The FSA (now the FCA) is also able to prosecute criminal offences other than insider dealing. This means that in an insider dealing prosecution, the indictment may contain counts specifying other offences (for example money laundering offences under the Proceeds of Crime Act 2002 ('POCA')) in addition to the insider dealing counts. **12.09**

This issue was considered by the Supreme Court in *R v Rollins*.[4] The FSA brought criminal proceedings against Mr Rollins for offences of insider dealing, contrary to s 52(1) CJA and also offences of money laundering, contrary to ss 327(d) and 328(e) of POCA. The insider dealing counts related to the sale of shares in a company by whom he was employed, in circumstances where he was in possession of inside information.[5] The money laundering counts related to the transfer of part of the proceeds of sale from his bank account to a bank account in his father's name. **12.10**

At a preparatory hearing, the trial judge ruled that the FSA had the power to prosecute the money laundering offences. Mr Rollins appealed, contending that the FSA's power to prosecute criminal offences was limited to the offences specifically referred to in ss 401 and 402 of FSMA. Section 401(2) provides that proceedings for an offence contained in FSMA may be instituted in England and Wales only by the Authority or the Secretary of State; or by, or with, the consent of the DPP. The defence contended that this provision operated to restrict the FSA's prosecution powers to the offences referred to therein. The Court of Appeal held that the FSA's powers were not limited in the way contended for by the defence and confirmed the Crown Court's decision that the FSA had the power to bring prosecutions in respect of other offences. Mr Rollins appealed to the Supreme Court. **12.11**

The Supreme Court held that it was unlikely that Parliament would have intended to restrict the power of the FSA to the prosecution only of offences mentioned in ss 401 and 402. The purpose of s 401 was not to *confer* the power to prosecute, but to *limit* the persons who might prosecute for offences under FSMA (or the subordinate legislation made under it). It was clear that ss 401 and 402 of FSMA did not exhaustively define the prosecutorial powers of the FSA, and it followed that the FSA had the power to prosecute offences of money laundering contrary to ss 327 and 328 of POCA. Plainly, this decision would equally apply to other offences which might arise in the context of an insider dealing case, such as offences under the Fraud Act 2006. **12.12**

---

[4] *R v Neil Rollins* [2010] UKSC 39, Supreme Court.
[5] CJA, s 52(1).

5. Conspiracy or substantive counts

12.13 Where the conduct alleged involves an agreement between two or more individuals the prosecution will need to consider whether to charge the alleged offenders with substantive insider dealing counts or a conspiracy to commit insider dealing contrary to s 1 of the Criminal Law Act 1977:

Conspiracy—Criminal Law Act 1977, s 1

1. The offence of conspiracy

(1) Subject to the following provisions of this Part of this Act, if a person agrees with any other person or persons that a course of conduct shall be pursued which, if the agreement is carried out in accordance with their intentions, either
  (a) will necessarily amount to or involve the commission of any offence or offences by one or more of the parties to the agreement, or
  (b) would do so but for the existence of facts which render the commission of the offence or any of the offences impossible,
he is guilty of conspiracy to commit the offence or offences in question.
(2) Where liability for any offence may be incurred without knowledge on the part of the person committing it of any particular fact or circumstance necessary for the commission of the offence, a person shall nevertheless not be guilty of conspiracy to commit that offence by virtue of subsection (1) above unless he and at least one other party to the agreement intend or know that that fact or circumstance shall or will exist at the time when the conduct constituting the offence is to take place.

12.14 A sample count of conspiracy to commit insider dealing might be drafted as follows:

Statement of Offence

Conspiracy to commit insider dealing, contrary to section 1 of the Criminal Law Act 1977.

Particulars of Offence

XY between the ... day of ... 20 ... and the ... day of ... 20 ... conspired with AB and CD, to deal as an insider in price affected securities relating to shares in Z Ltd, within the meaning of Part V of the CJA.

12.15 The general rule is that where there is a substantive offence which appropriately meets the conduct complained of and which will adequately reflect the criminality alleged, then a charge of conspiracy is undesirable (see *Verrier v DPP*;[6] *R v*

---

[6] *Verrier v DPP* [1967] 2 AC 195, HL.

Griffiths;[7] *R v Greenfield*;[8] *R v Watts*[9]). This rule applies to an insider dealing case just as much as to any other type of criminal case. However, each case must be considered on its own facts.[10] Where the allegation involves a completed course of conduct (for example, an agreement between the insider and the dealer(s) that the insider would supply the inside information and the dealers would trade on their joint behalf), in general terms, substantive offences will probably be more appropriate. This is particularly so since the introduction of Rule 14.2(2) of the Criminal Procedure Rules[11] which enables multiple trading in any stock to be charged in a single count:

> Criminal Procedure Rules 2005 (SI 2005 no 384) r 14.2
>
> Form and content of indictment
>
> (2) More than one incident of the commission of the offence may be included in a count if those incidents taken together amount to a course of conduct having regard to the time, place or purpose of commission.

12.16 This procedure avoids the need to charge multiple counts against the same individual(s) for sequential positions in the same stock and also avoids the need to charge specimen counts. It is suggested that this is a preferable course to the alternative process under the provisions of s 17 of the Domestic Violence, Crime and Victims Act 2004, of charging sample substantive counts confined to individual acts with the residue left to be determined by the trial judge alone in the event of conviction.

12.17 Alleging a conspiracy to commit insider dealing also arguably involves an additional layer of technicality as in addition to the elements of the statutory offence, the prosecution must also prove (1) the agreement, (2) that the defendant knew what he was agreeing to, and (3) that, when he joined the agreement, the defendant intended that he should carry the agreement out.

12.18 Pleading conspiracy also carries with it risks for the prosecution when the allegation is that two defendants have conspired only with each other and the jury are not sure of guilt in relation to one defendant, as this necessarily means the acquittal of both.

12.19 A further issue arises on an indictment alleging conspiracy to commit insider dealing, where one or more of the defendants relies on a statutory defence. As explained in Chapter 6[12] the statutory defences place a legal and evidential burden on the defendant. However, a conspiracy requires the prosecution to prove a criminal

---

[7] *R v Griffiths* [1966] 1 QB 589.
[8] *R v Greenfield*, 57 Cr App R 849 CA.
[9] *R v Watts, The Times* (London, 14 Apr 1995) CA.
[10] *R v Jones (J)*, 59 Cr App R 120 CA.
[11] Criminal Procedure Rules 2012.
[12] See Chapter 11, Section 6.

agreement. So, for example, in a case in which a defendant relies on the s 53(1)(c) CJA defence—that he would have traded in the stock in question even if he had not had inside information (perhaps because of some pre-arranged trading strategy)—the prosecution, as part of the need to prove the agreement to commit insider dealing, would need to disprove this defence. The practical effect of this would be to remove the reverse burden from the defence and place it (to the criminal standard) on the prosecution.

12.20 The only recent insider dealing trial in which the jury was asked to consider counts of conspiracy to commit insider dealing was the case of *R v Richard Joseph*.[13] In that case, Richard Joseph was charged with six counts of conspiracy to deal as an insider, spanning the period from September 2007 to July 2008 and in relation to shares in six companies. The allegation was that Mr Joseph agreed with the insider, who worked in the print room at JP Morgan Cazenove, that the insider would provide him with inside information relating to forthcoming corporate transactions and that Mr Joseph would then trade on their joint behalf on the basis of this information. They then proceeded to put this agreement into effect in relation to six different stocks. The insider was not tried as he had fled the jurisdiction, although he was named in the indictment as a co-conspirator. Given that this was a completed course of conduct, it was open to the prosecution to charge the substantive offence of insider dealing on the basis of joint enterprise, rather than a conspiracy. However, the prosecution evidence was strong and the jury convicted Mr Joseph of all allegations.

6. Summary proceedings: venue and time limit

12.21 Section 61A CJA provides that summary proceedings for insider dealing must be begun within three years of the commission of the offence, or within twelve months after the date on which evidence which is sufficient to justify the proceedings comes to the knowledge of the DPP, Secretary of State (or FCA). Given the seriousness and complexity of most (if not all) insider dealing cases, it is difficult to conceive of such a case being suitable for summary trial. There is no time limit for offences tried on indictment in the Crown Court.

---

[13] *R v Richard Joseph*, unreported, Southwark Crown Court, His Honour Judge Pegden QC and a jury, 30 Jan to 11 Mar 2013. FSA/PN/023/2013.

13

PENALTIES AND SENTENCING

1. Introduction	13.01	4. Sentences imposed in recent insider dealing cases	13.16
2. The penalty for offences of insider dealing (s 61 CJA)	13.02	5. Disqualification of company directors	13.17
3. Court of Appeal sentencing authorities	13.04	6. Confiscation issues in insider dealing cases	13.19
R v Smith, Spearman and Payne	13.05	Value of benefit obtained	13.20
R v Asif Nazir Butt	13.08	Apportionment between defendants	13.24
R v Christopher McQuoid—sentencing guidelines	13.12	Confiscation as part of a plea agreement	13.27
		7. Other FCA proceedings	13.28

1. Introduction

This Chapter deals with the sentencing of defendants convicted of insider dealing offences. It summarises the sentencing principles and provides examples of sentences imposed in previous cases. It also summarises the key ancillary issues likely to arise in an insider dealing case such as disqualification of company directors and confiscation orders. **13.01**

2. The penalty for offences of insider dealing (s 61 CJA)

The maximum penalties for insider dealing offences are contained in s 61 CJA: **13.02**

Section 61—Penalties

(1) An individual guilty of insider dealing shall be liable
   (a) on summary conviction, to a fine not exceeding the statutory maximum or imprisonment for a term not exceeding six months or to both; or
   (b) on conviction on indictment, to a fine or imprisonment for a term not exceeding seven years or to both.

13.03 During Parliamentary debates, the Minister stated:

> The maximum penalty reflects the seriousness with which the Government regard the crime of insider dealing ... Despite the relatively small number of convictions secured since 1980, I do not accept that our existing insider dealing legislation is a failure. Rather, it has played an important part in changing attitudes to the improper use of insider information, with the effect that insider dealing is universally accepted as being wrong, which it was not when it was made illegal in 1980.[1]

3. Court of Appeal sentencing authorities

13.04 There are only a few reported cases on sentencing for insider dealing offences. These cases, together with the sentences imposed at first instance, demonstrate the sentencing principles which a court will apply and the range of sentences imposed in other cases.

R v Smith, Spearman and Payne

13.05 The first reported case is *R v Smith, Spearman and Payne*[2] in which the appellants appealed sentences of immediate imprisonment imposed on them by the Crown Court. The appellants pleaded guilty to conspiracy to contravene s 52(1) CJA. Mr Smith and Mrs Spearman were partners in a builders' merchants business based in Essex. Mr Payne, who was a friend of Mr Smith, worked as a proof-reader at a firm of printers that printed financial documents containing inside information regarding impending takeover bids, mergers and other types of financial transactions. Mr Payne provided this information to Mr Smith and through Smith to Smith's business partner, Mrs Spearman, and both Smith and Spearman traded on the information.

13.06 The conspiracy ran for nearly three years between 1997 and 2000, and trading was conducted in twenty-seven different stocks. Mrs Spearman profited by some £130,000, Mr Smith by £36,000, and both paid a share of their profits to Mr Payne who received approximately £20,000.

13.07 The sentencing judge sentenced Mr Smith and Mrs Spearman to eighteen months' imprisonment and Mr Payne to thirty months' imprisonment. The sentencing judge accepted that the appellants were not city professionals but considered that the case was a carefully run fraud that required application and some ingenuity. The Court of Appeal refused the appeal against sentence as against Mr Smith and Mrs Spearman but allowed the appeal against Mr Payne to the extent that it reduced his sentence to twenty-one months' imprisonment. However, it agreed

---

[1] HC Deb, Session 1992–93, Standing Committee B, col 206.
[2] *R v Smith, Spearman and Payne* [2003] EWCA Crim 2893.

with the sentencing judge's observation that the good character of the appellants was significant mitigation but 'those with the advantages of a good position in society, a good education and good businesses cannot be expected to be treated leniently when they deliberately offend'. The Court agreed that an immediate custodial sentence was necessary for these offences, and that there needed to be an element of deterrence in the sentences passed:[3]

> There has been for some years now a good deal of publicity about the process of insider trading. It has been well-known for many years that it is conduct which is a serious criminal offence. We have little doubt that if the defendants had been professional city traders they could have expected a sentence significantly greater than the sentences which were imposed here. We have been referred to the fact that new legislation enables some insider trading to be dealt with by means of regulatory or disciplinary process. That does not mean that the activity ceases to be a criminal offence which is likely to be prosecuted and if prosecuted likely in appropriate cases to be met by substantial sentences of imprisonment. Overall insider trading is a serious matter. On a large scale it corrupts the whole of the market.

R v Asif Nazir Butt[4]

13.08 Mr Butt was convicted after a trial of conspiracy to commit insider dealing. He was sentenced to five years' imprisonment. Four co-accused were jointly charged and convicted of the same offence. Two received sentences of two years, one of twelve months' and one of nine months' imprisonment. All five of the defendants were of previous good character.

13.09 Mr Butt worked as a Vice President at the investment bank, Credit Suisse First Boston ('CSFB'). He worked in the compliance control room where he had access to inside information about the companies that CSFB advised. Over a period of three years, in what was described as a 'gross breach of trust', Mr Butt used this inside information to place spread bets referenced to the shares of these companies prior to this information becoming public knowledge. He used the co-accused to trade for him through dealing accounts which they opened in their own names. The profits were shared between them with Mr Butt receiving 80 per cent of the profits. Nineteen stocks were traded and the net total profit was £287,807 with Mr Butt's share being in excess of £237,000.

13.10 The Court of Appeal, hearing Mr Butt's appeal against the sentence imposed, referred to the case of *R v Clark*[5] (the guideline case on theft in breach of trust). It also referred to *R v Spearman and others*[6] and *R v Rigby and Bailey*[7], a misleading the market case which concerned an offence contrary to s 397(1) FSMA—recklessly

---

[3] *R v Spearman and others* [2003] EWCA Crim 2893.
[4] *R v Asif Nazir Butt* [2006] EWCA Crim 137, CA 12 Jan 2006.
[5] *R v Clark* [1998] 2 Cr App R (S) 95.
[6] *R v Spearman and others* (n 3).
[7] *R v Rigby and Bailey* [2006] EWCA Crim 1653.

making a statement, promise or forecast which was misleading, false, or deceptive in a material particular.

13.11 The Court of Appeal concluded that Butt's breach of trust was serious, flagrant, calculated, deliberate, and also protracted. However the Court accepted that the cases to which it had been referred, though plainly not as serious, did provide guidance which led the Court to conclude that the sentence of five years was manifestly excessive and that a sentence of four years was appropriate.

R v Christopher McQuoid—sentencing guidelines

13.12 In *R v Christopher McQuoid*,[8] the Court of Appeal took the opportunity to issue sentencing guidelines for offences of insider dealing. Mr McQuoid was a solicitor and general counsel to a company named TTP Communications Ltd ('TTP'). In the course of his employment, he became a party to inside information about a proposed takeover of TTP by another company. He passed the information to his father-in-law who purchased shares in TTP on their joint behalf prior to the announcement. They sold these after the announcement at a profit of £48,919 which they split equally. The appellant was convicted after a trial and was sentenced to eight months' imprisonment.

13.13 In dismissing his appeal against the sentence imposed, the Lord Chief Justice made the following remarks which are of relevance to sentencing for any insider dealing case:[9]

> Insider dealing had been an offence in England and Wales since 1980. ... Those who involve themselves in insider dealing are criminals, no more and no less. The principles of confidentiality and trust, which were essential to the operations of the commercial world, are betrayed by insider dealing and public confidence in the integrity of the system which was essential to its proper function is undermined by market abuse. Takeover arrangements are normally kept secret. Very few people were permitted to have advance knowledge of them. Those who are entrusted with advance knowledge are entrusted with that knowledge precisely because it is believed that they can be trusted. When they seek to make a profit out of the knowledge and trust reposed in them, or indeed when they do so recklessly, their criminality is not reduced or diminished merely because they are individuals of good character.
>
> In the present case, as a result of this breach of trust, the appellant made a substantial profit for himself and for his father-in-law. This fact demonstrates (if it needs to be demonstrated) that profits from even a single transaction of insider dealing can be very high indeed.
>
> We would therefore emphasise that this conduct does not merely contravene regulatory mechanisms. If there ever was a feeling that insider dealing was a matter to be covered by regulation, that impression should be rapidly dissipated. The message

---

[8] *R v Christopher McQuoid* 10 June 2009 [2009] EWCA Crim 1301; [2010] 1 Cr App R (S) 43.
[9] *R v Christopher McQuoid* (n 8) paras 8–10.

must be clear: when it is done deliberately, insider dealing is a species of fraud; it is cheating. Prosecution in open and public court will often, and perhaps much more so now than in the past, be appropriate. Although those who perpetrate the offence may hope, if caught, to escape with regulatory proceedings, they can have no legitimate expectation of avoiding prosecution and sentence.

13.14 The Court of Appeal also set out the considerations that would be relevant in determining the appropriate sentence in an insider dealing case:[10]

(1) the nature of the defendant's employment or retainer, or involvement in the arrangements which enabled him to participate in the insider dealing of which he was guilty;
(2) the circumstances in which he came into possession of confidential information and the use he made of it;
(3) whether he behaved recklessly or acted deliberately, and almost inevitably dishonestly;
(4) the level of planning and sophistication involved in his activity, as well as a period of trading and the number of individual trades;
(5) whether he acted alone or with others and, if so, his relative culpability;
(6) the amount of anticipated or intended financial benefit or loss avoided, as well as the actual benefit or loss avoided;
(7) although the absence of any identified victim was not normally a matter giving rise to mitigation, the impact (if any), where proved, on any individual victim; and
(8) the impact of the offence on overall public confidence in the integrity of the market; because of its impact on public confidence, it was likely that an offence committed jointly by more than one person trusted with confidential information would be more damaging to public confidence than an offence committed in isolation by one person acting on his own.

13.15 On the issue of a defendant's previous character the Court of Appeal observed:[11]

Age, and a guilty plea will always be relevant. So, too, will good character. However it must be borne in mind that it will often be the case that it is the individual of good character who has been trusted with information just because he or she is an individual of good character. By misusing the information, the trust reposed as a result of the good character had been breached ...

.... In assessing sentence, full weight must be given. ... to the impact on the appellant and his family, as well as the destruction of his professional reputation.

13.16 The Court declined to set out a series of stages at which sentences should move to different levels, but stated that sentencing judges might find valuable assistance in the decision of the Court in *R v Clark*[12] (allowing for inflation) and

---

[10] *R v McQuoid* (n 8), para 14.
[11] *R v McQuoid* (n 8), paras 14–15.
[12] *R v Clark* (n 5).

the Sentencing Guidelines Council's definitive guideline on Theft in Breach of Trust.[13]

4. Sentences imposed in recent insider dealing cases

Table of sentences imposed in recent insider dealing prosecutions

Case	Sentence	Guilty plea or trial	Relevant information
R v McQuoid[14] and Melbourne (2009)	McQuoid: 8 months' imprisonment. Melbourne: 8 months' imprisonment suspended for 12 months.	Trial	The defendants were convicted of a single count of insider dealing. McQuoid was a solicitor and general counsel to a company named TTP and had inside information about a proposed takeover of TTP by another company. He told Melbourne (his father in law), who traded on the information on their joint behalf making £48,919 profit.
R v Uberoi and Uberoi (2009)	Neel Uberoi: 2 years' imprisonment. Matthew Uberoi: 12 months' imprisonment.	Trial	The defendants (father and son) were convicted of 12 counts of insider dealing. Matthew Uberoi worked as an intern in the corporate broking department of Hoare Govett and passed inside information regarding forthcoming corporate events to his father who dealt in the companies concerned. Each count represented a single trade. The trading covered shares in 3 companies and spanned a number of months. The profit was around £110,000.
R v Calvert (2010)	21 months' imprisonment.	Trial	The defendant, a former partner of Cazenove and Co, was convicted of five counts of insider dealing, carried out over 3 years, which netted him a profit of approximately £104,000. He obtained inside information from an unknown source

---

[13] Sentencing Guidelines Council, Theft and Burglary in a building other than a dwelling, Definitive Guideline, Dec 2008, Ch E, 10 and 11.
[14] R v McQuoid (n 8).

Sentences imposed in recent insider dealing cases

Case	Sentence	Guilty plea or trial	Relevant information
			in the corporate broking department of Cazenove, and asked his friend to trade on their joint behalf.
R v Rollins (2011)	15- and 21-month sentences (to run concurrently) for insider dealing, with a further 6-month consecutive sentence for money laundering.	Trial	The defendant was a manager in an engineering company. He was convicted of insider dealing and money laundering. He took advantage of his knowledge of inside information to sell shares he held in the company, during a closed period, to avoid a loss of approximately £60,000.
R v Ahmad (2010)	10 months' imprisonment suspended for 2 years. £50,000 fine and 300 hours community service.	Guilty plea	The defendant was a trader in a hedge fund. He and a co-defendant (Rupinder Sidhu) carried out a joint plan in which Ahmad tipped inside information to Sidhu regarding stocks that the hedge fund was about to trade. This enabled Sidhu to place spread bets in advance of this trading, thereby profiting from the movement in price.
			A guilty plea to conspiracy to insider deal was entered at a very early stage in the investigation.
			The defendant had engaged in plea discussions within weeks of arrest and assisted the prosecution under a SOCPA (Serious Organised Crime and Police Act 2005) agreement.
			He made full and frank admissions pre-charge, and information was provided on the way in which the fraud (carried out by others) was conducted.
			The period covered by the conspiracy was 3 months, with a total profit gained of £265,700 (of which he received 40%).

(Continued)

Table *Continued*

Case	Sentence	Guilty plea or trial	Relevant information
			HHJ Rivlin QC stated in his sentencing remarks that a starting point of 30 months' to 3 years' imprisonment was appropriate. The sentence passed took into account the guilty plea, SOCPA agreement and mitigation.
R v Littlewood and others (2011)	The first defendant was sentenced to 3 years 4 months' imprisonment (reduced from a starting point of 5 years).	Guilty pleas	Guilty pleas were entered by three defendants to 8 counts of insider dealing over an 8-year period between March 2000 and August 2008.
			In the region of £2m was invested, yielding a profit of £590,000.
	The second defendant was sentenced to a suspended term of 12 months' imprisonment.		The first defendant was an approved person in senior roles in the corporate broking departments of two large corporate banks, often leading on the corporate finance deals which gave him access to inside information.
	The third defendant was sentenced to 2 years' imprisonment.		
			He passed inside information about these deals to his wife (the second defendant) and her close friend (the third defendant).
			These defendants traded in their own names on behalf of the trio. The profits were divided equally between the three.
			The sentencing judge stated that were it not for the particular personal mitigation of the second defendant, she would have received at least 2 years' imprisonment.
R v Rupinder Sidhu (2011)	2 years' imprisonment.	Trial	The circumstances are as set out above in relation to Anjam Ahmad.

---

[15] The Company Directors Disqualification Act 1986, s 2.

Sentences imposed in recent insider dealing cases

Case	Sentence	Guilty plea or trial	Relevant information
			Profits from his trading in fact amounted to some £500,000 (only a fraction of which he accounted to Ahmad).
R v James Sanders, Miranda Sanders and James Swallow (2012)	James Sanders: 4 years' imprisonment. Directors Disqualification Order 5 years.[15] Costs and Confiscation adjourned. Miranda Sanders: 10 months' imprisonment. James Swallow: 10 months' imprisonment.	Guilty pleas	James Sanders: 10 counts of insider dealing over a 16 months period, including 2 counts of encouraging dealing and 2 counts of disclosing inside information. Miranda Sanders: 5 counts of insider dealing jointly with her husband. Profits on the Sanders insider dealing were £1,533,749. James Swallow: 3 counts of insider dealing over a 12-month period (profit £382,253.) The defendants James Sanders and James Swallow were co-directors of an FSA authorised broking firm. Trades were in relation to five US companies on the basis of inside information obtained by James and Miranda Sanders from her sister in the US. The defendants traded for themselves and James Sanders had also encouraged clients of Blue Index to trade in two stocks generating profits of £10.2 million. All defendants were of good character. The trial judge sentenced on the basis that pleas had been entered at an early opportunity which should result in a 25% discount.
R v Mustafa, Saini, Paresh Shah, Neten Shah, Bijal Shah and Patel (2012)	Mustafa, Saini and Paresh Shah: 3 years 6 months' imprisonment. Neten Shah: 18 months' imprisonment. Bijal Shah and	Trial	The defendants obtained inside information from sources in the print rooms at two investment banks concerning proposed or forthcoming takeover bids. They then used a large number of accounts to place

(Continued)

Table *Continued*

Case	Sentence	Guilty plea or trial	Relevant information
	Patel: 2 years' imprisonment.		spread bets ahead of those announcements knowing that when the information became public knowledge the price would rise. The defendants were convicted of making a combined profit of £732,044.59 on trading between 1 May 2006 and 31 May 2008. It was a sophisticated and complex attempt to deal on inside information over a long period.
			The six defendants were convicted of offences of disclosure of inside information and dealing whilst in possession of it in respect of six stocks:
			Mustafa: 3 stocks
			Saini, Paresh Shah, Bijal Shah and Patel: 6 stocks.
			Neten Shah: 2 stocks.
R v Thomas Amman (2012)	2 years 8 months' imprisonment.	Guilty plea	2 Counts of Insider Dealing and 2 Counts of Encouraging Dealing. The judge stated that but for his guilty plea the sentence would have been 4 years' imprisonment.
			Amman worked as an investment banker at Mizuho and was advising Canon on its acquisition of Oce—a Dutch company. Amman encouraged two friends to trade on his behalf for a share of the profit—which netted him some 1 million Euros.
R v Paul Milsom (2013)	2 years' imprisonment.	Guilty plea	Senior equities trader at Legal and General. Pleaded guilty to 1 Count of disclosing inside information covering 28 separate instances of passing inside information relating to 14 stocks to a co-defendant, between October 2008 and March 2010.

Sentences imposed in recent insider dealing cases

Case	Sentence	Guilty plea or trial	Relevant information
			Milsom tipped his co-defendant in advance of large trades by Legal and General which had the potential to move the market. His co-defendant would then place spread bets or CFD trades to gain from the market move and the pair split the profit.
			Profits: £400,000 of which Milsom received £164,000 in cash.
			Plea agreement in which Milsom also volunteered involvement in a separate, similar arrangement with another individual, involving 15 transactions in 5 stocks resulting in a total profit of £160,000 of which he received £81,000. These 15 offences were taken into consideration by the sentencing judge.
			For pleading guilty at the earliest opportunity, Milsom received the full ⅓ discount, plus a further discount for entering into the plea agreement.
R v Richard Joseph (2013)	4 years' imprisonment.	Trial	Convicted of 6 counts of conspiracy to commit insider dealing over a 10-month period. The defendant received inside information regarding forthcoming corporate takeovers, from his co-conspirator who worked in the print room at an investment bank. The defendant placed spread bets on these stocks making total profits of £692,644. He paid £268,713 in cash to the insider for the information. At trial, the defendant claimed that these payments were in connection with an unrelated business deal, and that he had dealt in the six stocks as a result of his own research.

5. Disqualification of company directors

13.17 A defendant convicted of insider dealing may, in addition to any other sentence imposed, be disqualified from acting as the director of a company under ss 1 and 2 of the Company Directors Disqualification Act 1986. In *R v Goodman*,[16] the Court of Appeal stated that the correct test to apply when a Court is considering making a Directors Disqualification Order is whether the offence has some relevant factual connection with the company of which the defendant was a director at the relevant time.

13.18 In *R v Sanders*,[17] James Sanders was disqualified from acting as a company director for a period of five years on the basis that the 'encouraging' and 'disclosing' offences (s 52(2) CJA) to which he had pleaded guilty related to the management of his company Blue Index. On the facts of that case, this was plainly right, given that these offences were committed in order to encourage the clients of Blue Index to trade in the stocks about which James Sanders had inside information, in order that Blue Index would benefit from the clients' trading success. The Court declined to make a disqualification order in respect of one of the other co-defendant in that case—James Swallow. Although Swallow was also a co-director of Blue Index, the offences to which he had pleaded guilty related to insider dealing on his own account and did not involve allegations relating to the clients of Blue Index.

6. Confiscation issues in insider dealing cases

13.19 Defendants convicted of insider dealing offences are invariably made the subject of punitive confiscation orders which go well beyond the simple net profit of their trading. Although a discussion of the criminal confiscation regime under the Proceeds of Crime Act 2002 ('POCA'), is beyond the scope of this book, there are some general principles to keep in mind which are particularly relevant in an insider dealing case.

Value of benefit obtained

13.20 Where the defendant's offending involves the purchase or sale of shares, the 'benefit obtained' for the purposes of s 6(4)(c) POCA has been held by the Crown Court to be the full value of the shares, ie, the gross sale price, and not merely the profit gained

---

[16] *R v Goodman* [1993] 97 Cr App R 210.
[17] *R v Sanders and others*, unreported, Southwark Crown Court, Mr Justice Simon, 20 June 2012. FSA/PN/060/2012 & FSA/PN/067/2012.

or loss avoided.[18] In those cases, the prosecution relied on the principles set out in the House of Lords case of *R v May*,[19] and contended that the property obtained by the defendant as a result of his offending was the shares themselves and not just their increase in value. This has led to some severe confiscation orders. For example, in *R v Uberoi*,[20] a confiscation order in the sum of £288,000 was made in relation to trading in three stocks which had resulted in a total profit of only £110,000. In *R v Calvert*,[21] a confiscation order was made in the sum of £473,000 in relation to trading from which it was common ground the defendant had received only £103,000 (and which had netted £160,000 in total). In *R v Littlewood and others*,[22] confiscation orders were made against Mr and Mrs Littlewood in the sum of £767,000 each, when total profits from their trading amounted to only £590,000.

13.21 In *R v Calvert*, this point having been fully argued, the sentencing Judge certified leave to appeal, however Mr Calvert subsequently abandoned the appeal proceedings. The decisions on this issue are therefore all at first instance.

13.22 However, the recent Supreme Court Judgment in *R v Waya*,[23] means that there will be scope to revisit this issue in such cases on the grounds of proportionality. *R v Waya* was a case concerning mortgage fraud in which a mortgage to purchase a property was obtained by the making of false representations. The issue was whether in these circumstances the 'benefit obtained' was the full value of the property or whether what had been obtained was the increase in its value. The majority judgment held that it was the latter.

13.23 The Supreme Court also highlighted the requirement that there must be a reasonable relationship of proportionality between the means employed by the State in the deprivation of property as a form of penalty by way of a confiscation order, and the legitimate aim which is sought to be realised by the deprivation.[24] This approach accords with Article 1 of the First Protocol to the European Convention on Human Rights and the European Jurisprudence.[25] In summary, the Supreme Court decided that a confiscation order which did not conform to the test of proportionality would constitute a violation of these principles and that therefore it was the duty of the Crown Court not to make an order which involves such a

---

[18] *R v McQuoid and Melbourne*, unreported, Southwark Crown Court, His Honour Judge Testar, 30 Mar 2012; *R v Calvert*, unreported, Southwark Crown Court, His Honour Judge Testar, 7 May 2010 (the trial judge certified leave to appeal on this point but the defendant chose to abandon the appeal); *R v Uberoi*, unreported, Southwark Crown Court, His Honour Judge Testar, 7 July 2010.
[19] *R v May* [2008] UKHL 28. See also *R v Allpress* [2009] EWCA Crim 8; *R v Rooney* [2010] EWCA Crim 2.
[20] *R v Uberoi* (n 18).
[21] *R v Uberoi* (n 18).
[22] *R v Littlewood and others*, unreported, Southwark Crown Court, His Honour Judge Anthony Leonard QC, 20 Aug 2012. FSA/PN/082/2012.
[23] *R v Waya* [2012] UKSC 51.
[24] *R v Waya* (n 23) 10, para 12.
[25] See *Jahn v Germany* (2006) 42 EHRR 1084, para 93; *Pressos Compania Naviera SA and others v Belgium*, judgment of 20 Nov 1995, ser A no 332, 23, s 38.

violation.[26] The above principles may provide grounds to argue that a confiscation order, which represents the full value of the shares purchased (rather than the profit made), would be disproportionate. Note also, that if spread bets or CFDs have been traded, then no shares have actually been acquired, and therefore the starting point in calculating benefit can only be the profits actually made.

Apportionment between defendants

13.24 Where two or more defendants are indicted on a joint enterprise basis, the courts have held that each is liable for the full value of the benefit obtained, rather than the benefit being apportioned between them. This was the approach adopted in *R v Sidhu*,[27] in which the defendant was ordered to pay a confiscation order which amounted to the full value of the proceeds of the trading he conducted with his co-defendant Anjam Ahmad, in circumstances in which a confiscation order, representing only his share of the profit, had previously been made against Mr Ahmad. In such a case, the Court will have regard to the general observations of the Court of Appeal in *R v Allpress*:[28]

> Where two or more defendants obtained property jointly, each was to be regarded as obtaining the whole of it. Where property was received by one conspirator, what mattered was the capacity in which he received it, that is, whether it was for his own personal benefit, or on behalf of others, or jointly on behalf of himself and others. That had to be decided on the evidence. Two or more defendants might or might not obtain a joint pecuniary advantage; it would depend on the facts.

13.25 In *R v Rooney*,[29] Lord Justice Aikens remarked as follows in respect of the calculation of benefit in cases where there are multiple defendants:

> In short, the position is, as we understand it: (a) if a benefit is shown to be obtained jointly by conspirators, then all are liable for the whole of the benefit jointly obtained. (b) If, however, it is not established that the total benefit was jointly received, but it is established that there was a certain sum by way of benefit which was divided between conspirators, yet there is no evidence on how it was divided, then the court making the confiscation order is entitled to make an equal division as to benefit obtained between all conspirators. (c) However, if the court is satisfied on the evidence that a particular conspirator did not benefit at all or only to a specific amount, then it should find that is the benefit that he has obtained.

13.26 Given the majority judgment in *R v Waya*, it must be arguable whether a confiscation order which makes no allowance for apportionment would meet the requirement of proportionality.

---

[26] *R v Waya* (n 23) 11, para 14.
[27] *R v Rupinder Sidhu*, unreported, Southwark Crown Court, Confiscation order 8 May 2012, His Honour Judge Gledhill QC. FSA/PN/050/2012.
[28] *R v Clark* (n 5).
[29] *R v Rooney* (n 19) para 36.

Confiscation as part of a plea agreement

The FSA has demonstrated that, in an appropriate case, it is willing to consider a negotiated settlement of confiscation proceedings as part of a plea agreement and it is to be presumed that the FCA will continue this practice. In *R v Anjam Ahmad*,[30] the defendant entered into a co-operation agreement with the FSA under s 73 of the Serious and Organised Crime and Police Act 2005 ('SOCPA'). As part of that agreement, he pleaded guilty to a single count of conspiracy to commit insider dealing, and the FSA agreed a confiscation order in the sum of £106,000 which equaled his share of the proceeds of the trading conducted by his co-defendant Rupinder Sidhu on their joint behalf. As explained above, Sidhu was subsequently convicted after a trial, following which a confiscation order[31] of £572,000 was made which represented the full value of the profits made. In *R v Paul Milsom*,[32] an agreed confiscation order in the sum of £245,000 was made which equaled Mr Milsom's share of the profits from his insider trading. **13.27**

7. Other FCA proceedings

A defendant convicted of insider dealing who is an FCA approved person and/or who runs an FCA authorised firm will almost certainly be made the subject of an FCA Prohibition Order under s 56 FSMA[33] which has the effect of preventing the individual from working in any capacity within the Financial Services sector. The authorised firm may also be at risk of the FSA removing its permissions and cancelling its authorisation under s 55 FSMA.[34] **13.28**

---

[30] *R v Anjam Ahmad*, unreported, Southwark Crown Court, His Honour Judge Rivlin QC, the Honorary Recorder of Westminster, 22 June 2010.
[31] *R v Rupinder Sidhu* (n 26).
[32] *R v Paul Milsom*, unreported, Southwark Crown Court, His Honour Judge Pegden QC, 7 Mar 2013. FSA/PN/022/2013.
[33] See Chapter 24, Section 4.
[34] See Chapter 24, Section 4.

14

INSIDER DEALING—THE CIVIL MARKET ABUSE REGIME

1. Introduction	14.01	Part VIII of the FSMA	14.12
2. Legislative background	14.02	The Code of Market Conduct	14.13
The Market Abuse Directive	14.07	Other FSA/FCA publications	14.16
3. Legal and source materials	14.12	Previous cases	14.17

1. Introduction

14.01 This Chapter sets the scene for the UK's civil market abuse regime as it applies to insider dealing conduct. It explains how the legislation and the FCA's Code of Market Conduct ('MAR') work, and the available legal and source materials.

2. Legislative background

14.02 Proceedings for market abuse are variously and interchangeably referred to as 'civil', 'civil offences', 'regulatory', or 'disciplinary' proceedings. Whatever term is used, its meaning is the same. It refers to proceedings under the Financial Services and Markets Act 2000 ('FSMA') part VIII (ss 118–23) which contain the UK's civil market abuse provisions. These, together with the MAR contained within the FCA's Handbook of Rules and Guidance provide for the civil offence of 'market abuse'.

14.03 Prior to FSMA, market abuse was dealt with in two ways:

1. Criminal proceedings for insider dealing under Part V of the CJA or criminal proceedings for misleading statements and practices (essentially misleading the market) under the then s 47 of the Financial Services Act 1996 ('FS Act').
2. Supervisory and Disciplinary powers in respect of authorised firms and approved persons, exercised initially by a variety of self-regulatory bodies

(such as the Stock Exchange and the Securities and Investments Board), and later by the FSA following its creation in May 1997.

14.04 Despite the prominence given to the need for a criminal offence of insider dealing, it was not until FSMA was enacted in 2000, that a civil market abuse regime came into existence to sit alongside the criminal law. Given the paucity of successful criminal prosecutions, and the inadequacies of alternatives,[1] the need for a comprehensive civil regime as a means of dealing with market abuse was obvious.

14.05 The original version of the market abuse regime, contained in Part VIII of FSMA as original enacted, prescribed three types of behaviour:

1. Misuse of information—behaviour based on information that was not generally available to market users.
2. False or misleading impressions—behaviour which gave a false or misleading impression as to the price of investments.
3. Distortion—behaviour which distorted the markets.

14.06 This regime applied the 'regular user' test, namely that behaviour had to be such as would be likely to be regarded by a 'regular user' of the market as a failure on the part of the person or persons concerned, to observe the standard of behaviour reasonably to be expected of a person in his or their position, in relation to the market. 'Regular user' was defined in relation to a particular market as 'a reasonable person who regularly deals on that market in investments of the kind in question'.[2]

The Market Abuse Directive

14.07 The regime was significantly amended following the implementation of the Market Abuse Directive 2003[3] ('MAD') which was passed by the European Parliament on 14 March 2002.[4] The MAD entered into force in April 2003[5] and introduced a number of key changes to the existing market abuse regime. The implementation date for the MAD was 12 October 2004,[6] although implementation did not in fact take place in the UK until 1 July 2005.

---

[1] See Melanie Johnson, Economic Secretary to the Treasury, Standing Committee A, 2 November 1999 HMSO. See also Michael Blair QC, George Walker and Robert Purves *Financial Services Law* (2nd edn, OUP 2009) 8.01–8.14 for a discussion of the background to the current regime.

[2] Now contained in FSMA s 130A(3). The FSA's guidance at that time (The Code of Market Conduct contained in the MAR 1.2.21G) described the regular user test as importing an objective element into the judgement to be made while at the same time retaining some subjective elements relative to the market in question.

[3] Directive 2003/6/EC of the European Parliament and of the Council of 28 Jan 2003 on Insider Dealing and Market Manipulation (Market Abuse) (OJ 96, 12 Apr 2003).

[4] Europarl Daily Notebook 14 Mar 2002, 5.

[5] Implementing Directive 2003/124/EC.

[6] Directive (n 4) art 18.

14.08 The MAD required the adoption of common regulatory provisions by all EU Member States and also required co-operation between Member States to combat market abuse activity. At the time, there remained wide variations in the market abuse regimes adopted by different Member States, and at the same time new financial and technical developments enhanced the incentives, means, and opportunities for market abuse, through new products, new technologies, increasing cross-border activities, and the internet.

14.09 Like the Insider Dealing Directive 1989 ('IDD'),[7] the MAD Preamble focused on the importance of the single market, market integrity, and market confidence. It was also intended that the MAD should replace the IDD to ensure legislative consistency.

14.10 Although that may have been Europe's intention, in the UK that is not quite what happened. Although the existing civil legislation in Part VIII of FSMA was amended to reflect the requirements in the MAD, the criminal legislation was left entirely alone. This is why in the UK we have two separate regimes—the criminal insider dealing regime under Part V of the CJA (which has its origins in the IDD) and the civil market abuse regime under Part VIII of FSMA (which has its origins in MAD). Given that the FCA (and before that the FSA) is the lead Authority under both regimes, it is perhaps not surprising that this dual approach causes confusion at times in the minds of the subjects of FCA investigations and also their lawyers.

14.11 The civil and criminal regimes sit alongside each other and as explained in the Investigations Chapter,[8] the FSA (and now the FCA), will commonly conduct investigations on the joint basis of the criminal and civil offences. However, whereas the criminal offence can only be dealt with in the criminal courts, the civil offences give rise to the civil and disciplinary measures imposed by the FCA from which recourse may be had to the Upper Tribunal (Tax and Chancery Chamber) ('the Tribunal').[9] FSMA also provides the FCA with the power to bring proceedings for market abuse in the High Court.[10]

3. Legal and source materials

Part VIII of the FSMA

14.12 Market abuse is defined in s 118 FSMA. The section describes seven 'types of behaviour' which amount to market abuse. The first type of behaviour deals with

---

[7] Com Dir 89/592/EC.
[8] See Chapter 22 and also Chapter 23.
[9] See Chapter 24, Section 5 Tribunal Reference.
[10] See Chapter 24, Section 7 Civil Proceedings.

insider dealing, the second with improper disclosure of inside information, and the third preserves the 'regular' user provision which survives from the pre-MAD version of FSMA.[11] As the focus of this book is on insider dealing, it is these three types of market abuse that will be dealt with in the forthcoming chapters of this book. The remaining four types of market abuse—contained in s 118(5) to (8) of FSMA—are beyond the scope of this book.[12] Therefore references in this book to 'market abuse' and the 'market abuse regime' relate to the limited scope of this book rather than the entirety of the market abuse regime.

The Code of Market Conduct

14.13 Under s 119(1) FSMA, the FCA is required to prepare and issue a code containing such provisions as it considers will give appropriate guidance to those determining whether or not behaviour amounts to market abuse.

14.14 The FSA satisfied this requirement with the Code of Market Conduct ("MAR") which was contained within the FSA's Handbook of Rules and Guidance. At legal cutover on 1 April 2013, MAR became part of the FCA's Handbook. MAR considers each of the seven types of behaviour set out in s 118 FSMA and sets out (non-exhaustive) descriptions of behaviour that, in the opinion of the FCA, do, or do not, amount to market abuse, as well as factors to be taken into account in making that determination.

14.15 MAR also sets out certain 'safe harbours' that apply to different types of behaviour. The provisions of MAR are designated with letter codes.[13] 'E' indicates an evidential provision, 'G' represents FCA guidance, and 'C' indicates a safe harbour. Evidential provisions are indicative in nature in that they create rebuttable presumptions of compliance with, or contravention of the rules to which they relate. Guidance is used to explain the implications of other provisions or regulatory requirements or to indicate possible means of compliance. Guidance can be relied upon as an interpretive tool but it is not a basis for taking action in itself. A safe harbour provides for types of conduct which do not constitute market abuse and can be relied upon as such. Safe harbours are therefore particularly important to market participants because they amount to conclusive evidence that conduct falling within the safe harbour does not constitute market abuse.

---

[11] This is known as the 'sunset provision'.
[12] See Blair et al (n 1) for a fuller discussion of the entirety of the Market Abuse Regime. See also Edward J Swan and John Virgo, *Market Abuse Regulation* (2nd edn, OUP 2010); Barry Rider, Kern Alexander, Lisa Linklater, and Stuart Bazley, *Market Abuse and Insider Dealing* (Tottel 2009); Martyn Hopper, *A Practitioners Guide to the Regulation of Market Abuse* (Sweet & Maxwell 2013).
[13] For a full explanation of the codes used in the Handbook see 'Reader's guide: an introduction to the FCA Handbook', ch 6.

Other FSA/FCA publications

14.16 The FSA published a periodical called *Market Watch* which provides updates on current themes and issues with which the FSA Markets Division was concerned and also guidance to firms and individuals in respect of these. *Market Watch* continues as a publication under the FCA. Although primarily a news source, it is a useful insight into the FCA's views and the way in which it will be likely to approach particular issues. In addition, from time to time, *Market Watch* is used to issue formal guidance on particular topics.

Previous cases

14.17 Previous cases are another useful source of information. These are divided into two categories: Final Notices[14] issued by the FSA/FCA in cases where the subject has decided not to refer the matter to the Tribunal, or where there has been a final Tribunal determination; and Tribunal Decisions in which the subject has referred the FSA/FCA's Decision to take Enforcement action to the Tribunal for a complete rehearing of the matter.[15] Plainly, previous Tribunal decisions do not represent binding precedent in respect of future cases, but they do provide a useful resource in terms of how similar issues have been dealt with by the Tribunal in previous cases.

14.18 Between 2000 and 2010, such cases were heard by the Financial Services and Markets Tribunal which was an independent judicial body established under s 132 FSMA. In April 2010, this Tribunal was abolished and its functions were transferred to the Upper Tribunal (Tax and Chancery Chamber).[16]

---

[14] These can be found on the FCA website: <http://www.fca.gov.uk>.

[15] The procedure in relation to both of these is discussed in Chapter 24 The Enforcement Process—Market Abuse Proceedings. Note that between 2000 and 2010, cases were heard by the Financial Services and Markets Tribunal ('FSMT') which was an independent judicial body established under s 132 FSMA. In Apr 2010, this Tribunal was abolished and its functions were transferred to the Upper Tribunal (Tax and Chancery Chamber).

[16] FSMT Decisions can be found at: <http://www.tribunals.gov.uk/financeandtax/Decisions.htm#fs>; Upper Tribunal decisions can be found at: <http://www.tribunals.gov.uk/financeandtax/Decisions/Financial.htm>.

15

THE CIVIL OFFENCES

1. Introduction	15.01	3. Qualifying investments and prescribed markets	15.13
2. Part VIII of FSMA	15.02	Prescribed markets for s 118(2) and (3) behaviour	15.15
Section 118(1) FSMA	15.03		
Section 123 FSMA—'requiring or encouraging'	15.05	Qualifying investments	15.26
'Behaviour' (s 130A(3) FSMA)	15.06	Related investments	15.28
'Person'	15.07	4. Territorial scope	15.32

1. Introduction

This Chapter describes the circumstances in which behaviour by a person, which is described in s 118(2)–(4) of the Financial Services and Markets Act 2000 ('FSMA') will be caught by the market abuse regime. It deals with the overarching requirements of s 118(1) FSMA, describes the qualifying investments and prescribed markets which are covered by the civil market abuse regime and the territorial scope requirements contained in s 118A(1) FSMA. **15.01**

2. Part VIII of FSMA

As explained in Chapter 14,[1] the civil market abuse regime originally came into effect with the implementation of FSMA on 1 December 2001.[2] The market abuse provisions were redrafted however, in order to give effect to the provisions of the Market Abuse Directive 2003 ('MAD').[3] The 'new' (post-MAD) provisions took effect on 1 July 2005 in relation to all conduct occurring on or after that date. Given the lapse of time, it is unlikely that any current or future FCA case will involve the pre-MAD legislation and therefore this book focuses on the post-MAD regime. **15.02**

---

[1] Chapter 14, Section 2 Legislative Background.
[2] This date is known as 'N2'.
[3] Directive 2003/6/EC.

Section 118(1) FSMA

15.03 Section 118 FSMA describes the types of behaviour that amount to market abuse. As explained in Chapter 14,[4] this book focuses only on the first three types which are to be found in s 118(2)–(4) FSMA.

Section 118—Market Abuse

(1) For the purposes of this Act, Market Abuse is behaviour (whether by one person alone or by two or more persons jointly or in concert) which
   (a) occurs in relation to
      (i) qualifying investments admitted to trading on a prescribed market,
      (ii) qualifying investments in respect of which a request for admission to trading on such a market has been made, or
      (iii) in the case of subsection (2) or (3) behaviour, investments which are related investments in relation to such qualifying investments, and
   (b) falls within any one or more of the types of behaviour set out in subsections (2) to (8).

15.04 The two types of behaviour described at s 118(2) and (3) largely mirror the primary insider dealing and secondary 'disclosing' offences under Part V of the CJA. Section 118(4) expressly preserves the previous market abuse offence and 'regular user' test that had existed in the pre-MAD version of s 118. This is often referred to as the 'legacy offence'. Initially, this provision was subject to a 'sunset date' of 30 June 2008, meaning that it would cease to exist unless action was taken by the Treasury to retain it. This date was later extended to 31 December 2009 and subsequently to 31 December 2014.[5]

Section 123 FSMA—'requiring or encouraging'

15.05 Section 123(1) FSMA provides that if the FCA is satisfied that a person has engaged in market abuse it may impose on him a penalty of such amount as it considers appropriate. Section 123(1)(b) provides that a penalty may also be imposed on a person (A) who the FCA is satisfied, has required or encouraged another person or persons to engage in behaviour which would amount to market abuse had it been engaged in by A himself. Section 123(1)(b) therefore provides the market abuse version of the criminal 'encouraging' offence.

'Behaviour' (s 130A(3) FSMA)

15.06 Under s 130A(3) FSMA, 'behaviour' for the purposes of the market abuse regime includes both action and inaction.

---

[4] Chapter 14, Section 3 Legal and source materials.
[5] Words in s 118(9) substituted (31 Dec 2011) by the FSMA (Market Abuse) Regulations 2011 (SI 2011/2928) reg 2(2).

'Person'

15.07 Section 118(1) FSMA (unlike s 52 CJA) deliberately uses the word 'person' rather than 'individual'. This gives effect to the requirement in the MAD Article 1(6) that 'person' shall mean any natural or legal person. This also accords with Schedule 1 of the Interpretation Act 1978 which defines 'person' as including:

> any person, including a body of persons corporate or unincorporate (that is, a natural person, a legal person and, for example, a partnership).

15.08 This means that civil proceedings for market abuse can be taken against a company or other structure, as well as the individuals who have actually undertaken the behaviour in question.

15.09 The extent to which a company could be held vicariously liable for market abuse committed by its employees was considered by the FSA in the *Jabre* case.[6] The FSA found that Philippe Jabre had committed market abuse in relation to trading he conducted while he was an employee of GLG Partners LP ('GLG') and held the title 'Managing Director'. Mr Jabre was also a member of GLG's Management and Investment Management Committees. Mr Jabre was responsible for managing six of GLG's investment funds including the 'Market Neutral Fund' on whose behalf the trading in question was conducted.

15.10 The Final Notice[7] records that the FSA was satisfied that on the facts of this case, Mr Jabre's acts should be attributed to GLG. In reaching this conclusion, the FSA had particular regard to Mr Jabre's seniority and status within GLG; the fact that he plainly had authority to enter into the transactions in question and that he exercised a large degree of autonomy in relation to the deals he undertook on GLG's behalf.

15.11 Accordingly, the FSA concluded that misconduct on the part of Mr Jabre in relation to trading conducted for the GLG Market Neutral Fund also constituted misconduct attributable to GLG. The FSA therefore imposed fines of £750,000 on both GLG and Mr Jabre.

15.12 Principles of vicarious liability were also applied in the *Greenlight Capital Inc*[8] ('*Greenlight*') case in which the FSA imposed a financial penalty of £3,650,957 on Greenlight in respect of market abuse (insider dealing s 118(2)) carried out by Greenlight's owner David Einhorn. Greenlight was an investment management firm based in the US. The FSA's case was that Mr Einhorn had instructed Greenlight's traders to dispose of part of its holding in a company named Punch Taverns plc ('Punch') and that that instruction was given on the basis of inside

---

[6] *Philippe Jabre and GLG Partners LP*, FSA Final Notice, 1 Aug 2006 (pre-MAD case).
[7] *Jabre and GLG Partners* (n 6) para 6ff.
[8] *Greenlight Capital Inc*, Final Notice, 12 Jan 2012 (post-MAD case).

information that Mr Einhorn had received during a telephone call with Merrill Lynch International ('MLI'), in which he was informed of a forthcoming substantial new equity issuance by Punch. The FSA considered that Mr Einhorn's behaviour was attributable to Greenlight on the basis that he was the sole owner, the President, and sole portfolio manager, and was responsible for all Greenlight's investment decisions.[9]

3. Qualifying investments and prescribed markets

15.13 Under s 130A(1) FSMA, the Treasury may by order specify the markets that are prescribed markets for the purposes of s 118 FSMA and the investments that are qualifying investments in relation to those prescribed markets. The FSMA (Prescribed Markets and Qualifying Investments) Order 2001[10] ('PMQI') gives effect to this.

15.14 Section 118(1)(a)(i)–(ii) FSMA states that the behaviour in question must occur in relation to qualifying investments which are either admitted to dealing on a prescribed market or in respect of which a request for admission to trading on such a market has been made. In addition, MAR 1.2.5E suggests that behaviour prior to a request for admission to trading may also be covered by s 118(1)(a). A number of indicative factors are given which amount in effect to whether the behaviour in question occurs in circumstances where a request for admission is subsequently made, or whether the behaviour continues to have an effect once an application is made or the qualifying investments have been admitted (or, offered for sale, in the case of a prescribed auction platform).

Prescribed markets for s 118(2) and (3) behaviour

15.15 The prescribed markets for the purposes of behaviour falling under s 118(2) or (3) FSMA are set out in Article 4(1) of the PMQI:

a. All markets which are established under the rules of a UK recognised investment exchange.
b. The market known as OFEX.
c. All other markets which are regulated markets.

UK Recognised Investment Exchange

15.16 The FSA kept, and the FCA now keeps, a register of Recognised Investment Exchanges. Currently, this list comprises ICE Futures Europe, ICAP Securities

---

[9] *Greenlight Capital Inc*, Final Notice (n 12) para 2.1. A financial penalty was also imposed on Mr Einhorn (see Final Notice, 15 Feb 2012) (post-MAD case).
[10] SI 2001/996, para 4(3) of the Prescribed Markets Order. As at 31 Dec 2012, there is only one recognised auction platform—namely ICE Futures Europe.

and Derivatives Exchange Limited, LIFFE Administration and Management, London Stock Exchange plc, and the London Metal Exchange Limited.

OFEX/ICAP

15.17 The Off Exchange ('OFEX') was started in 1995 as a way for shareholders to deal in the shares of small companies that do not meet the stringent requirements of the Alternative Investment Market ('AIM') and the London Stock Exchange's ('LSE') Official List. OFEX subsequently became the PLUS Derivatives Exchange ('PLUS-DX'), which was recently acquired by ICAP and is now known as the ICAP Securities and Derivatives Exchange ('ISDX').

Regulated markets

15.18 The Markets in Financial Instruments Directive 2004 ('MiFID')[11] (Article 4(1)(14)) defines 'regulated market' for the purposes of MAD, as follows:

> (14) a multilateral system operated and/or managed by a market operator, which brings together or facilitates the bringing together of multiple third-party buying and selling interests in financial instruments—in the system and in accordance with its non-discretionary rules—in a way that results in a contract, in respect of the financial instruments admitted to trading under its rules and/or systems, and which is authorised and functions regularly and in accordance with the provisions of Title III of MiFID.

15.19 Article 47 of MiFID requires each Member State to draw up a list of the regulated markets for which it is the home Member State and to forward that list to the other Member States and the European Commission. The Commission is required to publish a list of all regulated markets in the Official Journal of the European Union and update it at least once a year. The Commission must also publish and update the list on its website, each time the Member States notify it of changes to their lists.

15.20 In the case of *Nilas and others*,[12] the ECJ confirmed that Article 4(1)(14) must be interpreted as meaning that a market in financial instruments which does not satisfy the requirements in Title III of MIFID does not fall within the concept of 'regulated market', as defined in that provision. Whether it does so or not is a question of fact regardless of whether the market in question appears on the list of regulated markets required by Article 47 of MIFID.

Recognised Auction Platforms

15.21 As from 18 June 2012, the PMQI was amended by the Recognised Auction Platforms Regulations 2011[13] ('RAPR') to include in the list of prescribed markets for

---

[11] MiFID 2004/39/EC.
[12] Case C-248/11 *Nilas and others*, 22 March 2012, reference for a preliminary ruling under Article 267 TFEU, from the Curtea de Apel Cluj (Romania), made by decision of 13 May 2011.
[13] FSMA (Recognised Auction Platforms) Regulations 2011 SI/2011/2699, para 4(3) of the Prescribed Markets Order. As at 31 Dec 2012, there is only one recognised auction platform—namely ICE Futures Europe.

the purposes of sections 118(2) and (3) of FSMA,[14] all recognised auction platforms and all other auction platforms which have been appointed under the emission allowance auctioning regulations. This covers auctions in EU Emission Allowances. These changes occurred as a result of the EU Emission Trading System ('EU ETS') which covers sectors responsible for around half of the UK's carbon dioxide emissions. The EU ETS is expected to deliver annual carbon savings measured in percentage terms from previous years. It works on a 'cap and trade' basis by which a cap is set on EU Member State's emissions, which declines over time. Emission Allowances ('EA') equal to each year's cap are then issued and allocated to sectors covered by the system. EAs can be allocated for free or auctioned by national governments. In November 2010, a regulatory framework for auctioning EAs was published in the EU Official Journal.[15] This required Member States, amongst other things, to extend national laws to include the auctioning of EAs within the market abuse regime and designate such auction platforms as regulated markets.

Prescribed Markets for s 118(4) behaviour

15.22 For s 118(4) behaviour, Article 4(2) of the PMQI provides that only the first two types of prescribed market apply, ie, UK Recognised Investment Exchange or OFEX/ISDX). Article 4(4) PMQI extends to recognised auction platforms only.

Multilateral and Organised Trading Facilities

15.23 One of the key limitations to the MAD that has emerged is that it is based on the concept of prohibiting insider dealing or market manipulation in financial instruments which are admitted to trading on a regulated market. However, since the adoption of MiFID,[16] financial instruments have been increasingly traded on Multilateral Trading Facilities ('MTF') and Organised Trading Facilities ('OTF')—neither of which are regulated markets under MAD and nor are they established under the rules of a UK recognised investment exchange, which means that trading on these facilities falls outside the Market Abuse regime.

15.24 A MTF is defined in Article 4(15) of MiFID. Essentially, it is a type of financial trading system that brings together and enables trading in financial instruments between multiple parties (eg retail investors or other investment firms). An OTF is any facility or system which is designed to bring together buying and selling interests or orders which relate to financial instruments. OTFs are focused on non-equities such as derivatives and cash bond markets. These systems can be crossing networks or matching engines that are operated by an investment firm or a market operator. Instruments may include shares, bonds, and derivatives.

---

[14] Para 3 added to the PMQI. Note this also applies to behaviour falling within ss 118(5), (6) and (7) FSMA.
[15] Commission Regulation (EU) no 0131/2010.
[16] Directive 2000/12/EC.

Qualifying investments and prescribed markets

One of the main advantages of MTFs is that they do not have listing requirements and also operate with low cost bases. MTFs have had a considerable impact on European share-trading, one of the key effects of which is a process known as fragmentation, where liquidity for a security is no longer concentrated on one exchange but is instead spread across multiple trading venues. MTFs and OTFs have therefore provided more competition to existing regulated markets. As a result, they have inevitably gained an increased share of liquidity and attracted a broader range of investors. In recognition of this, on 20 October 2010, the European Commission adopted a proposal for a Regulation of the European Parliament and of the Council on Insider Dealing and Market Manipulation (Market Abuse)[17] ('Draft Regulation' or 'Regulation'). It is proposed that this Draft Regulation will replace the current MAD and one of the key changes will be that MTFs and OTFs will be specifically included within the market abuse regime.[18]

15.25

Qualifying investments

Qualifying investments are described in Article 5 of the PMQI as all financial instruments within the meaning given in Article 1(3) of MAD as modified by Article 69 of MiFID.[19] The effect of this is that the following investments are deemed 'qualifying investments' for the purposes of the PMQI:

15.26

1. Transferable securities—Defined in Article 4(18) of MiFID as those classes of securities which are negotiable on the capital market, with the exception of instruments of payment, such as:
    (a) shares in companies and other securities equivalent to shares in companies, partnerships or other entities, and depositary receipts in respect of shares;
    (b) bonds or other forms of securitised debt, including depositary receipts in respect of such securities;
    (c) any other securities giving the right to acquire or sell any such transferable securities or giving rise to a cash settlement determined by reference to transferable securities, currencies, interest rates or yields, commodities or other indices or measures;
2. Units in collective investment undertakings,
3. Money-market instruments,
4. Financial-futures contracts, including equivalent cash-settled instruments,
5. Forward interest-rate agreements,
6. Interest-rate, currency and equity swaps,
7. Options to acquire or dispose of any instrument falling into these categories, including equivalent cash-settled instruments. This category includes in particular options on currency and on interest rates,

---

[17] COM(2011) 651 final.
[18] See Chapter 25, Section 4 The MAD's limitations.
[19] MiFID 2004/39/EC.

8. Derivatives on commodities,
9. Any other instrument admitted to trading on a regulated market in a Member State or for which a request for admission to trading on such a market has been made.

15.27 In addition, Article 5(2) of the PMQI prescribes as qualifying investments in relation to auction platforms, all auctioned products that are financial instruments within the meaning given in Article 4.1(17) of MiFID. These are listed in Annex 1 s C of MiFID.[20]

Related investments

15.28 In the case of market abuse falling within the first two types of behaviour (s 118(2) and (3) FSMA—insider dealing and improper disclosure), the scope is extended to cover 'related investments'.[21] Related investments are defined in s 130(A)(3) FSMA as an investment whose price or value depends on the price or value of the qualifying investment. The most obvious example of this would be derivative products such as contracts for difference ('CFDs') and would also include spread bets.

15.29 In summary, if the behaviour in question does not occur in relation to qualifying investments admitted to trading on a prescribed market (or where a request for admission has been made), or in relation to related investments, then the behaviour cannot amount to market abuse under s 118 FSMA.

15.30 This is demonstrated by the case of *Nicholas Kyprios*.[22] Mr Kyprios was the Head of Credit Sales at Credit Suisse Securities (Europe) Limited ('Credit Suisse'). He improperly disclosed information relating to a potential large Eurobond issue by Credit Suisse's client Liberty Global Inc ('Liberty'), the proceeds of which were likely to be used in part to fund Liberty's acquisition of a German cable television company named Unitymedia.

15.31 The information was price-sensitive in relation to outstanding Unitymedia Floating Rate Notes and Credit Default Swaps, neither of which were qualifying investments admitted to trading on a prescribed market as they were admitted to trading on the GEM segment of the Irish Stock Exchange.[23] It was not therefore possible

---

[20] Article 1(17) of MiFID 2004/39/EC states: 'Financial instrument' means those instruments specified in Section C of Annex I.
[21] Section 118(1)(3) FSMA. This follows Article 9 of MAD which required that the prohibitions should also apply to any financial instrument not admitted to trading on a regulated market in a Member State, but whose value depends on a financial instrument admitted to trading on a regulated market in at least one Member State, or for which a request for admission to trading on such a market has been made, irrespective of whether or not the transaction itself actually takes place on that market.
[22] *Nicholas James Kyprios* Final Notice 13 Mar 2012 (post-MAD case).
[23] See *Nicholas James Kyprios* (n 22) paras 20–2 for a full summary of the FSA's analysis and its reasons for not pursuing a Market Abuse allegation against Mr Kyprios.

to bring proceedings against Mr Kyprios for market abuse (improper disclosure s 118(3) FSMA). Instead, the FSA fined him £200,000 (discounted from £300,000 for early settlement) for breaching Principles 2 and 3 of its Statements of Principles for Approved Persons ('APER').

4. Territorial scope

The territorial scope provisions are contained in s 118A(1) FSMA: **15.32**

(1) Behaviour is to be taken into account for the purposes of this Part only if it occurs (a) in the United Kingdom, or (b) in relation to
  (i) qualifying investments which are admitted to trading on a prescribed market situated in, or operating in, the United Kingdom,
  (ii) qualifying investments for which a request for admission to trading on such a prescribed market has been made, or
  (iii) in the case of section 118(2) and (3), investments which are related investments in relation to such qualifying investments.
(2) For the purposes of subsection (1), as it applies in relation to section 118(4) and (8), a prescribed market accessible electronically in the United Kingdom is to be treated as operating in the United Kingdom.

The effect of these provisions is that for the behaviour to fall within the market abuse regime it must occur: **15.33**

1. In the UK; or
2. In relation to qualifying investments admitted to trading on a prescribed market situated or operating in the UK or for which a request for such admission has been made; or
3. (In the case of s 118(2) and (3) behaviour)—related investments to the above.

For the purposes of s 118(4) behaviour, if the prescribed market is accessible electronically in the UK, this is sufficient for it to be treated as 'operating in the UK'. **15.34**

The territorial scope of the market abuse regime was dealt with by the Tribunal in the *Jabre* case.[24] The decision in fact relates to the pre-MAD version of s 118(1) which referred to behaviour occurring 'in relation to qualifying investments traded on a prescribed market'. In that case, it was held that transactions undertaken by Mr Jabre on the Tokyo exchange in respect of shares that were also listed on the London Stock Exchange, fell within the market abuse regime as the behaviour had occurred in relation to qualifying investments (shares) which were traded on a prescribed market (the LSE). That being the case, it was immaterial that the actual trading itself had not taken place on a prescribed market. The same rationale would apply to the post-MAD s 118A(1) and would therefore be likely to lead to the same result. **15.35**

---

[24] *Philippe Jabre v FSA*, FSMT Case 036, 2006; decision on Market Abuse (pre-MAD case).

16

SECTION 118(2) FSMA; BEHAVIOUR—INSIDER DEALING

1. Introduction	16.01	Likely to have a significant effect on the price of the qualifying or related investments		16.47
2. Section 118(2) FSMA	16.02			
3. Insider	16.05			
4. Dealing or attempting to deal	16.14	Inside information with respect to commodity derivatives		16.61
5. 'On the basis of'	16.16	Inside information with respect to persons charged with the execution of orders		
6. Inside information	16.28			16.64
Information of a precise nature	16.30			
Not generally available	16.38	7. Section 118(2) FSMA behaviour—safe harbours		16.66
Relates directly or indirectly to an issuer of qualifying investments, or to one or more of the qualifying investments	16.46	Prior decisions to deal and pre-existing trading strategies		16.66
		Market makers and professional dealers		16.71
		Execution of client orders		16.77
		Takeover and merger activity		17.82

1. Introduction

16.01 This Chapter deals with the required elements of s 118(2) behaviour including what 'Insider' and 'Inside Information' mean in this context. It also deals with the circumstances in which dealing can be said to have occurred 'on the basis of' inside information. Lastly, it describes the safe harbours that are available in respect of this offence. The statutory defences available under FSMA are dealt with separately in Chapter 19.

2. Section 118(2) FSMA

16.02 Section 118(2) FSMA provides:

> The first type of behaviour is where an insider deals, or attempts to deal, in a qualifying investment or related investment on the basis of inside information relating to the investment in question.[1]

16.03 The elements of this offence are set out in Figure 4.

---

[1] MAR 1.3.20G and MAR 1.3.2E provide examples of behaviour which in the FSA's opinion would amount to s 118(2) behaviour.

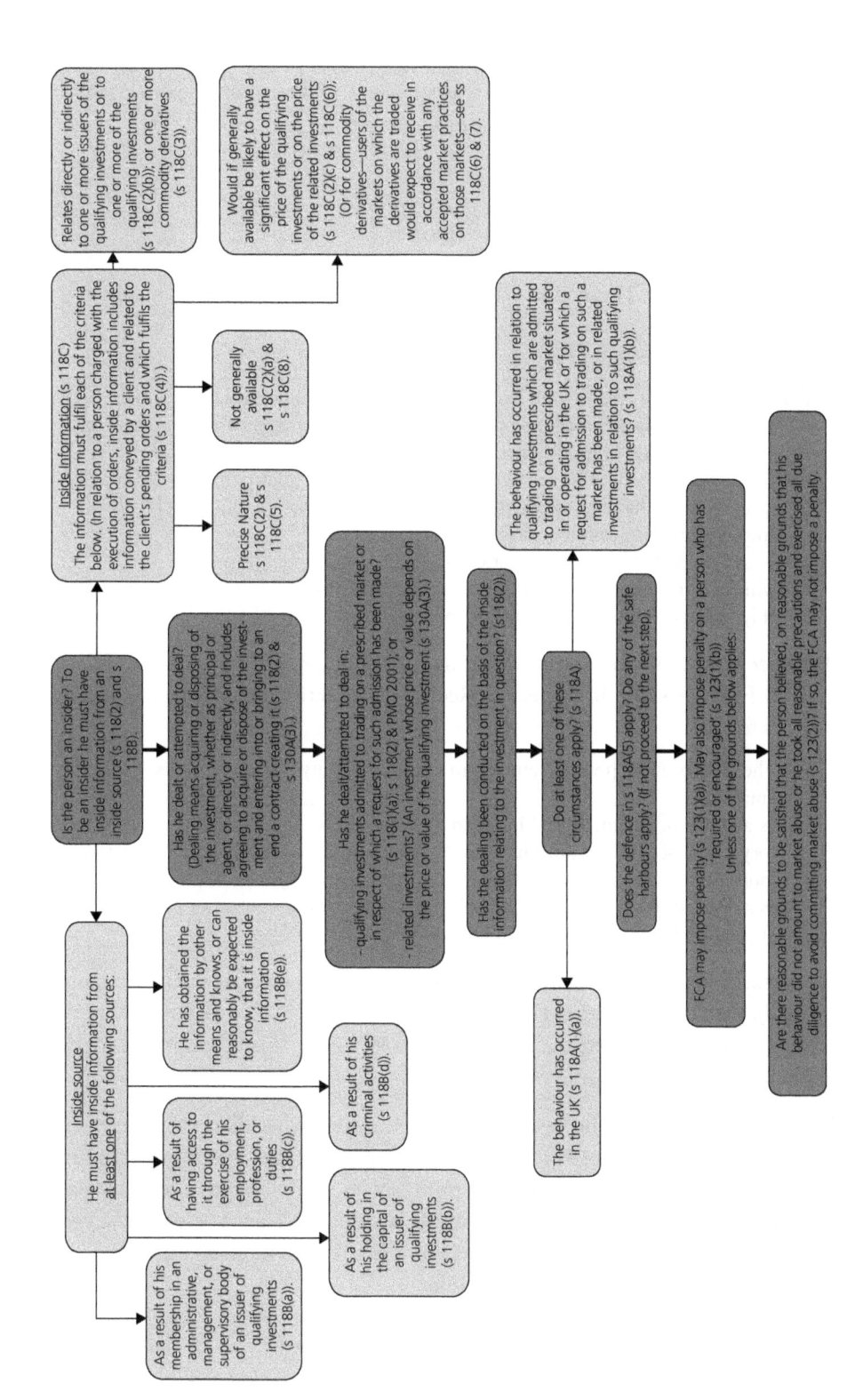

Figure 4. Flow chart for s 118(2) 'Dealing' offence

16.04 The flow chart demonstrates that the best way to analyse s 118(2) is firstly to determine whether the person in question is an insider, and thereafter go on to establish whether his behaviour falls within the other requirements.

3. Insider

16.05 An 'insider' is defined in section 118B FSMA:

> **118B—Insiders**
>
> For the purposes of this Part an insider is any person who has inside information
> (a) as a result of his membership of an administrative, management or supervisory body of an issuer of qualifying investments,
> (b) as a result of his holding in the capital of an issuer of qualifying investments,
> (c) as a result of having access to the information through the exercise of his employment, profession or duties,
> (d) as a result of his criminal activities, or
> (e) which he has obtained by other means and which he knows, or could reasonably be expected to know, is inside information.

16.06 The Recognised Auction Platform Regulations 2011 ('RAPR')[2] modify ss 118B(a) and (b) FSMA so that in respect of Recognised Auction Platforms, the section reads as follows:

> For the purposes of [market abuse] an [insider] is any person who has [inside information]:
> (a) as a result of his membership of an administrative, management or supervisory body of an [auction platform] or its operator, an auctioneer or auction monitor.
> (b) as a result of his holding in the capital of an [auction platform] or its operator, an auctioneer or auction monitor.

16.07 If a person is in possession of information in the circumstances set out in categories (a) to (d), then he is de facto deemed to be an insider and it is not necessary to prove that the person knew that the information was inside. This is confirmed by the guidance in MAR 1.2.9G.

16.08 In relation to s 118B(e), however, the position is somewhat different as *mens rea* (actual knowledge or constructive knowledge) is an integral part of the requirement. This category captures, and is presumably intended to capture, the category of secondary insider, who has received inside information from a person in categories (a) to (d) but who would otherwise, without this provision, be immune from culpability under the market abuse regime.

---

[2] FSMA (Recognised Auction Platform Regulations) 2011 SI 2011/2699.

16.09 Article 4 of the MAD,³ specifically required inclusion of this category of insider and its inclusion forestalls arguments about, for example, whether or not someone has had access to the information 'through the exercise of' his employment. This is demonstrated by the case of *John Shevlin v FSA*.⁴

16.10 The FSA imposed a financial penalty of £85,000 on Mr Shevlin for market abuse (insider dealing (s 118(2) FSMA)). Mr Shevlin was employed at the Body Shop plc ('Body Shop') as an IT technician and, as a result, he was able to gain access to the IT passwords of the Body Shop's Chairman and CEO. He used these to read their confidential emails which contained drafts of a forthcoming profits warning. On the basis of this information, he short-sold a substantial number of contracts for difference ('CFDs') prior to the announcement. He closed his position after the announcement and consequent share price fall, realising a profit of £38,472.

16.11 On the issue of whether Mr Shevlin was an insider, the FSA put its case in the alternative, asserting that either Mr Shevlin had obtained the information by having access to it through the exercise of his employment (s 118B(c)) or, alternatively, that he had obtained the information by other means, in circumstances in which he knew that the information was inside (s 118(b)(e)). This forestalled any argument as to whether the covert reading of the Chairman and CEO's emails amounted to having access to the information through the actual *exercise* of his employment.

16.12 The case is also interesting in that it was brought entirely on the basis of circumstantial evidence. The FSA accepted (as recorded in the Final Notice) that it had no direct evidence of Mr Shevlin having obtained inside information and pointed instead to a number of pieces of circumstantial evidence which painted a compelling picture. Although circumstantial evidence is a familiar concept in the criminal courts, it is clear from the careful and detailed way in which the Final Notice set out all relevant factors, that the Regulatory Decisions Committee ('RDC') of the FSA did not necessarily find this an easy concept. That said, it did feel able to conclude that in all the circumstances there was 'cogent and compelling evidence'⁵ against him. Mr Shevlin initially challenged the RDC's decision by referring the matter to the Tribunal; however, his case was subsequently struck out for failure to comply with the Tribunal's directions.⁶

---

³ Directive 2003/6/EC of 28 Jan 2003 on insider dealing and market manipulation (Market Abuse).
⁴ *John Shevlin v FSA*, Case 060, 12 June 2008 and see Final Notice 1 July 2008 (post-MAD case).
⁵ *Shevlin* Final Notice (n 4) para 11.2 (post-MAD case).
⁶ *Shevlin* (n 4).

16.13 MAR 1.2.8E provides guidance as to the factors that the FCA will take into account in determining whether or not a person could reasonably be expected to know that information in his possession is inside information. Essentially, these amount to an objective assessment based on whether a normal and reasonable person in the same position would or should have known the information was 'inside'. This assessment therefore is a question of fact and not law, which will need to be made on the basis of the available evidence and such inferences as can properly be drawn.

4. Dealing or attempting to deal

16.14 Section 130A(3) FSMA provides that 'dealing', in relation to an investment, means:

> acquiring or disposing of the investment whether as principal or agent or directly or indirectly, and includes agreeing to acquire or dispose of the investment, and entering into and bringing to an end a contract creating it.

16.15 This definition is sufficiently broadly drafted to capture trading in the broad range of qualifying investments described in the PMQI.[7] It is also broad enough to cover related investments such as CFDs and spread bets which are covered by the provision relating to the entering into and bringing to an end of a contract which creates the CFD or spread bet in question.

5. 'On the basis of'

16.16 The background to this requirement is contained in Article 2(1) of the MAD[8] which requires that:

> Member States shall prohibit any person referred to in the second subparagraph [*insiders*] who possesses inside information from using that information by acquiring or disposing of, or by trying to acquire or dispose of, for his own account or for the account of a third party, either directly or indirectly, financial instruments to which that information relates.

16.17 This concept of 'using' inside information was translated by the UK legislative draftsmen into dealing 'on the basis of' inside information (s 118(2) FSMA). This does not mean that the person engaging in the behaviour in question must have intended to commit market abuse.[9] This is confirmed by MAR 1.2.3G. This

---

[7] SI 2001/996. See Chapter 15, Section 3 Qualifying investments and prescribed markets, Qualifying investments.
[8] Dir 2003/6/EC (n 3).
[9] See MAR 1.2.3.

issue was considered by the European Court of Justice ('ECJ') in the context of Article 2(1) of MAD in the case of *Spector Photo Group NV and Chris Van Raemdonck v Commissie voor het Bank-, Financie- en Assurantiewezen (CBFA)*[10] ('*Spector* case'). Spector is a Belgian listed company, and the case concerned allegations of insider dealing in relation to a share buy-back programme operated by Spector in order to implement its staff stock options. The Brussels Court of Appeal referred a number of questions to the ECJ including a request for the ECJ to interpret the meaning of 'using inside information' contained in Article 2(1) of MAD.[11]

The referring court sought to determine whether it was sufficient for a transaction to be classed as prohibited insider dealing, if a primary insider in possession of inside information trades on the market in financial instruments to which that information relates or whether it is necessary in addition, to establish that that person has 'used' that information 'with full knowledge'. In answering this question, the ECJ set out some of the relevant background to the drafting of the MAD.[12] It was noted that the MAD sought to fill in some of the gaps identified in the Insider Dealing Directive 1989 ('IDD')[13] which sought to prohibit an insider from 'taking advantage of that information with full knowledge of the facts'. It was observed that the transposition of that provision into national law gave rise to variances in the interpretation by the Member States of the expression 'with full knowledge of the facts', which in certain national legal systems (the UK being one), was assimilated to a requirement of a mental element.[14] 16.18

Article 2(1) of the MAD[15] therefore removed this requirement on the ground that 'by nature [primary insiders] may have access to inside information on a daily basis and are aware of the confidential nature of the information that they receive'[16]. In addition, the use of the verb 'to use' in Article 2(1) of MAD demonstrated that the European Parliament had sought to remove any element of purpose or intention from the definition of insider dealing.[17] 16.19

The ECJ considered that the relationship of confidence which links the primary insider to the issuer of financial instruments to which his inside information relates, implies a specific responsibility on the insider's part. When such a person enters a market transaction, this is necessarily the result of a series of decisions which in principle, makes it possible to exclude the possibility that that person could have acted without being aware of his actions. Where such a market transaction is 16.20

---

[10] Case C-45/08 *Spector Photo Group NV and Chris Van Raemdonck v CBFA* [2010] All ER (D) 125 (Feb).
[11] Dir 2003/6/EC (n 3).
[12] Dir 2003/6/EC (n 3).
[13] Directive 89/592/EEC.
[14] *Spector* (n 10) para 33.
[15] Dir 2003/6/EC (n 3).
[16] *Spector* (n 10) para 34.
[17] *Spector* (n 10) para 34.

entered into while the author of that transaction is in possession of inside information, that information must, in principle, be deemed to have played a role in his decision-making.[18] Furthermore, given that the purpose of the MAD is to ensure the integrity of the European Community financial markets and to enhance investor confidence in those markets, the prohibition on insider dealing must be capable of effective sanction and application, achievable by basing it on a simple structure in which subjective grounds of defence are limited, not only to enable sanctions to be imposed but also to prevent infringements of that prohibition in an effective way.[19]

16.21 Therefore, once the constituent elements of insider dealing laid down in Article 2(1) of the MAD are satisfied, it is possible to assume an intention on the part of the author of that transaction. An insider who acquires or disposes of, or tries to acquire or dispose of, for his own account or for the account of a third party, either directly or indirectly, the financial instruments to which that information relates, has 'used that information' within the meaning of Article 2(1) of the MAD. The ECJ was careful not to define insider dealing as (in effect) a strict liability offence, by acknowledging that this interpretation was without prejudice to the rights of the defence (under Article 6(2) of the European Convention on Human Rights ('ECHR')) and in particular the right to be able to rebut the presumption (in appropriate cases).[20]

16.22 The effect of the *Spector* judgment can be seen in the FSA's case against David Einhorn.[21] Mr Einhorn was fined £3,638,000 for market abuse (insider dealing s 118(2) FSMA). Mr Einhorn was the owner of Greenlight Capital Inc ('Greenlight'), an investment management firm based in the US. The FSA's case was that he instructed Greenlight's traders to dispose of part of its holding in a company named Punch Taverns plc ('Punch') on the basis of inside information he received in a telephone call regarding a forthcoming new equity issuance by Punch. The FSA Final Notice stated that 'Mr Einhorn decided to sell on the basis of the inside information he received on the Punch call (albeit not solely on this basis)'.[22] Therefore, the FSA concluded:[23]

> The FSA's view is that Mr Einhorn's decision to deal was based on the inside information he received. It is sufficient that a decision to deal is materially influenced by the inside information, it need not be the sole reason for the trading.

16.23 Furthermore, in accordance with the judgment in the *Spector* case, '[i]n the view of the FSA [Mr Einhorn] has not rebutted the presumption that he dealt on the

---

[18] *Spector* (n 10) para 36.
[19] *Spector* (n 10) para 37.
[20] *Spector* (n 10) paras 37–46.
[21] *David Einhorn*, Final Notice 15 Feb 2012 (post-MAD case).
[22] *David Einhorn* (n 21) para 2.7.
[23] *David Einhorn* (n 21) para 4.19.

basis of [the inside] information'.[24] This demonstrates the potentially wide reach of the market abuse regime. Although the *Spector* case left open the possibility of this presumption being rebutted in an appropriate case, it declined to specify in what circumstances this might arise. It also placed the onus very much on the person who is the subject of the allegation. Once it has been proved that he is an insider and that he dealt or attempted to deal in the circumstances set out in s 118(1) and (2) FSMA, his behaviour is presumed to be on the basis of his inside information unless he proves otherwise.

Some assistance in this regard is provided by MAR 1.3.3E which gives some guidance as to the factors which the FCA considers might indicate that a person's behaviour is *not* 'on the basis of' inside information. These include whether the person made the decision to deal prior to being in possession of inside information and whether the person is dealing in order to satisfy a pre-existing legal or regulatory obligation. If it is the person's case that there were other (pre-existing) reasons for his dealing, then he will of course need to provide evidence to support this assertion. 16.24

MAR 1.3.3E also addresses the issue of organisations that deal in stocks in circumstances where another part of the same organisation has inside information. This provision states that, provided none of the individuals in possession of the inside information have any involvement in, influence on, or contact with, the decision to deal or those who deal, then it is likely that this dealing will not be regarded as being on the basis of inside information. This would of course cover the position of an Investment Bank whose Corporate Broking Department acts for a company in relation (for example) to a takeover, when at the same time, another part of the organisation deals in the same company's shares. Plainly, it will be necessary to demonstrate by way of evidence that there was no connection between these events. 16.25

MAR 1.3.5E deals specifically with 'Chinese Walls' and states that, provided the inside information is held behind an effective Chinese Wall, then this will be taken to indicate that dealing by persons on the other side of the Chinese Wall is not on the basis of inside information. A Chinese Wall is an information barrier implemented within a firm to separate and isolate persons who make investment decisions from persons who are privy to inside or confidential material information which may influence those decisions. Its purpose is to avoid conflicts of interest.[25] All authorised firms are required to develop, implement, and enforce reasonable Chinese Wall policies and procedures.[26] When a firm manages a conflict of interest 16.26

---

[24] *David Einhorn* (n 21) para 6.7.
[25] FCA's Principles for Business, Principle 8.
[26] FCA Handbook of Rules and Guidance—Conduct of Business Sourcebook ('COBS') 2.4.1G–2.4.7G; Senior Management Arrangements, Systems and Controls ('SYSC') 10.2.2R(1) & 10.2.2R(4).

using arrangements which take the form of a Chinese Wall, individuals on the 'other side of the wall' will not be regarded as being in possession of knowledge denied to them as a result of the Chinese wall.

16.27 Many firms rely on the provisions contained in MAR 1.3.3E and 1.3.5E in relation to the market abuse regime. However, these provisions were drafted prior to the judgment in the *Spector* case.[27] In the light of that judgment, the FSA published its views on whether amendments to the UK's market abuse regime were required.[28] The FSA's view was that FSMA itself did not require amendment but one evidential provision in MAR should be deleted. This was MAR 1.3.4E, which addressed the (pre-Spector) mental element of the insider dealing offence, indicating that for an offence to be committed inside information must be 'the reason for, or a material influence' on, the decision to deal. This provision was duly deleted from MAR on 6 March 2011; however, the FSA deliberately retained the remaining provisions of MAR which concern 'factors to be taken into account: "on the basis of"' (MAR 1.3.3E and 1.3.5E). This approach provides some comfort for firms and individuals that the factors set out in these provisions, if proved, would provide evidence with which to rebut the Spector presumption.

6. Inside information

16.28 Inside information is defined in s 118C FSMA. The definition differs depending on whether or not the qualifying investments in question are commodity derivatives. Where the qualifying investments are not commodity derivatives, s 118C(2) provides:

> (2) In relation to qualifying investments, or related investments, which are not commodity derivatives, inside information is information of a precise nature which
> (a) is not generally available,
> (b) relates, directly or indirectly, to one or more issuers of the qualifying investments or to one or more of the qualifying investments, and
> (c) would, if generally available, be likely to have a significant effect on the price of the qualifying investments or on the price of related investments.

16.29 This will be the section that is most commonly used in a market abuse (insider dealing) case. Section 118(C)(2) can be broken down into distinct elements:

1. Information of a precise nature
2. Which is not generally available

---

[27] *Spector* (n 10).
[28] Quarterly Consultation Paper of Oct 2010 (CP10/22).

3. Which relates directly or indirectly to one or more issuers of the qualifying investments or to one or more of the qualifying investments; and
4. Which would, if generally available, be likely to have a significant effect on the price of the qualifying investments or on the price of related investments.

Information of a precise nature

This is defined in s 118C(5) FSMA. Information is precise if it: 16.30

(a) indicates circumstances that exist or may reasonably be expected to come into existence or an event that has occurred or may reasonably be expected to occur, and
(b) is specific enough to enable a conclusion to be drawn as to the possible effect of those circumstances or that event on the price of qualifying investments or related investments.

This explanatory provision derives almost verbatim from the MAD Implementing Directive (Article 1(1))[29] ('Implementing Directive'). The Commission, (having consulted with the Committee of European Securities Regulators ('CESR'), decided that: 16.31

> Legal certainty for market participants should be enhanced through a closer definition of two of the elements essential to the definition of inside information, namely the precise nature of that information and the significance of its potential effect on the prices of financial instruments or related derivative financial instruments.[30]

The ECJ considered the application of Article 1(1) of the Implementing Directive in the case of *Markus Geltl v Daimler AG*[31] ('*Geltl* case'). This was a referral from the German Federal Court of Justice ('Federal Court'). The Federal Court asked whether, in the case of a protracted process which was intended, over the course of a number of intermediate steps, to bring about a particular circumstance or to generate a particular event, account should be taken only of whether that future circumstance or event is to be regarded as precise information, or whether the intermediate steps which already exist, or have already occurred, and which are connected with bringing about the future circumstance or event, also constitute precise information. 16.32

The ECJ decided that an interpretation of the terms 'set of circumstances' and 'event' which disregards the intermediate steps in a protracted process would risk undermining the objective of the MAD[32] which was to protect the integrity of 16.33

---

[29] 2003/124/EC, 22 Dec 2003, Implementing Directive 2003/6/EC of the European Parliament and of the Council as regards the definition and public disclosure of inside information and the definition of market manipulation.
[30] 2003/124/EC (n 29) Article 3 of the Preamble.
[31] C-19/11 *Markus Geltl v Daimler AG*, Judgment of the European Court (Second Chamber) of 28 June 2012.
[32] Dir 2003/6/EC (n 3).

Section 118(2) FSMA; Behaviour

the EU financial markets and to enhance investor confidence in those markets. The provisions in Article 1(1) of the Implementing Directive[33] must therefore be interpreted as meaning that, in the case of a protracted process intended to bring about a particular circumstance or to generate a particular event, not only may that future circumstance or future event be regarded as precise information within the meaning of those provisions, but also the intermediate steps of that process which are connected with bringing about the future circumstance or event in question.

16.34 The second question addressed by the ECJ was whether the expression, 'may reasonably be expected', required that the probability be assessed as predominant or high, or whether the degree of probability depended on the extent of the effects on the issuer such that, where prices are highly likely to be affected, it is sufficient if the occurrence of the future circumstance or event is uncertain but not improbable.

16.35 The ECJ decided the term 'may reasonably be expected', refers to future circumstances or events from which it appears, on the basis of an overall assessment of the factors existing at the relevant time, that there is a realistic prospect that they will come into existence or occur. This issue would need to be decided on a case-by-case basis. However, given that the criteria set out in Article 1(1) of the Implementing Directive are minimum conditions which must each be satisfied in order for information to be held to be 'inside' information within the meaning of Article 1(1) of the MAD, the question of whether the required probability of the occurrence of a set of circumstances or an event may vary depending on the magnitude of their effect on the prices of the financial instruments concerned, must be answered in the negative. The effect of this can be illustrated by the following example:

> Mr A receives information that Company X is in takeover discussions with Company Y. He buys shares in Company X based on that information. Later, he receives further information that the takeover discussions are proceeding well and that the takeover is likely to be at a significant premium to Company X's then share price. Mr A therefore buys more shares in Company X. Later, he receives further information that the takeover is agreed and will be announced imminently. He therefore buys more shares in Company X prior to that announcement.
>
> Applying the ratio in the *Geltl* Case, at each stage at which Mr A dealt, the information he had which formed the basis for his dealing is capable of being precise information provided it meets the test set out in s 118C(5) FSMA and will be inside information provided the other requirements contained in s 118C(2) are satisfied. Furthermore, in assessing whether each piece of information refers to an event that 'may reasonably be expected' to come into existence or occur, it is necessary to make an overall assessment of the factors existing at the relevant time and to decide whether, based on those factors, there is a realistic prospect that the circumstance or event will exist or occur.
>
> Applying this to the first piece of information Mr A receives, whether the fact that Company X is in takeover discussions with Company Y refers to an event that 'may

---

[33] 2003/124/EC (n 29).

> reasonably be expected' to occur will probably depend on the stage the discussions have reached, Company X's attitude to the approach, whether Company Y at that stage is offering a deal which would be likely to be seen as attractive, etc. This demonstrates that the assessment must be made on the basis of the surrounding facts and circumstances at the relevant time.

16.36 The second requirement (s 118C(5)(b) FSMA) was considered by the Upper Tribunal in the case of *David Massey v FSA*.[34] The Tribunal admitted that it did not find the statutory wording of that section easy to understand:[35]

> The phrase 'specific enough to enable a conclusion to be drawn' seems to introduce a strong note of definiteness, which is then effectively removed, or at least diluted, by the phrase 'as to the possible effect ... on the price'. We note that there is no requirement for a conclusion as to the actual or probable effect on the price, but only as to the possible effect. We also note that the statutory words contain no explicit guidance on how precise the conclusion needs to be. Is it enough that there be a conclusion merely that the event, when it becomes known, may alter the price? A risk of alteration is a 'possible effect', even if it is not known whether the occurrence of an alteration is more probable than not, or whether, if it occurs, it is more likely to be an increase or a decrease.

16.37 The Tribunal expressed doubts as to whether it would be right to read this element so literally, as it felt that to do so would arguably render the phrase 'specific enough to enable a conclusion to be drawn' almost empty of effect. It therefore assumed in Mr Massey's favour that the conclusion as to a possible effect on price must relate to an effect in a particular direction.[36] The Tribunal, however, expressly stated that it was not deciding the point, and therefore in an appropriate case, it must be open to argument whether 'possible effect' must mean a movement in a particular direction. If this requirement is set in the context of the other requirements for inside information (s 118C(2) FSMA) the approach becomes simpler. In addition to information being 'of a precise nature' it must also be 'likely to have a significant effect on the price of the qualifying or related investments'. If the information fulfils the latter criteria, then it must follow that the 'possible effect on the price' must relate to the likely significant effect—whether that be an upward or downward movement.

Not generally available

16.38 Section 118C(8) FSMA provides that:

> Information which can be obtained by research or analysis conducted by, or on behalf of, users of a market is to be regarded, for the purposes of this Part, as being generally available to them.

---

[34] *David Massey v FSA*, Upper Tribunal, 2 Feb 2011, paras 37–9 (post-MAD case).
[35] *David Massey* (n 34) para 38.
[36] *David Massey* (n 34) para 39.

16.39 Beyond this, and unlike Part V of the CJA,[37] FSMA does not attempt to further define the meaning of this term. Instead, MAR 1.2.12E[38] provides a (non exhaustive) list of factors to be taken into account in determining whether or not information is generally available. Whether, and to what extent, these factors apply will need to be decided on the facts of any given case. The factors include whether the information:

- Has been published via a Regulatory Information Service ('RIS'): This of course includes the London Stock Exchange's Regulatory News Service and the equivalents in relation to other regulated markets.
- Is contained in records which are open to inspection by the public: This would of course include information at Companies House or the Patents Registry, or Public Records held at the National Archives. Unlike the equivalent provision in the CJA (s 58(2)(b)), there is no requirement that the records be open to inspection by the public 'by virtue of any enactment'. This provision in MAR is therefore potentially wider in scope than the CJA and may include records which are open to inspection by the public as a result of convention or common practice, although it is difficult to envisage what these might be in this context.
- Is available on the internet, published in another form, or derived from information which has been made public: This provision would cover, for example, internet information sites such as ADVFN and Interactive Investor and publication by e-book or webinar. It would also cover information derived by research analysts from information that has been made public. Assuming that the sources from which the analyst has derived his opinion are publicly available, then the content of his report ought to fall within this provision and will not therefore be deemed to be inside information.
- Can be obtained by observation: This provision is perhaps of less importance given the speed at which information is picked up by the media and disseminated by reporting, blogging, tweeting, and the like.
- Can be obtained by analysing or developing other information which is generally available: This provision would also cover the position of the Research Analyst as described above.

16.40 MAR 1.2.13E provides that, in relation to the above factors, it is not relevant that the information is only generally available outside the UK. This means that the key question is whether the information in question is 'generally available' taking account of the above criteria, regardless of the geographical location of this availability. MAR 1.2.13E also provides that it is not relevant that analysis of the information would require above average financial resources, expertise, or competence.

---

[37] See Chapter 6, Sections 6 and 7.
[38] MAR 1.2.14G provides an example of a situation in which information would be considered to be generally available.

Market rumours

16.41 In *Arif Mohammed v FSA*[39] (a pre-MAD case), the Tribunal considered the issue of market rumour and whether rumour can amount to inside information. Mr Mohammed was an audit manager with the accountancy firm PriceWaterhouseCoopers ('PwC'). He purchased shares in a company called Delta plc ('Delta') at a time when he knew, as a result of confidential information obtained in the course of his employment with PwC, that Delta imminently intended to sell its electrical division.

16.42 Mr Mohammed contended that rumours of the disposal of the electrical division were already widespread when he purchased the shares. He pointed to minutes of a Board Meeting of Delta's electrical division which recorded concern about the level of rumours surrounding the sale. He also pointed to rumours in messages posted on the Interactive Investor bulletin board and comments by a broker on the Factiva information service which hinted that Delta's electrical division might be for sale.

16.43 The Tribunal concluded that there was a clear distinction to be drawn between market rumour and 'information' and that:

> The term 'information' in this context requires something which is precise in nature.[40]

16.44 In *Philippe Jabre and GLG Capital Partners LP*[41] the FSA agreed with the Tribunal's decision in *Arif Mohammed* and decided that 'the fact that there may have been "rumours that were extensive and well known" is of no relevance'.[42]

16.45 The issue of market rumour was also considered in the case of *Andre Scerri*.[43] Mr Scerri was fined £66,062.50 for market abuse (insider dealing (s 118(2) FSMA)). The case concerned the selling, by Mr Scerri (who was a private investor), of stock in an Alternative Investment Market ('AIM') listed oil and gas exploration company ('Amerisur') on the basis of inside information about a forthcoming discounted placing. This trading generated a profit (or loss avoided) of £46,062.50. The FSA's case was that the inside information was provided to Mr Scerri by an insider via a text message and a short telephone call. Mr Scerri asserted, however, that these communications had merely passed on a market rumour about the placing.

---

[39] *Arif Mohammed v FSA*, FSMT Case 012, 29 Mar 2005 (pre-MAD case).
[40] *Arif Mohammed v FSA* (n 39) para 67.
[41] *Philippe Jabre*, Final Notice, 1 Aug 2006 (pre-MAD case).
[42] *Philippe Jabre and GLG Partners LP*, FSA Final Notice, 1 Aug 2006, para 3.59 (pre-MAD case).
[43] *Andre Jean Scerri*, Upper Tribunal Case 0016, 21 May 2010; see also Final Notice 29 Oct 2010 (post-MAD case).

Section 118(2) FSMA; Behaviour

The Tribunal disbelieved this explanation in light of the other evidence, in particular the nature and timeliness of his trading.

Relates directly or indirectly to an issuer of qualifying investments, or to one or more of the qualifying investments

16.46 This issue will be a question of fact in each case. Note that the information must relate to either one or more of the issuers of the qualifying investments that have been traded, or must relate to the qualifying investments themselves. It is not necessary that the information should relate to both. However, in most cases, it is likely that the information will in fact relate to both the issuer and the investments—for example, information about a forthcoming takeover is information about the issuer (the company) but it is also information about the likely upward movement of the share price (the qualifying investment).[44]

Likely to have a significant effect on the price of the qualifying or related investments

16.47 This is the almost exact mirror of the requirement in the CJA.[45] However, unlike the CJA, FSMA does provide some explanation as to what this provision means. Section 118C(6) states:

> Information would be likely to have a significant effect on price if and only if it is information of a kind which a reasonable investor would be likely to use as part of the basis of his investment decisions.

16.48 Does this mean that, provided the information is of a kind which a reasonable investor would be likely to use, then that is sufficient, regardless of whether the information would (in fact) be likely to have a significant effect on price? If so, then this would appear to cast the ambit of the market abuse regime far wider than it was ever envisaged by the MAD.[46]

16.49 The Tribunal came close to this view in *David Massey v FSA*.[47] David Massey was a market professional who short-sold a large number of shares in a small, AIM listed company called Eicom plc ('Eicom'), whilst in possession of information that Eicom was about to undertake a heavily discounted placing (in which Mr Massey subsequently participated in order to close his short position). The FSA's case was that the information Mr Massey had about the forthcoming placing was inside information. Mr Massey's case was that the fact that Eicom needed to raise capital was generally available information. In addition, he contended that as previous

---

[44] See Chapter 6, Section 4 Relating to particular securities or issuers (s 56(1)(a) CJA) for a discussion of this element in relation to the criminal offence.
[45] See Chapter 6, Section 8 Likely to have a significant effect on price (s 56(1)(d) CJA)
[46] Dir 2003/6/EC (n 3).
[47] *David Massey* (n 34).

placings by Eicom had not moved its share price significantly, it followed that the information he had when he traded, would not have been likely to have had a significant effect on Eicom's share price.

The Tribunal initially approached the matter by considering the surrounding circumstances of this placing as against previous placings conducted by Eicom, and concluded on the facts that there was 'a substantial risk that it [Eicom's share price] would fall when the discounted issue became known'.[48] However, later in its decision,[49] the Tribunal approached the same issue rather differently, although arriving at the same result: 16.50

> We consider next whether the information was likely to have a significant effect on the price of the shares. Mr Massey's case is that it was not likely to have such an effect. We would have considerable sympathy with his view if the phrase 'likely to have a significant effect on the price' had been used in the Act in its ordinary sense. But we have to apply the specially extended meaning assigned to this expression by s 118C(6). Whether or not the information was (in the ordinary sense) likely to have a significant effect on the price, we consider it is clear that it was information 'of a kind which a reasonable investor would be likely to use as part of the basis of his investment decisions'. If a hypothetical reasonable investor in Mr Burge's [the person to whom Mr Massey short sold Eicom shares] position had known of Eicom's willingness and offer to issue three million shares at 3.5p, he would have been likely to use that information as part of the basis of his decisions about purchasing Eicom shares.
>
> For the above reasons we conclude that Mr Massey dealt with Allianz on the basis of 'inside information' as defined in s118C.

This paragraph of the decision suggests that the Tribunal considered that the 'significant price effect' requirement was in effect 'trumped' by the reasonable investor test, the latter thereby rendering the former somewhat otiose. For a number of reasons, this approach appears to be inconsistent with the European law. 16.51

The origin of the 'reasonable investor' test is to be found in the MAD's Implementing Directive.[50] The Preamble to this Directive states (following consultation with CESR) (so far as is relevant): 16.52

Whereas:

(1) Reasonable investors base their investment decisions on information already available to them, that is to say, on *ex ante* available information. Therefore, the question whether, in making an investment decision, a reasonable investor would be likely to take into account a particular piece of information should be appraised on the basis of the *ex ante* available information. Such an assessment has to take into consideration the anticipated impact of the

---

[48] *David Massey* (n 34) para 32.
[49] *David Massey* (n 34) paras 41 and 42.
[50] 2003/124/EC (n 29).

information in light of the totality of the related issuer's activity, the reliability of the source of information and any other market variables likely to affect the related financial instrument or derivative financial instrument related thereto in the given circumstances.

16.53 Therefore, Article 1(2) of the Implementing Directive stated that for the purposes of defining 'inside information' in MAD:

'information which, if it were made public, would be likely to have a significant effect on the prices of financial instruments or related derivative financial instruments' shall mean information a reasonable investor would be likely to use as part of the basis of his investment decisions.

16.54 Therefore the intention behind the reasonable investor test was that it should encapsulate the concept of 'significant price effect'. Information which a reasonable investor would take into account as part of the basis of his investment decisions is, by its very nature, information which would be likely to have a significant effect on the price of the investments in question. The reason is that a reasonable investor would only be likely to make investment decisions based on information which was likely to have such an effect. Therefore, if the reasonable investor test is satisfied, the element of 'likely to have a significant effect on price' in the definition of 'inside information' will also be satisfied.

16.55 Finally, Article 17(2) of the MAD[51] provides that implementing measures may be adopted on the basis of CESR guidance provided that any such measures do not modify the essential provisions of the MAD. This appears to complete the circle and demonstrates that the 'significant price effect' test is an integral and inalienable requirement, and to the extent that the Massey decision suggests otherwise, then it is open to question as to whether that decision should be used as a suitable template for future cases.

16.56 It is also worth noting that the FSA (and now the FCA) itself considers that the significant price effect is defined by the reasonable investor test. This is reflected in the wording of the FSA Final Notices in market abuse cases, which will invariably record that:[52]

the information [in question] was likely to have a significant effect on the price of [X Company's] shares as it was information which a reasonable investor would be likely to use as part of the basis of his investment decisions.

16.57 This wording reflects the fact that, in most cases, if information is of a type which a reasonable investor would be likely to use as part of the basis of his investment decisions, in all likelihood it will also be information that would be likely to have a significant effect on price. This is because, firstly, it can be assumed that all reasonable investors would be likely to act in the same way, on the basis of

---

[51] Dir 2003/6/EC (n 3).
[52] See eg *David Einhorn* (n 21) paras 4.6(iv) and 4.18.

the same information, and therefore regard can be had to the cumulative effect of the use of the information; and, secondly, a reasonable investor would only make investment decisions where the information concerned would be likely to have a significant (as opposed to *de minimis*) effect on the price of the qualifying investments.

16.58 Where this observation may fall down, however, is in the case of information regarding forthcoming placings, particularly as regards smaller AIM listed companies that regularly use placings as a means of raising finance (as in the *Massey* case). Given that this is an expected market practice, it cannot necessarily be assumed that the effect of a placing on the company's share price would necessarily be likely to be significant. This was in fact the argument put to the Tribunal by Mr Massey. However, it is equally the case that knowledge of a forthcoming placing may well be information that a reasonable investor would want to use as part of the basis for his investment decisions. Therefore, in such a case, particular attention will need to be paid to whether on the facts of that case and in all the circumstances, it is possible to assert to the requisite standard, that the information in question would be likely to have a significant effect on price.

16.59 The issue of 'significant price effect' was also addressed in the *Spector* case,[53] in which the ECJ ruled that the capacity to have a significant effect on price must be assessed a priori in light of the content of the information at issue and the context in which it occurs. It is thus not necessary, in order to determine whether information is inside information, to examine whether its disclosure actually had a significant effect on the price of the financial instruments to which it relates.

16.60 It follows from the foregoing, that an examination of whether or not its disclosure actually had a significant effect on the price of the financial instruments to which it relates, should be approached with caution (although in many cases the actual effect will be one of the factors a court or Tribunal will consider).

Inside information with respect to commodity derivatives

16.61 In the case of commodity derivatives, inside information is defined a little differently in s 118C(3) FSMA:[54]

> In relation to qualifying investments or related investments which are commodity derivatives, inside information is information of a precise nature which
> (a) is not generally available,
> (b) relates, directly or indirectly, to one or more such derivatives, and
> (c) users of markets on which the derivatives are traded would expect to receive in accordance with any accepted market practices on those markets.

---

[53] *Spector* (n 10).
[54] MAR 1.3.21G and MAR 1.3.23G provide examples of behaviour which in the FSA's opinion would fall within s 118(2) relating to commodity derivatives.

Section 118(2) FSMA; Behaviour

16.62 'Accepted market practices' is defined in s 130A(3) FSMA as:

> practices that are reasonably expected in the financial market or markets in question and are accepted by the [FCA] or, in the case of a market situated in another EEA State, the competent authority of that EEA State within the meaning of [MAD].

16.63 The above provisions recognise that there are differences in the nature of information that is important to commodity derivatives from that which is important to other markets. Therefore inside information is defined by reference to information that the market participants in the market in question would expect to receive.[55] Some clarification is provided by s 118C(7) FSMA which states that:

> For the purposes of subsection (3)(c), users of markets on which investments in commodity derivatives are traded are to be treated as expecting to receive information ... which is
> (i) routinely made available to the users of those markets, or
> (ii) required to be disclosed in accordance with any statutory provision, market rules, or contracts or customs on the relevant underlying commodity market or commodity derivatives market.

Inside information with respect to persons charged with the execution of orders

16.64 Section 118C(4) FSMA provides:[56]

> In relation to a person charged with the execution of orders concerning any qualifying investments or related investments, inside information includes information conveyed by a client and related to the client's pending orders which—
> (a) is of a precise nature,
> (b) is not generally available,
> (c) relates, directly or indirectly, to one or more issuers of qualifying investments or to one or more qualifying investments, and
> (d) would, if generally available, be likely to have a significant effect on the price of those qualifying investments or the price of related investments.

16.65 MAR 1.2.16E describes what the FCA considers is meant by the term 'pending order'. Fundamental is that the person in receipt of a pending order must have taken on a legal or regulatory obligation relating to the manner or timing of the execution of the transaction for which the order has been placed. This

---

[55] MAR 1.2.17G.
[56] For Registered Auction Platforms s 118C(4) as modified by the RAP Regulations reads: 'In relation to a person charged with the execution of bids ... [*inside information*] includes information conveyed by a client and related to the client's pending bids ...'. MAR 1.3.22G provides an example of conduct which, in the FSA's opinion, would fall within this provision.

would include, for example, a best and/or timely execution duty under the FCA's rules.[57]

7. Section 118(2) FSMA behaviour—safe harbours

Prior decisions to deal and pre-existing trading strategies

Recital (30) in the MAD preamble states: 16.66

> Since the acquisition or disposal of financial instruments necessarily involves a prior decision to acquire or dispose taken by the person who undertakes one or other of these operations, the carrying out of this acquisition or disposal should not be deemed in itself to constitute the use of inside information.

MAR 1.3.6C provides a 'safe harbour' which gives effect to this by providing that the carrying out of a person's own intention to deal is not of itself market abuse. Whether or not a person had made a prior decision to deal, or had a pre-existing trading strategy, will be a question of fact to be determined on the facts and circumstances of each case as the following cases demonstrate. 16.67

James Parker v FSA[58]

This was a case brought under the pre-MAD market abuse provisions. Mr Parker was a chartered accountant who was at the relevant time employed by Pace Micro Technology plc ('Pace') as its credit risk and treasury manager. He learned on 27 February 2002 that a possible takeover of Pace by a much larger competitor had been abandoned and that Pace, for other reasons, was very likely to issue a profit warning. Between then and the publication of the profits warning on 5 March 2002, he sold holdings of shares in his and his wife's names, adjusted spread bets he had previously placed and placed new spread bets. The FSA's case was that he had undertaken this trading on the basis of the inside information he had regarding the imminent profits warning. 16.68

Mr Parker claimed that he was carrying out a pre-conceived trading strategy of hedging shares that he and his wife owned and share options which had been granted to him and that the transactions he conducted after 27 February 2002 did not reveal any change in his strategy. He claimed therefore that he had a 'safe harbour' under the Code of Market Conduct ('COMC') which preceded the current version (the MAR). The Tribunal concluded that the evidence demonstrated that his explanation regarding a pre-determined trading strategy was in reality an attempt to provide *ex post facto* justification, in order to mask the real reason for his 16.69

---

[57] MAR 1.3.22G provides an example of inside information in the context of pending client orders.
[58] *James Parker v FSA*, FSMT Case 037, 2006 (pre-MAD case).

trading.[59] The Tribunal therefore concluded that Mr Parker did not fall within the safe harbour.

Philippe Jabre and GLG Capital Partners LP

16.70 In *Philippe Jabre and GLG Capital Partners LP*,[60] Mr Jabre contended that the short sales he executed in SMFG on behalf of the GLG Market Neutral Fund (and which were the subject of the Market Abuse allegation) were consistent with a pre-existing trading pattern or strategy and were not therefore based on relevant information he had acquired. This issue was the subject of much argument at the RDC stage and experts' reports were submitted by both the FSA and Mr Jabre. The RDC found that the information Mr Jabre received on 11 February was a material influence on his decision to deal and therefore his dealing was 'on the basis of' this information. It also considered that:

> in the absence of any definite orders to execute sales or trades at pre-determined market price levels, [the FSA did not consider] that the post facto assertion of an intention to sell or trade at a particular price level is in these circumstances sufficient evidence of a 'pre-existing trading pattern' to justify the short-selling which occurred in this case between Mr Jabre's wall-crossing by GSI and the public announcement of the new issue of stock by SMFG of whose intentions he had been given confidential and privileged advance information.[61]

Market makers and professional dealers

16.71 Recital 18 of the MAD Preamble provides:

> the mere fact that market-makers, bodies authorised to act as counter-parties, or persons authorised to execute orders on behalf of third parties with inside information confine themselves, in the first two cases, to pursuing their legitimate business of buying or selling financial instruments or, in the last case, to carrying out an order dutifully, should not in itself be deemed to constitute use of such inside information.

16.72 Therefore, MAR 1.3.7C provides a safe harbour for market makers and professional dealers for 'own account' dealing provided that they are pursuing their legitimate business of such dealing. This includes underwriting an issue. MAR 1.3.8G states that the above applies even if the person concerned in fact possesses trading information which is inside information. Trading information is information that investments have been or are to be bought or sold (or that this is the subject of consideration or negotiation) and includes information that investments have not been or are not to be bought or sold. It also includes information regarding the quantity, price, or price range, or the identity of the persons involved.[62] In essence,

---

[59] *James Parker* (n 58).
[60] *Philippe Jabre* (n 41).
[61] *Philippe Jabre* (n 41) para 3.77.
[62] FCA Glossary definition.

it is information which relates directly to the trading itself and not to the investment itself or the issuer of the investment.

16.73 The purpose of this safe harbour is to protect market makers and professional dealers who have knowledge of their client's orders and trading activity, and who take this information into account when engaging in market making activities or hedging their own exposure. There is, however, an obvious link—and therefore a narrow dividing line—between this safe harbour, on the one hand, and abusive behaviour such as front running, on the other.

16.74 In recognition of this, MAR 1.3.10E sets out a number of factors that should be taken into account as indicators that a person's behaviour is in pursuit of legitimate business. These include trading in order to hedge a risk, trading on the basis of inside information regarding a client's executed transaction which is not (or not yet) required to be published and trading which is connected to a client's transaction, where the trading has no impact on the price or where the client has been informed and has not objected to the trading taking place.

16.75 MAR 1.3.10E provides that the extent to which the person's behaviour was reasonable by the proper standards of conduct of the market concerned, should be taken into account. This will require an assessment of any relevant regulatory or legal obligations and whether the transaction is executed in a way that takes into account the need for the market as a whole to operate fairly and efficiently.

16.76 MAR also provides two indicators that behaviour is not in pursuit of legitimate business interests. The first indicator is MAR 1.3.9E—where the behaviour has occurred in relation to inside information that is not limited to trading information (except in relation to an agreement for the underwriting of an issue). The second is to be found in MAR 1.3.11E—where a person has acted in contravention of a relevant legal, regulatory or exchange obligation.

Execution of client orders

16.77 MAR 1.3.12C provides that the dutiful carrying out of, or arranging for the dutiful carrying out of, an order on behalf of another (including as portfolio manager), will not in itself amount to market abuse by the person carrying out the order. This applies equally to an order relating to a bid on a Registered Auction Platform.

16.78 The safe harbour in respect of the 'dutiful carrying out' of client orders[63] also derives from Recital 18 of the MAD. MAR 1.3.13G states that the safe harbour applies whether or not the person carrying out the order, or the person for whom he is acting, in fact possesses inside information. Furthermore, a person who carries out an order on behalf of another will not be considered to have any inside information held by that other person.

---

[63] MAR 1.3.12C.

16.79 Whether or not the execution is 'dutiful' is therefore key. MAR 1.3.15E lists a number of factors that should be taken into account in determining this. These include whether the person concerned has complied with the FCA's relevant Conduct of Business Rules or their equivalent in other jurisdictions, whether the person has agreed with his client that he will act in a particular way when carrying out his order, and whether the person's behaviour was with a view to facilitating or ensuring the effective carrying out of the client's order.

16.80 The other factors to consider are the extent to which the person's behaviour was reasonable by the proper standards of conduct of the market concerned and, if relevant, proportionate to the risk undertaken by him. Alternatively, whether, if the trading is connected with a client transaction, it either has no impact on the price, or has been adequately disclosed to the client and he has not objected.

16.81 Lastly, MAR 1.3.14E provides that if the inside information is not limited to trading information, then this may be taken as an indication that the behaviour is not 'dutiful carrying out'.

Takeover and merger activity

16.82 Recital 29 of the MAD[64] states:

> Having access to inside information relating to another company and using it in the context of a public takeover bid for the purpose of gaining control of that company or proposing a merger with that company should not in itself be deemed to constitute insider dealing.

16.83 MAR 1.3.17C gives effect to this by providing that behaviour in the context of a public takeover or merger bid, which is based on inside information relating to another company, but is carried out for the purpose of gaining control of, or proposing a merger with that company, does not of itself amount to Market Abuse.

16.84 MAR 1.3.19E provides indicators that the behaviour falls within this safe harbour. These are whether the transactions concerned are in the target company's shares; or whether the transactions concerned are for the sole purpose of gaining that control or effecting that merger. What this means is that a person is permitted to 'build a stake' with a view to achieving a takeover or merger, provided that that is the purpose behind the trading. So, for example, a Director of Company X who gives orders to acquire shares in Company Y with a view to achieving a takeover of Company Y, would fall within this safe harbour. If, however, in addition to this, he separately placed a spread bet or CFD trade referenced to the price of Company Y's shares, with a view to profiting from the increase in the price of Company Y's shares once the takeover is announced, then this would fall outside the safe harbour.

---

[64] Dir 2003/6/EC (n 3).

17

SECTION 118(3) FSMA; BEHAVIOUR—IMPROPER DISCLOSURE

1. Introduction	17.01	Disclosure in compliance with rules and regulatory obligations	17.11
2. Section 118(3) FSMA behaviour	17.02	Disclosure of seller's managerial responsibilities to a potential buyer	17.12
3. Section 118(3) FSMA behaviour—safe harbours	17.10		
Disclosure to certain public bodies	17.10		

1. Introduction

This Chapter deals with Improper Disclosure of inside information under s 118(3) FSMA and the available safe harbours with respect to this behaviour. **17.01**

2. Section 118(3) FSMA behaviour

Section 118(3) sets out the second type of behaviour: **17.02**

> The second is where an insider discloses inside information to another person otherwise than in the proper course of the exercise of his employment, profession or duties.

The elements of this offence are set out in Figure 5. **17.03**

This is the market abuse equivalent of the s 52(2)(b) CJA offence.[1] As with that offence, the key question is whether the disclosure was made improperly. MAR 1.4.2E provides descriptions of behaviour that the FCA considers would amount to improper disclosure.[2] In essence, these are disclosures which are in a social context and selective briefings of analysts. **17.04**

---

[1] See Chapter 5, Sections 3 and 5.
[2] MAR 1.4.2E describes behaviour which in the FCA's opinion amounts to this behaviour. MAR1.4.6G provides scenarios which in the FCA's opinion amounts to improper disclosure.

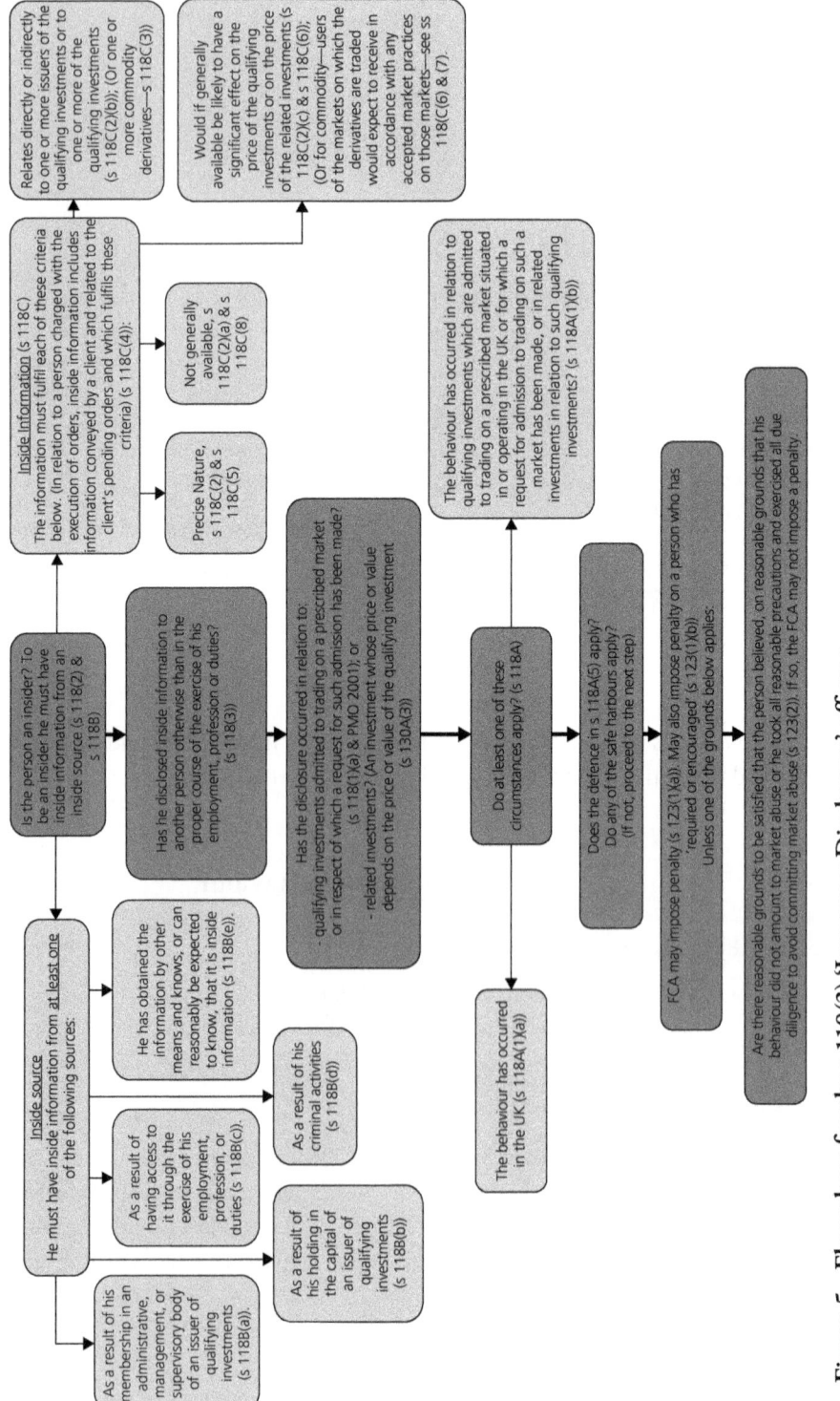

Figure 5. Flow chart for the s 118(3) 'Improper Disclosure' offence

17.05 MAR 1.4.5E lists the factors to be taken into consideration as indications that the disclosure in question was made in the proper course of the exercise of a person's employment, profession or duties. These include such factors as whether the disclosure is permitted by the rules of the market in question, the FCA or the Takeover Code, whether the disclosure imposes confidentiality requirements on the person to whom the disclosure is made, and whether the disclosure is reasonable and to enable the proper performance of functions in relation to a takeover bid, underwriting an issue or a legal obligation.

17.06 A further factor described in MAR 1.4.5E is whether the information disclosed is trading information.[3] If it is, then regard must be had to whether the disclosure is made only to the extent necessary and solely in order to offer to dispose of or acquire the investment from the person receiving the information. MAR 1.4.5A makes clear, however, that this last matter is only intended to apply to an actual offer of the investment. It is not therefore intended to apply to a disclosure of trading information to gauge potential interest in the investments to be offered or to help establish the likely price that will be obtained.

17.07 An example of a case in which the FSA took action in respect of behaviour falling within s 118(3) FSMA is the case of *Andrew Osborne*[4] against whom the FSA imposed a financial penalty of £350,000. At the relevant time, Mr Osborne was a Managing Director in the Corporate Broking Department of Merrill Lynch International ('MLI'). In May and June 2009, Mr Osborne led the corporate broking team at MLI in acting for Punch Taverns plc ('Punch') as joint book runner and co-sponsor in relation to a new equity issuance. His role included responsibility for wall-crossing certain US shareholders in respect of this. Specific wall-crossing procedures for the US shareholders were put in place by MLI requiring the US shareholders to agree to the terms of a written non-disclosure agreement ('NDA'). One of the US shareholders was Greenlight Capital. Despite the fact that Greenlight Capital and Mr Einhorn had previously refused to be wall-crossed, Mr Osborne arranged and participated in a conference call in which he nevertheless disclosed inside information about the forthcoming Punch equity issuance.

17.08 The FSA took the view that this behaviour amounted to improper disclosure in breach of s 118(3) FSMA, because this disclosure was not in the proper course of Mr Osborne's employment, profession, or duties. However, the Final Notice records that the improper disclosure by Mr Osborne was not deliberate or reckless and that he did not expect or intend Greenlight to deal on the basis of the information. These factors do not of themselves prevent the conduct from

---

[3] See FCA Glossary definition and Chapter 16, para 16.65.
[4] *Andrew Osborne*, Final Notice, 15 Feb 2012 (post-MAD case).

amounting to market abuse but will of course mitigate the level of penalty imposed.[5]

17.09 This case highlights the importance of whether the disclosure in question has been made in connection with the 'proper performance' of the person's employment, profession, or duties. There was no question in this case that the disclosures made by Mr Osborne were made in connection with his role at MLI. However, the circumstances of the disclosure breached MLI's wall-crossing procedures of which Mr Osborne was well aware, and furthermore the disclosure was made in circumstances in which he knew that Greenlight had refused to be wall-crossed. He ought therefore to have been aware of the significant legal and regulatory risk inherent in proceeding to nevertheless disclose inside information in such circumstances. Despite this, Mr Osborne did not take care regarding the information he disclosed, nor did he refer the contents of the call to senior management, internal compliance or legal personnel at MLI, as a matter of potential concern. This meant that his disclosures could not be said to be connected with the proper performance of his duties.

3. Section 118(3) FSMA behaviour—safe harbours

Disclosure to certain public bodies

17.10 MAR 1.4.3C provides that disclosure of inside information will not amount to market abuse (improper disclosure) if it is made to a government department, the Bank of England, the Competition Commission, the Takeover Panel or any other regulatory body or authority for the purposes of fulfilling a legal or regulatory obligation, or otherwise in connection with the performance of the functions of that body.

Disclosure in compliance with rules and regulatory obligations

17.11 MAR 1.4.4C provides that disclosure of inside information which is required or permitted by the Listing Rules (or any similar regulatory obligation) will not amount to improper disclosure under s 118(3) FSMA.

Disclosure of seller's managerial responsibilities to a potential buyer

17.12 MAR 1.4.4AC provides a safe harbour to enable a broker to disclose inside information to a potential buyer of qualifying investments, regarding the fact that the seller of qualifying investments is a person discharging managerial responsibilities (which means Director or Senior Executive), or the identity of the person

---

[5] *Andrew Osborne* (n 4) para 5.7. See also the ECJ case C-384/02 *Grongaard and Bang* [2005] ECR I-9939; [2006] 1 CMLR 30; [2006] CEC 241; [2006] IRLR 214, discussed in Chapter 5, Section 5, para 5.31.

discharging managerial responsibilities, or the purpose of the sale. However, the disclosure must be made only to the extent necessary, and solely in order to dispose of the investment. Furthermore, the illiquidity of the stock in question must be such that the transaction could not otherwise be completed; and the circumstances must be such that the transaction could not be otherwise completed without creating a disorderly market.

18

SECTION 118(4) FSMA; BEHAVIOUR—MISUSE OF INFORMATION

1. Introduction	18.01	*Robin Chhabra and Sameer Patel*	18.15
2. Section 118(4) FSMA behaviour	18.02	3. The regular user	18.17
Jason Smith and Robin Hutchings	18.08	4. 'Generally available'	18.18
Michael Thomas Davies	18.09	5. 'Based on'	18.19
Peter Bracken	18.10	6. 'Relevant information'	18.20
Robert Middlemiss	18.11	7. Standards of behaviour	18.22
Jonathan Mallins	18.12	8. Section 118(4) FSMA —safe harbours	18.23
David Isaacs	18.13		
Bertie Charles Hatcher	18.14		

1. Introduction

18.01 This Chapter deals with the elements that constitute s 118(4) behaviour. It focuses on how to approach this 'legacy' offence and when information might be 'RINGA' (relevant information, not generally available). It also deals with standards of behaviour and the safe harbours that are available in respect of this offence. This Chapter refers to a number of the cases under the pre-MAD market abuse regime to demonstrate the various elements of the offence and to show that in each case, the behaviour in question would be dealt with in the post-MAD[1] regime by the s 118(2) or (3) offences, thereby rendering s 118(4) perhaps somewhat otiose.

2. Section 118(4) FSMA behaviour

18.02 Section 118(4) FSMA describes the third type of behaviour:

The third is where the behaviour (not falling within subsection (2) or (3))

(a) is based on information which is not generally available to those using the market [auction platform][2] but which, if available to a regular user of the market

---

[1] Directive 2003/6/EC.
[2] As modified by the Recognised Auction Platform Regulations 2011 (SI 2011/2699).

[auction platform], would be, or would be likely to be, regarded by him as relevant when deciding the terms on which transactions in qualifying investments should be effected, and

(b) is likely to be regarded by a regular user of the market [auction platform] as a failure on the part of the person concerned to observe the standard of behaviour reasonably expected of a person in his position in relation to the market [auction platform].

(9) Subsections (4) and (8) and the definition of 'regular user' in section 130A(3) cease to have effect on 31 December 2014 and subsection (1)(b) is then to be read as no longer referring to those subsections.[3]

The elements of this offence are set out in Figure 6.   18.03

Section 118(4) FSMA expressly preserves the pre-MAD market abuse offence and 'regular user' test. This is often referred to as the 'legacy offence'. Initially, this provision was subject to a 'sunset date' of 30 June 2008, meaning that it would cease to exist unless action was taken by the Treasury to retain it. This date was later extended to 31 December 2009 and subsequently to 31 December 2014.   18.04

The reason given[4] for preserving the legacy offence was that the Treasury and the FSA considered that although the new MAD offences and the offences under the pre-MAD regime covered similar ground, their terms were not co-extensive. One of the reasons for retaining the legacy offence was that it was thought that the concept of 'relevant information not generally available' ('RINGA') used in the legacy offence is wider in scope than 'inside information' as defined in the post-MAD regime. A further reason given was that the legacy offence did not require the existence of an 'insider'. It was decided therefore that the pre-MAD offence should continue to exist (as s 118(4)), but would only apply in circumstances in which a person's conduct did not fall within any of the new post-MAD behaviour types.   18.05

The terms of s 118(4) FSMA are plainly wide enough to include dealing in qualifying investments based on RINGA (in circumstances where the information is not 'inside'), as well as improperly disclosing RINGA in circumstances where the conduct does not amount to s 118(2) behaviour—whether because the qualifying investment is of a kind where s 118(2) does not apply or because the relevant information is not 'inside'.[5]   18.06

---

[3] Words in s 118(9) substituted (31 Dec 2011) by the FSMA (Market Abuse) Regulations 2011 (SI 2011/2928), reg 2(2).
[4] For the full discussion, see HM Treasury, 'FSMA Market Abuse Regime: Final Impact Assessment on the Sunset Clauses' (June 2008).
[5] MAR 1.5.2E, 1.5.3G, and 1.5.10E provide examples of behaviour that would amount to s 118(4) behaviour.

Section 118(4) FSMA; Behaviour—Misuse of Information

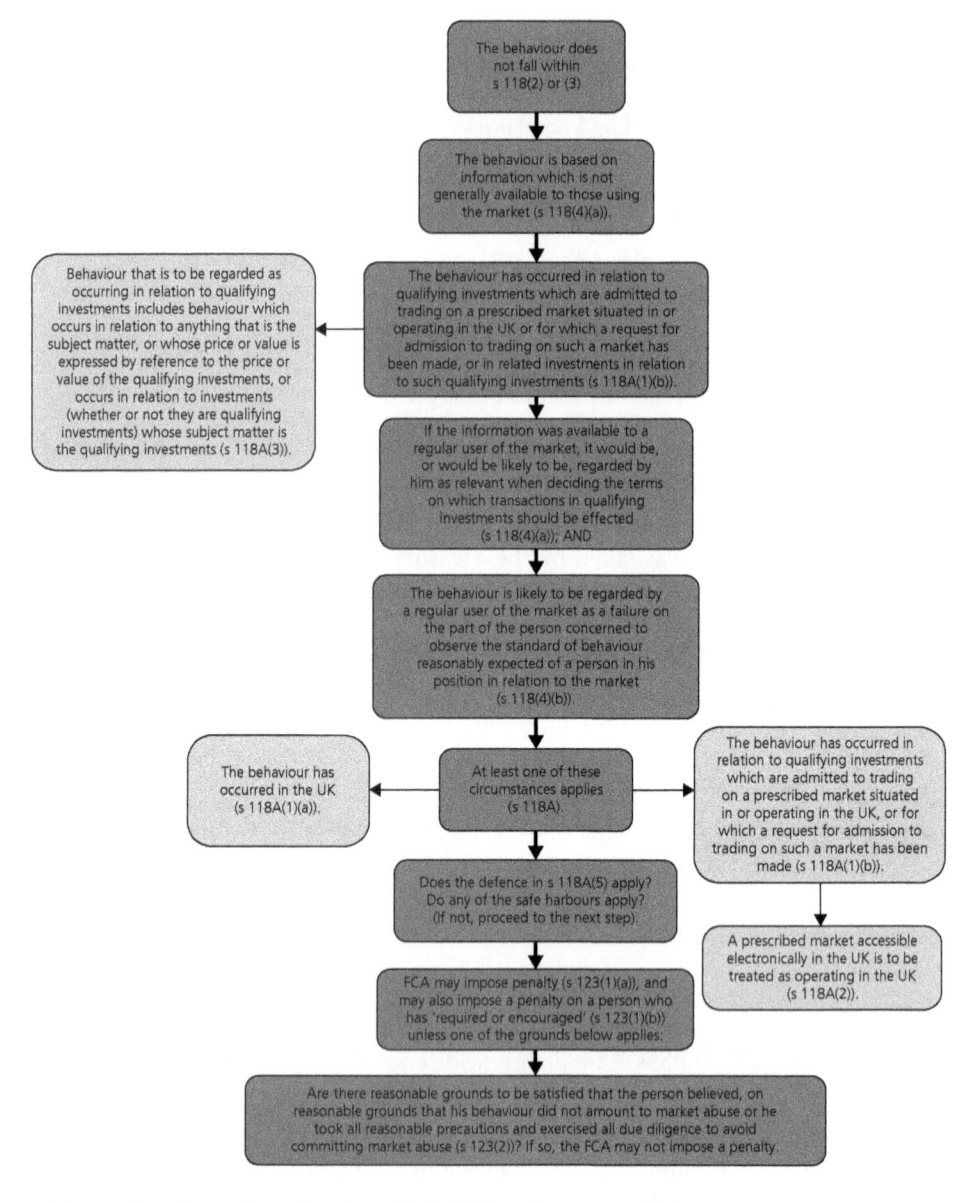

```
┌─────────────────────────┐
│ The behaviour does      │
│ not fall within         │
│ s 118(2) or (3)         │
└─────────────────────────┘
            │
            ▼
┌─────────────────────────┐
│ The behaviour is based on│
│ information which is not │
│ generally available to those using│
│ the market (s 118(4)(a)).│
└─────────────────────────┘
            │
            ▼
┌─────────────────────────────┐        ┌─────────────────────────────┐
│ Behaviour that is to be     │        │ The behaviour has occurred in relation to │
│ regarded as occurring in    │◄───────│ qualifying investments which are admitted to │
│ relation to qualifying      │        │ trading on a prescribed market situated in or │
│ investments includes        │        │ operating in the UK or for which a request for │
│ behaviour which occurs in   │        │ admission to trading on such a market has │
│ relation to anything that is│        │ been made, or in related investments in relation │
│ the subject matter, or whose│        │ to such qualifying investments (s 118A(1)(b)). │
│ price or value is expressed │        └─────────────────────────────┘
│ by reference to the price or│                      │
│ value of the qualifying     │                      ▼
│ investments, or occurs in   │        ┌─────────────────────────────┐
│ relation to investments     │        │ If the information was available to a │
│ (whether or not they are    │        │ regular user of the market, it would be, │
│ qualifying investments)     │        │ or would be likely to be, regarded by │
│ whose subject matter is     │        │ him as relevant when deciding the terms │
│ the qualifying investments  │        │ on which transactions in qualifying │
│ (s 118A(3)).                │        │ investments should be effected │
└─────────────────────────────┘        │ (s 118(4)(a)); AND │
                                       └─────────────────────────────┘
                                                      │
                                                      ▼
                                       ┌─────────────────────────────┐
                                       │ The behaviour is likely to be regarded by │
                                       │ a regular user of the market as a failure on │
                                       │ the part of the person concerned to │
                                       │ observe the standard of behaviour │
                                       │ reasonably expected of a person in his │
                                       │ position in relation to the market │
                                       │ (s 118(4)(b)). │
                                       └─────────────────────────────┘
                                                      │
                                                      ▼
┌──────────────────┐   ┌──────────────────┐   ┌─────────────────────────────┐
│ The behaviour has│◄──│ At least one of these│──►│ The behaviour has occurred in │
│ occurred in the UK│   │ circumstances applies│   │ relation to qualifying investments │
│ (s 118A(1)(a)).  │   │ (s 118A).            │   │ which are admitted to trading │
└──────────────────┘   └──────────────────┘   │ on a prescribed market situated │
                                │              │ in or operating in the UK, or for │
                                ▼              │ which a request for admission to │
                       ┌──────────────────┐   │ trading on such a market has been │
                       │ Does the defence in s 118A(5) apply? │   │ made (s 118A(1)(b)). │
                       │ Do any of the safe harbours apply? │   └─────────────────────────────┘
                       │ (If not, proceed to the next step). │                  │
                       └──────────────────┘                                     ▼
                                │                                  ┌─────────────────────────────┐
                                ▼                                  │ A prescribed market accessible │
                       ┌──────────────────┐                        │ electronically in the UK is to be │
                       │ FCA may impose penalty (s 123(1)(a)), and │ │ treated as operating in the UK │
                       │ may also impose a penalty on a person who │ │ (s 118A(2)). │
                       │ has 'required or encouraged' (s 123(1)(b))│ └─────────────────────────────┘
                       │ unless one of the grounds below applies: │
                       └──────────────────┘
                                │
                                ▼
           ┌─────────────────────────────────────────────────────┐
           │ Are there reasonable grounds to be satisfied that the person believed, on │
           │ reasonable grounds that his behaviour did not amount to market abuse or he │
           │ took all reasonable precautions and exercised all due diligence to avoid │
           │ committing market abuse (s 123(2))? If so, the FCA may not impose a penalty. │
           └─────────────────────────────────────────────────────┘
```

Figure 6. Flow chart for the s 118(4) 'Regular user' offence

18.07 Despite the availability of the s 118(4) offence, it has not been used since the post-MAD market abuse regime came into effect on 1 July 2005. It can be seen from a sample of the pre-MAD cases that, in each case, the conduct would today fall within either s 118(2) or (3) behaviour, and perhaps this explains why the legacy offence has not been used since those sections came into force.

Jason Smith and Robin Hutchings

In the case of *Smith*[6] and *Hutchings*,[7] Jason Smith was fined £15,000 and Robin Hutchings £18,000 for market abuse (misuse of information) under the pre-MAD regime. Mr Smith was a chartered accountant and the finance director and company secretary of a company named IFG. In April 2003, he tipped his friend (Hutchings) that IFG was going to release a holding announcement the following morning relating to a takeover approach. Several days later, he again tipped Hutchings that a final announcement of an agreed offer was imminent. Hutchings traded on the basis of this information making circa £5000 profit. Post-MAD, the case would have been dealt with under s 118(2) FSMA (as a joint enterprise), or alternatively under s 118(2) (Hutchings) and s 118(3) (Smith). **18.08**

Michael Thomas Davies[8]

The FSA imposed a nominal penalty of only £1000 on Mr Davies, the Group Financial Controller of Berkeley Morgan Group plc ('BMG') for market abuse (misuse of information) in respect of his dealing in January 2004 in the shares of BMG ahead of the announcement of its favourable third quarter results. Mr Davies made a small purchase of BMG shares just prior to the announcement and sold them shortly after, realising a profit of £420. In deciding on the level of the penalty, the Final Notice indicates that a penalty of £4000 would have been appropriate but for Mr Davies' full and frank admissions, his full co-operation with the FSA investigation and his financial resources and personal circumstances. Post-MAD, this case would have been dealt with under s 118(2) FSMA. **18.09**

Peter Bracken[9]

Peter Bracken was fined £15,000 for market abuse (misuse of information) in relation to his trading in shares of Whitehead Mann Group plc ('Whitehead Mann'), for whom he worked as Head of Communications. In 2002, Mr Bracken short sold shares in Whitehead Mann ahead of a negative announcement making a profit of circa £2500. Post MAD, this case would also have been dealt with under s 118(2) FSMA. **18.10**

Robert Middlemiss[10]

Robert Middlemiss was fined £15,000 for market abuse (misuse of information) in relation to his trading in April 2002 in shares in Profile Media Group plc ('PMG'). **18.11**

---

[6] *Jason Smith*, Final Notice 13 Dec 2004 (pre-MAD case).
[7] *Robin Mark Hutchings*, Final Notice 13 Dec 2004 (pre-MAD case).
[8] *Michael Thomas Davies*, Final Notice 28 July 2004 (pre-MAD case).
[9] *Peter Bracken*, Final Notice 7 July 2004 (pre-MAD case).
[10] *Robert Middlemiss*, Final Notice 10 Feb 2004 (pre-MAD case).

Mr Middlemiss was PMG's company secretary and he sold a substantial part of his shareholding in advance of a negative announcement thereby avoiding a potential loss of £6825. The Final Notice records that the FSA considered the appropriate penalty to be £20,000; however, this was reduced to £15,000 on account of Mr Middlemiss' financial resources and other personal circumstances. Post-MAD, this case would have been brought under s 118(2) FSMA.

Jonathan Mallins[11]

18.12 Jonathan Mallins was fined £25,000 for market abuse (misuse of information) in respect of his purchase of shares in Cambrian Mining plc ('Cambrian') ahead of two positive announcements. At the time of the dealing, in 2005, Mr Mallins was Cambrian's Finance Director. His profit—had he chosen to sell the shares after the second announcement—was calculated as £6400. The penalty was justified on the basis of the gross breach of a position of trust and a finding by the FSA that his actions were deliberate. Post MAD, this case would have been brought under s 118(2) FSMA.

David Isaacs[12]

18.13 David Isaacs was fined £15,000 for market abuse (misuse of information) relating to improper disclosure of confidential information relating to a company named Trafficmaster. Mr Isaacs was visiting the house of his friend Mr X, who was an employee of Trafficmaster, when he read a confidential document which contained positive news about one of Trafficmaster's key products. Thereafter, Mr Isaacs bought shares in Trafficmaster and at the same time posted strong hints about this information anonymously on the ADVFN bulletin board, presumably in order to 'ramp' the share price. The Final Notice does not record what (if any) profit he made from his activity. Post-MAD, this case would be dealt with under s 118(2) and possibly s 118(3) FSMA.

Bertie Charles Hatcher[13]

18.14 Mr Hatcher was an old friend of a man named Malcolm Calvert, who was a former partner of Cazenove and Co ('Cazenove'). Mr Calvert had obtained inside information regarding forthcoming takeovers from an unknown source connected to the Corporate Broking division of Cazenove. He asked Mr Hatcher to buy shares in the companies being acquired on their joint behalf and they split the profits. Mr Hatcher accepted a finding of market abuse (misuse of information) and was fined £56,098 which was the equivalent of his share of the profits. Mr Hatcher had entered into a restricted use undertaking agreement with the FSA in which he

---

[11] *Jonathan Mallins*, Final Notice 20 Dec 2005 (pre-MAD case).
[12] *David Isaacs*, Final Notice 28 Feb 2005 (pre-MAD case).
[13] *Bertie Charles Hatcher*, Final Notice 13 May 2008 (pre-MAD case).

agreed to give evidence at Mr Calvert's criminal trial in return for the FSA agreeing not to prosecute him. Mr Calvert was subsequently prosecuted and convicted of insider dealing under s 52(1) CJA. Post-MAD, Mr Hatcher's case would have been dealt with under s 118(2) FSMA.

Robin Chhabra and Sameer Patel[14]

18.15 Mr Chhabra was a research analyst at Evolution Securities Limited ('Evolution') and was responsible for covering two companies named Ebookers plc ('Ebookers') and Eidos plc ('Eidos'). Evolution acted as corporate broker to both companies. Mr Chhabra obtained information regarding both Ebookers and Eidos which he improperly disclosed to his friend Sameer Patel, who placed spread-bets referenced to these stocks making a net profit of £85,541. Mr Chhabra was fined £95,000 and Mr Patel was fined £180,541. Both men were also prohibited. Post-MAD, this case would have been dealt with under s 118(2) FSMA on the basis of joint enterprise, or alternatively s 118(2) (Patel) and s 118(3) FSMA (Chhabra).

18.16 The above cases demonstrate that, in every instance, the behaviour complained of would have fallen within either s 118(2) or s 118(3) FSMA. Given that s 118(4) will only apply in cases which fall outside these provisions, this history suggests that the future use of the s 118(4) offence is likely to be limited.

3. The regular user

18.17 Section 130A(3) FSMA provides that the 'regular user', in relation to a particular market, means a reasonable person who regularly deals on that market in investments of the kind in question. MAR 1.2.21G provides that the presence of the regular user imports an objective element into the elements listed in s 118(4) FSMA while retaining some subjective features of the markets for, or the auction of, the investments in question. This means that there must be some objective basis on which the attitude of the regular user can be assessed. Most likely, this will be in the form of evidence from other persons who would be reasonably considered to fall within that category, as to their view of the behaviour in question.

4. 'Generally available'

18.18 MAR 1.5.4E provides that the factors to be taken into account in deciding whether or not information is generally available for the purposes of the definition of inside

---

[14] *Robin Chhabra and Sameer Patel v FSA*, FSMT Case 072, 29 Dec 2009, and see Final Notice 16 Apr 2010 (pre-MAD case).

5. 'Based on'

18.19 MAR 1.5.5E states that the factors to be taken into account in deciding whether or not a person's behaviour is 'on the basis of' inside information,[16] will also be relevant when considering whether or not behaviour is 'based on' RINGA.

6. 'Relevant information'

18.20 MAR 1.5.6E sets out the factors that indicate that information is 'relevant'. The key indicator is whether the information could be said to be reliable. This will involve an assessment of how near the source the person providing the information is or appears to be, and the reliability of the source. An examination is also required of the content of the information itself. If it is new or fresh information, or relates to possible future developments, then an assessment is required of whether the information provides grounds to conclude (with reasonable certainty) that the possible future developments will, in fact, occur. This is another way of saying that information that is merely speculative, or rumour, will not be sufficient to qualify as 'relevant'.

18.21 MAR 1.5.6E also provides that a relevant consideration is whether there is any other material information which is already generally available to inform users of the market. This means that the test of whether the information is 'relevant' must be considered objectively in the context of the state of the market's knowledge at the time.

7. Standards of behaviour

18.22 MAR 1.5.7E provides for factors which indicate that behaviour is likely to be regarded by a regular user as failing to meet the expected standard. These include whether the information has to be, or will need to be, disclosed in accordance with any legal or regulatory requirement, or if the relevant information is, or will be, routinely the subject of a public announcement although not subject to any formal disclosure requirement. Again, this is an objective assessment which will need to be made on the available evidence. In particular, if it is asserted that the information

---

[15] See MAR 1.3.3 E—MAR 1.3.5 E, Chapter 16, Section 6.
[16] See MAR 1.3.3 E—MAR 1.3.5 E, Chapter 16, Section 5.

Safe harbours

is of a kind which would routinely be formally announced, then there will need to be evidence from which this conclusion can be drawn.

8. Section 118(4) FSMA—safe harbours

MAR 1.5.9C provides that the same safe harbours as are available in respect of s 118(2) are also available in respect of s 118(4) FSMA.[17] This means that the safe harbours which relate to prior decisions to deal and pre-existing trading strategies,[18] market makers, and professional dealers,[19] execution of client orders[20] and activity connected with takeovers and mergers[21] are all potentially available.

18.23

---

[17] See Chapter 16, Section 7.
[18] MAR 1.3.6C and see Chapter 16, Section 7.
[19] MAR 1.3.7C and see Chapter 16, Section 7.
[20] MAR 1.3.12C and see Chapter 16, Section 7.
[21] MAR 1.3.17C and see Chapter 16, Section 7.

19

MARKET ABUSE—STATUTORY DEFENCE AND POWER TO IMPOSE PENALTIES

1. Introduction	19.01	'Encouraging'	19.08
2. Statutory defence (s 118A(5) FSMA)	19.02	'Requiring'	19.12
		Circumstances in which a penalty may not be imposed (s 123(2) FSMA)	19.14
3. Power to impose penalties in cases of market abuse (s 123 FSMA)	19.06	4. Penalties imposed in market abuse cases	19.28
'Requiring or encouraging' (s 123(1)(b) FSMA)	19.07		

1. Introduction

19.01 This Chapter deals with the statutory defence contained in s 118A(5) FSMA which is available in respect of all s 118 behaviours. It also considers the power to impose financial penalties for market abuse contained in s 123(1) FSMA, and the scope of s 123(2) which provides for circumstances in which a penalty may not be imposed. Lastly, this Chapter provides a schedule of penalties imposed in previous market abuse cases.

2. Statutory defence (s 118A(5) FSMA)

19.02 Section 118A(5) FSMA provides that:

Section 118A(5)

Behaviour does not amount to market abuse for the purposes of this Act if

(a) it conforms with a rule which includes a provision to the effect that behaviour conforming with the rule does not amount to market abuse,
(b) it conforms with the relevant provisions of Commission Regulation (EC) No 2273/2003 of 22 December 2003 implementing Directive 2003/6/EC [MAD]

of the European Parliament and of the Council as regards exemptions for buy-back programmes and stabilisation of financial instruments, or

(c) it is done by a person acting on behalf of a public authority in pursuit of monetary policies or policies with respect to exchange rates or the management of public debt or foreign exchange reserves.

19.03 MAR 1.10.2G points out that there are no rules which permit or require a person to commit market abuse. However, as we have seen from the preceding Chapters, some rules contain a provision that behaviour conforming with that rule does not amount to market abuse. These include rules relating to Chinese Walls[1] and parts of the Disclosure Rules.[2]

19.04 Similarly, there are no rules in the Takeover Code which permit or require a person to behave in a way which amounts to market abuse;[3] however; behaviour conforming with particular specified rules will not amount to market abuse if the behaviour is expressly required or permitted by the rule and it conforms to any relevant General Principles.[4]

19.05 Lastly, behaviour conforming with Rule 4.2 of the Takeover Code relating to restrictions on dealing by offerors or parties acting in concert with them, will not of itself constitute market abuse to the extent that the behaviour is expressly permitted or required by that rule, provided that it conforms to any General Principle set out at s B of the Takeover Code.[5]

3. Power to impose penalties in cases of market abuse (s 123 FSMA)

19.06 Sections 123(1) and (3) FSMA empower the FCA to impose penalties in respect of behaviour amounting to market abuse:

(1) If the Authority is satisfied that a person ('A')—

(a) is or has engaged in market abuse, or
(b) by taking or refraining from taking any action has required or encouraged another person or persons to engage in behaviour which, if engaged in by A, would amount to market abuse, it may impose on him a penalty of such amount as it considers appropriate.

---

[1] FCA Handbook of Rules and Guidance—Conduct of Business Sourcebook ('COBS') 2.4.1G–2.4.7G; Senior Management Arrangements, Systems and Controls SYSC, 10.2.2R(1) & 10.2.2R(4). See Chapter 16, Section 6 'On the basis of', para 16.21.
[2] Those parts of the FSMA Part VI Rules which relating to disclosure announcement, communication, or release of information.
[3] MAR 1.10.3G.
[4] MAR 1.10.4C, 1.10.5C.
[5] MAR 1.10.6C.

(3) If the Authority is entitled to impose a penalty on a person under this section it may, instead of imposing a penalty on him, publish a statement to the effect that he has engaged in market abuse.

'Requiring or encouraging' (s 123(1)(b) FSMA)

19.07 Section 123(1)(b) FSMA also enables a financial penalty to be imposed on a person (A) who requires or encourages behaviour by another person which would amount to market abuse if undertaken by A himself.[6] The 'requiring' or 'encouraging' may occur by action or inaction. This section therefore provides the market abuse version of the 'encouraging' offence that is contained in s 52(2)(a) CJA.

'Encouraging'

19.08 Examples of where behaviour has been held to amount to 'encouraging' within the meaning of s 123(1)(b) FSMA are:

Alexei Krilov-Harrison[7]

19.09 Krilov-Harrison was fined £24,000 for market abuse in respect of behaviour while he was employed as a broker by Pacific Continental Securities (UK) Limited ('PCS'). In March 2007, he obtained inside information regarding an impending announcement that Provexis plc ('Provexis'), an Alternative Investment Market ('AIM') listed company, had entered into a collaboration agreement with a major international company. He improperly disclosed this inside information to clients of PCS (s 118(3) FSMA), and also encouraged these clients to purchase shares in Provexis (s 123(1)(b) FSMA).

Perry Bliss[8] and *William Coppin*[9]

19.10 The FSA fined Perry Bliss £30,000 (reduced from £60,000 on the grounds of his financial circumstances) and prohibited him in respect of behaviour amounting to market abuse (improper disclosure—s 118(3) FSMA) and for encouraging other persons to engage in behaviour which, if engaged in by himself, would have amounted to market abuse under s 123(1)(b) FSMA. Bliss was also a broker at Pacific Continental and engaged in conduct similar to that of Mr Krilov-Harrison. William Coppin, another broker at Pacific Continental, was also fined £70,000 and prohibited in respect of the same conduct.

Jeremy Burley[10]

19.11 Jeremy Burley was fined £144,200 in respect of behaviour amounting to market abuse (insider dealing s 118(2) FSMA), improper disclosure (s 118(3) FSMA), and

---

[6] MAR 1.2.23G provides examples of behaviour that might fall within the scope of s 123(1)(b).
[7] *Alexei Krilov-Harrison*, Final Notice 3 Nov 2009 (post-MAD case).
[8] *Perry John Bliss*, Final Notice 13 Dec 2010 (post-MAD case).
[9] *William James Coppin*, Final Notice 7 Dec 2010 (post-MAD case).
[10] *Jeremy Burley*, Final Notice 19 July 2010 (post-MAD case).

encouraging another person to engage in behaviour which, if engaged in by him, would have amounted to market abuse (s 123(1)(b) FSMA). He acquired inside information (negative drilling results) regarding a mining company named Tower Resources plc ('Tower'). He improperly disclosed this information to a Mr X and his father, Jeffery Burley,[11] and then instructed his father to sell his shares in Tower prior to the announcement of this information, thereby avoiding a loss of £21,700. He also encouraged Mr X to sell his own shareholding.

'Requiring'

Darwin Clifton[12] and *Byron Holdings*

19.12 Darwin Clifton was fined £59,900 and Byron Holdings £86,030 in respect of behaviour amounting to market abuse (insider dealing—s 118(2) FSMA. Mr Clifton was a founding Director of Desire Petroleum plc ('Desire') and also a director and shareholder in Byron Holdings. Mr Clifton became aware of positive inside information (a joint-venture drilling arrangement) relating to Desire. He directed Byron Holdings to purchase shares in Desire prior to the announcement of the information.

19.13 The FSA asserted that this behaviour amounted to market abuse (insider dealing s 118(2) FSMA) against Byron Holdings and conduct contrary to s 123(1)(b) FSMA against Mr Clifton on the grounds that, by directing Byron to purchase the shares, Mr Clifton took action to require Byron to engage in behaviour which would have amounted to market abuse if he had engaged in it himself. The FSA could also have taken action against Mr Clifton for market abuse (insider dealing) contrary to s 118(2) FSMA on the basis of s 118(1)—ie, that the behaviour was conduced by two or more persons acting jointly or in concert.

Circumstances in which a penalty may not be imposed (s 123(2) FSMA)

19.14 The circumstances in which a penalty may not be imposed are set out in s 123(2) FSMA:

> But the Authority may not impose a penalty on a person if, having considered any representations made to it in response to a warning notice, there are reasonable grounds for it to be satisfied that
>
> (a) he believed, on reasonable grounds, that his behaviour did not fall within paragraph (a) or (b) of subsection (1), or
> (b) he took all reasonable precautions and exercised all due diligence to avoid behaving in a way which fell within paragraph (a) or (b) of that subsection.

---

[11] Jeffery Burley was also fined (£35,000) for his role. *Jeffery Burley*, Final Notice 19 July 2010 (post-MAD case).
[12] *Darwin Lewis Clifton and Byron Holdings Limited*, Final Notice 27 Jan 2009 (post-MAD case).

19.15 Section 123(2) FSMA does not provide a defence to an allegation of market abuse, but instead provides an opportunity to the subject of such an allegation, to mitigate the penalty that might otherwise be imposed, on the grounds that he believed on reasonable grounds that his behaviour did not amount to market abuse, or that he took all reasonable precautions and exercised all due diligence to avoid behaving in a way which amounts to market abuse. It is plain from the wording of this section that it imposes a legal as well as an evidential burden on the subject to establish that he falls within one or other of these provisions.

19.16 The 'reasonableness' element of both subsections also imports an objective assessment. Thus, once the FCA has proved the elements of market abuse, the onus is on the person concerned to demonstrate in the case of s 123(2)(a) FSMA that he believed that his conduct did not amount to market abuse, and that that belief was reasonable, or under s 123(2)(b) FSMA, that he took all reasonable precautions and exercised all due diligence to avoid committing market abuse—which too will be assessed on an objective basis.

19.17 The Decisions Procedures and Penalties Manual of the FCA Handbook ('DEPP') 6.3.2 sets out a list of non-exhaustive criteria to which the FCA will have regard in determining this issue. These include:

1. Whether the behaviour is analogous to behaviour described in MAR.
2. Whether the FCA (or its predecessor the FSA) has published any guidance or other materials on the behaviour in question and if so whether and how far the person has followed or taken account of this.
3. Whether the behaviour complies with market rules or regulatory requirements.
4. The level of knowledge, skill, and experience to be expected of the person concerned.
5. Whether the person can demonstrate that the behaviour was undertaken for a legitimate and in a proper manner.
6. Whether the person followed internal consultation and escalation procedures in relation to the behaviour (for example, raising the matter with his line managers or his Firm's legal / compliance departments).
7. Whether the person sought and followed any appropriate expert legal or professional advice.
8. Whether the person sought and followed advice from the market authorities of any relevant prescribed market or the Takeover Panel.

19.18 Examples of how these considerations are applied in practice can be seen from the decided cases.

David Einhorn[13]

19.19 Mr Einhorn was the owner of Greenlight Capital Inc ('Greenlight'), an investment management firm based in the US. The FSA's case was that he instructed

---

[13] *David Einhorn*, Final Notice 15 Feb 2012 (post-MAD case).

Greenlight's traders to dispose of part of its holding in a company named Punch Taverns plc ('Punch') on the basis of inside information he received in a telephone call regarding a forthcoming new equity issuance by Punch. Following the issuing of the FSA's Warning Notice indicating a finding of market abuse (s 118(2) FSMA), Mr Einhorn made representations to the RDC under s 123(2)(b) FSMA, that he took all reasonable precautions and exercised all due diligence to avoid committing, and reasonably believed that he had not committed, market abuse. He pointed to the fact that he had refused to be 'wall-crossed' during the telephone call in which the inside information regarding Punch Taverns plc ('Punch') was imparted to him ('Punch call'), and that he had relied on Punch's management and the other insiders on the Punch call not to give him inside information, or to tell him if they inadvertently did so. No such concerns were raised during the call and none of the experienced parties on the call raised any concerns, even after he stated that he was considering selling Greenlight's holding in Punch.

Furthermore, Punch's management told him that they were talking only in general terms and were having an 'in-concept discussion', and therefore as a matter of market practice it was reasonable for him to place considerable weight on those disclaimers. Lastly, towards the end of the call he asked if the decision to issue equity had been made, and was told that no formal decision had been made, and that Punch was still consulting with various parties. He was also still being told at the end of the call that he was not wall-crossed. He took these comments as confirmation that he was 'nowhere close' to having inside information.[14] **19.20**

Mr Einhorn also stated that he did not consult with internal or external compliance staff because he believed, reasonably and in good faith, that there was no need. Further, the order to sell Greenlight's holding in Punch was relayed to the trader who served as Greenlight UK's compliance officer, and the sales were vetted by Greenlight's in-house counsel to make sure that the necessary regulatory filings were made.[15] **19.21**

The FSA did not criticise Mr Einhorn's approach to the Punch call and accepted that he did not believe that he had received inside information. However, it decided that following the call, Mr Einhorn should have been aware that he had been given inside information, or at the very least that there was a risk of this. That being the case, he should have taken further steps to ensure that the information he had been given was not inside before giving the instruction to deal in Punch. Therefore s 123(2)(b) FSMA was not made out as Mr Einhorn had not demonstrated that he took all reasonable precautions and exercised all due diligence to avoid committing market abuse, nor that his honestly held belief that he was not committing market abuse was reasonable.[16] **19.22**

---

[14] *David Einhorn* (n 13) para 6.8(i).
[15] *David Einhorn* (n 13) para 6.8(ii).
[16] *David Einhorn* (n 13) para 6.9.

Darren Morton[17]

19.23 Darren Morton was publicly censured by the FSA for market abuse (insider dealing s 118(2) FSMA), in respect of his authorisation of sales of Barclays Bank Floating Rate Notes ('FRN') ahead of a new Barclays FRN issue, in circumstances in which he was in possession of inside information regarding the new issue. At the relevant time, Mr Morton was a director of Dresdner Kleinwort, the investment banking division of Dresdner Bank AG ('Dresdner') and co-head of the Portfolio Management Team within Dresdner's Structured Investment Unit ('SCI') which managed the bank's Structured Investment Vehicle (K2).

19.24 Mr Morton made representations on the market practice prevalent at the time and also submitted under s 123(2)(a) FSMA that he believed on reasonable grounds that his conduct did not amount to market abuse. The FSA accepted that there was no industry guidance covering this situation and that the only specific guidance available to Mr Morton was the interim guidelines from Dresdner which stated that 'in the past it has been determined that the SCI was not routinely privy to price sensitive non-public [information]'. The FSA accepted therefore that Mr Morton was working in an environment in which the accepted view was that until a deal had closed, information of the type that Mr Morton had was not regarded as specific or price-sensitive, and therefore the view was that any activity related to such information could not be abusive.

19.25 However, the FSA found that although Mr Morton believed he had not received inside information, the FSA did not accept his representations that this belief was reasonable. The FSA took the view that Mr Morton had a responsibility to consider whether the information he had was capable of being inside information, regardless of the market practice and the guidance from his compliance department. The fact of the market practice at the time was not therefore sufficient to satisfy the FSA that there were reasonable grounds for it to be satisfied that Mr Morton did not engage in market abuse under s 123(2)(a) FSMA.[18]

19.26 That said, the FSA still took the view that a public censure was the appropriate penalty, which demonstrates that it must have had (at least), a considerable degree of sympathy with Mr Morton's position. This is reflected in the Final Notice which records that had the FSA found Mr Morton to have acted deliberately, recklessly or in breach of compliance department guidelines, this would have called into question his fitness and propriety as an approved person and would have resulted in a more severe penalty, including a financial penalty and a prohibition.

19.27 Mr Morton's colleague Christopher Parry[19] was also publicly censured for executing the sales in question. Mr Parry similarly stated that he did not believe that his

---

[17] *Darren Morton*, Final Notice 6 Oct 2009 (post-MAD case).
[18] *Darren Morton* (n 17) para 6.12.
[19] *Christopher Parry*, Final Notice 16 Oct 2009 (post-MAD case).

actions amounted to market abuse and the FSA accepted that this was a genuine belief.[20] However, as with Mr Morton, it took the view that this was not a reasonable belief in the circumstances. As with Mr Morton, the FSA decided that a public censure was the appropriate outcome for the same reasons.[21]

4. Penalties imposed in market abuse cases

The Table below summarises the market abuse cases brought by the FSA, the profits made or losses avoided, and the penalties imposed. This Table demonstrates that the financial penalties imposed in respect of market abuse have steadily increased in line with the FSA's tougher stance. The FCA's policy in respect of financial penalties is explained in Chapter 24.[22]

19.28

Market abuse cases: profits made/losses avoided, and penalties imposed

Company or individual	Date of FSA final notice	Amount of penalty	Conduct
Mr Robert Middlemiss	10/02/2004	£15,000	Market abuse pre-MAD (insider dealing), loss avoided £6825.
Mr Peter Bracken	07/07/2004	£15,000	Market abuse pre-MAD (insider dealing), profit £2824.
Mr Michael Davies	28/07/2004	£1000	Market abuse pre-MAD (insider dealing), profit £420.
Mr Jason Smith	13/12/2004	£15,000	Market abuse pre-MAD (improper disclosure).
Mr Robin Hutchings	13/12/2004	£18,000	Market abuse: pre-MAD (insider dealing), profit £4924.
Mr David Isaacs	28/02/2005	£15,000	Market abuse pre-MAD (insider dealing and possibly improper disclosure), profit unknown.
Mr Arif Mohammed	18/05/2005	£10,000	Market abuse pre-MAD (insider dealing), profit £3750. Tribunal Decision FSMT Case 012, 29 Mar 2005.
Jonathan Malins	20/12/2005	£25,000	Market abuse pre-MAD (insider dealing), potential profit £6400.
Mr Philippe Jabre	01/08/2006	£750,000	Market abuse pre-MAD (insider dealing) and breaching the FSA's Statements of Principle for Approved Persons. Profit $500,000 of which GLG's share was approximately $92,000. Tribunal decisions FSMT Case 035, 10 Jul 2006; Case 036, 10 Jul 2006.

(Continued)

---

[20] *Christopher Parry* (n 19) paras 6.3 and 6.13.
[21] *Christopher Parry* (n 19) para 7.
[22] Chapter 24, Section 4 Formal Enforcement Action, Financial Penalties.

Company or individual	Date of FSA final notice	Amount of penalty	Conduct
GLG Partners LP (GLG)	01/08/2006	£750,000	Market abuse pre-MAD (insider dealing) and breaching the FSA's Principles for Business.
James Boyd Parker	06/10/2006	£250,000	Market abuse pre-MAD (insider dealing), profit £121,742. Tribunal decision FSMT Case 037, 2006.
Sean Pignatelli	20/11/2006	£20,000	Breaches of Principles 2 and 3 of the FSA's Statements of Principle for Approved Persons (information not 'inside').
Bertie Hatcher	13/05/2008	£56,098	Market abuse pre-MAD (insider dealing), profit £56,098. Penalty equal to disgorgement of profit because Mr Hatcher entered into a restricted use undertaking with the FSA in which he agreed to give evidence in the FSA's prosecution of Malcolm Calvert for insider dealing.
John Shevlin	01/07/2008	£85,000	Market abuse post-MAD (insider dealing s 118(2)), profit £38,472. Tribunal Decision, FSMT Case 060, 12 Jun 2008.
Steven Harrison	08/09/2008	£52,500	Market abuse post-MAD (insider dealing s 118(2)), profit EUR 44,000.
Mr Richard Ralph	12/11/2008	£117,691.41	Market abuse post-MAD (insider dealing (s 118(2) and improper disclosure (s 118(3)), profit £12,691.
Mr Filip Boyen	12/11/2008	£81,982.95	Market abuse post-MAD (insider dealing (s 118(2)), profit £29,482.
Mr Stewart McKegg	16/12/2008	£14,411.25	Market abuse post-MAD (insider dealing s 118(2)), profit £14,411.
Mr Brian Valentine Taylor	16/12/2008	£4,642.50	Market abuse post-MAD (insider dealing s 118(2) and improper disclosure s 118(3)), profit £4462.
Mr Erik Boyen	12/01/2009	£176,254	Market abuse post-MAD (insider dealing s 118(2)), profit £127,254.
Mr Darwin Lewis Clifton OBE and Byron Holdings Ltd	27/01/2009	£59,500 & £86,030	Market abuse post-MAD (insider dealing s 118(2)), potential profit £86,030.
Darren Morton	06/10/2009	Public Censure	Market abuse post-MAD (insider dealing s 118(2)), loss avoided $66,000.
Christopher Parry	06/10/2009	Public Censure	Market abuse post-MAD (insider dealing s 118(2)), loss avoided $66,000.
Alexei Krilov-Harrison	03/11/2009	£24,000	Market abuse post-MAD (improper disclosure s 118(3) and encouraging s 123(1)(b)).
Mehmet Sepil	12/02/2010	£967,005	Market abuse post-MAD (insider dealing s 118(2)), profit £267,005.
Murat Ozgul	12/02/2010	£105,240	Market abuse post-MAD (insider dealing s 118(2)), profit £35,240.

Cases: penalties imposed

Company or individual	Date of FSA final notice	Amount of penalty	Conduct
Levent Akca	12/02/2010	£94,062	Market abuse post-MAD (insider dealing s 118(2)), profit £10,062.
Robin Chhabra	16/04/2010	£180,541	Market abuse pre-MAD (improper disclosure), profit made and loss avoided £85,541. Tribunal decision FSMT Case 036, 29 Dec 2012.
Sameer Patel	16/04/2010	£95,000	Market abuse pre-MAD (insider dealing), profit made and loss avoided £85,541. Tribunal decision FSMT Case 036, 29 Dec 2012.
Jeremy Burley	19/07/2010	£144,200	Market abuse post-MAD (insider dealing s 118(2) and encouraging s 123(1)(b)), loss avoided £21,700.
Jeffery Burley	19/07/2010	£35,000	Market abuse post-MAD (insider dealing s.118(2)), loss avoided £21,700.
Andre Jean Scerri	20/10/2010	£66,062.50	Market abuse post-MAD (insider dealing s 118(2)), profit £46.062. Tribunal decision Case 016, Upper Tribunal 21 May 2010 and 25 Aug 2010.
Perry John Bliss	14/12/2010	£30,000	Market abuse post-MAD (improper disclosure s 118(3) and encouraging s 123(1)(b)).
William James Coppin	14/12/2010	£70,000	Market abuse post-MAD (improper disclosure s 118(3) and encouraging s 123(1)(b)).
David Massey	27/02/2011	£150,000	Market abuse post-MAD (insider dealing s 118(2)), profit £111,474. Upper Tribunal Decision 2 Feb 2011.
David Einhorn	15/02/2012	£3,638,000	Market Abuse post-MAD (insider dealing s 118(2)), loss avoided £638,000.
Greenlight Capital Inc	15/02/2012	£3,650,795	Market Abuse post-MAD (insider dealing s. 118(2)), loss avoided £638,000.
Andrew Osborne	15/02/2012	£350,000	Market Abuse post-MAD (improper disclosure s 118(3)).
Nicholas James Kyprios	13/03/2012	£210,000	For improper market conduct in disclosing client confidential information ahead of a significant bond issue in Nov 2009. Not 'qualifying investments'.
Christian Arthur Littlewood	31/05/2012		Prohibition order having been convicted of s 52 CJA insider dealing.
Angie Littlewood aka Siew-Yoon Lew aka Angie Lew	31/05/2012		Prohibition order having been convicted of s 52 CJA insider dealing.

20

MARKET ABUSE PROCEEDINGS— ARTICLE 6 ECHR AND THE BURDEN AND STANDARD OF PROOF

1. Introduction	20.01	Burden of proof		20.12
2. Status of market abuse proceedings		Standard of proof		20.13
under Article 6 ECHR	20.02	Previous Tribunal cases		20.15
Davidson and Tatham v FSA	20.04	The effect of the House of Lords		
James Parker v FSA	20.06	Judgment in *Re B*		20.19
Legal assistance	20.10	The effect of the Supreme Court		
Privilege against self-incrimination	20.11	Judgment in *Re S-B* (Children) (Care Proceedings: Standard		
3. Burden and standard of proof in market abuse proceedings	20.12	of Proof)		20.23

1. Introduction

20.01 This Chapter deals with the status of market abuse proceedings for the purposes of Article 6 of the European Convention on Human Rights ('ECHR') and the burden and standard of proof in market abuse proceedings before the Upper Tribunal (Tax and Chancery Chamber) ('Tribunal').[1]

2. Status of market abuse proceedings under Article 6 ECHR

20.02 Article 6(1) ECHR provides that in determination of a person's civil rights and obligations or of any criminal charge against him, a person has certain fundamental rights. Articles 6(2) and (3) provide for further minimum rights in respect of a person 'charged with a criminal offence'. These are the presumption of innocence (Article 6(2)) and the 'equality of arms' provisions listed in Article 6(3), which relate to the conduct of proceedings.

---

[1] Formerly the Financial Services and Markets Tribunal ('FSMT').

The issue of whether market abuse proceedings should be treated as criminal in nature for the purposes of Article 6 ECHR has been considered by the Tribunal in two cases with the conclusion that such proceedings should be treated as a criminal charge for Convention purposes.

20.03

Davidson and Tatham v FSA[2]

In this case, the Tribunal considered the applicability of Article 6(2) and (3) ECHR as a preliminary issue. The Tribunal applied the reasoning of the Court of Appeal in *Han v Customs and Excise Commissioners*[3] ('*Han*') which concerned a civil penalty for dishonest evasion of tax. The issue in *Han* was whether such a civil penalty was a criminal charge for the purposes of Article 6 ECHR. Potter LJ gave the leading judgment which summarised the relevant jurisprudence of the European Court of Human Rights in Strasbourg and identified the criteria routinely applied by that Court for the purpose of determining whether an applicant was the subject of a criminal charge:[4]

20.04

1. The categorisation of the allegation in domestic law. The Tribunal observed that market abuse under Part VIII of the FSMA is not within the jurisdiction of the criminal courts. However, as Potter LJ observed in *Han*, this was nothing more than a starting point and is not decisive of the nature of the allegation.
2. If the offence is not criminalised by the national law, the court must determine whether it is none the less criminal in character for the purposes of Article 6 by proceeding to the second and third criteria, which are the nature of the offence and the severity of the penalty. As to these, Potter LJ stated that, the court must consider whether or not, under the law concerned, the 'offence' is one which applies generally to the public at large or is restricted to a specific group. If the former, then despite its 'decriminalisation' by the national law, it is apt to be regarded as criminal.
3. If a punitive and deterrent (as opposed to a compensatory) penalty is imposed, it is likely to be regarded as criminal in character, even in cases where the penalty is a fine rather than imprisonment.

Applying the second and third criteria, the Tribunal in *Davidson and Tatham v FSA* held that market abuse is a criminal charge for the purposes of Article 6 of the ECHR on the grounds that market abuse applies to the public at large and the penalty imposed of it is (and is intended to be) punitive and deterrent in nature.

20.05

James Parker v FSA.[5]

In this case, the FSA did not concede that an allegation of market abuse gave rise to a criminal charge within the meaning of Article 6 ECHR and maintained that such

20.06

---

[2] *Paul Davidson and Ashley Tatham v FSA*, FSMT Case 031, 16 May 2006, para 174 et seq (pre-MAD case).
[3] *Han v Customs and Excise Commissioners* [2001] EWCA Civ 1040.
[4] These criteria were approved by the ECJ in the cases of C-489/10 *Lukasz Marcin Bonda*, 5 June 2012 and C-617/10 *Aklagaren v Hans Akerberg Fransson*, 26 February 2013.
[5] *James Parker v FSA*, FSMT, Case 037, 18 Aug 2006, para 14ff (pre-MAD case).

proceedings were civil in nature. The FSA relied on the judgment of the Court of Appeal in *Fleurose v The Securities and Futures Authority Ltd*[6] ('*Fleurose*') which was decided after *Han*. Mr Fleurose had been found guilty by the Disciplinary Tribunal of the Securities and Futures Authority ('SFA') of improper conduct as a trader in securities during his employment with JP Morgan (specifically that he had breached Statements of Principle 1 and 3 that were then in force). He was suspended from acting as a 'registered person' for two years and ordered to pay £175,000 costs. Mr Fleurose appealed to the Court of Appeal (Civil Division), submitting that the Disciplinary Proceedings had been conducted in Breach of Article 6 of the ECHR.

20.07 In *Fleurose*, Schiemann LJ, gave the judgment of the court and quoted extensively from the judgment of Potter LJ in *Han*, in particular the three criteria he had extracted from the jurisprudence of the European Court of Human Rights, and a further Court of Appeal decision in *Official Receiver v Stern*.[7] Applying the criteria in *Han*, he concluded that the case was not a criminal charge because only a registered person was subject to the disciplinary authority of the tribunals, and that no punitive or deterrent penalty was imposed.

20.08 These fairly fundamental distinctions between the proceedings in *Fleurose* and market abuse proceedings were not lost on the Tribunal in the *Parker* case, which pointed out that a market abuse allegation can be brought against any member of the public (not just registered, or approved, persons), that the penalty imposed in a market abuse case is both punitive and deterrent in nature, and that the conduct alleged could also be dealt with as a criminal offence in the criminal courts.

20.09 Therefore, following the decisions in *Han* and *Davidson*, the Tribunal decided that an allegation of market abuse, even when punished in accordance with s 123 of FSMA and therefore by a route which is classed as civil for domestic law purposes, has to be treated as a criminal charge for Convention purposes.[8]

Legal assistance

20.10 Pursuant to the requirement in Article 6(3) ECHR, the Financial Services and Markets Tribunal (Legal Assistance) Regulations 2001[9] provide for legal assistance to be granted to Applicants in respect of market abuse proceedings, provided that the criteria set out in the Regulations are met. The purpose of this is to give effect to the equality of arms requirements in Article 6(3) ECHR.

---

[6] *Fleurose v The Securities and Futures Authority Ltd* [2001] EWCA Civ 2015.
[7] *Official Receiver v Stern* [2001] 1 All ER 633; [2000] 1 WLR 2230.
[8] This approach is consistent with the approach taken by the ECHR in competition law proceedings. See *Menarini Diagnostics SRL v Italy*, Application No 43509/08, 27 September 2011 in which the ECHR confirmed that the proceedings taken against Menarini by the Italian competition authority in respect of breaches of anti-competition rules had a 'criminal nature' for the purposes of Article 6 ECHR. The elements taken into account by the court to determine whether the procedure had a criminal nature were (i) the classification of the infringement by the national legislation; (ii) the nature of the offence; and (iii) the nature and severity of the applied penalty.
[9] SI 2001/3632.

Privilege against self-incrimination

Section 174 FSMA gives effect to Article 6(2) ECHR by providing that a statement made by a person in compliance with an information requirement imposed upon him under FSMA, is not admissible against him in market abuse proceedings. **20.11**

3. Burden and standard of proof in market abuse proceedings

Burden of proof

This issue was considered in both *Davidson* and *Parker*. In both cases there was no issue that the burden of proof in market abuse cases must lie with the FSA.[10] That is uncontroversial. **20.12**

Standard of proof

The standard of proof in a criminal case is that the prosecution must prove its case 'beyond reasonable doubt'. In a civil case, the standard of proof is the 'balance of probabilities'. FSMA does not specify which standard of proof is to be applied in market abuse cases and s 123 FSMA refers only to the FCA needing to be 'satisfied' that a person has engaged in market abuse—as the precondition for taking disciplinary action. **20.13**

At its inception, the FSA took the view that in market abuse cases, the burden of proof was on the FSA and that the civil, balance of probabilities standard applied.[11] In a number of market abuse cases, the Tribunal has considered the standard of proof in relation to proceedings for market abuse. **20.14**

Previous Tribunal cases

Arif Mohammed v FSA[12]

In this case, the Tribunal agreed with the FSA that the civil standard was the correct standard to be applied in a market abuse case, albeit adopting the 'sliding scale' which had been approved in previous Tribunal cases[13] and which found its roots in the (then) often cited judgment of Lord Nicholls in *Re H*.[14] **20.15**

---

[10] See in particular *Davidson and Tatham v FSA* (n 2) paras 185–86.
[11] FSA Policy Statement 59 (April 2001)—Code of Market Conduct Feedback on CP59 and CP76, para 4.11.
[12] *Arif Mohammed v FSA*, FSMT, Case 012, 29 Mar 2005 (pre-MAD case).
[13] The principle being that the more serious the allegation the more cogent the evidence needs to be to prove it: see *Hoodless and Blackwell v FSA*, FSMT, 3 Oct 2003, para 21; *Legal & General Assurance Soc Ltd v FSA*, FSMT, Jan 2005, para 19.
[14] *Re H* [1996] 1 All ER 1, 16–17. Ungoed-Thomas J expressed the principle neatly in *Re Dellow's Will Trusts, Lloyds Bank Ltd v Institute of Cancer Research* [1964] 1 All ER 771 773, [1964] 1 WLR 451 455: 'The more serious the allegation, the more cogent is the evidence required to overcome the unlikelihood of what is alleged and thus to prove it.'

Davidson and Tatham v FSA[15]

20.16 This was also the approach adopted in the *Davidson* case, in which the Tribunal conducted an extensive view of the authorities, concluding that the fact that it had classified the proceedings as a 'criminal charge' for the purposes of Article 6 ECHR, did not require that the criminal standard of proof should also apply. This is consistent with Lord Mance's judgment in *Han*:[16] 'The classification of a case as [criminal] is a classification for the purposes of the Convention only. It entitles the defendant to the safeguards provided expressly or by implication by that Article. It does not make the case criminal for all domestic purposes.'[17]

James Parker v FSA

20.17 In *Parker*, the Tribunal adopted the same approach.[18] As the Tribunal explained in *Davidson and Tatham*, the fact that conduct of a particular kind exposes the person committing it to what is regarded, for Convention purposes, as a criminal charge even though its classification in domestic law may be civil, does not lead to the conclusion that the standard of proof must be the domestic criminal standard. Article 6 ECHR bestows various rights and protections on an accused person; the requirement that the prosecuting authority establish the charge beyond reasonable doubt is not among them. The standard of proof is, therefore, not dictated by the Convention and one can look only to the domestic law.

20.18 The Tribunal Panels in both *Davidson* and *Parker* plainly derived a good deal of comfort from the application of the so called 'sliding scale' principle to the civil standard of proof, and both made clear that they regarded market abuse allegations as extremely serious and that therefore the sliding scale was (as it was put in *Parker*):

> very close to the upper end ... In a practical sense, even if not semantically, it is difficult to draw a meaningful distinction between the standard we must apply and the criminal standard.[19]

The effect of the House of Lords Judgment in Re B

20.19 The judgment of the House of Lords in *In re B (Children)*[20] (*'Re B'*) disavowed the (so-called) sliding scale and concluded that neither the seriousness of the allegation nor the seriousness of the consequences should make any difference to the standard of proof; and inherent probabilities were simply to be taken into account where relevant in deciding where the truth lay.

---

[15] *Davidson and Tatham v FSA* (n 2) para 174ff (pre-MAD case).
[16] *Han* (n 3).
[17] See also *B v Chief Constable of Avon and Somerset Constabulary* (2001) in which Lord Bingham stated at para 29, that the jurisprudence of the European Court of Human Rights did not, even in criminal proceedings, require member states to apply what United Kingdom courts called the criminal standard of proof if the standard of proof was sufficiently strong in the eyes of domestic law to establish what has to be established.
[18] *James Parker v FSA* (n 5) para 22.
[19] *James Parker v FSA* (n 5) para 23.
[20] *In re B (Children)* [2008] UKHL 35 at 13–15 (per Lord Hoffmann) and 69–73 (per Baroness Hale of Richmond).

20.20 Despite this judgment, the Tribunal still seemed to be adopting a version of the sliding scale:

Atlantic Law LLP and Andrew Greystoke v FSA

20.21 In *Atlantic Law*,[21] the Tribunal dealt with the burden and standard of proof as follows:

> It is for the FSA to prove its case to a civil standard on the balance of probabilities. In applying such a standard, the Tribunal will require persuasive evidence before being satisfied that a person has behaved fraudulently or in a reprehensible manner.

20.22 This was also the approach adopted in *Chhabra and Patel v FSA*[22] in which the allegation was market abuse:

> ... some things are inherently more likely than others and cogent evidence is generally required to satisfy a civil tribunal that a person has been fraudulent or behaved in a reprehensible manner. Generally speaking, people tend not to commit serious offences—not least because of the consequences likely to follow if they do—and someone with a good character is less likely to behave badly than someone with a bad character. Someone who values their reputation will be less likely to imperil it than someone known to be disreputable. The more inherently unlikely it is that something has happened the more persuasive the tribunal will need to find the evidence pointing that way before concluding it to be more likely than not.

The effect of the Supreme Court Judgment in *Re S-B (Children) (Care Proceedings: Standard of Proof)*

20.23 Subsequently, the issue of the seriousness of the allegations in relation to the standard of proof was considered again by the Supreme Court in In *Re S-B (Children) (Care Proceedings: Standard of Proof)* (2010)[23] ('*Re S-B*'). In that case, the Supreme Court held at paragraphs 10–13:

1. The House of Lords had decided in *Re B* that the standard of proof of past facts was the simple balance of probabilities, no more and no less.
2. Apart from cases which the law classed as civil but in which the criminal standard was appropriate,[24] as Lord Hoffman declared in *Re B*, 'the time has come to say, once and for all, that there is only one civil standard of proof and that is proof that the fact in issue more probably occurred than not.'[25]
3. This did leave a role for inherent probabilities in considering whether it was more likely than not that an event had taken place. But there was no necessary connection between seriousness and inherent probability.

---

[21] *Atlantic Law LLP and Andrew Greystoke v FSA*, Upper Tribunal, 1–10 Mar 2010, para 9. This was not a market abuse case but did concern quasi-fraudulent allegations.
[22] *Robin Chhabra and Sameer Patel v FSA*, FSMT Case 072, 29 Dec 2009.
[23] *Re S-B (Children) (Care Proceedings: Standard of Proof)* [2010] 1 AC 678.
[24] Into this category came sex offender orders and anti-social behaviour orders: see *B v Chief Constable of Avon and Somerset Constabulary* [2001] 1 WLR 340 and *R (McCann) v Crown Court at Manchester* [2002] UKHL 39, [2003] 1 AC 787.
[25] *Re B* (n 20) para 13.

4. Therefore the nostrum, 'the more serious the allegation, the more cogent the evidence needed to prove it', which had arisen since Lord Nicholls' decision in *Re H*[26] must be rejected.

Mark Ainley v FSA[27]

20.24 Here, the Tribunal considered the standard of proof in the light *Re S-B*. Ainley was an FSA approved person against whom the FSA wished to make a prohibition order and impose a financial penalty for allegations of breaches of the FSA's Statements of Principles for Approved Persons and the FSA's 'Threshold Conditions.'[28] On the appropriate standard of proof, the Tribunal decided:[29]

> The observations of the Tribunal in *Chhabra* predate the judgment of the 20 Supreme Court in *In Re S-B*. In that case, the Supreme Court clearly rejected the idea that the more serious the conduct alleged, the more inherently unlikely it is and the more cogent or persuasive the evidence needed to prove that it happened. Factors such as good character must be taken into account when assessing whether it is more likely than not that the conduct occurred, as the Tribunal did in *Chhabra*, but such factors do not necessarily make the conduct inherently improbable and do not lead to any requirement that the evidence required to prove such conduct must be more persuasive. We consider that the standard of proof to be applied in this case is, as the Supreme Court held in *In Re S-B*, the ordinary civil standard of proof namely whether the alleged misconduct more probably occurred than not.

20.25 Although this is undoubtedly a correct statement of the civil standard of proof following *Re B* and *Re S-B*, it does not necessarily resolve the matter so far as market abuse proceedings are concerned. In *Ainley*, the Tribunal took the view that those proceedings should not be classified as 'criminal' for the purposes of Article 6 ECHR. Applying the criteria set out by Lord Justice Potter in *Han*, this is plainly correct. However, as demonstrated above, the Tribunal in *Davidson* and *Parker* (and to an extent *Chhabra*), despite holding that the civil standard of proof should be applied, clearly took great comfort from the fact that the 'sliding scale' meant that in effect there was only a semantic difference between the civil and criminal standards. What is the position now that the 'sliding scale' has been expressly disavowed? The above analysis suggests that, there appears to be room to revisit the issue as to whether the appropriate standard of proof in market abuse cases should in fact be the criminal standard after all.

---

[26] See *Re H* (n 14). The Supreme Court considered that although this interpretation had become commonplace, it was in fact a misinterpretation of what Lord Nicholls had actually said in *Re H*.
[27] *Mark Ainley v FSA*, Upper Tribunal Decision, 13 July 2012. This approach to the standard of proof was cited with approval by the Tribunal in a subsequent case: *Andrew Jeffery v FSA*, Upper Tribunal Decision, 22 January 2013, FS/2010/0039.
[28] See Schedule 6 FSMA.
[29] See *Mark Ainley v FSA* (n 27) para 22.

21

DETECTION AND REFERRAL TO ENFORCEMENT

1. Introduction	21.01	6. Detection of insider dealing and market abuse	21.20
2. The FSA	21.02	SABRE and ZEN	21.23
3. The FSA—attitude to enforcement	21.07	Suspicious transaction reporting	21.25
4. Insider dealing prosecutions—the statistics	21.08	Record keeping: client orders and transactions	21.29
5. The PRA and the FCA	21.10	7. The Enforcement of Financial Crime division	21.34
The Prudential Regulation Authority	21.11	8. The process by which cases are referred to Enforcement for investigation	21.36
The FCA	21.12		
The Financial Services Act 2012	24.14		
The FCA's statutory objectives	21.16		
FCA—attitude to enforcement	21.17	9. Cases in which other authorities have an interest	21.38

1. Introduction

This Chapter puts market abuse and insider dealing in the context of the Financial Services Authority's ('FSA') and Financial Conduct Authority's ('FCA') statutory objectives and deals with the principle ways in which market abuse and insider dealing behaviour is detected and initially investigated. The Chapter concludes by addressing the criteria that will be employed when a decision is made to refer a case to Enforcement for investigation and in accepting a case into Enforcement. It also deals with the position when other authorities have an interest in a case which is being considered for Enforcement investigation. **21.01**

2. The FSA

Until 1 April 2013, the financial services industry in the UK was regulated by the FSA. The FSA was an independent non-governmental body, given statutory powers by the Financial Services and Markets Act 2000 ('FSMA'). It is a popular **21.02** misconception, however, that the FSA was a government body—it was not. It was a company limited by guarantee and financed by the financial services industry and individuals it regulated.

21.03 The FSA's overall policy was set by its Board, with day-to-day decisions overseen by the Executive Committee. The FSA was accountable to Treasury Ministers and, through them, to Parliament, and it derived its functions and powers from statute—FSMA—which provided it with a wide range of rule-making, investigatory, and enforcement powers in order to meet its four statutory objectives. FSMA was described by Lord Justice May as:

> a huge statute with 433 sections and 22 Schedules, occupying 488 pages of *Halsbury's Statutes* (not a great deal of which is editorial). On one view it is an example (regrettably not unique) of statutory overload. Quips about *War and Peace* come to mind.[1]

21.04 FSMA gave the FSA four regulatory objectives:[2]

1. Market confidence—maintaining confidence in the UK financial system.[3]
2. Financial stability—contributing to the protection and enhancement of stability of the UK financial system.[4]
3. Consumer protection—securing the appropriate degree of protection for consumers;[5] and
4. The reduction of financial crime—reducing the extent to which it is possible for a regulated business to be used for a purpose connected with financial crime.[6]

21.05 Under s 2 FSMA, the FSA's general functions were to make rules under FSMA, prepare and issue codes, give general guidance, and determine the general policy and principles by which it performs particular functions.[7] In addition, FSMA required the FSA to issue specific rules and guidance in relation to certain of its functions and activities. The FSA therefore published its 'FSA Handbook of Rules and Guidance' ('FSA Handbook') which sat alongside the provisions of FSMA.

21.06 Within the FSA, the Enforcement and Financial Crime Division ('EFCD') was responsible for investigating and taking disciplinary action for breaches of regulatory requirements or for market abuse and taking criminal action in respect of conduct amounting to criminal offences.

---

[1] *R (on the application of Uberoi and another) v City of Westminster Magistrates' Court* [2008] EWHC 3191 (Admin).
[2] FSMA, s 2 pre-amendment by Financial Services Act 2012 ('FS Act 2012').
[3] FSMA, s 3 pre-amendment by FS Act 2012.
[4] FSMA, s 3A pre-amendment by FS Act 2012.
[5] FSMA, s 5 pre-amendment by FS Act 2012.
[6] FSMA, s 6 pre-amendment by FS Act 2012.
[7] FSMA, s 2(4) pre-amendment by FS Act 2012.

3. The FSA—attitude to enforcement

21.07 In 2005, the arrival of Margaret Cole as Director of Enforcement changed the FSA's approach which until that point had been summed up by the mantra, 'We are not an Enforcement-led Regulator'.[8] Ms Cole replaced this with her strategy of 'credible deterrence'. An important part of this strategy was to make criminal prosecutions for insider dealing a key priority for the FSA. The strategy was summarised in a speech she made to the European Policy Forum in April 2008:[9]

> Where enforcement is key is where we need to be visible in the market place sending tough messages about wrongful behaviour and imposing sanctions (which doesn't just mean fines) which are severe enough to have deterrent effect. We recognise that we need to do enough enforcement cases of the right sort to have 'demonstration effect' to bring about our strategy of credible deterrence ...
>
> ... For the last two years or so I have been signalling our intention to use our powers as a criminal prosecutor. Why? It is a direct reaction to the findings of the market cleanliness study, anecdotal evidence from the marketplace and the media, the things we see as a result of real time market monitoring, and the belief that criminal prosecution where a custodial sentence is a real risk will act as a stronger deterrent than a civil/administrative market abuse prosecution under FSMA, even though we have the power to impose unlimited fines. I don't think this can be described as being enforcement averse. It is a significant shift of emphasis for the FSA and it comes with risk. Commentators are always eager to point out the UK's poor record on prosecutions for insider dealing.
>
> I have said that this is a long-term strategy. We cannot afford to change this strategy if we hit choppy waters. If we are to make a significant impact in this area we must prosecute a steady stream of insider dealing cases, gaining the invaluable experience that will bring, and learning what we need to learn from cases where we fail to gain convictions. The inevitable fact that not every case will be successful does not undermine the strategy.

4. Insider dealing prosecutions—the statistics

21.08 The effect of Cole's strategy can be seen in the statistics. Between 2000 and 2008, the FSA had not brought any prosecutions for insider dealing. A small number

---

[8] 'Delivering more transparent and better informed financial markets' 30 Sep 2004, Speech by Callum McCarthy, FSA Chairman; Financial Crime Newsletter, Issue No. 10—Jan 2008; 'Reaching Over to the Mainland—Unbundling in Continental Europe', Speech by Hector Sants Managing Director, Wholesale and Institutional Markets European Trader Forum's Winter Workshop, Brussels, 25 Feb 2005; FSA Annual Report 2009/10, Chairman's statement (Adair Turner).

[9] 'Enforcing Financial Services Regulation: The UK FSA Perspective', Speech by Margaret Cole, Director of Enforcement, FSA European Policy Forum, 4 Apr 2008; see also 'There is a view that people are not frightened of the FSA ... people should be very frightened of the FSA', Speech by Hector Sants (FSA CEO) at the Reuters Newsmakers seminar, 12 Mar 2009; *FT* (7 Sep 2010). See also 'Our strategy and key objectives for tackling market abuse', 26 Market Watch (Apr 2008) introduction by Sally Dewar, Managing Director, Wholesale and Institutional Markets.

of prosecutions had been brought by the Serious Fraud Office ('SFO') and the then Department of Trade and Industry ('DTI'):

Offence	Year	Found guilty
Insider dealing[10]	2000	6
	2001	5
	2002	2
	2003	4
	2004	5
	2005	4
	2006	2
	2007	6
	2008	0

21.09 Since 2008, the statistics show:

Year	Found guilty
2009	4
2010	2
2011	5
2012	10
2013	2 (plus 7 charged and awaiting trial)

5. The PRA and the FCA

21.10 At 'legal cutover' on 1 April 2013, the Financial Services Act 2012 ('FS Act 2012') replaced the FSA with a 'twin peaks' system of regulation in which the FSA's functions were split between two organisations:

The Prudential Regulation Authority

21.11 The Prudential Regulation Authority ('PRA') is part of the Bank of England and carries out the prudential regulation of financial firms, including banks, investment banks, building societies, and insurance companies.

The FCA

21.12 The FCA has responsibility for regulating financial firms, providing services to consumers, and maintaining the integrity of the UK's financial markets. Its focus is on the regulation of conduct by both retail and wholesale financial services firms.

Like the FSA, the FCA is a company limited by guarantee which is funded by the industries and individuals it regulates. The FCA has also taken over from the FSA as the UK's securities markets regulator. In addition, it has inherited responsibility for overseeing other exchange-traded markets and the over-the-counter derivatives market. However, responsibility for the supervision of clearing and settlement infrastructure has now moved to the Bank of England.[11]

21.13 The Enforcement and Financial Crime Division ('EFCD') of the FSA became part of the FCA at legal cutover and it is therefore the FCA that has responsibility for investigating and taking action—whether civil or criminal, in respect of insider dealing and market abuse.

The Financial Services Act 2012

21.14 The FS Act 2012 amended the Bank of England Act 1998, the Banking Act 2009, and FSMA to reflect the twin peaks system. For simplicity, the FS Act 2012 preserves, in so far as possible, FSMA's previous structure. The sections of FSMA which relate to Market Abuse and the Enforcement process are therefore essentially unchanged in substance. The relevant parts of the FSA Handbook were also carried over into the FCA Handbook, so that the Enforcement Guide ('EG'), the Decisions Procedures and Penalties Manual ('DEPP'), and the Code of Market Conduct ('MAR') are also largely unchanged.

21.15 Section 6 of the FS Act 2012 substitutes ss 1–18 FSMA with ss 1A–3R. Sections 1A–1T set out the FCA's objectives and general functions. Section 1A(1) makes the point that 'the body corporate previously known as the Financial Services Authority is renamed the Financial Conduct Authority'.

The FCA's statutory objectives

21.16 Section 1B(2) FSMA sets out the FCA's strategic objective which is 'ensuring that the relevant markets function well'. Relevant markets includes the financial markets.[12] Section 1B(3) provides that the FCA's operational objectives are

1. The consumer protection objective—securing an appropriate degree of protection for consumers.[13]
2. The integrity objective—protecting and enhancing the integrity of the UK financial system.[14] The UK financial system includes financial markets and exchanges and activities connected with financial markets and exchanges.[15]

---

[10] Statistics provided by the Ministry of Justice.
[11] *Journey to the FCA*, Approach Document, 46–47.
[12] FSMA, s 1F.
[13] FSMA, s 1C.
[14] FSMA, s 1D.
[15] FSMA, s 1I.

This objective includes ensuring that the UK financial system is not being used for a purpose connected with financial crime and is not being affected by behaviour that amounts to market abuse.[16] Financial crime includes any offence involving fraud or dishonesty, misconduct in, or misuse of information relating to a financial market, or handling the proceeds of crime.[17]

3. The competition objective—promoting effective competition in the interests of consumers in the markets.[18]

FCA—attitude to enforcement

21.17 In October 2012, the FSA published its Approach Document ('AD'), entitled *Journey to the FCA*. This document set out how the FCA would approach its objectives. The AD stated that the FCA 'will increase its focus on delivering good market conduct'.[19] This would include:

> Preventing market abuse—Good wholesale conduct relies on the effective policing of market abuse. Our approach to market conduct will reinforce the strong track record that we have built by tackling criminal and civil market abuse.[20]

21.18 All the indications are that 'Credible Deterrence' will remain very much at the heart of the FCA's Enforcement Strategy as confirmed by Tracey McDermott, the EFCD Director in a speech in November 2012:[21]

> Enforcement—in its traditional sense—will remain a core part of what we do. Our credible deterrence strategy will remain, taking tough and meaningful action against those firms and individuals who fall short of our standards and break the rules.
>
> The FCA will also take on all of the FSA's financial crime responsibilities, and we will be well placed, building on our recent work, to take a robust stance. Tackling financial crime will be a key task for the FCA, influencing who we allow to own and run financial firms, what questions we ask them, and our decisions to punish those who fall short.

21.19 These comments provide a further indication that the FCA is likely to continue the FSA's focus on insider dealing as a strategic priority with particular emphasis on misconduct by market professionals. In addition, as part of the FCA's future strategy, and as a signal that it intends to continue the FSA's work in using criminal prosecutions as a means of achieving 'credible deterrence', the EFCD now

---

[16] FSMA, s 1D(2).
[17] FSMA, s 1H(3).
[18] FSMA, s 1E.
[19] *Journey to the FCA* (n 12) ch 1, 12.
[20] *Journey to the FCA* (n 12) ch 1, 12.
[21] 'Combating Financial Crime: Key themes and Priorities for 2013', 15 Nov 2012; speech by Tracey McDermott, director of the Enforcement and Financial Crime Division at the APCIMS Conference. See also, 'The Changing Face of Financial Crime', speech by Martin Wheatley, FCA Chief Executive, at the FCA Financial Crime Conference and 'Keynote Address: Financial Crime in the FCA World', speech by Tracey McDermott, Director of the FCA Enforcement and Financial Crime Division, at the FCA Financial Crime Conference, both published 1 July 2013. See also Chapter 1, Section 4.

has a designated 'Criminal Prosecutions Team'. This team is led by David Kirk (the FCA's Chief Criminal Counsel), and comprises technical specialists with criminal law expertise, as well as other criminal law specialists and support staff. The role of this team will be to undertake the prosecution function with respect to the FCA's criminal proceedings and to oversee and advise on the work of the investigation teams with respect to criminal investigations.

6. Detection of insider dealing and market abuse

21.20 Within the FCA it is the Markets Division, which has primary responsibility for the supervision of market infrastructures, markets policy, the identification of market abuse, the function of the UK Listing Authority, and the client assets unit. This was also the position within the FSA. The Markets Division has the following responsibilities:

- Market Infrastructure and Policy;
- Wholesale Conduct Policy and Client Assets;
- Regulation of the UK Covered Bond programme;
- Market Surveillance and Monitoring; and
- the UK Listing Authority.

21.21 The Markets Division aims to fulfil its responsibilities through risk analysis, policy making, supervisory and enquiries functions. The Approach Document states that the Markets Division's intention is to carry forward its Enforcement-based approach to tackling market abuse behaviour and failures to disclose information to the markets.[22]

21.22 The FCA has, in addition to its Markets Division, a new Policy, Risk and Research Division which it is intended will act as a radar for what is happening in the markets and to consumers, and drive the actions that the FCA takes.[23] This new division is expected to gather and use a wide range of data and intelligence to help it identify and assess risks in financial markets, including information on consumers' behaviour, experiences, and concerns.

SABRE and ZEN

21.23 Until November 2011, the FSA used a market monitoring system, called 'Surveillance Analysis of Business Reporting' ('SABRE II'). SABRE II included a database of market transactions collected from authorised firms, regulated investment exchanges, and settlement systems. The transaction database held reportable equity, debt, and associated derivative trades (both on-exchange and over the counter).

---

[22] *Journey to the FCA* (n 12) 46–47.
[23] *Journey to the FCA* (n 12) 41.

21.24 In November 2011, the FSA's new surveillance and monitoring system, ZEN, went live and replaced the SABRE II system. ZEN is an enhanced version of SABRE II and provided the FSA with enhanced regulatory capabilities including a market abuse monitoring, alerting, and reporting function. The FCA continues to use ZEN to gather statistics on suspicious trading activity across the financial markets that operate in the UK.[24]

Suspicious transaction reporting

21.25 The Market Abuse Directive 2003 ('MAD')[25] required Member States to introduce wide ranging measures to require the reporting of suspicious transactions. These requirements sit alongside the requirements to report suspicious transactions that exist under the Proceeds of Crime Act 2002 ('POCA'). The MAD required that any professional who arranges transactions in financial instruments (which includes commodity derivatives), who reasonably suspects that a transaction constitutes market abuse, notify the competent authority (in the UK this is the FCA).[26]

21.26 This requirement was elaborated upon by a further EU Directive which required investment firms and credit institutions to 'decide on a case-by-case basis whether there are reasonable grounds for suspecting that a transaction involves insider dealing or market manipulation ... [and] shall be subject to the rules of notification'.[27] The FSA's Supervision Manual ('SUP')[28] implemented this requirement in the UK. The FSA's publication *Market Watch*[29] stated in 2009, that since the MAD was introduced in 2005, the FSA had received over 1000 Suspicious Transaction Reports ('STRs').

21.27 When a firm submits a STR, it may often choose to include additional information relevant to the circumstances of the transaction in order to explain why the firm considers the transaction suspicious and worthy of reporting. On receipt of an STR or other notification, the FCA will send an acknowledgement letter. This is often accompanied by a general request to the firm to retain any potentially relevant material.

21.28 Where the FCA's review of a transaction is prompted by some other source, or it requires more extensive information than is provided in the STR—for example further details of communications between the client and the firm relating to that particular transaction or perhaps to other earlier transactions—it will contact the

---

[24] *Journey to the FCA* (n 12) 47.
[25] MAD 2003/6/EC.
[26] MAD 2003/6/EC Article 9.
[27] Commission Directive 2004/72/EC, art 7.
[28] SUP 15.10; SUP 15.10.4 provided guidance on how to determine the basis for suspicion that the transaction might constitute market abuse. See also Code of Market Conduct ('MAR') and SUP 15 Annex 5G.
[29] 'Market Watch' 33 (Aug 2009).

firm to establish what further information it may hold, in particular recordings of conversations with the subject of the STR. The firm will be likely to be asked to retain or produce any additional relevant material.

Record keeping: client orders and transactions

The FCA's Conduct of Business Sourcebook[30] ('COBS') requires an investment firm to keep records of client orders and decisions to deal.   **21.29**

Recorded telephone calls

In March 2008, the FSA published a Policy Statement[31] entitled 'Telephone recording: recording of voice conversations and electronic communications'. This introduced rules requiring broking firms to record and retain for a period of six months, telephone conversations, and other electronic communications linked to taking client orders and dealing in financial instruments.   **21.30**

Plainly, records of phone conversations and electronic communications can play an important role in market abuse and insider dealing investigations, by providing context and helping to establish the facts. Taped records can provide evidence of the dealing and also of knowledge and intent—crucial elements in building a case but not always easy elements to establish. In any insider dealing or market abuse investigation, the FCA will obtain the taped records of communications between the suspects and their brokers.   **21.31**

Deal timetables and insider lists

When the Markets Division undertakes its preliminary enquiries in suspected cases of market abuse, particularly insider dealing, its primary aim is to establish whether there is a link between those who may have traded based on inside information and an 'insider' who may have passed that information on.   **21.32**

The FCA's Disclosure Rules and Transparency Rules ('DTR')[32] place an obligation on issuers to maintain a list of insiders both for itself and persons acting on its behalf.[33] This will be particularly important in relation to significant corporate events such as a takeover or merger. At the outset of its enquiries, the insider list will be likely to be among the first documents that the FCA will request firms to provide, together with a deal timetable for a transaction. The aim is to establish who had inside information, what the information was, and when it was known. This information enables a picture to be built of how widely disseminated the inside information was at any point in time. When it is suspected that inside information   **21.33**

---

[30] COBS 11.5.
[31] 08/01. See also FSA's 'Market Watch' 24 (Oct 2007).
[32] DTR 2.8.
[33] The FSA published guidance on interpreting these requirements, see 'Market Watch' 12 (June 2005) and 21 (July 2007).

may have leaked, and been acted on, the FCA uses the deal timetable to focus its enquiries on particular institutions or individuals who would have had the information when the suspicious trades were undertaken.

7. The Enforcement and Financial Crime Division

21.34 The EFCD conducts forensic investigations into suspected misconduct, compliance failures and financial crime, committed by firms and individuals. The Wholesale and Retail departments within the EFCD carry out administrative, civil, and criminal proceedings in the enforcement of FSMA, the FSA's rules and other regulatory requirements. Within the EFCD, the Financial Crime and Intelligence team comprises Policy, Intelligence, Sector, and Operations teams who together deal with any issues involving money laundering, fraud or dishonesty, or market abuse. The EFCD Legal Department is the specialist litigation department that conducts Legal Reviews of Enforcement Cases and proposed Enforcement action and also advises on and conducts litigation on behalf of the EFCD. The Legal Department also handles International co-operation issues. The EFCD also works with other regulatory bodies and law enforcement agencies in the UK and abroad.

21.35 There are a number of principles underlying the FCA's approach to the exercise of its Enforcement powers. These are contained within the Enforcement Guide ('EG') of the FCA Handbook.[34] They include the need to exercise enforcement powers in a manner that is transparent, proportionate, responsive to the issue, and consistent with its publicly stated policies and to deter future non-compliance by others.

8. The process by which cases are referred to Enforcement for investigation

21.36 Enforcement action is only one of a number of regulatory tools available to the FCA. As a risk based regulator with limited resources, the FCA must prioritise its resources in the areas which pose the biggest threat to its regulatory objectives[35]. Plainly, the FCA does not have the resources to take action in every case where suspicious circumstances are present. It follows therefore that not all cases in which the Markets Division conducts an initial investigation and gathers information, will be referred to the EFCD for formal investigation, or will be accepted for investigation by the EFCD. The actual decision as to whether to accept a case into EFCD for investigation will be a collaborative decision

---

[34] Enforcement Guide ('EG') of the FSA Handbook, 2.2.
[35] EG 2.3.

between staff from the referring department, the EFCD and, in some cases, from other areas of the FCA.

When the Markets Division decides to refer an insider dealing / market abuse case to the EFCD for investigation, and when the EFCD decides to accept a case, a number of criteria are taken into account. These are found in EG 2.5 to 2.10 which focus on strategic priorities and thematic work[36] and also in 'The Referral Criteria'.[37] The criteria are framed as a set of questions. They take into account the FCA's statutory objectives, business priorities and other relevant issues. Not all of the criteria will be relevant to every case and in addition there may be other considerations that are relevant to a particular case. The criteria include factors which will be particularly relevant to an insider dealing / market abuse case such as evidence of financial crime or risk of financial crime; whether the suspected misconduct could undermine public confidence in the orderliness of financial markets; whether there is evidence that the person has profited from the action; whether the issue is relevant to an FCA strategic priority; and whether Enforcement action is likely to further the FCA's aims and objectives. **21.37**

9. Cases in which other authorities have an interest

When considering whether to use its powers to conduct formal investigations into any misconduct, the FCA will take into account whether another regulatory authority is in a position to investigate and deal with the matters of concern.[38] Equally, in some cases, the FCA may investigate and/or take action in parallel with another domestic or international authority. The FSA previously agreed guidelines[39] that established a framework for liaison and cooperation in cases where one or more other authority (such as the Crown Prosecution Service or Serious Fraud Office) has an interest. The FCA is also a signatory to the Prosecutors' Convention,[40] which sets out the responsibilities of prosecutors where a suspect's conduct could be dealt with by criminal or civil/regulatory sanctions and/or where more than one prosecuting authority and investigating body share the power to take some action. The aim of the Prosecutors' Convention is to ensure that prosecuting authorities work together in an active and co-ordinated manner to ensure that cases are conducted in a way that is just and which best serves the overall public interest, so that the public can have confidence in the outcome. **21.38**

---

[36] EG 2.5–2.10.
[37] FCA, Enforcement Referral Criteria.
[38] EG 2.15.
[39] EG 12.11 and Annex 2.
[40] Prosecutors' Convention 2009.

21.39 Under EG Annex 2[41]—in relation to the indicators for deciding which agency should take action in any given case, two of the factors tending towards action by the FCA are:

- Where the allegations concern conduct that gives rise to concerns regarding market confidence.
- Where the allegations concern conduct which would best be dealt with by criminal prosecution of offences which the FCA has powers to prosecute by virtue of FSMA.

Plainly, proceedings for market abuse or insider dealing will be likely to meet both these criteria and it is difficult therefore to conceive of circumstances in which the FCA would defer to another authority in such a case.

---

[41] EG Annex 2, para 9.

22

THE ENFORCEMENT INVESTIGATION

1. Introduction	22.01	7. Protected items (s 413 FSMA)		22.18
2. Allocation to a case team	22.02	8. Banking confidentiality (s 175(5) FSMA)		22.20
3. Powers of investigation	22.03			
Power to appoint investigators to carry out investigations in particular cases	22.04	9. Sanctions for failure to comply (s 177 FSMA)		22.21
		10. Use of information		22.25
4. Notification of an investigation	22.06	Disclosure gateways		22.29
5. Use of statutory powers to require the production of documents, the provision of information, or the answering of questions	22.09	Other disclosure issues		22.32
		11. Search warrants		22.34
		12. Interviews		22.40
		Procedure in a compelled interview		22.44
Power to require information from authorised persons (s 165 FSMA)	22.11	Voluntary interviews with non suspects		24.45
Powers of persons appointed as a result of s 168(2) (s 173 FSMA)	22.14	Interviews with suspects		22.47
		Admissibility of compulsory interviews in criminal market or market abuse proceedings (s 174 FSMA)		
Supplementary powers (s 175 FSMA)	22.16			
6. Powers under the Regulation of Investigatory Powers Act 2000	22.17			22.50
		13. Witness statements		22.51

1. Introduction

This Chapter describes the steps in a market abuse / insider dealing Enforcement **22.01** investigation. It deals with the powers to appoint investigators, notification of the subject, the use of statutory powers under FSMA to require the production of documents or the provision of information, and the limits on these powers in certain circumstances. This Chapter also deals with the FCA's power to obtain search warrants in market abuse / insider dealing cases, interviews with suspects and non-suspects, and the obtaining of witness statements. It also deals with the use by the FCA of information obtained in the course of an investigation.

2. Allocation to a case team

22.02 When a market abuse / insider dealing case is accepted into the Enforcement and Financial Crime Division ('EFCD') for investigation, it will be allocated to one of the Wholesale Case Teams. Each team will comprise a Manager, at least one Technical Specialist (a Senior lawyer with specialist expertise in the Wholesale field), associate lawyers, forensic investigators, and support staff. The case team will decide on the scope of the investigation and will conduct the investigation. At regular intervals, the case team will report on the progress of the investigation to the 'Project Sponsor' who will be one of the two Heads of the Wholesale Department. In addition, particular actions, such as applications for and conduct of search warrants, will require the particular approval of the Project Sponsor. Therefore, whilst the case team has significant autonomy in the conduct of the investigation, there is a strong reporting line up the chain of command.

3. Powers of investigation

22.03 The FCA's powers of investigation and information gathering are found in Part XI of FSMA. In addition, the Enforcement Guide ('EG') contained in the FCA's Handbook of Rules and Guidance describes the FCA's approach to exercising these powers. This section focuses on the powers that are likely to be used in an insider dealing / market abuse investigation.

Power to appoint investigators to carry out investigations in particular cases

22.04 At the outset of an insider dealing / market abuse investigation, it will probably not be known what the outcome will be and whether, ultimately, the case will be pursued as a criminal prosecution under Part V of the CJA or as a market abuse case under Part VIII of FSMA. That decision will probably not be made until much later on, towards the end of the investigation. At the outset therefore, investigators will be appointed under s 168(2)(a) or (b) FSMA.[1] The threshold for the exercise of the power to appoint investigators under s 168(2) is set at a relatively low level. The power of investigation in these cases is not limited to the affairs of authorised persons and nor is it subject to any jurisdictional limits.

---

[1] See also EG, 3.8–3.9.

Under s 168(2) FSMA, the FCA may appoint investigators to conduct an investigation on its behalf if it appears to it that there are circumstances suggesting that: **22.05**

- An offence under Part V of the CJA 2003 (insider dealing) may have been committed (s 168(2)(a) FSMA).
- Market abuse may have taken place (s 168(2)(d) FSMA).

4. Notification of an investigation

Section 170 FSMA[2] provides for the notice requirements that the FCA is required to give the subject of the investigation. Essentially, the FCA must give written notice to a subject of the appointment of an investigator (known as a 'Memorandum of Appointment') or the change in scope of an investigation, unless the investigator is appointed as a result of s 168(2) FSMA, or the FSA believes that the investigation would be frustrated by the giving of written notice.[3] If Notice is given it must specify the provisions under which the investigator was appointed and state the reasons for his appointment.[4] **22.06**

Although the FCA is not required to give the subject written notice of the appointment of investigators appointed as a result of s 168(2), once the subject becomes aware of the investigation (usually following arrest and / or execution of search warrants), the FCA will normally provide a written notice to the subject notifying them that they are under investigation. **22.07**

Accompanying the Memorandum of Appointment will be a Notice of Appointment of Investigators. The Notice informs the subject that investigators have been appointed and that he will be informed if there is any significant change in the scope of the investigation unless the FCA believes that such notice would be likely to result in the investigation being frustrated. The Notice also informs the subject of the investigators' powers, which include powers to compel attendance at interview to answer questions, to compel the production of documents, and to otherwise compel the provision of information as well as the consequences of failure to comply. **22.08**

---

[2] See EG, 4.1–4.6.
[3] FSMA, s 170(3)(a).
[4] FSMA, s 170(4).

5. Use of statutory powers to require the production of documents, the provision of information, or the answering of questions

22.09 The FCA's standard practice is to use statutory powers to require the production of documents, the provision of information or the answering of questions in interview.[5] Exceptions to this are:

- Where individuals are suspects or possible suspects in criminal or market abuse investigations.
  Here statutory powers will generally be used to obtain pre-existing documents but questioning of those suspected of a criminal offence will be conducted under caution. This preserves the individual's privilege against self-incrimination. Suspects in market abuse cases in which it is clear that there will be no criminal prosecution will be interviewed either under caution or on a voluntary basis rather than by the use of compulsory powers. This is because the privilege against self-incrimination in such cases is expressly preserved by s 174 of FSMA.
- The FCA will usually seek information voluntarily from third parties who have no professional connection with the financial services industry, such as the victims of an alleged fraud or misconduct.
- Requests to the FCA by overseas regulators to obtain documents or conduct interviews on their behalf. Here the FCA will consider with the overseas regulator the most appropriate method for obtaining evidence for use in the overseas regulator's jurisdiction.

22.10 Authorised firms and approved persons have an obligation to be open and co-operative with the FCA (as a result of Principle 11 of the FCA's Principles for Businesses, and Statement of Principle 4 for Approved Persons, respectively). In these cases, the FCA will make it clear to the firm or individual concerned whether it requires them to produce information or answer questions pursuant to compulsory powers under FSMA or whether the provision of answers or information is purely voluntary.

Power to require information from authorised persons (s 165 FSMA)

22.11 Under s 165 FSMA, the FCA may give a notice in writing to an authorised person requiring him to provide information and / or produce documents.[6] The information or documents required must be specified in the notice.

22.12 The FCA may also require the information or documents to be supplied without delay (known as a 'here and now' request), provided that the information or documents are

---

[5] EG 4.8–4.11, 4.15.
[6] See EG 3.2–3.3.

reasonably required in connection with the exercise of the functions conferred on it by FSMA. The power is exercisable against authorised persons; however, s 165(8) defines 'authorised person' as including a person who was at one time an authorised person but has now ceased to be so. The power also extends to persons 'connected' with an authorised person and this definition extends to a membership of the authorised person's group, a controller of an authorised person, a partnership with the authorised person, and other specific types of relationship identified in Part 1 of Schedule 15 of FSMA (which includes the employees and agents of the authorised person).[7]

22.13 Preliminary enquiries by the Markets Division will be conducted under s 165 FSMA. However, once the case has been accepted into Enforcement for investigation and investigators are appointed under s 168(2), investigators will use s 173 powers for the purposes of a formal investigation.

Powers of persons appointed as a result of s 168(2) (s 173 FSMA)

22.14 Under s 173 FSMA, a requirement may be imposed on any person if an investigator considers that person is, or may be able, to give, information which is, or may be, relevant to the investigation. An investigator may require any such person to:

- attend for questioning;
- otherwise provide such information as he may require for the purposes of the investigation;
- produce any documents specified in a notice which appear to the investigator to relate to any matter relevant to the investigation;
- provide all assistance in connection with the investigation which the person is reasonably able to give.

22.15 By s 174(5) FSMA these requirements are known as 'information requirements'. Section 173 is widely drawn. It is important, however, that the FCA is able to justify, if necessary, that the information request relates to information that 'is or may be relevant to the investigation'. In addition, the exercise of these powers is also subject to overarching laws of natural justice. This was confirmed by Chadwick LJ in *R (on the application of Clegg) v Secretary of State for Trade and Industry*.[8] Here, the Court of Appeal was concerned with the conduct of inspectors appointed under the provisions of s 442(1) of the Companies Act 1985. Chadwick LJ said:

> Section 177 of the Financial Services Act (now repealed and replaced by section 168 of the Financial Services and Markets Act 2000) contained a power to much the same effect in respect of insider dealing. It is not in dispute that inspectors appointed under those provisions have a duty to act fairly towards those whose conduct they may criticise in the report they are required to make.

---

[7] See FSMA, s 165(7)(a) and (11).
[8] *R (on the application of Clegg) v Secretary of State for Trade and Industry* [2002] EWCA Civ 519; [2002] All ER (D) 114.

Supplementary powers (s 175 FSMA)

22.16 Where the FCA has power to require production of a document but it appears that the document is in possession of a third party, s 175 FSMA enables an investigator to:

- obtain documents from third parties;
- take copies or extracts from documents;
- require an explanation of a document to be provided;
- require a person who fails to produce a document to state where the document is to the best of his knowledge and belief;
- require a lawyer to furnish the name and address of his client;
- produce banking documents or provide banking information (s 175(5) FSMA sets out the circumstances in which these can be required).

6. Powers under the Regulation of Investigatory Powers Act 2000

22.17 In addition to its investigatory powers under FSMA, the FCA is one of a number of public authorities who are entitled under the Regulation of Investigatory Powers Act 2000 ('RIPA') to obtain 'communications data' from providers of communications services such as the post, telephone, and email. Access to communications data is regulated by the provisions of RIPA, and the FCA is required to comply with its provisions in obtaining authorisation for the use of its powers to obtain details of subscribers to such services and the details of communications made via them. The FCA has no power to authorise the interception of communications, although it would not be prevented from working in conjunction with other organisations who do have such powers (such as the Serious Organised Crime Agency ('SOCA')).

7. Protected items (s 413 FSMA)

22.18 The power to require the production of documents and information under FSMA are restricted in respect of two categories of documents:

- protected items
- documents/information subject to banking confidentiality

22.19 Section 413 FSMA states that a person cannot be required to produce, disclose, or permit the inspection of protected items. Sections 413(2) and (3) FSMA define a protected item which essentially amounts to a statutory form of legal professional privilege protecting communications made between a professional legal adviser, his client, and other persons who represent his client. The communication must be in connection with the giving of legal advice to the client, or in connection with, or in contemplation of, legal proceedings and be made for the purposes of those proceedings. The privilege extends to items that are enclosed with or referred to in such communications provided the item is in the possession of a person entitled to have them. Section 413(4) FSMA provides that a communication or item is not a protected item if it is held with the intention of furthering a criminal purpose.

8. Banking confidentiality (s 175(5) FSMA)

A bank is generally not permitted to disclose details of a customer's account except in very limited circumstances. This obligation continues even following closure of the account. Section 175(5) FSMA provides a number of exceptions to this and enables the FCA to obtain the documents or information in circumstances in which: 22.20

- the bank itself is the subject of the investigation or is a member of a group of companies and one of its group is the subject of the investigation;
- the person to whom the obligation of confidence is owed (the account holder) is the person under investigation or a member of that person's group;
- the person to whom the obligation of confidence is owed consents to the disclosure; or
- the requirement to disclose has been specifically authorised by the FCA.

9. Sanctions for failure to comply (s 177 FSMA)

Under s 177(3) FSMA it is an offence for a person to: 22.21

a) falsify, conceal, destroy or otherwise dispose of a document which he knows or suspect is, or would be, relevant to the investigation; or
b) cause or permit the falsification, concealment, destruction or disposal of such a document.

Both instances apply unless the person shows that he had no intention of concealing facts disclosed by the documents from the investigators.

In addition, it is an offence under s 177(4) FSMA for a person who, in purported compliance with a requirement placed on him under FSMA, knowingly or recklessly gives information, which is false or misleading in a material particular. 22.22

Under s 177(2) FSMA, failure to comply with a requirement imposed without reasonable excuse may be certified in writing to the High Court and the person may be 22.23

dealt with as if he were in contempt of court and may be imprisoned, fined, or have his assets seized. Under s 177(5) FSMA, a person guilty of an offence under s 177(3) or (4) may be liable on summary conviction, to imprisonment for a term not exceeding six months or a fine not exceeding the statutory maximum or both, or on conviction on indictment, to imprisonment for a term not exceeding two years or a fine, or both.

22.24 In addition, in the case of an authorised firm or approved person, such failure may result in disciplinary action for breach of Principle 11 for Businesses and/or Statement of Principle 4 for Approved Persons.[9]

10. Use of information

22.25 The FCA's ability to obtain, use, and disclose information are wide reaching. There are, however, no corresponding provisions that enable a person to prevent the FCA from obtaining or using information, or to discover when disclosures have been made. The main provisions governing the treatment of information obtained by the FCA are set out in ss 348 and 349 FSMA and in the FSMA (Disclosure of Confidential Information) Regulations 2001 ('DOCIR').

22.26 Section 348 FSMA provides protection against disclosure by the FCA of confidential information and by persons obtaining information directly or indirectly from the FCA (subject only to the consent of the person who provided the information or, if different, the person to whom the information relates). Confidential information is widely defined in s 348(2) and (4) FSMA as being:

- information which relates to the business or other affairs of any person;
- was received by the primary recipient for the purposes of, or in discharge of, any functions of the FCA or the Secretary of State under any provision made by or under FSMA;
- has not already been made available to the public; or
- is not in a form that would make it impossible to ascertain whether it relates to any particular person.

22.27 Primary recipient is defined in s 348(5) FSMA as meaning not only the FCA, but also the Secretary of State and various other categories of persons, such as those the FCA appoints or employs. Breach of s 348 is a criminal offence.[10] There are a number of circumstances in which confidential information may lawfully be disclosed. These are as follows:

1. Where the person from whom the information was obtained, and (if different) the person to whom it relates, consents (s 348(1) FSMA).

---

[9] See EG 4.11.
[10] See FSMA, s 352.

2. Where the information is already available to the public from other sources. (s 348(4)(a) FSMA).
3. Where the information is in the form of a summary or collection of information so framed that it is not possible to ascertain from it information relating to any particular person (s 348(4)(b) FSMA).

22.28 Section 349 FSMA also permits disclosure of confidential information subject to two requirements. These are that the disclosure must be made for the purpose of facilitating the carrying out of a public function. Public function is defined in s 349(5) FSMA and includes public functions conferred by the laws of countries and territories outside the UK. The disclosure must also be permitted by the DOCIR.[11]

Disclosure gateways

22.29 The DOCIR provides for a number of 'gateways' through which confidential information may be disclosed. The gateways are wide-reaching and complex. They are intended to provide a code that deals with all possible situations, and persons to whom, the disclosure of confidential information may be necessary. The gateways are permissive in that the FCA is permitted to disclose information in certain circumstances, but is not compelled to do so. Regulation 7 of the DOCIR provides that when making a disclosure, the FCA can impose conditions on how the information may be used.

22.30 The gateways define the persons to whom disclosure can be made and the purpose for which disclosure can be made in a number of different ways. In some instances, a particular person or body is specifically listed together with the purpose for which disclosures can be made to that person or body. In other instances, the regulations allow disclosure for a particular purpose without specifying any particular person or body.

22.31 The most common gateways are:

1. The 'self-help' gateway.[12] This permits disclosure by or to the FCA, the Secretary of State, or the Treasury to enable or assist the FCA to carry out its public functions.
2. Disclosures in relation to criminal matters.[13] This permits disclosure for the purposes of any criminal proceedings or investigations in the UK or elsewhere. This regulation is very widely drafted. There is no requirement for the criminal investigation to already be underway, although it should at least be under consideration.

---

[11] SI 2001/2188.
[12] DOCIR para 3.
[13] DOCIR para 4.

3. Disclosure in relation to other types of proceedings.[14] These gateways permit disclosure for the purposes of civil proceedings in the High Court, the Tribunal, other civil proceedings to which the FCA is a party, Directors disqualification proceedings, and Insolvency proceedings.
4. Disclosures to other regulatory bodies (in the UK and abroad).[15] These gateways permit disclosure for the purposes of discharging the regulatory bodies' particular functions. This is a very widely drawn gateway; however, the FCA will only make the permitted disclosures to overseas regulatory authorities where there is a co-operation agreement in place and an 'equivalent' condition met that when received, the information will be subject to guarantees of professional secrecy at least equivalent to those set out in the FSMA, DOCIR, and the EU Single Market Directives.

Other disclosure issues

22.32 The FCA is also bound by the Data Protection Act 1998 ('DPA'). This protects personal data (ie, data about living individuals) and places restrictions on the FCA's ability to disclose personal data within the UK and overseas. The DPA also provides individuals with a right of access to data (including regulatory information) relating to them, other than in certain cases, for example where disclosure would prejudice the FCA's regulatory functions or a criminal investigation. Information subject to statutory restrictions on disclosure is excluded from any requirement to disclose imposed by any Freedom of Information legislation.

22.33 Like any other UK public body, the FCA is obliged to comply with a court witness summons, requiring it to provide oral evidence or documents in civil or criminal litigation to which it is not a party. However, the FCA can only be compelled to provide evidence by way of witness summons in circumstances in which it would be permitted to disclose that information in accordance with FSMA or DOCIR.

11. Search warrants

22.34 Section 176 FSMA empowers the FCA to obtain a search warrant from a magistrates' court, provided the court is satisfied, on information given on oath, that there are reasonable grounds for believing that one of the three 'sets of conditions' given in s 176(2), (3) or (4) FSMA is satisfied.[16] These conditions are:

1. A person has failed to comply with an information requirement and that the information or document required is on the premises specified in the warrant.[17]

---

[14] DOCIR para 5.
[15] DOCIR Schedules 1 and 2.
[16] EG 4.28–4.29.
[17] FSMA, s 176(2).

2. The premises specified in the warrant are the premises of an authorised person or appointed representative and that:[18]
   a. There are on the premises documents or information in relation to which an information requirement could be imposed.
   b. If it were imposed, it would not be complied with or the documents or information to which it relates would be removed, tampered with, or destroyed.
3. An offence mentioned in s 168 FSMA has been committed, for which the maximum sentence for conviction on indictment is two years' imprisonment or more, and that:[19]
   a. There are on the premises specified in the warrant documents or information relevant to whether that offence has been or is being committed.
   b. An information requirement could be imposed.
   c. If it were imposed it would not be complied with or the documents or information would be removed, tampered with or destroyed.

22.35 By s 176(5) FSMA, a warrant authorises a constable to enter the premises specified in the warrant, search the premises, and take possession of any documents or information appearing to be of a kind specified in the warrant (referred to as 'the relevant kind'), or to take steps to preserve or prevent interference with these. In addition, the warrant permits copies or extracts to be taken from these documents and to require any person on the premises to provide an explanation of any document or information appearing to be of a relevant kind, or state where it may be found. Section 176(5)(e) FSMA provides that a constable is authorised to use such force as may be reasonably necessary in order to execute the warrant.

22.36 It is common for insider dealing investigations to commence with the obtaining and execution of a search warrant as this maintains an element of 'surprise' and is therefore most likely to produce the evidence needed to substantiate a prosecution. However, as set out above, although the FCA has the power to obtain search warrants, it has no power to execute them and therefore warrants must be executed by the relevant police force who will attend at the premises together with the FCA investigators.[20] The search is conducted by the FCA investigators but the police are required to remain on the premises for the duration of the search as, otherwise, the search is rendered unlawful.

22.37 In 2010, the Complaints Commissioner upheld a complaint[21] relating to one incident that occurred on 10 April 2008 when FSA investigators attended the home address of the director of an authorised firm. The FSA had a warrant to search the

---

[18] FSMA, s 176(3).
[19] FSMA, s 176(4).
[20] Police and Criminal Evidence Act ('PACE'), Part II, s 16. S 15(5) to (8) PACE also apply to warrants under s 176 FSMA.
[21] FSA Complaints Commissioner's Annual Report 2009/2010.

home address, but the director told the Enforcement staff that the information specified on the warrant was at a nearby business centre. Two FSA Enforcement staff remained and searched the home, while the accompanying police officers and a number of other FSA Enforcement staff went to search the business centre premises. The director of the firm complained that the FSA team had illegally executed the search warrant at his home address. The Complaints Commissioner upheld the complaint. In a decision letter dated 10 July 2009, the FSA stated: 'The FSA accepts that the FSA investigators who remained at the property and continued to execute the warrant, in the absence of the Police Constables, acted unlawfully, it being a requirement that a constable should have been present throughout the search.'

22.38 The FSA and the Association of Chief Police Officers of England and Wales ('ACPO') previously agreed a Memorandum of Understanding[22] the purpose of which was to record the agreed best practice for co-operation between the police and the FSA with regard to the arrest of suspects and the execution of search warrants. This Memorandum has since been adopted by the FCA. If a search warrant is obtained and executed it is likely that the police will also arrest the suspects, following which they will be taken to a designated police station and detained for interview under caution.

22.39 Section 176(8) FSMA[23] provides that any document that is taken pursuant to a search warrant may be retained for as long as it is necessary to retain it.

12. Interviews

22.40 There are two types of persons in respect of whom the FCA will conduct an interview in connection with an insider dealing / market abuse investigation. The first type is a person who is being treated as a potential witness and the second type is the subject of the investigation.

22.41 For potential witnesses, there are two types of interview that the FCA will conduct in connection with an insider dealing / market abuse investigation. These are a 'Compulsory Interview' conducted under s 173 FSMA, or a 'Voluntary Interview' in which the person interviewed agrees to attend on a voluntary basis.

22.42 If the FCA decides to conduct an interview with a person, then this will normally take place by arrangement. This will be the case whether the person is a potential witness or the subject of the investigation, unless the FCA intends to ask the police

---

[22] Memorandum of Understanding, Association of Chief Police Officers of England and Wales and the FSA, Aug 2005.
[23] As amended by FS Act 2012, Schedule 12.

to arrest the subject, in which case the first interview will be conducted at the police station. Thereafter, further interviews with the subject will normally be conducted by arrangement. The FCA will usually send the person concerned a letter which sets out which statutory powers are being used and the reason why the interview is being conducted.

22.43 The FCA is only required to provide the interviewee with sufficient information about the interview to enable him to seek appropriate legal advice. It is not therefore required to provide disclosure of documentation, questions, or issues in advance of the interview, although in many cases some pre-interview disclosure will be provided to assist the interview process. A person required to attend an interview by the use of statutory powers has no entitlement to insist that the interview takes place voluntarily. Similarly, a person asked to attend an interview on a purely voluntary basis is not entitled to insist that he be served with a requirement.[24] Whatever type of interview is being conducted, the person being interviewed is always entitled to have a legal advisor present.

Procedure in a compelled interview

22.44 At the start of a compelled interview, the person being interviewed will be told that the interview is being conducted under statutory powers, the section of FSMA under which the investigator has been appointed and the various powers that the appointment entitles the investigator to exercise. He will also be informed of the consequences under s 177 FSMA of failing to comply with the requirement to answer questions without reasonable excuse. A compulsory interview will be recorded and the person will be given a copy of the audio recording of the interview and, where a transcript is made, a copy of the transcript.[25]

Voluntary interviews with non-suspects

22.45 Where a voluntary interview is carried out with a person who is not the subject of the investigation, the interviewee must be told that the interview is voluntary and there is therefore no obligation to answer questions. The person must also be informed that any answers they do give will be admissible in any proceedings.

22.46 If the person being interviewed is not a suspect in a criminal or market abuse investigation, then, if that person refuses to attend the interview or to answer questions, the FCA will instead probably interview the person on a compelled basis. When this happens, the investigator will normally stop the voluntary interview and arrange for the compelled interview to be held on a different date in consultation with the person and his legal adviser.

---

[24] EG 4.18–4.19.
[25] EG 4.20.

Interviews with suspects

22.47 Interviews with suspects in an insider dealing/market abuse investigation will invariably be conducted under caution.[26] The subject is entitled to be accompanied by his legal adviser. The interview will be recorded and, as soon as practicable after the interview, the interviewee will be provided with a transcript of the interview and a copy of the audio recording. The FCA conducts interviews under caution in the following two ways:

1. at a police station either following arrest by the police, or following the suspect surrendering into custody from police bail for further interview; or
2. voluntary attendance at the FCA (or other place).

22.48 When the suspect agrees to attend the FCA for interview voluntarily, he will be told at the outset that he is not under arrest and is therefore free to leave at any time. Where a suspect refuses to attend an interview under caution in a criminal case, the FCA will then consider whether to request that the police arrest the person in order to interview him at the police station.

22.49 When the FCA conducts an interview under caution with a suspect detained at a police station, the interview will be conducted by FCA Investigators and a representative of the police will be present during the interview. The conduct of the interview will be governed by the Police and Criminal Evidence Act 1984 Codes of Practice.

Admissibility of compulsory interviews in criminal market or market abuse proceedings (s 174 FSMA)

22.50 Section 174 FSMA deals with the admissibility of statements made to investigators by a person in compliance with an information requirement. Section 174(1) states that such statements are admissible in evidence in any proceedings so long as they comply with any requirements governing the admissibility of evidence in the circumstances in question. However, under s 174(2) and (3) FSMA, in criminal proceedings in which that person is charged with a criminal offence[27] or in market abuse proceedings taken under s 123 FSMA, no evidence relating to the statement may be adduced and no question relating to it may be asked by or on behalf of the prosecution unless evidence relating to it is adduced or a question relating to it is asked in the proceedings by or on behalf of that person. This preserves the privilege against self-incrimination.

---

[26] See EG 4.21–4.27.
[27] FSMA, s 174(3). This applies to all offences save for those listed—which are offences under s 177(4) or 398 FSMA, s 5 of the Perjury Act 1911, s 44(2) of the Criminal Law (Consolidation) Scotland Act 1995, or Article 10 of the Perjury (Northern Ireland) Order 1979.

13. Witness statements

22.51 As explained above, the FCA is likely to conduct initial enquiries of potential witnesses by way of compulsory or voluntary interview or information requests. If the case ultimately proceeds as a market abuse case, the FCA will normally use the transcripts of these interviews for the purposes of preparation of its Investigation Report and the subsequent Regulatory Decisions Committee Proceedings.[28] Normally, it is not until a case is referred to the Tribunal that the FCA will obtain witness statements from witnesses for use in the Tribunal proceedings. Where however the case is pursued as a criminal prosecution, witness statements will need to be obtained at a much earlier stage as they will need to form part of the evidence at Committal.

22.52 Note that, although the FCA has the power to compel witnesses to attend for interview, it does not have the statutory power under FSMA to compel witnesses to provide witness statements for use in legal proceedings. For this, the FCA will need to use the witness summons procedure applicable in the relevant proceedings.

---

[28] See Chapter 24, Section 5.

23

CRIMINAL PROCEEDINGS

1. Introduction	23.01	Co-operation agreements—case examples	23.22
2. The decision to commence criminal proceedings	23.02	5. Plea discussions	23.29
3. Factors which may influence the decision	23.06	6. The role of the RDC Chairman	23.31
4. Co-operation agreements	23.15	7. Instituting criminal proceedings	23.35
Full immunity from prosecution (s 71 SOCPA)	23.19	8. Restraint proceedings	23.38
Restricted use undertakings (s 72 SOCPA)	23.20	9. Issuing a caution	23.39
Agreements for plea and reduction in sentence (s 73 SOCPA)	23.21	10. Decisions not to prosecute	23.41

1. Introduction

23.01 This Chapter deals with criminal proceedings for insider dealing. It sets out the factors relevant to the decisions whether and who to prosecute and when and how these decisions are likely to be taken. It also describes some of the ways in which it might be possible to influence this decision. The Chapter concludes by describing the process by which a decision to institute criminal proceedings is taken and the practical steps involved.

2. The decision to commence criminal proceedings

23.02 When deciding whether to commence criminal proceedings, the Financial Conduct Authority ('FCA') will apply the two-stage test as set out in the Code for Crown Prosecutors:[1] namely, the evidential and public interest tests. The

---

[1] Code for Crown Prosecutors 2013 (previously 2009).

consideration of this two-stage test may be conducted internally by a senior lawyer in the Enforcement and Financial Crime Division ('EFCD') Legal Department or may involve advice from external Counsel. If external Counsel is instructed, Counsel will advise on the evidential test and express a view in relation to the public interest test; however, the final decision on public interest will be taken by the FCA. This is because the FCA as a public body, takes decisions on matters of public interest.

23.03 In addition to the Code for Crown Prosecutors, the FCA will also have regard to the provisions of the Enforcement Guide ('EG') of the FCA Handbook of Rules and Guidance.[2] EG 12.8 lists a number of factors to which the FCA must additionally have regard. EG 12.9 provides that these factors are non-exhaustive and nor are they cumulative. The importance attached by the FCA to these factors will vary from case to case. In many respects, the factors listed overlap the considerations that will already have been considered under the Code for Crown Prosecutors. However, several focus specifically on particular matters relevant to offences of insider dealing / market abuse:

- EG 12.8(4). The FCA considers that a criminal prosecution may be more likely to be appropriate where the alleged misconduct has resulted in significant distortion or disruption to the market and / or has significantly damaged market confidence. Note, however, that in general terms, the FCA is likely to consider that insider dealing by its very nature is damaging to market confidence. However, if the suspect is not a market professional and the trading is limited in extent, duration, and profit, then these factors may provide grounds for the FCA to consider that the case could be dealt with without the need for a criminal prosecution.[3]
- EG 12.8(7)—The person's previous criminal or disciplinary record. This provision records that a relevant factor in deciding to take criminal proceedings is whether the person has previously been cautioned or convicted for market misconduct offences or has been the subject of previous civil or regulatory proceedings. Note, however, that most suspects in insider dealing cases are of previous good character, and therefore this matter may not be as relevant in such cases. It will, however, be relevant if the suspect has a previous disciplinary history with the FCA, FSA, or another professional body, or has been previously warned about similar conduct. It may also be relevant if the suspect has come to the attention of the FCA or FSA in relation to similar conduct in the past but where no action was taken.
- EG 12.8(10). This provision refers to the degree of co-operation demonstrated by the person under investigation. It states that voluntary co-operation with

---

[2] EG 12.7 and 12.8.
[3] See Chapter 23, Section 3 Factors which may influence the decision.

the FCA, in particular in the taking of corrective measures, will be taken into account. However, it will not be possible to avoid a prosecution simply because the person concerned has taken such measures—particularly if they amount to no more than the fulfilment of a statutory duty.

- EG 12.8(12A). This provision records the FCA's approach to co-operation type agreements. This applies in cases in which the misconduct in question has been carried out jointly by two or more individuals, and one of those individuals offers to provide full information and assistance in the FCA's prosecution of the other(s). This is a factor that the FCA will take into account when deciding whether, it is appropriate to prosecute the individual who has provided assistance, or whether, instead, market abuse proceedings should be brought against him.[4] This provision and its potential effects, is dealt with in Section 5 below.
- EG12.8(13). States that the personal circumstances of the individual in question may be a relevant factor in deciding whether to bring criminal proceedings against him. This of course would be relevant if, for example, the individual was suffering from a serious or terminal illness or there are other factors which ought properly to be considered.

23.04 EG 12.10 states that it is the FCA's policy not to impose a sanction for market abuse where a person is being prosecuted or has been convicted or acquitted of essentially the same allegations. Similarly, it is the FCA's policy not to commence a prosecution for insider dealing where it has brought or is seeking to bring disciplinary proceedings for market abuse arising in respect of the same matter. This means that the decision is an 'either/or', and suspects and their advisers can safely approach discussions with the FCA about the appropriate route for a case on this basis.

3. Factors which may influence the decision

23.05 The starting point is that the FCA's stated aim is to continue the 'credible deterrence' agenda, and taking action in respect of cases of insider dealing is at the heart of this.[5] This will be particularly so if the suspects in question are market professionals as this impacts directly on the FCA's integrity objective.[6] This must also be seen in the context of the current financial crisis and in particular the LIBOR scandal which has brought the behaviour of certain market professionals into sharp focus.

23.06 The FCA's great advantage is that in nearly all insider dealing / market abuse investigations, it has the option as to whether to pursue a case as a criminal prosecution

---

[4] See Chapter 23, Section 3 Factors which may influence the decision.
[5] See Chapter 21, Section 5 The PRA and the FCA, FCA—attitude to enforcement.
[6] See Chapter 21, Section 5 The PRA and the FCA, The FCA's statutory objectives.

or as a regulatory market abuse case under Part VIII of the Financial Services and Markets Act 2000 ('FSMA'). In this, the FCA has the advantage over other organisations such as the Serious Fraud Office ('SFO') or the Fraud Prosecution Unit of the Crown Prosecution Service ('CPS'). Those organisations, in most cases, have a stark choice—to prosecute or do nothing. The FCA, however, can choose which route is more appropriate for each given case, according to its stated priorities, the issues at stake, and the state of the evidence. That said, the FCA does not have infinite resources and it certainly does not have either the financial or human resources to investigate and prosecute every possible case.

23.07 There is no hard and fast rule as to when the decision whether or not to commence criminal proceedings is likely to be taken. In an insider dealing/market abuse investigation, although the case will be investigated as a joint criminal and regulatory matter, the FCA will be likely to consider the prospect of a criminal prosecution given its stated priorities in this field. This was certainly the position under the FSA. However, the final decision as to which route a case will take, may not be taken until towards the end of the investigation. By this point, sufficient evidence should have been obtained and analysed and the suspects will have been interviewed and their explanations considered. When taking the decision, the FCA will apply the two-stage test in the Code for Crown Prosecutors as well as the specific matters set out in the Enforcement Guide.[7]

23.08 An opportunity for a suspect to make representations as to the route the case may take will therefore be prior to, or at, the point at which the FCA is considering the two-stage test. Representations on behalf of a suspect may be made orally or in writing but in any event would probably do well to focus on the matters contained in the Code for Crown Prosecutors and EG 12.8. A suspect who actively wishes to persuade the FCA to adopt the market abuse route will also need to be prepared to offer settlement proposals.

23.09 A willingness on behalf of a suspect to co-operate with the FCA, accept a finding of market abuse, and pay a financial penalty might, in an appropriate case, have the effect of avoiding a criminal prosecution. Certainly, under the FSA, this has been employed successfully. An example of this can be seen in the case of *Richard Ralph* and *Filip Boyen*,[8] a market abuse case in which the FSA imposed financial penalties on both men in respect of s 118(2) FSMA behaviour (insider dealing).

23.10 The facts of the case were straightforward. Richard Ralph was the Executive Chairman of Monterrico Metals Plc ('Monterrico') a UK resource development company whose shares were quoted on AIM. On or about 28 January 2007, Ralph asked his friend Filip Boyen to buy shares in Monterrico on his behalf on the basis

---

[7] EG 12.8.
[8] *Richard Ralph* Final Notices 12 Nov 2008; *Filip Boyen*, Final Notice 12 Nov 2008.

of inside information which Mr Ralph had relating to a forthcoming takeover announcement. After the takeover was announced, Mr Boyen sold these shares at a considerable profit for them both.

23.11 The evidence in the case was strong, Mr Ralph had acted in gross breach of trust, and the case appeared to have all the hallmarks of a criminal prosecution. The Final Notice in respect of both men recorded a number of factors that would all have justified a criminal prosecution. These included the fact that in Mr Ralph's case he occupied a position of trust as Executive Chairman and a director of Monterrico. He traded in contravention of the company's share dealing restrictions, the provisions of the Model Code, Disclosure Rules, Transparency Rules, and the Takeover Code despite having received advice from the company's advisers regarding his obligations in these respects. The FSA considered that Mr Ralph's behaviour was deliberate and that he asked Mr Boyen to buy shares on his behalf in order to conceal his own involvement. In Mr Boyen's case, he had committed insider dealing in circumstances where he was an experienced investor and businessman. Furthermore, the FSA considered that the conduct damaged market confidence as other market users were disadvantaged because they would have made investment decisions without having access to the same information that Mr Ralph and Mr Boyen had.

23.12 Given that these are all factors which might have caused the FSA to consider that the case was suitable for a criminal prosecution, why was this not the outcome? It is plain from the Final Notices that both men avoided criminal proceedings by virtue of their full admissions and voluntary co-operation with the FSA's enquiries.

23.13 In addition, in both cases the Final Notices record that:

> But for that co-operation, the FSA would have proposed to impose a greater financial penalty. Alternatively, the FSA may have brought criminal proceedings against [Ralph and Boyen].[9]

And therefore:

> The FSA has decided not to prosecute [Ralph and Boyen] for the criminal offence of insider dealing in light of the high degree of co-operation [they] provided to the FSA's investigation.[10]

23.14 As a result, the FSA imposed a financial penalty of £117,691.41 on Richard Ralph. The financial penalty consisted of the disgorgement of financial benefit arising from the market abuse of £12,691.41 (being the profit derived by him from the purchase and sale of the shares in question), and an additional penalty element of

---

[9] *Richard Ralph* (n 8) para 3.5; *Filip Boyen* (n 8) para 3.4.
[10] *Richard Ralph* (n 8) para 3.6; *Filip Boyen* (n 8) para 3.5.

£105,000. Mr Ralph agreed to settle at an early stage of the FSA's investigation. He therefore qualified for a 30 per cent (Stage 1) reduction in the additional penalty element of the financial penalty under the FSA's executive settlement procedures.[11] Were it not for this discount, the Final Notice records that the FSA would have imposed a financial penalty consisting of the disgorgement and an additional penalty element of £150,000. Filip Boyen was fined £81,982.95 for engaging in market abuse (insider dealing) contrary to s 118(2) FSMA and improper disclosure of information contrary to s 118(3). This represented a disgorgement of financial benefit arising from the market abuse of £29,482.95 (being the profit derived by Mr Boyen from the purchase and sale of the shares), and an additional penalty element of £52,500. Both men therefore received hefty financial penalties in addition to the disgorgement of their profits, but by coming forward at an early stage and fully co-operating with the FSA's investigation, they were able to avoid a criminal prosecution and possible prison sentence.

4. Co-operation agreements

23.15 EG 12.8(12A) provides that where the misconduct in question was carried out by two or more individuals acting together, and one of the individuals provides information and gives full assistance in the FCA's prosecution of the other(s), the FCA will take this co-operation into account when deciding whether to prosecute or bring market abuse proceedings against the individual who has given assistance.

23.16 The power to enter into co-operation agreements with suspects who wish to ameliorate their positions by providing information and assistance to a prosecuting authority has always existed at Common Law. In insider dealing cases, this power is especially valuable. Insider dealing cases are by their very nature difficult, time consuming, and expensive to investigate and prosecute. This is particularly so, given that, for the most part, such cases are built on circumstantial evidence. Given this, it is not surprising that the FSA previously demonstrated its willingness to engage in co-operation agreements with suspects in order to assist in building a case against other offenders, particularly those higher up the chain of culpability.

23.17 Sections 71 to 74 of the Serious Organised Crime and Police Act 2005 ('SOCPA') provide a statutory mechanism for offenders who are willing to assist in the investigation or prosecution of others. These powers are intended to be used in relation to serious offending only, that is in relation to indictable offences (whether indictable only or triable either way). Powers under ss 71 to 74 SOCPA were originally given only to certain specified prosecutors, the Director of Public Prosecutions the Director of the SFO, and the Director

---

[11] See Chapter 24, Section 6 The Executive Settlement Process.

of Public Prosecutions for Northern Ireland. SOCPA was subsequently amended by the Coroners and Justice Act 2009. This extended the powers under ss 71–74 to the Secretary of State for Business, Innovation and Skills ('BIS') and the FSA—and now by extension the FCA.

23.18 In deciding whether to exercise its powers under ss 71–74 SOCPA, the FCA will apply the considerations set out in the Prosecutor's guidance, agreed by the Attorney-General.[12] This sets out the common approach of the specified prosecutors to the exercise of theses powers. Key considerations for the FCA will be the strength of the prosecution case with and without the information from the potential accomplice/witness, and whether it can be satisfied that the person is able and prepared to provide reliable evidence on significant aspects of the case and would be a credible witness.

Full immunity from prosecution (s 71 SOCPA)

23.19 Section 71 SOCPA provides that a 'specified prosecutor' may give a suspect an immunity notice if he thinks that for the purposes of the investigation or prosecution of any offence it is appropriate to offer any person immunity from prosecution. The FCA is not able to offer a person immunity under this section unless the Attorney General has given his consent to the granting of the immunity in accordance with s 71(6)(c) SOCPA.

Restricted use undertakings (s 72 SOCPA)

23.20 Section 72 SOCPA provides that a specified prosecutor may give a suspect a restricted use undertaking if he thinks that for the purposes of the investigation or prosecution of any offence it is appropriate to offer any person an undertaking that information of any description will not be used in any criminal or confiscation proceedings or civil recovery under Part 5 of the Proceeds of Crime Act 2002 ('POCA'). The information obtained from the person following the grant of the undertaking must not be used against that person except in circumstances specified in the notice,[13] but a restricted use undertaking ceases to have effect if the person to whom it relates fails to comply with any conditions specified in the undertaking.[14]

Agreements for plea and reduction in sentence (s 73 SOCPA)

23.21 These agreements provide that a defendant who pleads guilty pursuant to a written agreement with a specified prosecutor in which he provides or offers to provide

---

[12] Queen's Evidence—Immunities, Undertakings and Agreements under the Serious Organised Crime and Police Act 2005.
[13] SOCPA, s 72(3).
[14] SOCPA, s 72(3).

assistance to an investigator or prosecutor, is eligible to receive a reduction in sentence. If the offender fails to comply with the conditions of the agreement he may be referred back to the sentencing court for reconsideration of his sentence pursuant to s 74 SOCPA. Where the FCA proposes to enter into plea discussions with a suspect, it will consider the factors set out in the 'Attorney General's Guidelines on Plea Discussions in cases of Serious or Complex Fraud'.[15]

Co-operation agreements—case examples

R v Malcolm Calvert

23.22 Malcolm Calvert was a former partner of Cazenove and Co ('Cazenove'). He obtained inside information on forthcoming takeovers from an unknown source in the Corporate Broking Department of Cazenove. In order to conceal his own involvement he asked his friend Bertie Hatcher to deal for him and they split the profits. The FSA's investigation revealed a circumstantial case; however, it considered that the evidence was insufficient to found a realistic prospect of conviction. The FSA therefore entered into a Common Law Restricted Use Undertaking with Mr Hatcher. The FSA considered that Mr Hatcher was secondary to Mr Calvert in terms of culpability, and that without this agreement, it would not have sufficient evidence to prosecute either suspect. At the time, the FSA was not a specified prosecutor for the purposes of SOCPA and therefore the agreement with Mr Hatcher was entered into under common law powers.

23.23 Pursuant to the Restricted Use Undertaking, the FSA agreed that in return for his co-operation, it would treat Mr Hatcher as a witness in any criminal proceedings. The undertaking was conditional on Mr Hatcher fully disclosing and admitting his involvement in the matters being investigated, providing a truthful and complete account and continuing to co-operate throughout the investigation and prosecution of Mr Calvert. In addition, Mr Hatcher was required to disgorge all profits retained by him from his trading, which would be paid by way of a financial penalty for market abuse under s 123 FSMA.

23.24 In consequence of this, on 13 May 2008, the FSA issued a Final Notice[16] confirming that it had decided to impose on Mr Hatcher a financial penalty of £56,098 which equalled his share of the profits from the insider dealing that he had engaged in on the basis of inside information provided by Mr Calvert. The Final Notice specifically recorded that the FSA had taken account of the fact that Mr Hatcher had provided valuable evidence that had assisted the FSA's investigation into Mr Calvert and that Mr Hatcher had undertaken to provide ongoing assistance

---

[15] Published 18 Mar 2009. See also CPS Guidance to Accompany the Attorney-General's Guidelines, Updated 24 May 2012.
[16] *Bertie Hatcher*, Final Notice 13 May 2008.

to the investigation and to give evidence if required at any subsequent criminal or regulatory proceedings.[17] The Final Notice also stated:

> The FSA is mindful of the need to encourage others to provide the FSA with information that may assist in the investigation and prosecution of suspected cases of insider dealing and market abuse, especially where it is suspected that the misconduct has occurred as a result of two or more persons acting in concert to commit market abuse.[18]

23.25 By the time Mr Calvert's criminal trial commenced, Mr Hatcher had become seriously ill and was unfit to give evidence. A successful application to read Mr Hatcher's witness statement was made by the Prosecution pursuant to the hearsay provisions of s 116 of the Criminal Justice Act 2003 ('CJA 2003'). Mr Calvert was ultimately convicted by the jury following a trial. When making the application to read Mr Hatcher's statement, the prosecution conceded that, without his evidence, the case against Mr Calvert was insufficient to found a realistic prospect of conviction.

R v Anjam Ahmad

23.26 In January 2010, the FSA together with the City of London Police, executed search warrants on addresses associated with Anjam Ahmad and another suspect, Rupinder Sidhu, in respect of suspected insider dealing in a large number of stocks on the basis of inside information originating from a hedge fund in which Ahmad was employed as a trader. In February 2010, Ahmad's solicitor approached the FSA and indicated a willingness to co-operate. Plea discussions were conducted and Mr Ahmad subsequently entered into a plea and co-operation agreement under s 73 SOCPA in which he pleaded guilty to conspiracy to commit insider dealing and agreed to give evidence for the FSA at the trial of Mr Sidhu.

23.27 In return for this assistance, Mr Ahmad received a sentence of ten months' imprisonment suspended for two years, and a £50,000 fine. The sentencing Judge made clear in his sentencing remarks[19] that this sentence was imposed as a direct result of the considerable credit to which Ahmad was entitled pursuant to the SOCPA agreement and that without this the sentence would have been an immediate custodial sentence within the range of thirty months to three years.

23.28 This was not a case in which the FSA would have been likely to agree not to prosecute Mr Ahmad in exchange for his assistance. For one thing, the circumstantial evidence against Mr Sidhu was sufficiently strong that, ultimately, the FSA decided not to call Mr Ahmad at Mr Sidhu's trial. Another factor was that Mr Ahmad

---

[17] See *Bertie Hatcher* (n 16) para 4.9.
[18] See *Bertie Hatcher* (n 16) para 4.10.
[19] *R v Anjam Ahmad*, unreported, Southwark Crown Court, His Honour Judge Rivlin QC, the Honorary Recorder of Westminster, *R v Anjam Ahmad* sentencing hearing, 22 June 2012. See also *R v Dougall* [2012] EWCA Crim 1048.

appeared to be at least equally complicit in the offending, or quite probably the instigator of it. In such circumstances it would be unlikely for the FSA to consider it appropriate to offer total immunity from prosecution. What Mr Ahmad did achieve, however, was a much lighter sentence, an agreed confiscation order which amounted only to disgorgement of his share of the profits from the dealing, and also the early settlement of an unrelated misconduct matter.[20]

5. Plea discussions

23.29 The FSA has also demonstrated a willingness in an appropriate case, to enter into plea discussions pursuant to the Attorney General's Guidelines on Plea Discussions in Cases of Serious or Complex Fraud[21] and it is to be assumed that the FCA will continue this practice. This process may be initiated by the suspect or the FCA and, once initiated, will follow the procedure set out in the Guidelines. This procedure was recently successfully employed in the case of *R v Paul Milsom*.[22] Mr Milsom was a Senior equities trader at Legal and General. He pleaded guilty to one count of disclosing inside information covering twenty-eight separate instances of passing inside information relating to fourteen stocks to a co-accused who was a broker at another institution between October 2008 and March 2010.

23.30 According to the written plea agreement, Mr Milsom tipped his co-accused in advance of large trades by Legal and General which had the potential to move the market. His co-accused would then place spread bet or CFD trades to gain from the market move and the pair split the profit. Profits from this trading amounted to £400,000 of which Mr Milsom received £164,000 in cash. As part of the plea agreement, Mr Milsom also volunteered involvement in a separate, similar arrangement with another individual, involving fifteen transactions in five stocks resulting in a total profit of £160,000 of which he received £81,000. These matters were taken into consideration by the sentencing judge. He was sentenced to two years' imprisonment. By entering into plea discussions and subsequently a formal plea agreement, Mr Milsom was able to agree the wording of the written agreement that set out the level of his culpability. He was also able to agree the amount of the confiscation order with the FSA (which by agreement was limited to the profits from his trading.) He also of course benefitted from a sentencing discount for pleading guilty.[23] He received the maximum ⅓ discount for pleading

---

[20] See *R v Anjam Ahmad* (n 19) and also *Anjam Saeed Ahmad*, Final Notice 22 June 2010.
[21] Attorney General's Guidelines on Plea Discussions in Cases of Serious or Complex Fraud, 18 Mar 2009.
[22] *R v Paul Milsom*, unreported, Southwark Crown Court, His Honour Judge Pegden QC, 7 Mar 2013. FSA/PN/022/2013.
[23] Sentencing Guidelines Council, Reduction in Sentence for a Guilty Plea, Definitive Guidance, Revised 2007.

guilty at the earliest opportunity plus a further discount for entering into the plea agreement.

6. The role of the RDC Chairman

23.31 Criminal proceedings are instituted by the FCA in accordance with EG 12.4A. A decision to commence criminal proceedings is normally made by the Chairman of the Regulatory Decisions Committee ('RDC').[24] Amongst other matters, the RDC's role is to decide whether it is appropriate for the FCA to issue Enforcement Notices or take criminal or civil proceedings.

23.32 The Chairman will usually be provided with draft charges or a draft indictment, and information regarding the facts of the case, the evidential merits and the public interest test.

23.33 It may be that the proposed defendant or his lawyers will also have made written representations at this stage. These will probably follow from an earlier dialogue with the investigation case team. It will be important for any written submissions to address the Code for Crown Prosecutors two stage test and the EG 12.8 criteria, as these will be provided to the RDC for the Chairman to consider along with the papers submitted by the Enforcement case team.

23.34 Once the RDC Chairman has considered these documents, he normally meets with the case team to discuss any issues or concerns. Provided he is satisfied that there is sufficient evidence to provide a realistic prospect of conviction against each suspect on each charge and that a prosecution is in the public interest, he will confirm his agreement to the institution of proceedings.

7. Instituting criminal proceedings

23.35 Criminal Proceedings for insider dealing will usually be commenced either by charge, where the suspect has been arrested and is on bail or remand, or by Summons. The FCA cannot charge a suspect. However, under the Memorandum

---

[24] The FSMA requires the investigation and recommendation functions to be carried out separately from the taking of decisions and issuing of statutory notices. The RDC decides whether the FCA should give the statutory and other notices described as within its scope by the Handbook, any regulatory guide or legislation. The RDC is a Committee of the FCA board and reports directly to the board. The board appointed the RDC Chairman and members, who represent the public interest and are drawn from practitioners and non-practitioners. See Chapter 24, Section 5 The enforcement process.

of Understanding with ACPO,[25] the police will charge a suspect on the FCA's behalf. The advantage of this is that the police have the ability to impose bail conditions or to remand a suspect in custody prior to the first court hearing.

23.36 Criminal Proceedings for insider dealing may also begin with the laying of an Information at a Magistrates Court (usually City of Westminster Magistrates Court). The Magistrates Court will then issue a Summons, a copy of which will be served on the defendant, with a return date at which all parties should attend at Court for the first appearance and in order to deal with matters such as bail.

23.37 FCA prosecutions are committed or sent to Southwark Crown Court for trial, on the basis of a protocol previously agreed between the FSA and that Court, on the grounds that these cases generally require the particular expertise and case management of the leading fraud Court Centre.

8. Restraint proceedings

23.38 It is common for the FCA to apply for Restraint Orders to restrain and freeze a suspect's assets under Part 2 POCA. Usually, this will occur at the time search warrants are executed and initial arrests made. The FCA has a number of accredited Financial Investigators who are able to deal with these applications.

9. Issuing a caution

23.39 The FCA is entitled to issue a caution as an alternative to prosecution if it is satisfied that the public interest can be properly served by disposing of the case in this manner. If it does so, then the police will be asked to formally administer the caution in order to ensure that it is recorded on the Police National Computer. There are three requirements that must be satisfied before a caution may be issued:

1. the evidential stage criteria must be satisfied, ie there must be a realistic prospect of conviction on each charge;
2. the subject must admit the offence; and
3. the subject must understand that a caution is a recordable offence.

23.40 If the subject does not accept the offer of a caution, the FCA will withdraw the offer and either take no further action or commence criminal proceedings. To

---

[25] Memorandum of Understanding, Association of Chief Police Officers of England and Wales and the FSA Aug 2005.

date, neither the FSA nor the FCA have issued a caution in relation to any criminal allegation of insider dealing, and it is doubtful whether it would ever do so in an insider dealing case given the serious view it takes of such offences. However, this may be an aspect to consider in an exceptional case.

10. Decisions not to prosecute

23.41 If the FCA decides not to prosecute a suspect, it can either take no further action, issue a private warning or take other Enforcement action. Where the FCA decides to issue a private warning, it will send the suspect a Warning Letter which states that the matter will be taken into account should further conduct occur in future and would also be relevant when deciding what action to take in respect of the future matter and in deciding on the appropriate penalty.

24

THE ENFORCEMENT PROCESS—MARKET ABUSE PROCEEDINGS

1. Introduction	24.01	Written representations to the RDC	24.35
2. Range of enforcement actions	24.02	Oral representations	24.36
3. Informal enforcement action	24.03	Decision Notice	24.41
Private Warnings	24.04	Tribunal Reference	24.43
		Final Notice	24.44
4. Formal enforcement action	24.09	6. The Executive Settlement Process	24.45
Financial penalties	24.10	The settlement discount scheme applied	
Prohibition orders	24.14	to financial penalties	24.50
Withdrawal of approval	24.16	Mediation	24.56
Cancellation of permission	24.19	7. Civil proceedings	24.57
Suspension and restriction orders	24.20		
5. The enforcement process	24.21	8. Publicity	24.59
Preliminary findings letters and		Publicity during an FCA investigation	24.59
preliminary investigation reports	24.22	Publicity during or upon the conclusion	
The Legal Review	24.23	of regulatory action	24.60
The Regulatory Decisions Committee	24.24	Challenges to the publication of	
Warning Notices	24.29	enforcement notices	24.61
Enforcement Submissions Document	24.30	Publicity during or upon the conclusion	
Warning Notice Meeting	24.31	of civil action	24.64
Material disclosed to the subject	24.32	Publicity during or upon the conclusion	
		of criminal action	24.65

1. Introduction

This Chapter provides a step-by-step guide to the Enforcement process in respect of market abuse proceedings brought under Part VIII of FSMA. It deals with the range of available Enforcement actions, in particular the structured regime for the calculation of financial penalties, and describes how the Executive Settlement process applies. This Chapter also deals with proceedings for market abuse which may be taken in the High Court. Lastly, this Chapter deals with the issue of publicity in relation to a market abuse case. **24.01**

2. Range of enforcement actions

24.02 Under FSMA, the FCA has an extensive range of disciplinary, and civil powers to take action against authorised and non-authorised firms and individuals. Examples of those powers include:

- Variation and cancellation of a firm's Part IV permission on the Authority's own initiative ('OIVOP') pursuant to s 55J FSMA.[1] The FCA may exercise this power to vary a firm's Part IV permission to remove any or all of a firm's permissions if it appears to it that (amongst other things):
  - The firm is failing or is likely to fail to satisfy the Threshold Conditions contained in Schedule 6 FSMA.
  - It is desirable to exercise the power in order to meet any of the FCA's regulatory objectives. Section 55(7) FSMA provides that if as a result of an OIVOP there are no longer any regulated activities for which the firm has permissions, the FCA must cancel the firm's Part IV permission once it is satisfied that it is no longer necessary to keep the permissions in force.
- Fully or partially prohibiting an individual from performing functions in relation to regulated activities under s 56 FSMA.[2]
- The power to suspend a firm for up to twelve months from undertaking specific regulated activities or impose such limitations or other restrictions in relation to the carrying on of regulated activity as the FCA deems appropriate (s 206A FSMA).
- The power to suspend an individual for up to two years from undertaking specific regulated activities or impose such limitations or other restrictions in relation to the performance by him of any function to which any approval relates under s 66(3)(aa) and (ab) FSMA.
- Withdrawal of an individual's approval under s 63 FSMA.[3]
- The power to censure firms and individuals through public statements. Section 205 FSMA provides that if the FCA considers that an authorised person has contravened a requirement imposed by or under FSMA it may publish a statement to that effect. Section 66(3)(b) FSMA provides for the power to publish a public statement in respect of an individual.
- Imposition of financial penalties under s 206 FSMA (for contravention of relevant requirements by firms), s 66(3)(a) (on individuals who are guilty of misconduct), or under s 123 FSMA (penalties for Market Abuse). The FCA also

---

[1] This power was used against Blue Index in the Sanders case on the grounds that the authorised firm was being used for the purposes of Market Abuse, given that James Sanders (one of the two co-directors) was encouraging Blue Index's clients to trade in the stocks about which he had inside information.

[2] See Chapter 24, Section 4 Formal enforcement action; Prohibition orders, withdrawal of approval, suspension and restriction orders.

[3] See Chapter 24, Section 4 Formal enforcement action; Prohibition orders, withdrawal of approval, suspension and restriction orders.

has the power to require a market abuser to pay restitution under s 384 FSMA although this has never been exercised in a s 118(2)–(4) case.[4]
- Applying to the High Court for an asset freezing and restraining injunction, and remedial order.[5]

3. Informal enforcement action

Some cases will be discontinued without any formal disciplinary action. When this happens, the subject will be provided with a notice of discontinuance of the investigation. **24.03**

Private Warnings

In certain cases, despite concerns about a person's behaviour or evidence of a rule breach, the FCA may decide that it is not appropriate to take formal action in the form of a public censure. In such cases, it may give a subject or firm a private warning, the purpose of which is to make the person aware that they came close to being subject to formal action and that, should there be a repeat of this type of behaviour in the future, then the fact that they have received a private warning would be taken into account in deciding whether to take Enforcement action in respect of the new matter. **24.04**

Typically, the FCA might give a private warning rather than take formal action where the matter giving cause for concern is minor in nature or degree, or where the person has taken full and immediate remedial action. Generally, private warnings are issued in the context of firms and approved persons. However, in cases of potential market abuse, the FCA may decide to issue a private warning to a non-authorised firm or non-approved individual. **24.05**

Private warnings are non-statutory in nature and therefore whether or not to issue a private warning is in the discretion of the FCA. If the FCA decides that a private warning is appropriate, it will identify and explain its concerns about a person's conduct and/or procedures, and inform the subject that the FCA has seriously considered formal steps to impose a penalty or censure and the reasons why instead it considers that a private warning is appropriate. **24.06**

A private warning is not a final determination. However, the fact of a private warning will be kept on record and will form part of any consideration as to whether to commence action for a penalty or censure in relation to any future breaches. It may also be considered an aggravating factor in relation to the level of a penalty imposed in respect of a similar issue that is the subject of FCA action in the future. **24.07**

---

[4] See Chapter 24, Section 4 Formal enforcement action, Financial penalties.
[5] See Chapter 24, Section 7 Civil proceedings.

24.08 The FCA's normal practice is to follow a 'minded-to' procedure before deciding whether to give a private warning. This means that it will notify the subject (or firm) in writing, informing them that it has concerns about their conduct and that the FCA proposes to give the warning. The subject or firm will then have an opportunity to comment. The FCA will then consider any response to its initial letter before it decides whether to give the warning. The final decision whether to issue a private warning will be taken by an EFCD Head of Department or Senior EFCD staff member.

4. Formal enforcement action

24.09 In a market abuse case, a financial penalty is most commonly imposed.[6] In addition to this, the FCA will, in an appropriate case, make a prohibition order or withdraw an approved person's approval, or, in the case of an authorised firm, withdraw the firm's authorisation.

Financial penalties

24.10 The Decisions Procedures and Penalties Manual of the FCA's Handbook of Rules and Guidance ('DEPP') 6.2 lists a number of non-exhaustive factors that the FCA will consider when determining whether or not to impose a financial penalty or public censure. These include the nature, seriousness, and impact of the suspected breach, whether the breach was deliberate or reckless and the level of profits made. DEPP 6.2.2 provides that, when deciding whether to take action for market abuse, the FCA may consider additional factors such as the degree of sophistication of the users of the market in question, the size and liquidity of the market, the susceptibility of the market to market abuse, and the deterrent effect that such a penalty may have on other market users and on standards of market conduct.

24.11 In determining the level of a financial penalty to be imposed on an individual in respect of behaviour amounting to market abuse, the FCA will follow a five-step process which is set out in DEPP 6.5C:

> Step 1: Disgorgement. This step takes account of the benefit the person has derived as a direct result of the market abuse. This may include the profit made or loss avoided, where it is practicable to quantify this. The FCA will ordinarily also charge interest on the benefit.
>
> Step 2: Seriousness. The level of penalty in respect of this element will be determined based on the seriousness of the behaviour in question and whether or not it was referable to the individual's employment. The FCA considers that where an individual has been put into a position where he

---

[6] FSMA, s 123.

can commit market abuse because of his employment then this should be reflected in the fine imposed. The approach taken in such a case is to take as a reference point the gross amount of all benefits derived from that employment. The Step 2 figure will be calculated as the greater of a figure based on a percentage of the individual's relevant income (the gross amount of all benefits received from his employment during the period of the market abuse),[7] or a multiple of the profit made or loss avoided 'profit multiple', or £100,000 for the most serious offences (for example where the market abuse was committed deliberately).

24.12 Where the market abuse was not referable to the individual's employment, the figure for the purposes of Step 2 will be the greater of: a multiple of the profit made or loss avoided (the 'profit multiple') or £100,000 for cases which the FCA assesses to be serious. The FCA will determine the profit multiple which will apply by considering the seriousness of the market abuse and choosing a multiple between 0 and 4. DEPP 6.5C.2G sets out the considerations which will be applied in determining the appropriate multiple. These include such matters as the nature of the market abuse, its impact on the market and market confidence and whether the behaviour was committed deliberately or recklessly.

Step 3: Mitigating and Aggravating Factors. The FCA may increase or decrease the amount of the financial penalty arrived at after Step 2, to take into account factors which aggravate or mitigate the market abuse. A number of (non exhaustive) aggravating or mitigating factors are listed in DEPP 6.5C.3G. These include the degree of cooperation with the FCA, the previous regulatory or disciplinary history of the person in question and whether the behaviour relates to conduct about which the FCA (or FSA) has previously published concerns. Any adjustment to take account of aggravating or mitigating factors may only be in respect of the Step 2 figure and not in respect of the disgorgement element.

Step 4: Adjustment for Deterrence. If the FCA considers that the figure arrived at after Step 3 is insufficient to deter the subject or others from committing further or similar market abuse in future, then the penalty may be increased. DEPP 6.5C.4G lists some examples of when this situation might arise such as a case in which the overall amount is too small to amount to 'credible deterrence', where the FCA (or FSA) has taken previous similar action in respect of other cases which have failed to improve market standards, and where the penalty might not act as a deterrent in light of the size of the individual's income or net assets.

Step 5: Settlement Discount. The FCA operates an 'Executive Settlement' Process under which the FCA and the person concerned may agree the

---

[7] DEPP 6.5C.2G.

amount of the penalty to be imposed and other terms.[8] Where settlement has been achieved, the penalty will be reduced by a percentage which reflects the stage in the process at which settlement was reached. The settlement discount does not apply to the disgorgement element of the penalty.

24.13 Where an individual or firm claims that payment of the penalty proposed will cause them serious financial hardship, the FCA will consider whether to reduce the proposed penalty to reflect this.[9] This reflects the principle that a penalty imposed should be proportionate to the breach. The individual or firm will need to provide verifiable evidence to substantiate a claim of serious financial hardship and co-operate with any requests for further information. Where the subject is an individual, DEPP 6.5D.2 provides that the FCA will consider whether the individual would be in a position to pay the penalty over a three year period. Its starting point in such a case is that serious financial hardship does not arise unless, as a result of the penalty, an individual's net annual income would fall below £14,000 and his capital below £16,000. In an appropriate case, the FCA will also consider reasonable proposals for payment by installments.

Prohibition orders

24.14 In cases against individuals, including market abuse cases, the FCA may make a prohibition order under s 56 FSMA as well as impose a financial penalty.[10] Section 56 provides that a prohibition order may be made if it appears to the FCA that an individual is not a fit and proper person to perform functions in relation to regulated activities. A prohibition order may be made in terms which prevent a person from performing any functions or regulated activities, or may be limited to certain functions or activities only. It is also possible to limit the time period for which a prohibition order will run, although this will only usually happen as part of a negotiated settlement.

24.15 Under s 56(4) FSMA, performing or agreeing to perform a function in breach of a prohibition order is a criminal offence punishable on summary conviction to a fine not exceeding level 3 on the standard scale. Under s 56(7) FSMA, an individual who is subject to a prohibition order may apply to the FCA to vary or revoke it.

Withdrawal of approval

24.16 In an appropriate case, the FCA can also withdraw a person's approval under s 63 FSMA. This may be in addition to any financial penalty imposed[11] and it may be instead of or in addition to, a prohibition order. The power to withdraw a person's

---

[8] DEPP 6.5C.5 and see Chapter 24, Section 6 The Executive Settlement Process.
[9] DEPP 6.5D.
[10] See EG, ch 9.
[11] See EG, ch 9.

The enforcement process

approval may be exercised if it appears to the FCA that the person concerned is not a fit and proper person to perform the function to which the approval relates.

The criteria for assessing whether an individual is fit and proper are set out in the 'Fit and Proper Test for Approved Persons' ('FIT') in the FCA's Handbook. At a high level, these criteria fall under three headings: **24.17**

1. Honesty, integrity and reputation.[12]
2. Competence and capability.[13]
3. Financial soundness.[14]

EG 9 sets out the factors that the FCA will consider when deciding to make a prohibition order or withdraw a person's approval. Broadly these amount to a consideration of all the relevant circumstances and are specifically stated to be non exhaustive given the extremely broad factors that will inevitably be relevant to this decision. **24.18**

Cancellation of permission

If the behaviour said to amount to market abuse has been committed by an authorised firm, the FCA may cancel the firm's authorisation to conduct regulated activities under s 55 FSMA. In an appropriate case, the FCA may intervene during the investigation stage by varying a firm's permissions to conduct regulated activities and thereafter to cancel the firm's authorisation altogether under ss 55J and s 55Q FSMA. An example of when this might occur is when a firm is being run as a vehicle for insider dealing and / or is run by the subjects of an insider dealing/market abuse investigation.[15] **24.19**

Suspension and restriction orders

Under ss 66 and 206A FSMA, the FCA has power to suspend or restrict an individual's or authorised firm's ability to perform regulated activities. DEPP 6A sets out the factors to which the FCA will have regard when considering whether to make such an order and the length of the order. In the case of an individual, the period of the suspension must not exceed two years, and in respect of an authorised firm, it must not exceed twelve months. **24.20**

5. The enforcement process

When deciding to take formal disciplinary action against a firm or individual, the FCA is required to follow a prescribed enforcement procedure and in addition, to comply with the Human Rights Act 1998. The procedure is designed as a staged **24.21**

---

[12] FIT 2.1.
[13] FIT 2.2.
[14] FIT 2.3.
[15] See n 1.

Enforcement—Market Abuse Proceedings

process that aims to ensure that each side is clear about the how the proceedings are progressing. This section focuses on the procedure post investigation, and once a decision has been made that the case is to be pursued as a market abuse case under ss 118 and 123 FSMA.

Preliminary findings letters and preliminary investigation reports

24.22 Once the investigation is complete, the EFCD case team will usually send a preliminary findings letter ('PFL') to the subject of the investigation.[16] The letter will normally annex the investigators' preliminary investigation report ('PIR'). The PFL and PIR will set out the facts that the case team consider relevant to the matters under investigation. The subject will be invited to comment on these and those views will then be considered.

The Legal Review

24.23 After the PFL and PIR have been provided to the subject and he has had an opportunity to comment, the case team will need to decide whether, in the light of these comments, it is appropriate to proceed with the case, or whether the case should be amended or restated to reflect the matters raised. Assuming that a decision is taken that the case should proceed, the next stage is for the case to be referred to the Regulatory Decisions Committee ('RDC'). Prior to this, the case will go through a process known as the 'Legal Review'. This process arose out of a recommendation of the FSA's Enforcement Process Review[17] (known as the 'Strachan Report'). One of the Strachan Report's recommendations was that, before a case is referred to the RDC, it must be reviewed by a lawyer who has not been part of the investigation team and who therefore can be bring a fresh view and judgement to bear. To give effect to this, all cases are reviewed by a lawyer within the EFCD Legal Department, or occasionally by external Counsel.

The Regulatory Decisions Committee

24.24 Decisions to take Enforcement action against a firm or individual are taken by the RDC. This is because FSMA requires that, in relation to an Enforcement case, the investigation and recommendation functions must be carried out separately from the taking of decisions and issuing of statutory notices.[18] The purpose of this is that the procedure must be designed to secure, among other things, that the decision which gives rise to the obligation to give any such notice is taken by a person not directly involved in establishing the evidence on which that decision is based.

---

[16] EG 4.30–4.33.
[17] Published 19 July 2005.
[18] FSMA, s 395.

24.25 The FSA Board created the RDC in order to give effect to this provision. The RDC is an administrative decision making body which now reports directly to the FCA Board. The Board appoints the Chairman and members of the RDC, who include industry specialists and those outside the industry with particular specialist knowledge. Apart from its Chairman, none of the members of the RDC are FCA employees.[19] The RDC has its own legal advisers and support staff and RDC staff are separate from the FCA staff who are involved in conducting investigations and making recommendations to the RDC.[20]

24.26 The RDC meets as often as necessary to discharge its functions. Members of the public are not permitted to attend RDC meetings.[21] The RDC may meet as a full committee, but will usually meet as a panel of three or five members. Each meeting is usually chaired by the Chairman or a Deputy Chairman.[22] The composition and size of a panel will vary depending on the nature of the particular matter under consideration. Where the RDC has issued a Warning Notice and the subject then chooses to make oral representations, the panel that hears these will usually include additional members of the RDC who have not previously considered the matter.[23]

24.27 It is important to remember that the RDC is an administrative decision maker, not a judicial or Tribunal body. It has no power under FSMA to require persons to attend before it or provide information. It will make a decision based on all the relevant information available to it, which may include views of FCA staff and the subject and his lawyers, about the relative quality of witness and other evidence.

24.28 The EFCD Case Team will submit papers to the RDC, which will include an Investigation Report ('IR'), which takes account of the subject's response to the PIR, a draft Warning Notice and an Enforcement Submissions Document ('ESD'). The RDC will consider these documents and decide whether the material provided is adequate to support the action proposed. It may seek additional information or clarification if required.[24]

Warning Notices

24.29 Under s 126 FSMA, if the FCA proposes to take action against a person under s 123 for Market Abuse, it must give him a Warning Notice. The Warning Notice must state the reasons why the FCA proposes to take action and if a financial penalty is to be imposed, then it must state the amount of the penalty. The Warning

---

[19] DEPP 3.1.2G.
[20] DEPP 3.1.3G.
[21] DEPP 3.2.1G.
[22] DEPP 3.2.2G.
[23] DEPP 3.2.3G.
[24] DEPP 2.2.3G.

Enforcement Submissions Document

24.30 The purpose of the ESD is to provide the RDC with the background to the investigation and such other matters as are relevant to their consideration of the proposed action but which would not normally be appropriate to include in a Warning Notice. For example, this may include the reason why an investigation has changed in scope over time, why particular aspects were not pursued, or why action is or is not being taken against other persons.

Notice must also state whether it is proposed that any other action is to be taken—for example the making of a prohibition order under s 56 FSMA.

Warning Notice Meeting

24.31 Once the RDC has considered the papers submitted, it will then hold a formal meeting with the EFCD case team (known as a 'Warning Notice Meeting'). The subject is not entitled to attend this meeting. The purpose of this meeting is to discuss the case and to raise any points of concern. The RDC is free to decide whether or not to take the action proposed by the case team, or take different action, or defer a decision pending further information. The RDC will need to satisfy itself that the action it is being asked to take is appropriate in all the circumstances.[25]

Material disclosed to the subject

24.32 If the RDC decides that the action is appropriate it will finalise the draft Warning Notice and send it out to the subject.[26] The Warning Notice may be in the same terms as the draft or it may be in different terms. It is also possible for the RDC to decide to increase or decrease the penalty proposed depending on the view it takes of the case.[27] The subject also has the right to access material relied on by the RDC in taking its decision together with secondary material which might undermine that decision.[28] What this usually means is that the subject will be provided with a copy of the papers that the EFCD case team originally submitted to the RDC (usually the Draft Warning Notice, the ESD and any other documents). He will also be provided with a note of the Warning Notice meeting.

24.33 There are four types of material that the FCA may withhold from disclosure:[29]

1. 'Excluded material'—which relates to material obtained under the Regulation of Investigatory Powers Act 2000 ('RIPA').

---

[25] DEPP 2.2.3G.
[26] FSMA, s 126.
[27] DEPP 2.2.3G.
[28] FSMA, ss 394(1), 391(1)(b).
[29] FSMA, s 394(7).

2. 'Comparison material'—which relates to cases involving a person other than the recipient of the Warning Notice and which was taken into account by the FCA in the instant case for comparison purposes only.
3. 'Protected items'.[30]
4. 'Public interest material'—material which in the FCA's opinion, it would not be in the public interest to disclose or that it would be unfair to disclose having regard to its significance to the recipient of the Notice and the potential prejudice to the commercial interests of the other person.[31]

24.34 In relation to protected items and public interest material, the FCA is required to inform the subject of the existence of this material, but is not required to provide him with copies of it.

Written representations to the RDC

24.35 Following receipt of these documents, the firm or individual concerned then has twenty-eight days[32] within which to make written representations to the RDC on any aspect of the Warning Notice, including the conduct alleged and the penalty proposed. This period may be extended upon application. Requests for an extension must normally be made within fourteen days of receipt of the Warning Notice.[33] If the subject does submit written representations, then the EFCD case team will be given the opportunity to submit written representations, in response. If the subject makes no representations in response to the Warning Notice the FCA will regard the matters set out in the notice as undisputed.[34] The FCA will then give the person a Decision Notice.[35]

Oral representations

24.36 If the recipient of a Warning Notice indicates that he wishes to make oral representations, the RDC will hold an 'Oral Representations Meeting' at which the subject and his legal advisers or other representatives may attend and make such representations as they wish.[36] The Chair of the RDC Panel has a good deal of discretion as to how he wishes to conduct the meeting,[37] provided it is conducted in such a manner as to enable the recipient of the Warning Notice to make representations, and the FCA case team to respond. The FCA case team is also entitled to deal with any matters raised by the subject during the meeting. The RDC panel members are

---

[30] See Chapter 22, Section 7 Protected items (s 143 FSMA).
[31] FSMA, s 394(3).
[32] FSMA, s 387(2); DEPP 3.2.15G.
[33] DEPP 3.2.16G.
[34] DEPP 3.2.22G.
[35] DEPP 2.3.2G.
[36] DEPP 3.2.17G.
[37] DEPP 3.2.18G.

Enforcement—Market Abuse Proceedings

also entitled to raise any points or questions about the matter (whether in response to particular representations or more generally), with the subject and also the case team, and invite both sides to deal with the points raised.[38]

24.37 As the RDC is an administrative decision-making body, it is important to remember that this is not a judicial forum. However, the meeting itself does follow a fairly formal structure. Normally, the RDC Chair will introduce the matter and the other RDC panel members. He will then ask the FCA representatives and the subject and his representatives to introduce themselves. Often a subject will attend with his lawyers and also (if appropriate), with representatives of his employer.

24.38 Generally, the RDC Chair will ask the subject and his advisers to make their submissions first. It is entirely a matter for the subject as to who makes representations on his behalf and how they are made. In general terms, however, it is likely to be far more persuasive if the subject himself addresses the panel at least in relation to matters to which he can speak directly, such as why he traded, what was in his mind at the time he did so, etc. During this process, the RDC will ask questions of the subject and his representatives in relation to matters of specific concern or interest. The FCA case team is generally not permitted to question the subject or his representatives directly. The Chair will then ask the FCA case team to address the panel and to deal with any particular matters raised. There will then usually be an opportunity for closing remarks.

24.39 In general terms, the opportunity at this stage of the proceedings for a subject to attend in person and make representations to the RDC is one that a subject should consider carefully as an opportunity to present himself to the RDC and set out his position in person. At worst, the subject will receive a Decision Notice in the same terms as the Warning Notice. At best however, he may achieve a lesser penalty, or a finding on less serious grounds, or perhaps persuade the RDC not to take any action at all. If he does decide to attend however, he should bear in mind that the purpose of an Oral Representations Meeting is for him to give his own account of events and respond in person to questions from the RDC, certainly on issues of fact and therefore it would generally be wise for the subject not to leave the submissions entirely to his lawyers.

24.40 In appropriate cases, the Chairman of the RDC may ask those present to provide additional information in writing after the meeting. If he does so, he will specify the time within which that information is to be provided.[39] Once a Warning Notice has been issued to the subject, the RDC will not meet with the FCA case team or discuss the matter without other relevant parties being present or otherwise having the opportunity to respond.[40]

---

[38] DEPP 3.2.18G.
[39] DEPP 3.2.20G.
[40] DEPP 3.2.21G.

Decision Notice

Section 128 FSMA requires that if the FCA decides to take action against a person **24.41** under s 123 FSMA, it must give him a Decision Notice. If a financial penalty is imposed it must state the amount of the penalty and must also set out any other action it has decided to take together with reasons.

Following the Oral Representations Meeting, the RDC will consider whether a **24.42** Decision Notice should be issued and if so, in what terms.[41] It will be the responsibility of the RDC to settle the wording of the notice. The notice will include a brief summary of the key representations made and how the RDC has dealt with these. It is the RDC's responsibility to ensure that the notice complies with the relevant provisions of FSMA.[42]

Tribunal Reference

Following receipt of a Decision Notice, the subject has the right to refer the Decision **24.43** to the Upper Tribunal (Tax and Chancery Chamber) ('the Tribunal').[43] The subject has twenty-eight days within which to make this referral (known as a 'Reference'). The Tribunal is a judicial body which is wholly independent of the FCA. At the hearing of the Tribunal Reference, evidence is presented to the Tribunal by both sides and the Tribunal must determine afresh, what (if any,) is the appropriate action for the FCA to take in relation to the matter referred to it.[44] On determining the Reference, the Tribunal must remit the matter to the FCA with such directions as the Tribunal considers appropriate to give effect to its determination.[45]

Final Notice

If, following receipt of the Decision Notice, the subject does not refer the matter **24.44** to the Tribunal, then the FCA will issue a Final Notice. This will set out the FCA's findings, the basis for the action and the type and amount of the penalty. The Final Notice will be published on the FCA's website.

6. The Executive Settlement Process

On 20 October 2005, the FSA introduced the Executive Settlement Process which **24.45** provides for discounts to financial penalties in exchange for early settlement. From 6 March 2011, the process was extended to cover the length of any suspension imposed

---

[41] DEPP 3.2.23G.
[42] DEPP 3.2.24G.
[43] FSMA, s 128(4).
[44] FSMA, s 133.
[45] FSMA, s 133.

on an approved person or authorised firm. The scheme does not apply to the disgorgement element of a financial penalty, to public censure, prohibition orders, withdrawal of authorisation or approval or the payment of compensation or redress. It also does not apply to High Court Civil Proceedings or to Criminal Proceedings.

24.46 A significant proportion of the FSA's Enforcement cases were concluded by way of settlement, and this will continue to be an important part of the process under the FCA. The FCA has finite financial and human resources and it is not possible to investigate and litigate every matter that is referred to Enforcement to the fullest extent. Other benefits include the fact that settled outcomes enable the FCA to get key messages out to the financial services industry in a timely manner as well as negating the litigation risk inherent in any contested Enforcement case.

24.47 Settlement can also be beneficial for the subject of the investigation in terms of saving financial and other resources and achieving the early resolution of an investigation. It also provides certainty of outcome and the possibility of being able to negotiate the wording of the Final Notice and any press release. It is important to remember that in the FCA context, a settlement is a regulatory decision, it is not the same as an 'out of court' settlement in the commercial context which puts an end to a commercial dispute. An FCA settlement amounts to an agreed regulatory decision whereby the firm or individual accepts the terms of the FCA's decision and gives up its right to make representations or refer the matter to the Tribunal. For its part, the FCA agrees to accept settlement in the terms agreed and issue a Final Notice in those terms.

24.48 Therefore, whereas a regulatory settlement will inevitably involve some degree of commercial negotiation, the FCA, as a public authority with statutory responsibilities, is in a different position to an ordinary commercial litigant. The FCA will need to ensure that the proposed settlement is consistent with its statutory and strategic objectives. Before reaching a settlement the FCA will also need to take into account past cases and other cases that are currently being investigated, as well as its overall strategy. Cases will not therefore be looked at in isolation, but as part of an overall strategic picture.

24.49 What this means in practice is that the FCA will not 'cut a deal' by making concessions and giving penalty discounts in the way that a commercial litigant can.

The settlement discount scheme applied to financial penalties

24.50 Settlement can be considered at any time after the FCA has a sufficient understanding of the nature and gravity of the issue to make a reasonable assessment of the appropriate outcome.[46] Settlement discussions are possible at any time if

---

[46] EG 5.7.

both parties agree[47] although the FCA generally considers that the earlier such discussions can take place the better from a public interest perspective.

24.51 The FCA's approach to settlement is to firstly calculate the appropriate financial penalty in respect of the conduct concerned. This starting figure will take no account of the existence of the settlement discount scheme. This assessment of the appropriate penalty will be provided to the subject together with an indication of the alleged breaches. The amount will then be reduced by a set percentage depending on the stage in the process at which settlement is agreed. There are four stages for these purposes:[48]

> Stage 1: the period from commencement of an investigation until the FCA has a sufficient understanding of the nature and gravity of the breach to make a reasonable assessment of the appropriate penalty and in addition has communicated that assessment to the person concerned and allowed a reasonable opportunity to reach agreement as to the amount of the penalty. The FCA normally considers that twenty-eight days is a reasonable period within which to agree settlement and extensions will usually only be granted in exceptional circumstances. Settlement at Stage 1 will result in a thirty per cent reduction on the proposed penalty.
> Stage 2: the period from the end of Stage 1 until the expiry of the period for making written representations or, if sooner, the date on which the written representations are sent in response to the giving of a warning notice. Settlement at Stage 2 will result in a twenty per cent reduction on the proposed penalty.
> Stage 3: the period from the end of Stage 2 until the giving of a decision notice. Settlement at Stage 3 will result in a ten per cent reduction on the proposed penalty.
> Stage 4: the period after the end of Stage 3, including proceedings before the Tribunal and any subsequent appeals. Settlement at Stage 4 or beyond will result in no reduction.

24.52 The FCA appoints Settlement Decision Makers ('SDMs') who are its ultimate decision makers in connection with any settlement negotiations between the investigation team and the firm/individual. The SDMs will be two decision makers of at least Director of Division level, one of whom will normally be the Director of EFCD. The SDMs will be briefed by the investigation team on the issues in the case, and will normally have sight of any draft Warning Notice, Investigation Report, or other such documentation. The SDM will give authority to the investigation team to negotiate within the financial or other limits given and for the issue of a Notice on substantially the terms seen by the SDMs. The investigation team is,

---

[47] EG 5.6–5.7.
[48] DEPP 6.7.3G.

however, able to agree amendments to a draft Warning Notice provided approval has been given by the Project Sponsor.

24.53 Settlement discussions are conducted on a 'without prejudice' basis.[49] Therefore, if the matter was to be subsequently considered by a Court or Tribunal, neither FCA staff nor the person concerned should seek to rely, against the other, on any admissions or statements made during discussions if the matter were subsequently to be considered by the courts, the RDC, or the Tribunal. However, the fact that discussions are 'without prejudice' will not prevent the FCA from following up on any new issues of regulatory concern which come to light during settlement discussions.

24.54 There is no concept of 'without prejudice' in criminal proceedings. Therefore, in a market abuse investigation that has been commenced on a dual criminal/market abuse basis, settlement discussions will typically only take place after a decision has been taken to proceed solely on a market abuse basis and notice of change of scope has been given.

24.55 Once settlement has been reached, this will be recorded in a settlement agreement. This will record the stage at which settlement was reached and the discount that has been applied.[50] These details will also be recorded in the Final Notice.[51]

Mediation

24.56 DEPP 5.1.9 G and EG 5.20 state that the FCA is committed to mediation as a way of facilitating settlement in appropriate cases. This method is rarely used and is probably unlikely to be used in preference to the Executive Settlement Process.

7. Civil proceedings

24.57 Under s 381 FSMA (injunctions in cases of market abuse), the FCA may apply to the High Court for an order restraining a course of conduct, to take steps to remedy a course of conduct and to secure assets.[52] The FCA's policy in relation to such applications is set out in EG 10.3. The broad test it will apply is whether the application would be the most effective way to deal with the FCA's concerns. The FCA's Enforcement Guide ('EG') 10.3 sets out a non-exhaustive list of factors that the FCA will consider in making this assessment. In cases of market abuse, the nature and seriousness of the misconduct and its impact on the financial system will be particularly relevant. Given that the proceedings are injunctive in nature, key

---

[49] DEPP 5.1.4G & EG 5.9.
[50] DEPP 6.7.4G.
[51] DEPP 6.7.4G.
[52] See EG 10.2.

considerations will also be urgency and the need to restrain ongoing conduct as well as the need to freeze assets which are the proceeds from the conduct in order to prevent them being dissipated.

In a market abuse case in which the behaviour complained of falls within s 118(2)–(4), a further key issue will be whether the conduct can be adequately addressed by other disciplinary powers such as a financial penalty or public censure. This will be the position in most such cases. Furthermore, the fact that an investigation would be commenced on a joint criminal / market abuse basis means that the powers of the Crown Court to restrain a subject's assets under the Proceeds of Crime Act 2002 ('POCA') would be an available mechanism and it is this process which is more commonly used in these cases. Neither the FSA nor the FCA have used s 381 powers in respect of a case falling within s 118(2)–(4) FSMA, but the procedure has been used in relation to other types of market abuse.[53]

8. Publicity

Publicity during an FCA investigation

The FCA will not normally publicise the fact that it is investigating a particular person or matter except in certain exceptional circumstances.[54] Nor will it normally publish the results of its investigations, unless certain exceptional circumstances exist.[55]

Publicity during or upon the conclusion of regulatory action

Section 391 FSMA requires the FCA to publish such information about a Warning Notice, Decision Notice or Final Notice as it considers appropriate. However, s 391 FSMA provides that the FCA cannot publish information if such publication would, in its opinion, be unfair to the person against whom the action was taken, or be prejudicial to consumers or detrimental to the stability of the UK financial system. Once published, the Final Notice will remain on the FCA's website for at least six years. The power to publish information regarding a Warning Notice is a new power which was granted to the FCA by the FS Act 2012. By publicising the matter at the Warning Notice stage, the FCA aims to improve transparency about its enforcement processes and also to be seen to be taking timely action. However, this power brings with it an increased reputational risk to the person concerned

24.58

24.59

24.60

---

[53] *FSA v Da Vinci Invest Ltd* [2011] EWHC 2674; *Barnett Michael Alexander*, Final Notice 14 June 2011 and FSA/PN/053/2011.
[54] EG 6.1–6.6.
[55] EG 6.6.

Enforcement—Market Abuse Proceedings

because publication in these circumstances will occur at an early stage of investigation, before the person has even had the opportunity to put its case before the RDC.

Challenges to the publication of enforcement notices

24.61 In the case of *Canada Inc and Peter Beck*,[56] the Applicants applied to the High Court for permission to apply for judicial review of the decision of the FSA to publish a Decision Notice. The High Court granted permission to bring judicial review proceedings on condition that firstly, the Claimants should apply to the Upper Tribunal for directions that there be no publication of the Decision Notice and that the FSA be restrained from publishing the Decision Notice until either determination of the Tribunal proceedings or the Judicial Review proceedings (whichever was the earlier).

24.62 The applicants therefore made this application to the Tribunal who refused it. The Tribunal decided that, in applying Rule 14(1) of the Upper Tribunal Rules[57] ('Order Prohibiting Disclosure or Publication'), there was an overall public interest in the openness of proceedings and a strong presumption that Tribunal references would be dealt with in public. Consequently, the onus was on an applicant to demonstrate the need for privacy and unfairness and cogent evidence to this effect would be required.[58] The applicants subsequently made a further application to the High Court for an interim injunction to restrain the FSA from publishing the Decision Notice. The High Court dismissed this application.[59]

24.63 A point to note is that, thus far, challenges to the publication of a Decision Notice have always related to proceedings in which it might be said that there was a consumer interest in publicising at that stage—perhaps because the proceedings related to an unauthorised investment scheme and therefore investors needed to know to contact the FSA regarding their investment, or in order to prevent further investors from investing in the same or similar schemes. The position might be considered to be different in a market abuse case, in which in all probability the conduct complained of will have already happened and may not therefore present the same ongoing risk. In such a case, it is open to the subject to the FCA to justify the reasons why it considers that the requirements of s 391 FSMA are satisfied and in particular why it does not consider that such publication would be unfair to the person concerned. These reasons can then be examined, and may in an appropriate

---

[56] *Canada Inc and Peter Beck v FSA*, Upper Tribunal, 2 Aug 2011. See also *Arch Financial Products LLP v FSA*, Upper Tribunal [2013] All ER (D) 67.
[57] The Tribunal Procedure (Upper Tribunal) rules 2008 SI 2008 No 2698 as amended.
[58] *Sachin Karpe and others v FSA*, 15 May 2002 FIN/2010/0019; *Theophilus Folagbade Sonaike v FSA* (13 July 2005); *Eurolife Assurance Company Ltd v FSA* (26 July 2002).
[59] *Canada Inc, R (on the application of) v The Financial Services Authority* [2011] EWHC 2766 (Admin).

case provide grounds for a submission to the Tribunal or High Court, that the FCA should be prevented from publishing the Decision Notice in the circumstances.

Publicity during or upon the conclusion of civil action

24.64 High Court proceedings are invariably conducted in open court and will therefore be in the public domain from an early stage. The FCA will therefore generally consider it appropriate to publish details of these proceedings in the absence of a compelling reason.[60]

Publicity during or upon the conclusion of criminal action

24.65 The FCA will normally publicise the outcome of public hearings in criminal prosecutions. When conducting a criminal investigation the FCA will generally make a public announcement when suspects are arrested, when search warrants are executed and when charges are laid. A public announcement may also be made at other stages of the investigation when this is considered appropriate.[61]

---

[60] EG 6.16.
[61] EG 6.17–6.17A.

25

THE FUTURE

1. Introduction	25.01	Powers of competent authorities	25.22
2. New European legislation	25.02	Sanctions	25.23
3. The Draft Regulation	25.06	4. The Draft Directive	25.24
Scope of the Regulation	25.14	Potential effect on the UK's criminal	
Insider dealing	25.17	insider dealing regime	25.27
Inside information	25.19	5. Conclusion—the next five years	25.28

1. Introduction

25.01 This Chapter summarises the European Commission's current legislative proposals for a harmonised European Market Abuse regime which will extend significantly beyond the scope of the current Market Abuse Directive 2003 ('MAD').[1] It considers the potential future effect of this on the UK's current civil and criminal legislation.

2. New European legislation

25.02 On 20 October 2011, the European Commission adopted a proposal for a Regulation of the European Parliament and of the Council on Insider Dealing and Market Manipulation (Market Abuse) ('Draft Regulation' or 'Regulation').[2] It is proposed that this Draft Regulation will replace the current MAD.

25.03 The Draft Regulation seeks to create a single, directly applicable EU-wide rulebook for market abuse (insider dealing and market manipulation), enforced by national

---

[1] Market Abuse Directive 2003, Directive 2003/6/EC.
[2] COM (2011) 651 final. On 25 July 2012, the proposal was amended to extend the coverage of the Regulation to include the manipulation of benchmarks which would include LIBOR and EURIBOR (COM(2012) 421 Final; 2011/0295 COD).

administrative sanctions. Accompanying it is a Directive on Criminal Sanctions for Insider Dealing and Market Manipulation[3] ('Draft Directive' or 'Directive').

On 8 October 2012, the European Parliament's Economic Affairs Committee voted in favour of both the Draft Regulation and Directive and the Council of the European Union agreed its general approach on 7 December 2012.[4] On 25 June 2013, the Proposal for the Draft Regulation was provisionally agreed by the European Parliament and Council, with some amendments.[5] Once the Draft Regulation and Directive have been adopted, the Regulation would apply after two years, by which time Member States would also have to transpose the Directive into national law. This means that the application of the new rules created by the Regulation and the Directive could be expected to take effect from 2015 at the earliest, although this estimate can be regarded as no more than provisional at this stage. **25.04**

As matters currently stand, the UK has exercised an 'opt-out' in relation to the Draft Directive on the grounds that at present it is not possible to ascertain sufficiently the scope and implications of the Directive and its match with other financial regulations.[6] The UK Government also considers our current Market Abuse regime and criminal legislation to be effective and fit for purpose. However, the Government has said that it will keep its position under review as the drafting and agreement process progresses in Europe. **25.05**

3. The Draft Regulation

Article 1 of the Draft Regulation[7] summarises its intended purpose: **25.06**

> This Regulation establishes a common regulatory framework on insider dealing, misuse of inside information and market manipulation as well as measures to prevent market abuse to ensure the integrity of financial markets in the Union and to enhance investor protection and confidence in those markets.

As the Proposal[8] for the Draft Regulation makes clear, the Draft Regulation arises directly out of the current global economic and financial crisis which has highlighted the importance of market integrity. In particular, gaps have emerged in **25.07**

---

[3] COM 2011 (654/3) 7 Dec 2012, Interinstitutional File 2011/0297 (COD). On 25 July 2012, the proposal was amended to extend the coverage of the Directive to include the manipulation of benchmarks (see n 2; COM(2012) 420 Final, 2011/0297 (COD)).
[4] COM 2011 (654/3). File 2011/0297 (COD).
[5] Council of European Union, 25 June 2013, 11384/13, 2011/0295 (COD).
[6] House of Commons Standard Note, Market Abuse Directive, 15 June 2012 (SN/BT/3271); European Scrutiny Committee, 57th Report, HMT (33282) Financial Services: Market Abuse.
[7] Draft Regulation (n 2) as amended by the European Parliament and Council, 25 June 2013, 11384/13, 2011/0295 (COD).
[8] Proposal for a Regulation of the European Parliament and of the Council COM(2011) 651 final; 2011/0295; SEC(2011)1217, 1218 final.

the current legislation (MAD),[9] in relation to new markets, platforms, and over the counter ('OTC') instruments, commodities, and related derivatives, together with an inconsistent approach to Regulation and Disciplinary Sanctions across the Member States.[10]

25.08 One of the key limitations of the MAD that has emerged is that it is based on the concept of prohibiting insider dealing or market manipulation in financial instruments which are admitted to trading on a regulated market. However, since the adoption of the Markets in Financial Instruments Directive 2004 ('MiFID'),[11] financial instruments have been increasingly traded on Multilateral Trading Facilities ('MTF') and Organised Trading Facilities ('OTF'), neither of which are Regulated Markets under MAD.[12]

25.09 The increase in trading across different venues has made it more difficult to monitor such trading for possible market abuse. These problems have been highlighted by a number of reports published by influential entities such as the Committee of European Securities Regulators ('CESR') on the nature and extent of the supervisory powers of Member States under the MAD[13] and on the options and discretions of the MAD regime used by Member States,[14] a report by the European Securities Markets Expert Group ('ESME') which assessed the effectiveness of the MAD in achieving its primary objectives, identified certain weaknesses and made suggestions for improvement.[15] The Proposal also takes into account responses received to a 2009 call for evidence on the review of the MAD.[16]

25.10 Therefore the Draft Regulation extends the scope of the market abuse framework to any financial instrument admitted to trading on a MTF or an OTF, as well as to any related financial instruments traded OTC which can have an effect on the underlying covered market.[17] The Proposal states that this is necessary to avoid any regulatory arbitrage among trading venues, to ensure that the protection of investors and the integrity of markets are preserved on a level playing field in the entire European Union, and to ensure that the market manipulation of such financial instruments through derivatives traded OTC, such as Credit Default Swaps, is clearly prohibited.[18]

---

[9] Dir 2003/6/EC (n 1).
[10] Proposal (n 8) para 1.
[11] Directive 2000/12/EC.
[12] See Chapter 15, Section 3, paras 15.22–15.24.
[13] Ref CESR/07-380, June 2007, available at <http://www.cesr-eu.org>.
[14] Ref CESR/09-1120.
[15] Issued June 2007 and entitled 'MMarket Abuse EU legal framework and its implementation by Member States: a first evaluation'.
[16] See <http://www.ec.europa.eu/internal_market/consultations/2009/market_abuse_en.htm>.
[17] Proposal (n 8) para 3.4.1.1.
[18] Proposal (n 8) para 3.4.1.1.

25.11 It is also proposed that the Regulation will deal specifically with commodity derivatives and related spot commodity contracts.[19] A spot market is a commodities or securities market in which goods are sold for cash and delivered immediately. Contracts bought and sold on these markets are immediately effected and delivery must be effected within one month or less. Examples of spot markets include Crude oil and also the Energy market. Spot and related derivative markets are highly interconnected yet the existing rules on transparency and market integrity only apply to financial and derivatives markets and not to the related spot markets. It is not proposed that the Regulation should cover the spot market itself, but would cover transactions or behaviours in those spot markets which are related to, and have an effect on, financial and derivatives markets which are within its scope.

25.12 Emission allowances will also be included by being reclassified as financial instruments under MiFID, which will bring them within the market abuse framework. Therefore, a specific definition of inside information for emissions allowances is introduced in the Regulation.

25.13 The Regulation also aims to ensure better detection of market abuse by requiring minimum standards to ensure that competent authorities are provided with all necessary powers to investigate and take action in respect of market abuse.

Scope of the Regulation

25.14 As stated above, the Regulation will significantly increase the scope of the current market abuse regime. Article 2 of the Regulation specifically extends beyond financial instruments traded on a Regulated Market and includes financial instruments traded on a MTF or OTF in at least one Member State, or for which a request for admission to trading on a MTF has been made, and behaviour or transactions that relate to such instruments regardless of whether the behaviour or transaction actually takes place on a Regulated Market, MTF, or OTF. Article 2 also specifically includes behaviour or transactions, including bids, relating to the auctioning of emissions allowances or other auctioned products based thereon; it also includes spot commodity contracts.

25.15 The insider dealing prohibitions in the Regulation will also apply to the acquisition or disposal of financial instruments not falling within the above, but whose value relates to one of these. This of course would include derivative instruments such as spread bets and Contracts for Differences.

25.16 As regards territorial scope, the Draft Regulation proposes that the prohibitions and requirements shall apply to actions carried out in the European Union or outside the Union. This will significantly expand the extraterritorial reach of the

---

[19] Proposal (n 8) para 3.4.1.2.

EU market abuse regime, since the Regulation will apply to insider dealing taking place entirely outside the EU simply because the trading relates to an instrument which happens also to be admitted to trading on a trading facility in the EU—regardless of whether the conduct takes place on an EU trading facility or actually has any effect on EU markets.

Insider dealing

25.17 Article 9 of the Draft Regulation provides for a prohibition on insider dealing and improperly disclosing inside information. Its wording adopts in essence the same prohibitions as are currently present in the MAD, namely engaging in insider dealing, recommending or inducing another person to engage in insider dealing, or improperly disclosing inside information. Article 9 also specifically prohibits the onward disclosure of recommendations or inducements when the person concerned knows or ought to know that it was based on inside information. Article 9 also prohibits attempting to do any of these things.

25.18 Article 7 of the Regulation provides for the definition of insider dealing and improper disclosure of inside information. It adopts the current definition in the MAD but then provides for certain extensions to the definition to include:

- The use of inside information to cancel or amend an order concerning a financial instrument to which the information relates where the order was placed before the person concerned possessed the inside information.
- Attempting to engage in insider dealing or attempting to cancel or amend an order on the basis of inside information.
- In relation to auctions of emission allowances or other auctioned products based thereon, using inside information by submitting, modifying, or withdrawing a bid.

Inside information

25.19 Inside information is defined in Article 6 of the Draft Regulation. Again, the definitions broadly follow those used in the MAD; however, these have been extended to include:

- in relation to derivatives on commodities, information which would be likely to have a significant effect on the price of such derivatives or related spot commodity contracts; which would include information reasonably expected to be disclosed in accordance with legal or regulatory provisions, rules; or customs at the Union or national level, on the commodity derivatives or spot markets concerned.
- in relation to emission allowances or auctioned products based thereon, inside information relating, directly or indirectly, to one or more of these instruments.

25.20 The original Proposal provided for a significant extension to the MAD definition by including information which does not fall within one of the specific definitions but which, if it were available to a reasonable investor who regularly deals on the market and in the financial instrument or a related spot commodity contract concerned, would be regarded by that person as relevant when deciding the terms on which transactions in the financial instrument or a related spot commodity contract should be effected. In so doing, the Draft Regulation would provide a 'stay of execution' in respect of the 'Legacy Offence' that is currently contained in s 118(4) FSMA and whose demise is currently set for December 2014,[20] although whether this provision will survive into the final version of the Regulation is open to question given that it has been deleted by the agreed amendments made by the Parliament and Council.[21]

The Draft Regulation also proposes to define 'precise information'[22] and 'significant effect'.[23] The definitions proposed are identical in terms to those already contained in s 118C FSMA although the definition is extended to specifically include, the steps in a protracted process intended to bring about, or that results in, a particular circumstance or a particular event, as well as the particular circumstance or event itself. **25.21**

Powers of competent authorities[24]

It is proposed that the Regulation will significantly extend the powers available to competent authorities to investigate and detect market abuse. This includes a power to enter private premises and seize documents. This is a power which the FCA already enjoys by virtue of s 176 FSMA;[25] however, a number of other Member States do not have similar provisions. It is also proposed that the Regulation should introduce a level playing field in the internal market in relation to the access by competent authorities to telephone and existing data traffic records held by a telecommunication operator or by an investment firm. Again, the FCA already has this power under the Regulation of Investigatory Powers Act 2000 ('RIPA').[26] Lastly specific requirements are proposed to require Member States to co-operate with each other. **25.22**

Sanctions[27]

Currently, there is a wide divergence among Member States as regards administrative and criminal sanctions for market abuse. The Regulation will therefore introduce minimum rules for administrative measures, sanctions and fines. Member **25.23**

---

[20] See Chapter 18, Section 2, paras 18.04–18.05.
[21] 25 June 2013, 11384/13, 2011/0295 (COD).
[22] Draft Regulation (n 2) art 6(2).
[23] Draft Regulation (n 2) art 6(3).
[24] Proposal (n 8) para 3.4.4.1 and Draft Regulation Chapter 5.
[25] See Chapter 22, Section 11 Search Warrants.
[26] See Chapter 22, Section 6 Regulation of Investigatory Powers Act 2000.
[27] Proposal (n 8) para 3.4.5.1 and Draft Regulation Chapter 5.

States will not be prevented from fixing higher standards. As a minimum, the Regulation provides for financial penalties in the form of disgorgement of any profits plus interest and a punitive/deterrent element which must exceed any profit gained or loss avoided.

4. The Draft Directive

25.24 In addition to the requirements set out in the Draft Regulation, the Commission considers that criminal sanctions have a stronger deterrent effect than administrative measures and sanctions. Therefore the Directive will require Member States to put in place criminal sanctions for the most serious insider dealing and market manipulation offences. The Directive will also provide for minimum criminal sanctions to be determined at EU level.

25.25 Paragraph 10 of the Preamble to the Directive provides that Member States should be under an obligation to provide that (as a minimum), serious cases of insider dealing, market manipulation, and unlawful disclosure of inside information should constitute criminal offences when committed with intent.[28] Paragraph 10a proposes that a case be deemed 'serious' when the impact on the integrity of the market, the actual or potential profit derived or loss avoided, the level of damage caused to the market, or the overall value of the financial instruments traded is high.

25.26 Paragraph 12 will require Member States to ensure that their criminal regimes encompass inciting as well as aiding and abetting the criminal offences. Paragraph 14 requires that Member States should also extend liability for the offences to legal persons where such offences have been committed for their benefit, through the imposition of criminal or non-criminal sanctions or measures.

Potential effect on the UK's criminal insider dealing regime

25.27 If the UK Government ultimately decides to 'opt in' to the Directive, the UK will be required to implement domestic legislation which will extend the UK's current criminal regime in some significant respects. Firstly, given that Part V of the CJA is based on the now defunct Insider Dealing Directive 1989 ('IDD'),[29] it is likely that rather than amend the current criminal legislation (the CJA), the UK Government will either draft new legislation or make amendments to Part VIII of FSMA to incorporate the extended requirements of the Regulation and the Directive. In practical terms, either option would mean that the UK's criminal insider dealing regime would bear a striking similarity to the current UK market abuse regime. The effect of

---

[28] Draft Directive (n 3).
[29] Com Dir 89/592/EC.

the Directive's requirements would also mean that the UK's criminal regime would need to cover certain areas that are currently beyond the scope of the CJA such as:

1. Financial instruments admitted to trading on an MTF or OTF or for which a request for admission has been made.[30]
2. Financial instruments whose price or value depends on, or has an effect on, the price or value of financial instruments traded on a regulated market, MTF or OTF, would also be included.[31]
3. Behaviour or transactions, including bids, relating to the auctioning of emissions allowances or other auctioned products based thereon would be included.[32]
4. The criminal regime will be required to apply irrespective of whether the transaction, behaviour, or order actually takes place on a trading venue, systematic internaliser,[33] or is over the counter trading.[34]
5. The use of inside information by cancelling or amending an order concerning a financial instrument to which the information relates where the order was placed before the person concerned possessed the inside information, would also be included as insider dealing.[35]
6. In relation to auctions of emissions allowances or other auctioned products based thereon, the use of inside information referred to in item 5 would also include modifying or withdrawing a bid by a person for its own account or for the account of a third party.[36]
7. Given that it is proposed that the definition of 'inside information' should be extended to include information that a reasonable investor would use as part of the basis for his investment decisions,[37] this would extend the definition beyond the current criminal offences which relate only to the more restrictive definition of inside information.
8. The Directive requires that Member States ensure that attempting, inciting and aiding abetting also be criminalised.[38] The UK's current criminal law on inchoate offences will be likely to be sufficient in this respect.
9. Member States will be required to ensure that legal persons can be held liable when the insider dealing offence in question is committed for their benefit by any person, acting either individually or as part of an organ of the legal

---

[30] Draft Directive (n 3) art 1(2).
[31] Draft Directive (n 3) art 1(2).
[32] Draft Directive (n 3) art 1(4).
[33] An investment firm trading on its own account. Will be defined in art 2(1)(3) of the Regulation (n 2).
[34] Draft Directive (n 3) art 1(6).
[35] Draft Directive (n 3) art 3(4).
[36] Draft Directive (n 3) art 3(5).
[37] Draft Directive (n 3) art 6.
[38] Draft Directive (n 3) art 5.

person, and having a leading position within the legal person.[39] The UK's current criminal law applies only to individuals.[40]

10. Member States will also be required to ensure that legal persons can be held liable where the lack of supervision or control has made the commission of an insider dealing offence possible for the benefit of the legal person, by a person under its authority.[41]

5. Conclusion—the next five years

25.28 As matters currently stand, the UK has opted out of the Draft Directive and takes the view that its current criminal legislation offences covers all of the offences currently proposed therein. This may not be entirely correct as the above paragraphs demonstrate. However, for now and for the foreseeable future, all the indications are that the UK will continue with its current dual regimes—Criminal (Part V CJA) and Market Abuse (Part VIII of FSMA).

25.29 Maintaining this attitude may well become increasingly difficult, however, given the inevitable pressure from Europe. As time passes and the scope of Europe's proposals are revised and clarified, the Government's current stance will need to be revisited. The new Regulation and Directive will come into force at some point in the next few years and when they do, the UK's criminal insider dealing regime, based as it is on the outdated and now effectively defunct IDD, will look increasingly archaic. It will also be increasingly difficult for the UK to continue to claim that its current criminal legislation is fit for purpose, particularly when it does not cover types of financial instruments and trading which were simply never envisaged in 1993 but which are now an integral part of the financial system.

25.30 I predict therefore that the UK legislators will in time recognise a need for a streamlined and harmonised civil and criminal regime based on the new European legislation, and which takes account of the realities of trading in the twenty-first century. As a result, I predict that we will see draft domestic legislation to this effect within the next few years. If this is sufficiently flexibly drafted to cope with ever more innovative variations on the traditional forms of trading, it is likely to be an attractive prospect for the legislators, market participants and the Enforcement agencies. This would in turn provide for a clarity and unity in approach which would surely be welcomed by all market participants, their advisers, the Regulators / Prosecutors and of course the Courts. Time will tell.

---

[39] Draft Directive (n 3) art 7.
[40] See Chapter 5, Section 3, paras 5.8–5.10.
[41] Draft Directive (n 3) art 7(2).

Appendices

1. Glossary of Terms Commonly Encountered in
   Insider Dealing Cases   291
2. Legislation
   A. Insider Dealing Directive (Dir 89/592/EC)   296
   B. Criminal Justice Act 1993, Part V   301
   C. Criminal Justice Act 1993, Schedule 2   306
   D. Insider Dealing (Securities and
      Regulated Markets) Order 1994
      (SI No 187) (as amended)   308
3. Financial Services and Markets Act 2000
   Part VIII (as amended)   312
4. FSMA 2000 (Prescribed Markets and
   Qualifying Investments) Order 2001   322

APPENDIX 1

Glossary of Terms Commonly Encountered in Insider Dealing Cases

Term	Description
All cash offer	Proposal, either hostile or friendly, to acquire a target company through the payment of cash for the stock of the target.
All share offer	In a takeover—an offer by a firm to give one security, such as a bond or preferred stock, in exchange for another security, such as shares in the target company.
Alternative Investment Market ('AIM')	Launched by the LSE in the mid 1990s to appeal to smaller, newer companies that may not have the track record of those on the Main Market. As such, it has more flexible requirements.
Average Daily Volume	The cumulative number of shares traded over a given time period, divided by the number of trading sessions in that period. Time frames for calculating average daily volume can vary, monthly, quarterly and annual averages are common.
Bid / offer price	Price quoted for a stock by a broker or other market participant for an immediate purchase (bid) and immediate sale (offer).
Bid / offer quote	The price at which a broker or other market participant is prepared to buy a security *and* to sell a security.
Broker	A firm that arranges or executes transactions between a buyer and a seller and charges a fee or a commission for doing so.
Chinese Walls	Arrangements in the form of procedures, systems, management, and physical location which are intended to act as barriers within a firm to ensure that confidential information which is generated by one part of the firm or obtained from a client in one part of the firm does not penetrate another part of the firm.
Commitment Committee ('Com Com')	Part of the internal control procedures established by a merchant bank to manage the firm's risks within its corporate finance business. Its principal role is to provide independent review of important decisions taken within the corporate finance department.
Company	A company is an artificial legal 'person' with rights and obligations distinct from those of the people who run it. The company is owned by its shareholders who take shares but the company itself owns its business. A company is run by its directors.
Contract for Difference ('CFD')	A contract between two parties, typically a broker and client, to settle for cash the difference between the opening price and closing price of a specific referenced underlying security, eg an equity.
Corporate Broker	Advises companies on fund raising (eg new issues of shares). Tries to generate interest among investors for the company's securities. Stands prepared to buy and sell companies' shares.

(*Continued*)

Appendix 1

Term	Description
Corporate Finance	Advising on and executing transactions in the UK market relating to listed and AIM quoted companies including mergers, acquisitions and disposals and equity related financings and giving advice to corporate clients on their market related activities.
Derivative	A security whose price is dependent upon or derived from one or more underlying assets. So a single-share spread bet is a derivative whose price is dependent upon the price of the underlying share.
Discretionary dealing	A discretionary broker buys and sells shares on behalf of the client and also has the authority to make investment decisions without the prior approval of the client.
Down bet	Another term for selling a security or taking a short position. Common spread betting terminology.
Equity or equities	Another name for a share or group of shares.
Execution-only dealing	An execution-only broker merely buys and sells shares on the instructions of the client.
FTSE100	An index of the 100 largest firms (by market capitalisation) listed on the London Stock Exchange.
Fundamental analysis	A method of determining a trading strategy by a detailed analysis of the economic situation of the share or commodity.
Guaranteed stop loss	Used in spread betting and CFD trading as a means of limiting risk. For a premium, the agreed stop loss price will be guaranteed by the broker regardless of whether the market moves beyonvd the stop loss price.
Hedge fund	An aggressively managed portfolio of investments that uses advanced investment strategies with the aim of generating high returns. Hedge funds are typically open to a limited number of investors who are often required to provide a very large initial investment.
High cap	Also known as 'large cap', this refers to the market capitalisation of a company. There is no absolute value for a high cap company but it would typically have a market value bigger than £3 to £5 billion.
Holding Announcement	The announcement to the market that talks are taking place between two companies which may or may not lead to the announcement of an offer or that a potential bidder is considering making an offer.
ICAP Securities and Derivatives Exchange ('ISDX')	A London-based stock exchange which provides a range of fully listed and growth markets. ISDX allows a company to raise capital on its primary market and investors are able to trade in the company's shares on an active secondary market. The requirements for listing are not as stringent as those on the other markets and therefore companies may start here with a view to moving up to AIM or the LSE Main Market in the future.
Illiquid Market	A market in which there is little volume traded. An illiquid market in a particular share means that it may be a more difficult share to trade, particularly in large size, as there are not always many buyers and sellers willing to trade in that share at any one time.
Initial Public Offering ('IPO')	The first sale of stock by a private company to the public.

Glossary of Terms

Term	Description
Initial margin	Also known as 'deposit margin', in relation to CFDs or spread sets, it represents a percentage of the full value of a transaction that a broker requires his client to pay in order to trade eg if the initial margin is 20 per cent, a client is only required to initially pay £20 for every £100 that the transaction is worth.
Investor	The owner of an asset. An investor normally buys a share with a view to a longer-term capital return or dividend income stream.
Limit or limit order	The maximum price a client will pay to buy a security or the minimum price at which a client will offer to sell a security.
Liquid Market	A high level of trading activity, allowing buying and selling with minimum price disturbance. Also, a market characterised by the ability to buy and sell with relative ease. A liquid market in a particular share means that it is an easy share to trade, with many buyers and sellers willing to trade in that share at any one time.
Listed company	A company whose shares are listed on an exchange.
Listing prospectus	Before a company's shares are first allowed to be listed on a stock market, it has to publish a listing prospectus which contains detailed information on the company, its business, and financial situation. The purpose of a listing prospectus is to provide all relevant information that a prospective investor needs to decide whether or not to invest in the company.
London Stock Exchange ('LSE')	The UK's six regional exchanges joined together in 1973 to form the stock exchange of Great Britain and Ireland, later named the LSE.
Long or long position	Another term for buying a security or indicating that you own a security.
Low cap	Also known as 'small cap' or possibly 'mid cap', this refers to the market capitalisation of a company. There is no absolute value for a low cap company but it would typically be below £500 million.
Main Market (LSE)	Also known as the LSE Official List. Aimed at larger, more established companies.
Management Buyout	Acquisition of a company by the management team supported by venture capital investment and/or bank debt financing.
Margin	When a trader opens a CFD or spread bet position, rather than pay the full value of a transaction the client only needs to pay a percentage of the total value of the transaction when opening the position. This is called 'Initial Margin'. This margin allows leverage or 'gearing', which means that a trader can access a larger amount of shares for a smaller amount of money than he would be able to do if he was actually buying or selling the shares themselves.
Margin call	If the CFD trader's or spread better's position moves against him so that he is below the required margin level on a trade, then he will be subject to a 'margin call', and he will have to pay additional money into his trading account to keep the position open, or he may be forced to close his position (called 'closing out').
Market capitalisation	A measurement of the value of the ownership interest that shareholders hold in a publicly traded company. It is equal to the share price times the number of shares outstanding.

(Continued)

Appendix 1

Term	Description
Market maker	One who maintains firm bid and offer prices in a given share by standing ready to buy or sell round lots at publicly quoted prices. Market makers create a marketplace for the buying and selling of shares to match supply and demand. Market makers cannot deal with the general public and will deal through brokers.
Merger	The coming together of two or more enterprises for the purpose of mutual sharing of the risks and rewards provided the combined enterprise.
Non-guaranteed stop loss	Used in spread betting or CFD trading. In this case the broker will try to close the client's position at the stop loss price, but if the market trades rapidly through that price, any additional loss is borne by the client. There is usually no charge for a non-guaranteed stop.
Normal Market Size ('NMS')	The minimum number of securities for which a market maker is obliged to quote firm bid and offer prices.
Per point	Spread bets are quoted in an amount of money per point. In the UK a point represents a penny. In other countries where the Euro is the unit of currency a point represents a Euro cent (ie one-hundredth of a Euro). A bet of £10 per point on a UK share represents a bet of £10 for every 1p movement in the price of the UK share.
Placing	A method of raising finance by selling shares and other financial securities in the primary market.
Private company	A company whose shares are owned only by its founders, management, or private investors,
Public limited company ('plc')	A company whose shares can be bought and sold by the public.
Regulatory News Service ('RNS')	Transmits regulatory and non-regulatory information published by companies and organisations, allowing them to comply with local market transparency legislation. It is owned by the London Stock Exchange and distributes over 90 per cent of UK company news and results announcements. Its purpose is to ensure that all market users simultaneously have the ability to access information released by companies.
Regulatory Information Service ('RIS')	An approved newswire service for the transmission of market information.
Share / Security / Equity / Stock	A single unit which signifies a portion of ownership of a company.
Share capital	The amount of shares in a company is known as its 'share capital'.
Short or short position	Another term for selling a security or indicating that you have sold a security you do not own.
Short selling	Where the trader sells an asset that he does not own in the expectation that the price will fall and he can buy the asset back at a cheaper price and thereby 'cover' his short position.
Spread bet	In financial terms, a bet on the future price movement of a security.
Spread	The difference between the price at which a broker will buy a security (the bid price), and the price at which he will sell a security (the offer price).

Glossary of Terms

Term	Description
Stockbroker	Someone who acts on behalf of clients to buy and sell shares and other securities on a stock exchange.
Stock exchange	Electronic trading systems that enable people to trade in shares either directly with each other on an order-driven basis, or with market participants, under the overall regulatory umbrella of the particular stock exchange's rules and its regulatory requirements.
Stop loss	A price at which a broker closes a client's losing position in order to avoid any further losses.
Takeover	In a takeover (or acquisition) the acquiring company buys a controlling stake in the acquired company. The acquired company is also referred to as the 'target company'. In a friendly acquisition the target company is told formally about the acquisition and there is an agreement on corporate management and finance control.
Technical analysis	An approach to trading that concentrates on price charts and market patterns as a way of predicting price movements. (Also known as chartist analysis).
Trading	The buying and selling of an asset with a view to profit.
Trailing stop loss	A stop loss that adjusts in price in order to protect unrealised profits (ie a trade where the market has moved in the client's favour but where the profit has not been taken by closing the position).
Up bet	Another term for buying a security or taking a long position. Common spread betting terminology.
Variation margin	An additional margin payment that a broker may require from his client if the client's bet is losing money, ie the price has moved against him.
Volume	The number of shares of a security that change hands between a buyer and a seller during a given period of time.

APPENDIX 2A

Council Directive 89/592/EEC of 13 November 1989 coordinating regulations on insider dealing

Official Journal L 334, 18/11/1989 p. 0030–0032
Finnish special edition: Chapter 6 Volume 3 p. 0010
Swedish special edition: Chapter 6 Volume 3 p. 0010

*****

COUNCIL DIRECTIVE

of 13 November 1989
coordinating regulations on insider dealing
(89/592/EEC)

The Council of the European Communities,

Having regard to the Treaty establishing the European Economic Community, and in particular Article 100a thereof,

Having regard to the proposal from the Commission (1),

In cooperation with the European Parliament (2),

Having regard to the opinion of the Economic and Social Committee (3),

Whereas Article 100a (1) of the Treaty states that the Council shall adopt the measures for the approximation of the provisions laid down by law, regulation or administrative action in Member States which have as their object the establishment and functioning of the internal market;

Whereas the secondary market in transferable securities plays an important role in the financing of economic agents;

Whereas, for that market to be able to play its role effectively, every measure should be taken to ensure that market operates smoothly;

Whereas the smooth operation of that market depends to a large extent on the confidence it inspires in investors;

Whereas the factors on which such confidence depends include the assurance afforded to investors that they are placed on an equal footing and that they will be protected against the improper use of inside information;

Whereas, by benefiting certain investors as compared with others, insider dealing is likely to undermine that confidence and may therefore prejudice the smooth operation of the market;

Whereas the necessary measures should therefore be taken to combat insider dealing;

Whereas in some Member States there are no rules or regulations prohibiting insider dealing and whereas the rules or regulations that do exist differ considerably from one Member State to another;

Whereas it is therefore advisable to adopt coordinated rules at a Community level in this field;

Whereas such coordinated rules also have the advantage of making it possible, through cooperation by the competent authorities, to combat transfrontier insider dealing more effectively;

Whereas, since the acquisition or disposal of transferable securities necessarily involves a prior decision to acquire or to dispose taken by the person who undertakes one or other of these operations, the carrying-out of this acquisition or disposal does not constitute in itself the use of inside information;

Whereas insider dealing involves taking advantage of inside information; whereas the mere fact that market-makers, bodies authorised to act as counterparty, or stockbrokers with inside information confine themselves, in the first two cases, to pursuing their normal business of buying or selling securities or, in the last, to carrying out an order should not in itself be deemed to constitute use of such inside information; whereas likewise the fact of carrying out transactions with the aim of stabilising the price of new issues or secondary offers of transferable securities should not in itself be deemed to constitute use of inside information;

Whereas estimates developed from publicly available data cannot be regarded as inside information and whereas, therefore, any transaction carried out on the basis of such estimates does not constitute insider dealing within the meaning of this Directive;

Whereas communication of inside information to an authority, in order to enable it to ensure that the provisions of this Directive or other provisions in force are respected, obviously cannot be covered by the prohibitions laid down by this Directive,

HAS ADOPTED THIS DIRECTIVE:

Article 1

For the purposes of this Directive:

1. 'inside information' shall mean information which has not been made public of a precise nature relating to one or several issuers of transferable securities or to one or several transferable securities, which, if it were made public, would be likely to have a significant effect on the price of the transferable security or securities in question;
2. 'transferable securities' shall mean:
    (a) shares and debt securities, as well as securities equivalent to shares and debt securities;
    (b) contracts or rights to subscribe for, acquire or dispose of securities referred to in (a);
    (c) futures contracts, options and financial futures in respect of securities referred to in (a);
    (d) index contracts in respect of securities referred to in (a),

when admitted to trading on a market which is regulated and supervised by authorities recognised by public bodies, operates regularly and is accessible directly or indirectly to the public.

Article 2

1. Each Member State shall prohibit any person who:
    - by virtue of his membership of the administrative, management or supervisory bodies of the issuer,
    - by virtue of his holding in the capital of the issuer, or
    - because he has access to such information by virtue of the exercise of his employment, profession or duties,

    possesses inside information from taking advantage of that information with full knowledge of the facts by acquiring or disposing of for his own account or for the account of a third party, either directly or indirectly, transferable securities of the issuer or issuers to which that information relates.
2. Where the person referred to in paragraph 1 is a company or other type of legal person, the prohibition laid down in that paragraph shall apply to the natural persons who take part in the decision to carry out the transaction for the account of the legal person concerned.
3. The prohibition laid down in paragraph 1 shall apply to any acquisition or disposal of transferable securities effected through a professional intermediary.

Each Member State may provide that this prohibition shall not apply to acquisitions or disposals of transferable securities effected without the involvement of a professional intermediary outside a

market as defined in Article 1 (2) in fine.
4. This Directive shall not apply to transactions carried out in pursuit of monetary, exchange-rate or public debt-management policies by a sovereign State, by its central bank or any other body designated to that effect by the State, or by any person acting on their behalf. Member States may extend this exemption to their federated States or similar local authorities in respect of the management of their public debt.

Article 3

Each Member State shall prohibit any person subject to the prohibition laid down in Article 2 who possesses inside information from:
(a) disclosing that inside information to any third party unless such disclosure is made in the normal course of the exercise of his employment, profession or duties;
(b) recommending or procuring a third party, on the basis of that inside information, to acquire or dispose of transferable securities admitted to trading on its securities markets as referred to in Article 1 (2) in fine.

Article 4

Each Member State shall also impose the prohibition provided for in Article 2 on any person other than those referred to in that Article who with full knowledge of the facts possesses inside information, the direct or indirect source of which could not be other than a person referred to in Article 2.

Article 5

Each Member State shall apply the prohibitions provided for in Articles 2, 3 and 4, at least to actions undertaken within its territory to the extent that the transferable securities concerned are admitted to trading on a market of a Member State. In any event, each Member State shall regard a transaction as carried out within its territory if it is carried out on a market, as defined in Article 1 (2) in fine, situated or operating within that territory.

Article 6

Each Member State may adopt provisions more stringent than those laid down by this Directive or additional provisions, provided that such provisions are applied generally. In particular it may extend the scope of the prohibition laid down in Article 2 and impose on persons referred to in Article 4 the prohibitions laid down in Article 3. Article 7

The provisions of Schedule C5 (a) of the Annex to Directive 79/279/EEC (1) shall also apply to companies and undertakings the transferable securities of which, whatever their nature, are admitted to trading on a market as referred to in Article 1 (2) in fine of this Directive.

Article 8

1. Each Member State shall designate the administrative authority or authorities competent, if necessary in collaboration with other authorities to ensure that the provisions adopted pursuant to this Directive are applied. It shall so inform the Commission which shall transmit that information to all Member States.
2. The competent authorities must be given all supervisory and investigatory powers that are necessary for the exercise of their functions, where appropriate in collaboration with other authorities.

Article 9

Each Member State shall provide that all persons employed or formerly employed by the competent authorities referred to in Article 8 shall be bound by professional secrecy. Information covered by professional secrecy may not be divulged to any person or authority except by virtue of provisions laid down by law.

Article 10

1. The competent authorities in the Member States shall cooperate with each other whenever necessary for the purpose of carrying out their duties, making use of the powers mentioned in Article 8 (2). To this end, and notwithstanding Article 9, they shall exchange any information required for that purpose, including information relating to actions prohibited, under the options given to Member States by Article 5 and by the second sentence of Article 6, only by the Member State requesting cooperation. Information thus exchanged shall be covered by the obligation of professional secrecy to which the persons employed or formerly employed by the competent authorities receiving the information are subject.
2. The competent authorities may refuse to act on a request for information:
   (a) where communication of the information might adversely affect the sovereignty, security or public policy of the State addressed;
   (b) where judicial proceedings have already been initiated in respect of the same actions and against the same persons before the authorities of the State addressed or where final judgment has already been passed on such persons for the same actions by the competent authorities of the State addressed.
3. Without prejudice to the obligations to which they are subject in judicial proceedings under criminal law, the authorities which receive information pursuant to paragraph 1 may use it only for the exercise of their functions within the meaning of Article 8 (1) and in the context of administrative or judicial proceedings specifically relating to the exercise of those functions. However, where the competent authority communicating information consents thereto, the authority receiving the information may use it for other purposes or forward it to other States' competent authorities.

Article 11

The Community may, in conformity with the Treaty, conclude agreements with non-member countries on the matters governed by this Directive.

Article 12

The Contact Committee set up by Article 20 of Directive 79/279/EEC shall also have as its function:

(a) to permit regular consultation on any practical problems which arise from the application of this Directive and on which exchanges of view are deemed useful;
(b) to advise the Commission, if necessary, on any additions or amendments to be made to this Directive.

Article 13

Each Member State shall determine the penalties to be applied for infringement of the measures taken pursuant to this Directive. The penalties shall be sufficient to promote compliance with those measures.

Article 14

1. Member States shall take the measures necessary to comply with this Directive before 1 June 1992. They shall forthwith inform the Commission thereof.
2. Member States shall communicate to the Commission the provisions of national law which they adopt in the field governed by this Directive.

Article 15

This Directive is addressed to the Member States.

Made at Brussels, 13 November 1989.

For the Council

The President

P. BÉRÉGOVOY

(1) OJ No C 153, 11.6.1987, p 8 and OJ No C 277, 27.10.1988, p 13.
(2) OJ No C 187, 18.7.1987, p 93 and Decision of 11 October 1989 (not yet published in the Official Journal).
(3) OJ No C 35, 8.2.1989, p 22.
(1) OJ No L 66, 16.3.1979, p 21.

APPENDIX 2B

Criminal Justice Act 1993 (as amended)

Chapter 36

Part V
Insider Dealing

The offence of insider dealing

52 The offence

(1) An individual who has information as an insider is guilty of insider dealing if, in the circumstances mentioned in subsection (3), he deals in securities that are price-affected securities in relation to the information.
(2) An individual who has information as an insider is also guilty of insider dealing if
    (a) he encourages another person to deal in securities that are (whether or not that other knows it) price-affected securities in relation to the information, knowing or having reasonable cause to believe that the dealing would take place in the circumstances mentioned in subsection (3); or
    (b) he discloses the information, otherwise than in the proper performance of the functions of his employment, office or profession, to another person.
(3) The circumstances referred to above are that the acquisition or disposal in question occurs on a regulated market, or that the person dealing relies on a professional intermediary or is himself acting as a professional intermediary.
(4) This section has effect subject to section 53.

53 Defences

(1) An individual is not guilty of insider dealing by virtue of dealing in securities if he shows
    (a) that he did not at the time expect the dealing to result in a profit attributable to the fact that the information in question was price-sensitive information in relation to the securities, or
    (b) that at the time he believed on reasonable grounds that the information had been disclosed widely enough to ensure that none of those taking part in the dealing would be prejudiced by not having the information, or
    (c) that he would have done what he did even if he had not had the information.
(2) An individual is not guilty of insider dealing by virtue of encouraging another person to deal in securities if he shows
    (a) that he did not at the time expect the dealing to result in a profit attributable to the fact that the information in question was price-sensitive information in relation to the securities, or
    (b) that at the time he believed on reasonable grounds that the information had been or would be disclosed widely enough to ensure that none of those taking part in the dealing would be prejudiced by not having the information, or
    (c) that he would have done what he did even if he had not had the information.
(3) An individual is not guilty of insider dealing by virtue of a disclosure of information if he shows
    (a) that he did not at the time expect any person, because of the disclosure, to deal in securities in the circumstances mentioned in subsection (3) of section 52; or

(b) that, although he had such an expectation at the time, he did not expect the dealing to result in a profit attributable to the fact that the information was price-sensitive information in relation to the securities.

(4) Schedule 1 (special defences) shall have effect.
(5) The Treasury may by order amend Schedule 1.
(6) In this section references to a profit include references to the avoidance of a loss.

Interpretation

54 Securities to which Part V applies

(1) This Part applies to any security which
  (a) falls within any paragraph of Schedule 2; and
  (b) satisfies any conditions applying to it under an order made by the Treasury for the purposes of this subsection;
  and in the provisions of this Part (other than that Schedule) any reference to a security is a reference to a security to which this Part applies.
(2) The Treasury may by order amend Schedule 2.

55 'Dealing' in securities

(1) For the purposes of this Part, a person deals in securities if
  (a) he acquires or disposes of the securities (whether as principal or agent); or
  (b) he procures, directly or indirectly, an acquisition or disposal of the securities by any other person.
(2) For the purposes of this Part, 'acquire', in relation to a security, includes
  (a) agreeing to acquire the security; and
  (b) entering into a contract which creates the security.
(3) For the purposes of this Part, 'dispose', in relation to a security, includes
  (a) agreeing to dispose of the security; and
  (b) bringing to an end a contract which created the security.
(4) For the purposes of subsection (1), a person procures an acquisition or disposal of a security if the security is acquired or disposed of by a person who is
  (a) his agent,
  (b) his nominee, or
  (c) a person who is acting at his direction,
  in relation to the acquisition or disposal.
(5) Subsection (4) is not exhaustive as to the circumstances in which one person may be regarded as procuring an acquisition or disposal of securities by another.

56 'Inside information', etc

(1) For the purposes of this section and section 57, 'inside information' means information which
  (a) relates to particular securities or to a particular issuer of securities or to particular issuers of securities and not to securities generally or to issuers of securities generally;
  (b) is specific or precise;
  (c) has not been made public; and
  (d) if it were made public would be likely to have a significant effect on the price of any securities.
(2) For the purposes of this Part, securities are 'price-affected securities' in relation to inside information, and inside information is 'price-sensitive information' in relation to securities, if and only if the information would, if made public, be likely to have a significant effect on the price of the securities.
(3) For the purposes of this section 'price' includes value.

57 'Insiders'

(1) For the purposes of this Part, a person has information as an insider if and only if
  (a) it is, and he knows that it is, inside information, and
  (b) he has it, and knows that he has it, from an inside source.

(2) For the purposes of subsection (1), a person has information from an inside source if and only if
   (a) he has it through
      (i) being a director, employee or shareholder of an issuer of securities; or
      (ii) having access to the information by virtue of his employment, office or profession; or
   (b) the direct or indirect source of his information is a person within paragraph (a).

58 Information 'made public'

(1) For the purposes of section 56, 'made public', in relation to information, shall be construed in accordance with the following provisions of this section; but those provisions are not exhaustive as to the meaning of that expression.
(2) Information is made public if
   (a) it is published in accordance with the rules of a regulated market for the purpose of informing investors and their professional advisers;
   (b) it is contained in records which by virtue of any enactment are open to inspection by the public;
   (c) it can be readily acquired by those likely to deal in any securities
      (i) to which the information relates, or
      (ii) of an issuer to which the information relates; or
   (d) it is derived from information which has been made public.
(3) Information may be treated as made public even though
   (a) it can be acquired only by persons exercising diligence or expertise;
   (b) it is communicated to a section of the public and not to the public at large;
   (c) it can be acquired only by observation;
   (d) it is communicated only on payment of a fee; or
   (e) it is published only outside the United Kingdom.

59 'Professional intermediary'

(1) For the purposes of this Part, a 'professional intermediary' is a person
   (a) who carries on a business consisting of an activity mentioned in subsection (2) and who holds himself out to the public or any section of the public (including a section of the public constituted by persons such as himself) as willing to engage in any such business; or
   (b) who is employed by a person falling within paragraph (a) to carry out any such activity.
(2) The activities referred to in subsection (1) are
   (a) acquiring or disposing of securities (whether as principal or agent); or
   (b) acting as an intermediary between persons taking part in any dealing in securities.
(3) A person is not to be treated as carrying on a business consisting of an activity mentioned in subsection (2)
   (a) if the activity in question is merely incidental to some other activity not falling within subsection (2); or
   (b) merely because he occasionally conducts one of those activities.
(4) For the purposes of section 52, a person dealing in securities relies on a professional intermediary if and only if a person who is acting as a professional intermediary carries out an activity mentioned in subsection (2) in relation to that dealing.

60 Other interpretation provisions

(1) For the purposes of this Part, 'regulated market' means any market, however operated, which, by an order made by the Treasury, is identified (whether by name or by reference to criteria prescribed by the order) as a regulated market for the purposes of this Part.
(2) For the purposes of this Part an 'issuer', in relation to any securities, means any company, public sector body or individual by which or by whom the securities have been or are to be issued.
(3) For the purposes of this Part
   (a) 'company' means any body (whether or not incorporated and wherever incorporated or constituted) which is not a public sector body; and

(b) 'public sector body' means
   (i) the government of the United Kingdom, of Northern Ireland or of any country or territory outside the United Kingdom;
   (ii) a local authority in the United Kingdom or elsewhere;
   (iii) any international organisation the members of which include the United Kingdom or another member State;
   (iv) the Bank of England; or
   (v) the central bank of any sovereign State.
(4) For the purposes of this Part, information shall be treated as relating to an issuer of securities which is a company not only where it is about the company but also where it may affect the company's business prospects.

Miscellaneous

61 Penalties and prosecution

(1) An individual guilty of insider dealing shall be liable
   (a) on summary conviction, to a fine not exceeding the statutory maximum or imprisonment for a term not exceeding six months or to both; or
   (b) on conviction on indictment, to a fine or imprisonment for a term not exceeding seven years or to both.
(2) Proceedings for offences under this Part shall not be instituted in England and Wales except by or with the consent of
   (a) the Secretary of State; or
   (b) the Director of Public Prosecutions.
(3) In relation to proceedings in Northern Ireland for offences under this Part, subsection (2) shall have effect as if the reference to the Director of Public Prosecutions were a reference to the Director of Public Prosecutions for Northern Ireland.

61A Summary proceedings: venue and time limit for proceedings

(1) Summary proceedings for an offence of insider dealing may (without prejudice to any jurisdiction exercisable apart from this subsection) be brought against an individual at any place at which the individual is for the time being.
(2) An information relating to an offence of insider dealing that is triable by a magistrates' court in England and Wales may be so tried if it is laid
   (a) at any time within three years after the commission of the offence, and
   (b) within twelve months after the date on which evidence sufficient in the opinion of the Director of Public Prosecutions or the Secretary of State (as the case may be) to justify the proceedings comes to that person's knowledge.
(3) Summary proceedings in Scotland for an offence of insider dealing
   (a) must not be commenced after the expiration of three years from the commission of the offence;
   (b) subject to that, may be commenced at any time
      (i) within twelve months after the date on which evidence sufficient in the Lord Advocate's opinion to justify the proceedings came to that person's knowledge, or
      (ii) where such evidence was reported to the Lord Advocate by the Secretary of State, within twelve months after the date on which it came to the knowledge of the latter.

Section 136(3) of the Criminal Procedure (Scotland) Act 1995 (date when proceedings deemed to be commenced) applies for the purposes of this subsection as for the purposes of that section.

(4) A magistrates' court in Northern Ireland has jurisdiction to hear and determine a complaint charging the commission of a summary offence of insider dealing provided that the complaint is made
   (a) within three years from the time when the offence was committed, and

(b) within twelve months from the date on which evidence sufficient in the opinion of the Director of Public Prosecutions for Northern Ireland or the Secretary of State (as the case may be) to justify the proceedings comes to that person's knowledge.
(5) For the purposes of this section a certificate of the Director of Public Prosecutions, the Lord Advocate, the Director of Public Prosecutions for Northern Ireland or the Secretary of State (as the case may be) as to the date on which such evidence as is referred to above came to that person's notice is conclusive evidence.][1]

62 Territorial scope of offence of insider dealing

(1) An individual is not guilty of an offence falling within subsection (1) of section 52 unless
   (a) he was within the United Kingdom at the time when he is alleged to have done any act constituting or forming part of the alleged dealing;
   (b) the regulated market on which the dealing is alleged to have occurred is one which, by an order made by the Treasury, is identified (whether by name or by reference to criteria prescribed by the order) as being, for the purposes of this Part, regulated in the United Kingdom; or
   (c) the professional intermediary was within the United Kingdom at the time when he is alleged to have done anything by means of which the offence is alleged to have been committed.
(2) An individual is not guilty of an offence falling within subsection (2) of section 52 unless
   (a) he was within the United Kingdom at the time when he is alleged to have disclosed the information or encouraged the dealing; or
   (b) the alleged recipient of the information or encouragement was within the United Kingdom at the time when he is alleged to have received the information or encouragement.

63 Limits on section 52

(1) Section 52 does not apply to anything done by an individual acting on behalf of a public sector body in pursuit of monetary policies or policies with respect to exchange rates or the management of public debt or foreign exchange reserves.
(2) No contract shall be void or unenforceable by reason only of section 52.

64 Orders

(1) Any power under this Part to make an order shall be exercisable by statutory instrument.
(2) No order shall be made under this Part unless a draft of it has been laid before and approved by a resolution of each House of Parliament.
(3) An order under this Part
   (a) may make different provision for different cases; and
   (b) may contain such incidental, supplemental and transitional provisions as the Treasury consider expedient.

---

[1] Inserted by Companies Act 2006 (Consequential Amendments, Transitional Provisions and Savings) Order 2009 SI 2009/1941.

APPENDIX 2C

Criminal Justice Act 1993 (as amended)

Schedule 2 Securities
Section 54

Shares

1. Shares and stock in the share capital of a company ('shares').

Debt securities

2. Any instrument creating or acknowledging indebtedness which is issued by a company or public sector body, including, in particular, debentures, debenture stock, loan stock, bonds and certificates of deposit ('debt securities').

Warrants

3. Any right (whether conferred by warrant or otherwise) to subscribe for shares or debt securities ('warrants').

Depositary receipts

4. (1) The rights under any depositary receipt.
(2) For the purposes of sub-paragraph (1) a 'depositary receipt' means a certificate or other record (whether or not in the form of a document)
   (a) which is issued by or on behalf of a person who holds any relevant securities of a particular issuer; and
   (b) which acknowledges that another person is entitled to rights in relation to the relevant securities or relevant securities of the same kind.
(3) In sub-paragraph (2) 'relevant securities' means shares, debt securities and warrants.

Options

5. Any option to acquire or dispose of any security falling within any other paragraph of this Schedule.

Futures

6. (1) Rights under a contract for the acquisition or disposal of relevant securities under which delivery is to be made at a future date and at a price agreed when the contract is made.
(2) In sub-paragraph (1)
   (a) the references to a future date and to a price agreed when the contract is made include references to a date and a price determined in accordance with terms of the contract; and
   (b) 'relevant securities' means any security falling within any other paragraph of this Schedule.

Contracts for differences

7. (1) Rights under a contract which does not provide for the delivery of securities but whose purpose or pretended purpose is to secure a profit or avoid a loss by reference to fluctuations in
   (a) a share index or other similar factor connected with relevant securities;
   (b) the price of particular relevant securities; or
   (c) the interest rate offered on money placed on deposit.
   (2) In sub-paragraph (1) 'relevant securities' means any security falling within any other paragraph of this Schedule.

APPENDIX 2D

1994 No 187

Insider Dealing (Securities and Regulated Markets) Order 1994 (as amended)

Made—1 February 1994

Whereas a draft of this Order has been approved by a resolution of each House of Parliament pursuant to section 64(2) of the Criminal Justice Act 1993;

Now, therefore, the Treasury, in exercise of the powers conferred on them by sections 54(1), 60(1), 62(1) and 64(3) of that Act and of all other powers enabling them in that behalf, hereby make the following Order

UK Parliament SIs 1990–1999/1994/151-200/Insider Dealing (Securities and Regulated Markets) Order 1994 (SI 1994/187)/1

1. Title, commencement and interpretation

This Order may be cited as the Insider Dealing (Securities and Regulated Markets) Order 1994 and shall come into force on the twenty eighth day after the day on which it is made.

2

In this Order a 'State within the European Economic Area' means a State which is a member of the [European Union][1] and the Republics of Austria, Finland and Iceland, the Kingdoms of Norway and Sweden and the Principality of Liechtenstein.

3. Securities

Articles 4 to 8 set out conditions for the purposes of section 54(1) of the Criminal Justice Act 1993 (securities to which Part V of the Act of 1993 applies).

4

The following condition applies in relation to any security which falls within any paragraph of Schedule 2 to the Act of 1993, that is, that it is officially listed in a State within the European Economic Area or that it is admitted to dealing on, or has its price quoted on or under the rules of, a regulated market.

5

The following alternative condition applies in relation to a warrant, that is, that the right under it is a right to subscribe for any share or debt security of the same class as a share or debt security which satisfies the condition in article 4.

6

The following alternative condition applies in relation to a depositary receipt, that is, that the rights under it are in respect of any share or debt security which satisfies the condition in article 4.

---

[1] Substituted by Treaty of Lisbon (Changes in Terminology) Order 2011, SI 2011/1043.

7

The following alternative conditions apply in relation to an option or a future, that is, that the option or rights under the future are in respect of

(a) any share or debt security which satisfies the condition in article 4, or
(b) any depositary receipt which satisfies the condition in article 4 or article 6.

8

The following alternative condition applies in relation to a contract for differences, that is, that the purpose or pretended purpose of the contract is to secure a profit or avoid a loss by reference to fluctuations in

(a) the price of any shares or debt securities which satisfy the condition in article 4, or
(b) an index of the price of such shares or debt securities.

9. Regulated markets

The following markets are regulated markets for the purposes of Part V of the Act of 1993

[(a)] any market which is established under the rules of an investment exchange specified in the Schedule to this Order;
[(b)] the market known as OFEX...²]³.

10. United Kingdom regulated markets

The regulated markets which are regulated in the United Kingdom for the purposes of Part V of the Act of 1993 are any market which is established under the rules of

[(a) the London Stock Exchange Limited;]⁴
(b) LIFFE Administration & Management; ...⁵
(c) OMLX, the London Securities and Derivatives Exchange Limited [... ⁶
(d) [virt-x Exchange Limited];⁷]⁸
[(e) [the exchange known as COREDEALMTS];⁹

together with the market known as OFEX ... ¹⁰].¹¹

SCHEDULE

REGULATED MARKETS

Article 9

Any market which is established under the rules of one of the following investment exchanges:

Amsterdam Stock Exchange.
Antwerp Stock Exchange.
Athens Stock Exchange.

---

² Deleted words revoked by Insider Dealing (Securities and Regulated Markets) (Amendment) Order 2002, SI 2002/1874.
³ Inserted (as n 2) Order 2000, SI 2000/1923.
⁴ Substituted (as n 2) Order 1996, SI 1996/1561.
⁵ Deleted word revoked (as n 2) Order 1996, SI 1996/1561.
⁶ Deleted word revoked (as n 2) Order 2000, SI 2000/1923.
⁷ Substituted (as n 2) Order 2002, SI 2002/1874.
⁸ Inserted (as n 2) Order 1996, SI 1996/1561.
⁹ Substituted (as n 2) Order 2002, SI 2002/1874.
¹⁰ Deleted words revoked (as n 2) Order 2002, SI 2002/1874.
¹¹ Inserted (as n 2) Order 2000, SI 2000/1923.

Barcelona Stock Exchange.
Bavarian Stock Exchange.
Berlin Stock Exchange.
Bilbao Stock Exchange.
Bologna Stock Exchange.
...[12]
Bremen Stock Exchange.
Brussels Stock Exchange.
Copenhagen Stock Exchange.
[The exchange known as COREDEALMTS.][13]
Dusseldorf Stock Exchange.
[The exchange known as EASDAQ.][14]
Florence Stock Exchange.
Frankfurt Stock Exchange.
Genoa Stock Exchange.
...[15]
Hamburg Stock Exchange.
Hanover Stock Exchange.
Helsinki Stock Exchange.
[Iceland Stock Exchange.
The Irish Stock Exchange Limited.][16]
...[17]
...[18]
Lisbon Stock Exchange.
LIFFE Administration & Management.
[The London Stock Exchange Limited.][19]
Luxembourg Stock Exchange.
Lyon Stock Exchange.
Madrid Stock Exchange.
...[20]
Milan Stock Exchange.
...[21]
...[22]
Naples Stock Exchange.
The exchange known as NASDAQ.
[The exchange known as the Nouveau Marche.][23]
OMLX, the London Securities and Derivatives Exchange Limited.
Oporto Stock Exchange.
Oslo Stock Exchange.
Palermo Stock Exchange.
Paris Stock Exchange.

---

[12] Entry revoked (as n 2) Order 1996, SI 1996/1561.
[13] Substituted (as n 2) Order 2000, SI 2000/1923.
[14] Inserted (as n 2) Order 2000, SI 2000/1923.
[15] Entry revoked (as n 2) Order 1996, SI 1996/1561.
[16] Substituted (as n 2) Order 1996, SI 1996/1561.
[17] Entry revoked (as n 2) Order 1996, SI 1996/1561.
[18] Entry revoked (as n 2) Order 1996, SI 1996/1561.
[19] Inserted (as n 2) Order 1996, SI 1996/1561.
[20] Entry revoked (as n 2) Order 1996, SI 1996/1561.
[21] Entry revoked (as n 2) Order 1996, SI 1996/1561.
[22] Entry revoked (as n 2) Order 1996, SI 1996/1561.
[23] Inserted (as n 2) Order 1996, SI 1996/1561.

Insider Dealing (Securities and Regulated Markets) Order 1994

Rome Stock Exchange.
...[24]
Stockholm Stock Exchange.
Stuttgart Stock Exchange.
[The exchange known as SWX Swiss Exchange.][25]
[...[26]][27]
Trieste Stock Exchange.
Turin Stock Exchange.
Valencia Stock Exchange.
Venice Stock Exchange.
Vienna Stock Exchange.
[virt-x Exchange Limited.][28]

---

[24] Entry revoked (as n 2) Order 2000, SI 2000/1923.
[25] Inserted (as n 2) Order 2002, SI 2002/1874.
[26] Entry revoked (as n 2) Order 2002, SI 2002/1874.
[27] Inserted (as n 2) Order 1996, SI 1996/1561.
[28] Inserted (as n 2) Order 2002, SI 2002/1874.

APPENDIX 3

Financial Services and Markets Act 2000 (as amended)

Part VIII
Penalties for Market Abuse
Market abuse

[118 Market abuse

(1) For the purposes of this Act, market abuse is behaviour (whether by one person alone or by two or more persons jointly or in concert) which
   (a) occurs in relation to
       (i) qualifying investments admitted to trading on a prescribed market,
       (ii) qualifying investments in respect of which a request for admission to trading on such a market has been made, or
       (iii) in the case of subsection (2) or (3) behaviour, investments which are related investments in relation to such qualifying investments, and
   (b) falls within any one or more of the types of behaviour set out in subsections (2) to (8).
(2) The first type of behaviour is where an insider deals, or attempts to deal, in a qualifying investment or related investment on the basis of inside information relating to the investment in question.
(3) The second is where an insider discloses inside information to another person otherwise than in the proper course of the exercise of his employment, profession or duties.
(4) The third is where the behaviour (not falling within subsection (2) or (3))
   (a) is based on information which is not generally available to those using the market but which, if available to a regular user of the market, would be, or would be likely to be, regarded by him as relevant when deciding the terms on which transactions in qualifying investments should be effected, and
   (b) is likely to be regarded by a regular user of the market as a failure on the part of the person concerned to observe the standard of behaviour reasonably expected of a person in his position in relation to the market.
(5) The fourth is where the behaviour consists of effecting transactions or orders to trade (otherwise than for legitimate reasons and in conformity with accepted market practices on the relevant market) which
   (a) give, or are likely to give, a false or misleading impression as to the supply of, or demand for, or as to the price of, one or more qualifying investments, or
   (b) secure the price of one or more such investments at an abnormal or artificial level.
(6) The fifth is where the behaviour consists of effecting transactions or orders to trade which employ fictitious devices or any other form of deception or contrivance.
(7) The sixth is where the behaviour consists of the dissemination of information by any means which gives, or is likely to give, a false or misleading impression as to a qualifying investment by a person who knew or could reasonably be expected to have known that the information was false or misleading.
(8) The seventh is where the behaviour (not falling within subsection (5), (6) or (7))
   (a) is likely to give a regular user of the market a false or misleading impression as to the supply of, demand for or price or value of, qualifying investments, or
   (b) would be, or would be likely to be, regarded by a regular user of the market as behaviour that would distort, or would be likely to distort, the market in such an investment,

and the behaviour is likely to be regarded by a regular user of the market as a failure on the part of the person concerned to observe the standard of behaviour reasonably expected of a person in his position in relation to the market.
(9) Subsections (4) and (8) and the definition of 'regular user' in section 130A(3) cease to have effect on [31 December 2014][1] and subsection (1)(b) is then to be read as no longer referring to those subsections.][2]

[118A Supplementary provision about certain behaviour

(1) Behaviour is to be taken into account for the purposes of this Part only if it occurs
    (a) in the United Kingdom, or
    (b) in relation to
        (i) qualifying investments which are admitted to trading on a prescribed market situated in, or operating in, the United Kingdom,
        (ii) qualifying investments for which a request for admission to trading on such a prescribed market has been made, or
        (iii) in the case of section 118(2) and (3), investments which are related investments in relation to such qualifying investments.
(2) For the purposes of subsection (1), as it applies in relation to section 118(4) and (8), a prescribed market accessible electronically in the United Kingdom is to be treated as operating in the United Kingdom.
(3) For the purposes of section 118(4) and (8), the behaviour that is to be regarded as occurring in relation to qualifying investments includes behaviour which
    (a) occurs in relation to anything that is the subject matter, or whose price or value is expressed by reference to the price or value of the qualifying investments, or
    (b) occurs in relation to investments (whether or not they are qualifying investments) whose subject matter is the qualifying investments.
(4) For the purposes of section 118(7), the dissemination of information by a person acting in the capacity of a journalist is to be assessed taking into account the codes governing his profession unless he derives, directly or indirectly, any advantage or profits from the dissemination of the information.
(5) Behaviour does not amount to market abuse for the purposes of this Act if
    (a) it conforms with a rule which includes a provision to the effect that behaviour conforming with the rule does not amount to market abuse,
    (b) it conforms with the relevant provisions of Commission Regulation (EC) No 2273/2003 of 22 December 2003 implementing Directive 2003/6/EC of the European Parliament and of the Council as regards exemptions for buy-back programmes and stabilisation of financial instruments, or
    (c) it is done by a person acting on behalf of a public authority in pursuit of monetary policies or policies with respect to exchange rates or the management of public debt or foreign exchange reserves.
(6) Subsections (2) and (3) cease to have effect on [31 December 2014][3].][4]

[118B Insiders

For the purposes of this Part an insider is any person who has inside information
(a) as a result of his membership of an administrative, management or supervisory body of an issuer of qualifying investments,
(b) as a result of his holding in the capital of an issuer of qualifying investments,

---

[1] Substituted by Financial Services and Markets Act 2000 (Market Abuse) Regulations 2011, SI 2011/2928.
[2] Substituted (as n 1) 2005, SI 2005/381.
[3] Substituted (as n 1) 2011, SI 2011/2928.
[4] Substituted (as n 1) 2005, SI 2005/381.

(c) as a result of having access to the information through the exercise of his employment, profession or duties,
(d) as a result of his criminal activities, or
(e) which he has obtained by other means and which he knows, or could reasonably be expected to know, is inside information.]⁵

[118C Inside information

(1) This section defines 'inside information' for the purposes of this Part.
(2) In relation to qualifying investments, or related investments, which are not commodity derivatives, inside information is information of a precise nature which—
    (a) is not generally available,
    (b) relates, directly or indirectly, to one or more issuers of the qualifying investments or to one or more of the qualifying investments, and
    (c) would, if generally available, be likely to have a significant effect on the price of the qualifying investments or on the price of related investments.
(3) In relation to qualifying investments or related investments which are commodity derivatives, inside information is information of a precise nature which
    (a) is not generally available,
    (b) relates, directly or indirectly, to one or more such derivatives, and
    (c) users of markets on which the derivatives are traded would expect to receive in accordance with any accepted market practices on those markets.
(4) In relation to a person charged with the execution of orders concerning any qualifying investments or related investments, inside information includes information conveyed by a client and related to the client's pending orders which
    (a) is of a precise nature,
    (b) is not generally available,
    (c) relates, directly or indirectly, to one or more issuers of qualifying investments or to one or more qualifying investments, and
    (d) would, if generally available, be likely to have a significant effect on the price of those qualifying investments or the price of related investments.
(5) Information is precise if it
    (a) indicates circumstances that exist or may reasonably be expected to come into existence or an event that has occurred or may reasonably be expected to occur, and
    (b) is specific enough to enable a conclusion to be drawn as to the possible effect of those circumstances or that event on the price of qualifying investments or related investments.
(6) Information would be likely to have a significant effect on price if and only if it is information of a kind which a reasonable investor would be likely to use as part of the basis of his investment decisions.
(7) For the purposes of subsection (3)(c), users of markets on which investments in commodity derivatives are traded are to be treated as expecting to receive information relating directly or indirectly to one or more such derivatives in accordance with any accepted market practices, which is
    (a) routinely made available to the users of those markets, or
    (b) required to be disclosed in accordance with any statutory provision, market rules, or contracts or customs on the relevant underlying commodity market or commodity derivatives market.
(8) Information which can be obtained by research or analysis conducted by, or on behalf of, users of a market is to be regarded, for the purposes of this Part, as being generally available to them.]⁶

---

⁵ Substituted (as n 1) 2005, SI 2005/381.
⁶ Substituted (as n 1) 2005, SI 2005/381.

The code

119 The code

(1) The *Authority* [*FCA*][7] must prepare and issue a code containing such provisions as the *Authority* [*FCA*][8] considers will give appropriate guidance to those determining whether or not behaviour amounts to market abuse.

(2) The code may among other things specify
 (a) descriptions of behaviour that, in the opinion of the *Authority* [*FCA*][9], amount to market abuse;
 (b) descriptions of behaviour that, in the opinion of the *Authority* [*FCA*][10], do not amount to market abuse;
 (c) factors that, in the opinion of the *Authority* [*FCA*][11], are to be taken into account in determining whether or not behaviour amounts to market abuse;
 [(d) descriptions of behaviour that are accepted market practices in relation to one or more specified markets;
 (e) descriptions of behaviour that are not accepted market practices in relation to one or more specified markets][12].

[(2A) In determining, for the purposes of subsections (2)(d) and (2)(e) or otherwise, what are and what are not accepted market practices, the *Authority* [*FCA*][13] must have regard to the factors and procedures laid down in Articles 2 and 3 respectively of Commission Directive 2004/72/EC of 29 April 2004 implementing Directive 2003/6/EC of the European Parliament and of the Council.][14]

(3) The code may make different provision in relation to persons, cases or circumstances of different descriptions.

(4) The *Authority* [*FCA*][15] may at any time alter or replace the code.

(5) If the code is altered or replaced, the altered or replacement code must be issued by the *Authority* [*FCA*][16].

(6) A code issued under this section must be published by the *Authority* [*FCA*][17] in the way appearing to the *Authority* [*FCA*][18] to be best calculated to bring it to the attention of the public.

(7) The *Authority* [*FCA*][19] must, without delay, give the Treasury a copy of any code published under this section.

(8) The *Authority* [*FCA*][20] may charge a reasonable fee for providing a person with a copy of the code.

120 Provisions included in the Authority's [FCA's][21] code by reference to the City Code

(1) The *Authority* [*FCA*][22] may include in a code issued by it under section 119 ('the *Authority's* [*FCA's*][23] code') provision to the effect that in its opinion behaviour conforming with the City Code

---

[7] Repealed and substituted by Financial Services Act 2012, not yet in force.
[8] As n 7.
[9] As n 7.
[10] As n 7.
[11] As n 7.
[12] Inserted (as n 1) 2005, SI 2005/381.
[13] As n 7.
[14] Inserted (as n 1) 2005, SI 2005/381.
[15] As n 7.
[16] As n 7.
[17] As n 7.
[18] As n 7.
[19] As n 7.
[20] As n 7.
[21] As n 7.
[22] As n 7.
[23] As n 7.

(a) does not amount to market abuse;
(b) does not amount to market abuse in specified circumstances; or
(c) does not amount to market abuse if engaged in by a specified description of person.
(2) But the Treasury's approval is required before any such provision may be included in the *Authority's* [*FCA's*][24] code.
(3) If the *Authority's* [*FCA's*][25] code includes provision of a kind authorised by subsection (1), the *Authority* [*FCA*][26] must keep itself informed of the way in which the Panel on Takeovers and Mergers interprets and administers the relevant provisions of the City Code.
(4) 'City Code' means the City Code on Takeovers and Mergers issued by the Panel as it has effect at the time when the behaviour occurs.
(5) 'Specified' means specified in the *Authority's* [*FCA's*][27] code.

121 Codes: procedure

(1) Before issuing a code under section 119, the *Authority* [*FCA*][28] must publish a draft of the proposed code in the way appearing to the *Authority* [*FCA*][29] to be best calculated to bring it to the attention of the public.
(2) The draft must be accompanied by
 (a) a cost benefit analysis; and
 (b) notice that representations about the proposal may be made to the *Authority* [*FCA*][30] within a specified time.
(3) Before issuing the proposed code, the *Authority* [*FCA*][31] must have regard to any representations made to it in accordance with subsection (2)(b).
(4) If the *Authority* [*FCA*][32] issues the proposed code it must publish an account, in general terms, of
 (a) the representations made to it in accordance with subsection (2)(b); and
 (b) its response to them.
(5) If the code differs from the draft published under subsection (1) in a way which is, in the opinion of the *Authority* [*FCA*],[33] significant
 (a) the *Authority* [*FCA*][34] must (in addition to complying with subsection (4)) publish details of the difference; and
 (b) those details must be accompanied by a cost benefit analysis.
(6) Subsections (1) to (5) do not apply if the *Authority* [*FCA*][35] considers that there is an urgent need to publish the code.
(7) Neither subsection (2)(a) nor subsection (5)(b) applies if the *Authority* [*FCA*][36] considers
 (a) that, making the appropriate comparison, there will be no increase in costs; or
 (b) that, making that comparison, there will be an increase in costs but the increase will be of minimal significance.
(8) The *Authority* [*FCA*][37] may charge a reasonable fee for providing a person with a copy of a draft published under subsection (1).
(9) This section also applies to a proposal to alter or replace a code.

---

[24] As n 7.
[25] As n 7.
[26] As n 7.
[27] Repealed and substituted by Financial Services Act 2012, not yet in force.
[28] As n 7.
[29] As n 7.
[30] As n 7.
[31] As n 7.
[32] As n 7.
[33] Repealed and substituted by Financial Services Act 2012, not yet in force.
[34] As n 7.
[35] As n 7.
[36] As n 7.
[37] As n 7.

(10) 'Cost benefit analysis' means an estimate of the costs together with an analysis of the benefits that will arise
  (a) if the proposed code is issued; or
  (b) if subsection (5)(b) applies, from the code that has been issued.
[(10) 'Cost benefit analysis' means
  (a) an analysis of the costs together with an analysis of the benefits that will arise—
    (i) if the proposed code is issued, or
    (ii) if subsection (5)(b) applies, from the code that has been issued, and
  (b) *subject to subsection (10A), an estimate of those costs and of those benefits.*
(10A) *If, in the opinion of the FCA*
  (a) *the costs or benefits referred to in subsection (10) cannot reasonably be estimated, or*
  (b) *it is not reasonably practicable to produce an estimate, the cost benefit analysis need not estimate them, but must include a statement of the FCA's opinion and an explanation of it.*][38]
(11) 'The appropriate comparison' means
  (a) in relation to subsection (2)(a), a comparison between the overall position if the code is issued and the overall position if it is not issued;
  (b) in relation to subsection (5)(b), a comparison between the overall position after the issuing of the code and the overall position before it was issued.

122 Effect of the code

(1) If a person behaves in a way which is described (in the code in force under section 119 at the time of the behaviour) as behaviour that, in the *Authority's* [*FCA's*][39] opinion, does not amount to market abuse that behaviour of his is to be taken, for the purposes of this Act, as not amounting to market abuse.
(2) Otherwise, the code in force under section 119 at the time when particular behaviour occurs may be relied on so far as it indicates whether or not that behaviour should be taken to amount to market abuse.

Power to impose penalties

123 Power to impose penalties in cases of market abuse

(1) If the *Authority* [*FCA*][40] is satisfied that a person ('A')
  (a) is or has engaged in market abuse, or
  (b) by taking or refraining from taking any action has required or encouraged another person or persons to engage in behaviour which, if engaged in by A, would amount to market abuse,
  it may impose on him a penalty of such amount as it considers appropriate.
(2) But the *Authority* [*FCA*][41] may not impose a penalty on a person if, having considered any representations made to it in response to a warning notice, there are reasonable grounds for it to be satisfied that
  (a) he believed, on reasonable grounds, that his behaviour did not fall within paragraph (a) or (b) of subsection (1), or
  (b) he took all reasonable precautions and exercised all due diligence to avoid behaving in a way which fell within paragraph (a) or (b) of that subsection.
(3) If the *Authority* [*FCA*][42] is entitled to impose a penalty on a person under this section it may, instead of imposing a penalty on him, publish a statement to the effect that he has engaged in market abuse.

---

[38] Substituted by Financial Services Act 2012, not yet in force.
[39] As n 7.
[40] As n 7.
[41] As n 7.
[42] Repealed and substituted by Financial Services Act 2012, not yet in force.

Appendix 3

Statement of policy

124 Statement of policy

(1) The *Authority* [FCA][43] must prepare and issue a statement of its policy with respect to—
  (a) the imposition of penalties under section 123; and
  (b) the amount of penalties under that section.
(2) The *Authority's* [FCA's][44] policy in determining what the amount of a penalty should be must include having regard to
  (a) whether the behaviour in respect of which the penalty is to be imposed had an adverse effect on the market in question and, if it did, how serious that effect was;
  (b) the extent to which that behaviour was deliberate or reckless; and
  (c) whether the person on whom the penalty is to be imposed is an individual.
(3) A statement issued under this section must include an indication of the circumstances in which the *Authority* [FCA][45] is to be expected to regard a person as
  (a) having a reasonable belief that his behaviour did not amount to market abuse; or
  (b) having taken reasonable precautions and exercised due diligence to avoid engaging in market abuse.
(4) The *Authority* [FCA][46] may at any time alter or replace a statement issued under this section.
(5) If a statement issued under this section is altered or replaced, the *Authority* [FCA][47] must issue the altered or replacement statement.
(6) In exercising, or deciding whether to exercise, its power under section 123 in the case of any particular behaviour, the *Authority* [FCA][48] must have regard to any statement published under this section and in force at the time when the behaviour concerned occurred.
(7) A statement issued under this section must be published by the *Authority* [FCA][49] in the way appearing to the *Authority* [FCA][50] to be best calculated to bring it to the attention of the public.
(8) The *Authority* [FCA][51] may charge a reasonable fee for providing a person with a copy of a statement published under this section.
(9) The *Authority* [FCA][52] must, without delay, give the Treasury a copy of any statement which it publishes under this section.

125 Statement of policy: procedure

(1) Before issuing a statement of policy under section 124, the *Authority* [FCA][53] must publish a draft of the proposed statement in the way appearing to the *Authority* [FCA][54] to be best calculated to bring it to the attention of the public.
(2) The draft must be accompanied by notice that representations about the proposal may be made to the *Authority* [FCA][55] within a specified time.
(3) Before issuing the proposed statement, the *Authority* [FCA][56] must have regard to any representations made to it in accordance with subsection (2).

---

[43] As n 7.
[44] As n 7.
[45] As n 7.
[46] As n 7.
[47] As n 7.
[48] As n 7.
[49] As n 7.
[50] As n 7.
[51] As n 7.
[52] As n 7.
[53] As n 7.
[54] As n 7.
[55] As n 7.
[56] As n 7.

(4) If the *Authority* [FCA][57] issues the proposed statement it must publish an account, in general terms, of
   (a) the representations made to it in accordance with subsection (2); and
   (b) its response to them.
(5) If the statement differs from the draft published under subsection (1) in a way which is, in the opinion of the *Authority* [FCA],[58] significant, the *Authority* [FCA][59] must (in addition to complying with subsection (4)) publish details of the difference.
(6) The *Authority* [FCA][60] may charge a reasonable fee for providing a person with a copy of a draft published under subsection (1).
(7) This section also applies to a proposal to alter or replace a statement.

Procedure

126 Warning notices

(1) If the *Authority* [FCA][61] proposes to take action against a person under section 123, it must give him a warning notice.
(2) A warning notice about a proposal to impose a penalty must state the amount of the proposed penalty.
(3) A warning notice about a proposal to publish a statement must set out the terms of the proposed statement.

127 Decision notices and right to refer to Tribunal

(1) If the *Authority* [FCA][62] decides to take action against a person under section 123, it must give him a decision notice.
(2) A decision notice about the imposition of a penalty must state the amount of the penalty.
(3) A decision notice about the publication of a statement must set out the terms of the statement.
(4) If the *Authority* [FCA][63] decides to take action against a person under section 123, that person may refer the matter to the Tribunal.

Miscellaneous

128 Suspension of investigations

(1) If the *Authority* [FCA][64] considers it desirable or expedient because of the exercise or possible exercise of a power relating to market abuse, it may direct a recognised investment exchange or recognised clearing house
   (a) to terminate, suspend or limit the scope of any inquiry which the exchange or clearing house is conducting under its rules; or
   (b) not to conduct an inquiry which the exchange or clearing house proposes to conduct under its rules.
(2) A direction under this section
   (a) must be given to the exchange or clearing house concerned by notice in writing; and
   (b) is enforceable, on the application of the *Authority* [FCA],[65] by injunction or, in Scotland, by an order under section 45 of the Court of Session Act 1988.

---

[57] As n 7.
[58] As n 7.
[59] As n 7.
[60] As n 7.
[61] As n 7.
[62] As n 7.
[63] Repealed and substituted by Financial Services Act 2012, not yet in force.
[64] As n 7.
[65] As n 7.

(3) The *Authority's [FCA's]*⁶⁶ powers relating to market abuse are its powers
    (a) to impose penalties under section 123; or
    (b) to appoint a person to conduct an investigation under section 168 in a case falling within subsection (2)(d) of that section.

129 Power of court to impose penalty in cases of market abuse

(1) The *Authority [FCA]*⁶⁷ may on an application to the court under section 381 or 383 request the court to consider whether the circumstances are such that a penalty should be imposed on the person to whom the application relates.
(2) The court may, if it considers it appropriate, make an order requiring the person concerned to pay to the *Authority [FCA]*⁶⁸ a penalty of such amount as it considers appropriate.

130 Guidance

(1) The Treasury may from time to time issue written guidance for the purpose of helping relevant authorities to determine the action to be taken in cases where behaviour occurs which is behaviour
    (a) with respect to which the power in section 123 appears to be exercisable; and
    (b) which appears to involve the commission of an offence under section 397 of this Act [Part 7 of the Financial Services Act 2012]⁶⁹ or Part V of the Criminal Justice Act 1993 (insider dealing).
(2) The Treasury must obtain the consent of the Attorney General and the Secretary of State before issuing any guidance under this section.
(3) In this section 'relevant authorities'
    (a) in relation to England and Wales, means the Secretary of State, the *Authority [FCA]*,⁷⁰ the Director of the Serious Fraud Office and the Director of Public Prosecutions;
    (b) in relation to Northern Ireland, means the Secretary of State, the *Authority [FCA]*,⁷¹ the Director of the Serious Fraud Office and the Director of Public Prosecutions for Northern Ireland.
(4) Subsections (1) to (3) do not apply to Scotland.
(5) In relation to Scotland, the Lord Advocate may from time to time, after consultation with the Treasury, issue written guidance for the purpose of helping the *Authority [FCA]*⁷² to determine the action to be taken in cases where behaviour mentioned in subsection (1) occurs.

[130A Interpretation and supplementary provision

(1) The Treasury may by order specify (whether by name or description)
    (a) the markets which are prescribed markets for the purposes of specified provisions of this Part, and
    (b) the investments that are qualifying investments in relation to the prescribed markets.
(2) An order may prescribe different investments or descriptions of investment in relation to different markets or descriptions of market.
(3) In this Part

'accepted market practices' means practices that are reasonably expected in the financial market or markets in question and are accepted by the *Authority [FCA]*⁷³ or, in the case of a market situated in another EEA State, the competent authority of that EEA State within

---

⁶⁶ As n 7.
⁶⁷ As n 7.
⁶⁸ As n 7.
⁶⁹ As n 7.
⁷⁰ As n 7.
⁷¹ As n 7.
⁷² As n 7.
⁷³ As n 7.

the meaning of Directive 2003/6/EC of the European Parliament and of the Council of 28 January 2003 on insider dealing and market manipulation (market abuse),

'behaviour' includes action or inaction,

'dealing', in relation to an investment, means acquiring or disposing of the investment whether as principal or agent or directly or indirectly, and includes agreeing to acquire or dispose of the investment, and entering into and bringing to an end a contract creating it,

'investment' is to be read with section 22 and Schedule 2,

'regular user', in relation to a particular market, means a reasonable person who regularly deals on that market in investments of the kind in question,

'related investment', in relation to a qualifying investment, means an investment whose price or value depends on the price or value of the qualifying investment.

(4) Any reference in this Act to a person engaged in market abuse is to a person engaged in market abuse either alone or with one or more other persons.][74]

131 Effect on transactions

The imposition of a penalty under this Part does not make any transaction void or unenforceable.

[131A Protected Disclosures

(1) A disclosure which satisfies the following three conditions is not to be taken to breach any restriction on the disclosure of information (however imposed).
(2) The first condition is that the information or other matter
    (a) causes the person making the disclosure (the discloser) to know or suspect, or
    (b) gives him reasonable grounds for knowing or suspecting, that another person has engaged in market abuse.
(3) The second condition is that the information or other matter disclosed came to the discloser in the course of his trade, profession, business or employment.
(4) The third condition is that the disclosure is made to the *Authority* [*FCA*][75] or to a nominated officer as soon as is practicable after the information or other matter comes to the discloser.
(5) A disclosure to a nominated officer is a disclosure which is made to a person nominated by the discloser's employer to receive disclosures under this section, and is made in the course of the discloser's employment and in accordance with the procedure established by the employer for the purpose.
(6) For the purposes of this section, references to a person's employer include any body, association or organisation (including a voluntary organisation) in connection with whose activities the person exercises a function (whether or not for gain or reward) and references to employment must be construed accordingly.][76]

---

[74] Inserted (as n 1) 2005, SI 2005/381.
[75] As n 7.
[76] Inserted (as n 1) 2005, SI 2005/381.

APPENDIX 4

2001 No 996
Financial Services and Markets Act 2000 (Prescribed Markets and Qualifying Investments) Order 2001 (as amended)

Made 15 March 2001

Laid before Parliament 15 March 2001

Coming into force in accordance with article 2

The Treasury, in exercise of the powers conferred upon them by section 118(3) of the Financial Services and Markets Act 2000, hereby make the following Order:

UK Parliament SIs 2000-2009/2001/951-1000/Financial Services and Markets Act 2000 (Prescribed Markets and Qualifying Investments) Order 2001 (SI 2001/996)/1 Citation

1 Citation

This Order may be cited as the Financial Services and Markets Act 2000 (Prescribed Markets and Qualifying Investments) Order 2001.

2 Commencement

This Order comes into force on the day on which section 123 of the Act (power to impose penalties in cases of market abuse) comes into force.

3 Interpretation

In this Order

'the Act' means the Financial Services and Markets Act 2000;

['auctioned products' has the meaning given in Article 4 of Commission Regulation (EU) No 1031/2010 on the timing, administration and other aspects of auctioning of greenhouse gas emission allowances pursuant to Directive 2003/87/EC of the European Parliament and of the Council establishing a scheme for greenhouse gas emission allowances trading within the Community;

'emission allowance auctioning regulation' means Commission Regulation (EU) No 1031/2010 of 12 November 2010 on the timing, administration and other aspects of auctioning of greenhouse gas emission allowances pursuant to the emission allowance trading directive;

'recognised auction platform' means a recognised investment exchange in relation to which there is in force a recognition order made under regulation 2 of the Recognised Auction Platforms Regulations 2011 (recognition orders);][1]

['regulated market' has the meaning given in [Article 4.1.14 of the markets in financial instruments directive][2];][3] and

---

[1] Inserted by Recognised Auction Platforms Regulations 2011, SI 2011/2699.
[2] Substituted by Financial Services and Markets Act 2000 (Markets in Financial Instruments) Regulations 2007, SI 2007/126.
[3] Inserted by Financial Services and Markets Act 2000 (Market Abuse) Regulations 2005, SI 2005/381.

'UK recognised investment exchange' means a body corporate or unincorporated association in respect of which there is in effect a recognition order made under section 290(1)(a) of the Act (recognition orders in respect of investment exchanges other than overseas investment exchanges).

[4 Prescribed Markets [and auction platforms][4]

[(1) There are prescribed, as markets to which subsections (2), (3), (5), (6) and (7) of section 118 apply
  (a) all markets which are established under the rules of a UK recognised investment exchange,
  (b) the market known as OFEX,
  (c) all other markets which are regulated markets.
(2) There are prescribed, as markets to which subsections (4) and (8) of section 118 apply
  (a) all markets which are established under the rules of a UK recognised investment exchange;
  (b) the market known as OFEX.
[(3) There are prescribed, as auction platforms to which subsections (2), (3), (5), (6) and (7) of section 118 (as modified by the Recognised Auction Platform Regulations 2011) apply, all recognised auction platforms, and all other auction platforms which have been appointed under the emission allowance auctioning regulation.
(4) There are prescribed, as auction platforms to which subsections (4) and (8) of section 118 (as modified by the Recognised Auction Platform Regulations 2011) apply, all recognised auction platforms.
(5) There are prescribed, as auction platforms to which subsection (8A) of section 118 as inserted by the modifications made to that section by the Recognised Auction Platforms Regulations 2011 applies, all auction platforms which have been appointed under the emission allowance auctioning regulation.]5]6

[4A

...][7]

[5 Qualifying Investments]

[[(1)][8] There are prescribed, as qualifying investments in relation to the markets prescribed by [article 4(1) and (2)],[9] all financial instruments within the meaning given in Article 1(3) of Directive 2003/6/EC of the European Parliament and the Council of 28 January 2003 on insider dealing and market manipulation (market abuse) [as modified by Article 69 of Directive 2004/39/EC on markets in financial instruments].[10]
[(2) There are prescribed, as qualifying investments in relation to the auction platforms prescribed by article 4(3) and (4), all auctioned products which are financial instruments within the meaning given in Article 4.1(17) of the market in financial instruments directive.

---

[4] Inserted (n 1).
[5] Inserted (n 1).
[6] Substituted (n 3).
[7] Substituted (n 3).
[8] Numbered by Recognised Auction Platforms Regulations 2011, SI 2011/2699.
[9] Substituted by Recognised Auction Platforms Regulations 2011, SI 2011/2699.
[10] Inserted by Definition of Financial Instrument Order 2008, SI 2008/3053.

(3) There are prescribed, as qualifying investments in relation to the auction platforms prescribed by article 4(5), all auctioned products which are not financial instruments within the meaning given in Article 4.1(17) of the market in financial instruments directive.][11]][12]

David Clelland

Clive Betts

Two of the Lords Commissioners of Her Majesty's Treasury

15 March 2001.

---

[11] Inserted (n 1).
[12] Substituted (n 3).

INDEX

acquisitions and disposals:
   dealing in securities defined 9.05–9.10
   procuring defined 9.10–9.19
   special defence for dealings to
     facilitate 11.33–11.34
Ainley (Mark) v FSA, standard of proof
   20.23–20.24
Alternative Investment Market (AIM) 2.14
analysts and inside information 6.36–6.38
apportionment of penalties between
   defendants 13.24–13.26
Arif Mohammed v FSA, standard of proof 20.15
Article 6 of European Convention on Human
   Rights (market abuse proceedings):
   burden of proof 20.12, 20.21–20.22
   introduction to 20.01
   legal assistance (Art 6(3)) 20.10
   privilege against self-incrimination
     (Art 6(2)) 20.11
   standard of proof 20.13–20.25
   status of proceedings 20.02–20.10
Atlantic Law LLP v FSA, burden and standard of
   proof 20.21
authorized persons
   power to require information from
     22.11–22.13
   withdrawal of authorization 24.16–24.18

banking confidentiality, FCA enforcement
   powers 22.20
behaviour:
   amounting to market abuse 15.04
   defined 15.06
   improper disclosure, *see* Section 118(3) of
     Financial Services and Markets Act 2000
   insider dealing, *see* Section 118(2) of Financial
     Services and Markets Act 2000
   misuse of information, *see* Section 118(4) of
     Financial Services and Markets Act 2000
   safe harbours, *see* safe harbours
'benefit obtained' defined 13.20–13.23
bets, *see* spread bets
bid price defined 2.23
Bliss, Perry, 'encouraging' market abuse
   offence 19.10
Boesky, Ivan, case of 1.03–1.05
Bracken, Peter, misuse of information 18.10

brokers' commission on CFD trades 2.38
burden of proof:
   information not made public 6.65–6.67,
     6.93–6.108
   market abuse proceedings 20.12, 20.21–20.22
   standard of proof, market abuse
     proceedings 20.13–20.25
   statutory defences 11.42–11.49
Burley, Jeremy, 'encouraging' market abuse
   offence 19.11
Byron Holdings, 'requiring' market abuse
   offence 19.12–19.13

cancellation of firm's authorization 24.19
cautions, issuing of 23.40–23.41
chartist (technical) analysis defined 2.28
Chhabra, Robin
   burden and standard of proof 20.22
   misuse of information 18.15
City Code on Take-Overs and Mergers,
   compliance 3.17–3.19
civil market abuse regime:
   civil offences, *see* Financial Services and
     Markets Act 2000
   Code of Market Conduct (MAR) 14.13–14.15
   Final Notices 14.17
   Financial Services and Markets Tribunal 14.18
   introduction to 14.01
   legislative background 14.02–14.11
   market abuse defined (s 118 FSMA 2000) 14.12
   Market Watch 14.16
   Tribunal decisions 14.17
   Upper Tribunal (Tax and Chancery
     Chamber) 14.18
client orders, safe harbour as to execution
   of 16.77–16.81
Clifton, Darwin, 'requiring' market abuse
   offence 19.12–19.13
closing (down) bet defined 2.51–2.52
closing out defined 2.37
co-operation agreements 23.15–23.28
Code of Market Conduct (MAR):
   content of 14.14
   issuing of 14.13
   safe harbours as to insider dealing
     behaviour 14.15, 16.66–16.84; *see also* safe
     harbours

Index

Cohen Committee recommendations 3.13
commodity derivatives, behaviour as to
   16.61–16.63
companies:
   company defined 6.12
   directors, *see* directors
   Part V of Companies Act 1980 3.31–3.36
   private company shares defined 2.09
Company Securities (Insider Dealing)
   Act 1985 3.37–3.40
Conduct of Business Sourcebook (COBS), record
   keeping requirements 21.29
confiscation, *see* penalties
conspiracy, prosecution 12.13–12.20
contracts for difference (CFDs):
   broker's commission 2.38
   closing out 2.37
   defined 8.13–8.14
   example trades 2.40
   gearing (leverage) 2.36, 2.39
   guaranteed stop loss 2.43
   IDO 1994 8.38–8.46
   initial margin 2.36
   insider dealing 2.40
   limit order 2.46
   limiting losses 2.42–2.46
   margin 2.35
   margin call 2.37
   non-guaranteed stop loss 2.44–2.45
   parties 2.34
   price 2.34
   slippage 2.44
   stop loss 2.42–2.43
   taxation 2.38
   trailing stops 2.45
   unsuccessful trade 2.41
   usage 2.33
Coppin, William, 'encouraging' market abuse
   offence 19.10
Court of Appeal sentencing authorities
   13.04–13.16
Criminal Justice Act 1993:
   Part V, *see entries for specific sections*; Part V of
      Criminal Justice Act 1993
   Schedule 2, *see* Schedule 2 of Criminal Justice
      Act 1993
criminal proceedings:
   co-operation agreements 23.15–23.28
   commencement of 23.36–23.38
   decision to commence 23.02–23.05
   decisions not to prosecute 23.42
   factors influencing decision to
      prosecute 23.05–23.06
   full immunity from prosecution
      (s 71 SOCPA 2005) 23.19
   introduction to 23.01
   issuing of cautions 23.40–23.41

   plea agreements (s 73 SOCPA 2005) 23.21
   plea discussions 23.29–23.30
   reduction in sentence (s 73 SOCPA 2005) 23.21
   Regulatory Decisions Committee Chairman's
      role 23.31–23.34
   Restraint Orders 23.38
   restricted use undertakings (s 72 SOCPA
      2005) 23.20
   suspect's representations 23.08–23.14
   timing of 23.07
cumulative preference shares defined 2.07

data protection, FCA enforcement
   powers 22.32
Davidson and Tatham v FSA, standard of
   proof 20.16
Davies, Michael Thomas, misuse of
   information 18.09
deal timetables, requirement on firms
   21.32–21.33
dealers, *see* professional intermediaries
dealing, *see* insider dealing
debt securities (bonds) defined 8.04–8.05
Decision Notices as to market abuse 24.41–24.42
defences:
   CJA 1993, *see* Section 53 of Criminal Justice
      Act 1993
   market abuse, power to impose 19.01–19.05
depositary receipts defined 8.06–8.07
derivatives:
   commodity derivatives, behaviour as
      to 16.61–16.63
   Contracts for Difference (CFDs), *see* Contracts
      for Difference (CFDs)
   ICAP Securities and Derivatives Exchange
      (ISDX) 2.15
detection and enforcement, *see* enforcement;
   Financial Conduct Authority (FCA)
directors:
   disqualification 13.17–13.18
   Executive Settlement Process 24.45–24.56
   inside information 6.33–6.35
   as insiders 7.21–7.22
disclosure:
   to certain public bodies 17.10
   compliance with rules and regulatory
      obligations 17.11
   disclosure duty and *Percival v Wright* 3.12, 3.15
   improper disclosure, *see* Section 118(3) of
      Financial Services and Markets Act 2000
   seller's managerial responsibilities to potential
      buyer 17.12
Disclosure Rules and Transparency Rules (DTR),
   deal timetables and insider lists 21.32–21.33
disposals, *see* acquisitions and disposals
   (s 55(1)–(3) CJA 1993)
down (closing) bet defined 2.51–2.52

Index

Draft Directive:
  potential effect 25.27
  proposals 25.24–25.26
Draft Regulation:
  competent authorities' powers 25.22
  inside information 25.19–25.21
  insider dealing 25.17–25.18
  proposals 25.10–25.09
  purpose 25.06
  sanctions 25.23
  scope of 25.14–25.16

economic theory of insider dealing 3.03–3.09
Efficient Capital Market Hypothesis, information dissemination in relation 1.17–1.21
Einhorn, David, non-imposition of market abuse penalty 19.19–19.22
electronic trading:
  investors 2.27
  stock exchanges 2.11
employees as insiders 7.23
'encouraging' market abuse offence 19.07–19.11
enforcement; *see also* **civil market abuse regime; criminal proceedings:** 1970s 3.17–3.19
  allocation to case team 22.02
  appoint of investigators (s 168(2) FSMA 2000) 22.04–22.05
  banking confidentiality (s 175(5) FSMA 2000) 22.20
  data protection 22.32
  deal timetables 21.32–21.33
  detection of insider dealing and market abuse 21.20–21.33
  disclosure gateways 22.29–22.32
  Enforcement and Financial Crime Division (EFCD) 21.06, 21.13, 21.34–21.37
  FCA, *see* Financial Conduct Authority (FCA)
  FSA's approach 21.07
  information powers 22.09–22.16
  information use 22.25–22.33
  Insider Dealing Directive proposals 4.24
  insider lists 21.32–21.33
  interviews, *see* interviews
  introduction to 21.01
  introduction to enforcement investigation 22.01
  investigation powers of FCA (Part XI FSMA 2000) 22.03–22.04
  investigators' powers (s 173 FSMA 2000) 22.14–22.15
  market abuse, *see* market abuse
  monitoring systems, SABRE II and ZEN 21.23–21.24
  more than one authority 21.38–21.39
  notification of investigation 22.03–22.05
  notification of investigation (s 170 FSMA 2000) 22.06–22.08
  power to require information from authorized persons (s 165 FSMA) 22.11–22.13
  protected information (s 143 FSMA 2000) 22.18–22.19
  publicity during investigations, *see* publicity
  record keeping, requirement on firms 21.29
  recorded telephone calls 21.30–21.31
  referral of cases for investigation 21.36–21.37
  RIPA 2000 powers as to communications data 22.17
  sanctions for non-compliance (s 177 FSMA 2000) 22.21–22.24
  search warrants 22.34–22.39
  supplementary powers as to information gathering (s 175 FSMA) 22.16
  suspicious transaction reporting 21.25–21.28
  tougher approach to 1.25–1.27
  witness statements 22.51–22.53
Enforcement Submissions Documents 24.30
equities, *see* **shares**
European Convention on Human Rights (ECHR), *see* Article 6 of European Convention on Human Rights
European legislation:
  Draft Directive, *see* Draft Directive
  Draft Regulation, *see* Draft Regulation
  introduction to 25.01
  MAD, *see* Market Abuse Directive 2003 (MAD)
  MiFID *see* Markets in Financial Instruments Directive 2004 (MiFID)
  new legislation 25.02–25.05
execution of client orders, safe harbour as to 16.77–16.81
Executive Settlement Process 24.45–24.56

Fama, Eugene, Efficient Capital Market Hypothesis 1.18
Final Notices:
  FCA practice contained in 14.17
  market abuse 24.44
Financial Conduct Authority (FCA):
  approach to enforcement 21.17–21.19
  cases in which other authorities have interest 21.38–21.39
  Conduct of Business Sourcebook 30 (COBS) 21.29
  deal timetables, requirement on firms 21.32–21.33
  detection of insider dealing and market abuse 21.20–21.33
  Disclosure Rules and Transparency Rules (DTR) 21.32–21.33
  Enforcement and Financial Crime Division (EFCD) 21.13, 21.34–21.37
  enforcement role 21.12
  Financial Services Act 2012 21.14–21.15
  insider lists, requirement on firms 21.32–21.33

Index

Financial Conduct Authority (FCA): (cont.)
  market abuse regime, see civil market abuse
    regime
  as non-party witness 22.33
  objectives 21.16
  Prohibition Orders 13.28
  proposed powers in Draft Regulation 25.22
  record keeping, requirement on firms 21.29
  recorded telephone calls, policy
    statement 21.30–21.31
  referral of cases for investigation 21.36–21.37
  suspicious transaction reporting 21.25–21.28
  ZEN 21.24
financial markets:
  Insider Dealing Directive proposals 4.19–4.21
  key trading principles introduced 2.01
  Market Cleanliness Statistic, see Market
    Cleanliness Statistic
  prescribed markets 15.13–15.25
  regulated markets defined 10.04, 15.18–15.19
  regulated markets provisions 8.29–8.36
  shares, see shares
  stock exchanges, see stock exchanges
financial penalties for market abuse 24.10–24.12
Financial Services Act 1986 3.41–3.43
Financial Services Act 2012, effect of 21.14–21.15
Financial Services and Markets Act 2000:
  behaviour amounting to market abuse 15.04
  'behaviour' defined 15.06
  behaviour defined 15.06
  civil offences introduced 15.01
  enforcement investigation, see enforcement
  improper disclosure, see Section 118(3) of
    Financial Services and Markets Act 2000
  insider dealing, see Section 118(2) of Financial
    Services and Markets Act 2000
  market abuse defence (s 118A(5) 19.02–19.05
  market abuse defined (s 118(1)) 14.12, 15.03
  misuse of information, see Section 118(4) of
    Financial Services and Markets Act 2000
  Part VIII overviewed 15.02–15.12
  Part VIII text Appendix 3
  'person' defined 15.07–15.12
  power to impose penalties for market abuse
    (s 123) 19.06–19.27; see also market abuse
  prescribed markets 15.13–15.25
  qualifying investments 15.13–15.14,
    15.26–15.27
  related investments 15.28–15.31
  'requiring or encouraging' others in market
    abuse (s 123) 15.05
  safe harbours, see safe harbours
  territorial scope (s 118A(1)) 15.32–15.33
Financial Services and Markets Act 2000
  (Prescribed Markets and Qualifying
  Investments) Order 2001 (PMQI 2001):
    amendment 15.21

improper disclosure see Section 118(3) of
  Financial Services and Markets Act 2000
inside information see Section 118C of Financial
  Services and Markets Act 2000
insider dealing behaviour see Section 118(2) of
  Financial Services and Markets Act 2000
misuse of information see Section 118(4) of
  Financial Services and Markets Act 2000
prescribed markets 15.13, 15.15, 15.22
qualifying investments 15.13, 15.26–15.27, 16.15
text Appendix 4
Financial Services and Markets Tribunal,
  abolition 14.18
Financial Services Authority (FSA):
  approach to enforcement 21.07
  Enforcement and Financial Crime Division
    (EFCD) 21.06
  general functions 21.05
  insider dealing prosecutions 21.08–21.09
  market abuse regime, see civil market abuse
    regime
  policy direction 21.03
  regulatory objectives 21.04
  replacement 21.10
  status 21.02
  'Surveillance Analysis of Business Reporting'
    (SABRE II) 21.23
  ZEN 21.24
fund managers and inside information 6.36–6.38
fundamental analysis defined 2.28
futures contracts defined 8.10–8.13

gearing (leverage):
  CFD trading 2.39–2.40
  defined 2.36
glossary Appendix 1
Greystoke (Andrew) v FSA, burden and standard of
  proof 20.21
guaranteed stop loss defined 2.43

harmonization, see European legislation
Hatcher, Bertie Charles, misuse of
  information 18.14
Hutchings, Robin, misuse of information 18.08

ICAP Securities and Derivatives Exchange (ISDX):
  overview of 2.15
  as prescribed market 15.17
immunity from prosecution (s 71
  SOCPA 2005) 23.19
improper disclosure, see Section 118(3) of Financial
  Services and Markets Act 2000
information:
  availability of 2.16–2.22
  behaviour as to, see behaviour
  disclosure, see disclosure
  Efficient Capital Market Hypothesis 1.17–1.21

Index

enforcement and investigation powers as to, *see* enforcement
generally available 18.18
importance of 1.15–1.16
informal sources of 2.22
inside information at time of dealing 7.10–7.16
inside information defined 16.28–16.29
insider dealing behaviour, *see* Section 118C of Financial Services and Markets Act 2000
Insider Dealing Directive proposals 4.17–4.18
knowledge requirement 7.03–7.09
likely to significantly effect price of qualifying or related investments 16.47–16.60
made public, *see* Part V of Criminal Justice Act 1993
market rumours 16.41–16.45
misuse of, *see* Section 118(4) of Financial Services and Markets Act 2000
not generally available 16.38–16.45
not made public, *see* Section 56 of Criminal Justice Act 1993
offences, *see* Section 52 of Criminal Justice Act 1993
precise nature 16.30–16.37
Regulatory Information Service (RIS) 2.20–2.21
relating directly or indirectly to issuer of qualifying investments or to qualifying investments 16.46
relevant information 18.20–18.21
s 56 CJA 1993, *see* Section 56 of Criminal Justice Act 1993
significantly affecting price, *see* Section 56 of Criminal Justice Act 1993
initial margin defined 2.36
Initial Public Offering (IPO) defined 2.09
inside information, *see* information; Section 56 of Criminal Justice Act 1993; Section 118C of Financial Services and Markets Act 2000
inside source defined 7.15–7.18
insider dealing; *see also* **market abuse:**
alleged cases 3.38
behaviour, *see* behaviour; Section 118(2) of Financial Services and Markets Act 2000
criminal proceedings, *see* criminal proceedings
dealing defined 9.02–9.10, 16.02–16.04, 16.14–16.15
Directive, *see* Insider Dealing Directive (IDD)
economic theory 3.03–3.09
enforcement action, *see* enforcement
European legislation, *see* European legislation
example cases 1.03–1.14
future legislative approach 25.28–25.30
glossary Appendix 1
information, *see* information
introduction to 1.01
legislation, *see* legislation

Market Cleanliness Statistic, *see* Market Cleanliness Statistic
moral objection to 3.10–3.11
offences, *see* Part V of Criminal Justice Act 1993
penalties, *see* penalties
practical definition 1.02
prevalence in UK 1.22–1.27
prosecution, *see* prosecution
Insider Dealing Directive (IDD):
background to 4.04–4.07
inside information proposals 4.17–4.18
insiders proposals 4.12–4.13
introduction to 4.01
monitoring and enforcement proposals 4.24
Part V of CJA 1993 in relation 4.02–4.03
prohibitions proposals 4.14–4.16
Proposal 4.08–4.24
Recitals 4.25–4.28
s 56 CJA 1993 in relation 6.02
securities and markets proposals 4.19–4.21
territorial scope proposals 4.22–4.23
text Appendix 2A
Insider Dealing (Securities and Regulated Markets) Order 1994 (IDO 1994):
approach to cases arising under 8.01
contracts for difference 8.38–8.46
entry into force 8.26
purpose 8.27
regulated markets defined 10.04
regulated markets provisions 8.29–8.36
Schedule 2 of CJA 1993 in relation 8.25
securities other than shares 8.37
security defined 8.28
text Appendix 2D
insider defined 7.01–7.02, 16.05–16.13
insider lists, requirement on firms 21.32–21.33
insiders, *see* Section 57 of Criminal Justice Act 1993
interviews:
admissibility of compulsory interviews in criminal market or market abuse proceedings (s 174 FSMA 2000) 22.50
by arrangement 22.42
compelled interviews procedure 22.44
information disclosure in advance 22.43
interviews with suspects 22.47–22.49
persons interviewed 22.40
types of 22.41
voluntary interviews with non suspects 22.45–22.46
investigation, *see* **enforcement**
investment:
qualifying investments 15.13–15.14, 15.26–15.27
related investments 15.28–15.31
investors; *see also* **shareholders:**
electronic trading 2.27

Index

investors (cont.)
  investing defined 2.29
  range of 2.26
  share sales to outside investors 2.09–2.10
  trading, *see* trading
Isaacs, David, misuse of information 18.13
issuer defined 6.11

Jenkins Report recommendations 3.14–3.16
journalists and insider dealing 6.82–6.84
Justice Committee Report recommendations 3.20–3.23

knowledge, *see* information
Krilov-Harrison, Alexei, 'encouraging' market abuse offence 19.09

legal assistance in market abuse proceedings 20.10
Legal Review as to market abuse 24.23
legislation:
  Cohen Committee Report 3.13
  company law reform 3.31–3.36
  consolidation of insider dealing provisions 3.37–3.40
  economic theory 3.03–3.09
  financial services legislation 3.41–3.43
  introduction to 3.01
  Jenkins Report 3.14–3.16
  Joint Statements 3.24–3.26
  Justice Committee Report 3.20–3.23
  moral basis of 3.10–3.11
  Percival v Wright 3.12, 3.15
  privatization and Thatcherism in relation 3.27–3.30
  supervision in 1970s 3.17–3.19
  US developments 3.02
leverage, *see* gearing (leverage)
limit order defined 2.46
Littlewood, Christian and Angie, case of 1.08–1.09
London Stock Exchange (LSE):
  Alternative Investment Market (AIM) 2.14
  Joint Statements 3.24–3.26
  Official List (Main Market) 2.13
  supervisory role 3.19
long trading:
  going long 2.51
  long trade defined 2.30
losses, Contracts for Difference (CFDs) 2.42–2.46

Mallins, Jonathan, misuse of information 18.12
Manne, Henry, economic theory of insider dealing 3.03–3.09
margin:
  defined 2.35
  initial margin 2.36
  margin call 2.37

margin call defined 2.37
market abuse, *see also* civil market abuse regime:
  behaviour amounting to 15.04; *see also* behaviour
  cancellation of firm's authorization 24.19
  civil offences, *see* Financial Services and Markets Act 2000
  civil proceedings 24.57–24.58
  Decision Notices 24.41–24.42
  disclosure to subject by FCA 24.32–24.34
  'encouraging' 19.07–19.11
  enforcement process 24.21–24.44
  Enforcement Submissions Documents 24.30
  Executive Settlement Process 24.44–24.55
  Final Notices 24.44
  financial penalties 24.10–24.12
  formal enforcement action 24.04–24.19
  harmonized regime, *see* European legislation
  informal enforcement action 24.03–24.08
  introduction to enforcement 24.01
  Legal Review 24.23
  mediation 24.56
  non-imposition of penalty 19.14–19.27
  oral representations to RDC 24.36–24.40
  penalties imposed 19.28
  power to impose penalties 19.06–19.27
  preliminary findings letters (PFLs) 24.22
  preliminary investigation reports (PIRs) 24.22
  private warnings 24.04–24.08
  proceedings, *see* Article 6 of European Convention on Human Rights
  prohibition orders 24.14–24.15
  publicity as to enforcement action, *see* publicity
  range of enforcement actions 24.02
  RDC decisions 24.24–24.27
  representations to RDC 24.35–24.40
  'requiring' 19.07, 19.12–19.13
  restriction orders 24.20
  Settlement Discount Scheme 24.50–24.55
  statutory defence 19.01–19.05
  suspension orders 24.20
  Tribunal References 24.43
  Warning Notice Meetings 24.31
  Warning Notices 24.29
  withdrawal of approval 24.15–24.17
  written representations to RDC 24.35
Market Abuse Directive 2003 (MAD):
  background 14.07–14.11
  limitations 25.07–25.09
Market Cleanliness Statistic:
  decline 1.24
  measurement 1.23
  reporting 1.22
market makers:
  defined 2.23–2.25
  safe harbour 16.71–16.76
  special defence 11.25–11.27
market rumours, behaviour as to 16.41–16.45
Market Watch 14.16

Index

markets, *see* financial markets
Markets in Financial Instruments Directive 2004 (MiFID):
    regulated market defined 15.18–15.19
    transferable securities defined 15.26
mediation as to market abuse 24.56
mergers, *see* takeovers and mergers
mid price defined 2.23
Middlemiss, Robert, misuse of information 18.11
misuse of information, *see* Section 118(4) of Financial Services and Markets Act 2000
monitoring systems, SABRE II and ZEN 21.23–21.24
moral objection to insider dealing 3.10–3.11
Morton, Darren, non-imposition of market abuse penalty 19.23–19.27
Multilateral Trading Facilities (MTFs) as prescribed markets 15.23–15.25

negotiated settlement of confiscation proceedings 13.28
non-guaranteed stop loss defined 2.44–2.45

Off Exchange (OFEX) as prescribed market 15.17, 15.22
offences, *see* Part V of Criminal Justice Act 1993
offer price defined 2.23
'on the basis of' defined 16.16–16.22
options defined 8.07–8.10
ordinary shares:
    dividends 2.04
    profit motive 2.07
Organized Trading Facilities (OTFs) as prescribed markets 15.23–15.25

Panel on Takeovers and Mergers:
    City Code supervision role 3.17–3.19
    Joint Statements 3.24–3.26
Parker (James) v FSA, standard of proof 20.17–20.18
Part V of Companies Act 1980 3.31–3.36
Part V of Criminal Justice Act 1993:
    acquisitions and disposals (s 55(1)–(3)), *see* acquisitions and disposals (s 55(1)–(3) CJA 1993)
    approach to cases arising under 8.01
    dealings in pursuit of monetary policies, defence of (s 63) 11.39–11.41
    defences, *see* Section 53 of Criminal Justice Act 1993
    information made public (s 58) 6.69–6.81
    information treated as made public (s 58(3)) 6.85–6.92
    inside information, *see* Section 56 of Criminal Justice Act 1993
    Insider Dealing Directive in relation 4.02–4.03
    insiders, *see* Section 57 of Criminal Justice Act 1993
    introduction to 5.01
    'made public' defined (s 58) 6.68–6.81
    offences, *see* Section 62 of Criminal Justice Act 1993
    overview of 5.02–5.05
    professional intermediaries 9.20–9.26
    securities defined 8.03–8.24
    territorial scope, *see* Section 62 of Criminal Justice Act 1993
    text Appendix 2B
Patel, Sameer:
    burden and standard of proof 20.22
    misuse of information 18.15
penalties:
    apportionment between defendants 13.24–13.26
    'benefit obtained' defined 13.20–13.23
    confiscation orders 13.19–13.26
    Court of Appeal sentencing authorities 13.04–13.16
    disqualification of directors 13.17–13.18
    insider dealing (s 61 CJA) 13.02–13.03
    introduction to 13.01
    market abuse, power to impose 19.06–19.27
    negotiated settlement of confiscation proceedings 13.28
    Prohibition Orders 13.28
    recent cases 13.16
    reduction in sentence (s 73 SOCPA 2005) 23.21
Percival v Wright:
    Jenkins Report 3.15
    ruling 3.12
'person' defined 15.07–15.12
persons charged with execution of orders, behaviour as to 16.64–16.65
persons in possession of market information, special defence 11.28–11.32
placing defined 2.10
plea agreements:
    discussions as to 23.29–23.30
    s 73 SOCPA 2005 23.21
PLUS Derivatives Exchange (PLUS-DX) as prescribed market 15.17
pre-existing trading strategies, safe harbour as to 16.66–16.70
preference shares:
    cumulation 2.07
    value 2.06
preliminary findings letters (PFLs) for market abuse 24.22
preliminary investigation reports (PIRs) for market abuse 24.22
prescribed markets 15.13–15.25
price-affected securities defined 6.127
price stabilization, special defence 11.35–11.38
pricing information, *see* information
primary offence (s 52(1)), *see* Section 52 of Criminal Justice Act 1993 (offences)

Index

prior decisions to deal, safe harbour as to 16.66–16.70
private company shares defined 2.09
private warnings for market abuse 24.04–24.08
privatization and insider dealing legislation in relation 3.27–3.30
privilege against self-incrimination in market abuse proceedings 20.11
proceedings as to market abuse, *see* Article 6 of European Convention on Human Rights
procuring defined 9.10–9.19
professional intermediaries:
   defined (s 59 CJA 1993) 9.23–9.26
   Part V of Criminal Justice Act 1993 9.20–9.26
   safe harbour 16.71–16.76
Prohibition Orders 13.28
prohibition orders for market abuse 24.13–24.14
proof, *see* burden of proof
prosecution:
   consent for 12.05–12.08
   conspiracy 12.13–12.20
   FSA 21.08–1.09
   introduction to 12.01
   numbers of prosecutions 1987 to 1993 3.38
   offences connected to insider dealing 12.09–12.12
   prosecuting bodies 12.02–12.04
   summary proceedings 12.21
Prudential Regulation Authority (PRA), enforcement role 21.11
public offering (placing) defined 2.10
public sector body defined 6.13
publicity:
   challenges to publication of enforcement notices 24.61–24.63
   during FCA investigation 24.59
   during or at conclusion of civil action 24.64
   during or at conclusion of criminal action 24.65
   during or at conclusion of regulatory action 24.60

qualifying investments 15.13–15.14, 15.26–15.27

R v Anjam Ahmad, co-operation agreement 23.26–23.28
R v Asif Nazir Butt, sentencing 13.08–13.11
R v Christopher McQuoid, sentencing guidelines 13.12–13.16
R v Malcolm Calvert, co-operation agreement 23.22–23.25
R v Smith, Spearman and Payne, sentencing 13.05–13.07
Rajaratnam, Raj, case of 1.06–1.07
re B (Children), standard of proof 20.19–20.20
Re S-B (Children), standard of proof 20.23
recognized auction platforms as prescribed market 15.21–15.22

Recognized Investment Exchanges as prescribed markets 15.16, 15.22
record keeping, requirement on firms 21.29
recorded telephone calls, FCA policy statement 21.30–21.31
redeemable shares defined 2.08
reduction in sentence (s 73 SOCPA 2005) 23.21
regular user:
   defined 18.17
   offence 18.06
regulated markets, *see* financial markets
Regulation of Investigatory Powers Act 2000 (RIPA 2000), FCA powers as to communications data 22.17
Regulatory Decisions Committee (RDC):
   Chairman's role 23.31–23.34
   decisions as to market abuse 24.24–24.28
   oral representations to 24.36–24.40
   written representations to 24.35
Regulatory Information Service (RIS):
   announcements via 2.20
   monitoring of announcements 2.21
'requiring' market abuse offence 19.07, 19.12–19.13
Restraint Orders 23.38
restricted use undertakings (s 72 SOCPA 2005) 23.20
restriction orders for market abuse 24.20
risk as to spread bets 2.54

safe harbours:
   disclosure of seller's managerial responsibilities to potential buyer 17.12
   disclosure to certain public bodies 17.10
   disclosures in compliance with rules and regulatory obligations 17.11
   execution of client orders 16.77–16.81
   guidance as to 14.15
   market makers 16.71–16.76
   misuse of information 18.23
   prior decisions to deal and pre-existing trading strategies 16.66–16.70
   professional dealers 16.71–16.76
   takeover and merger activity 16.82–16.84
Sanders, James, case of 1.10–1.14
Schedule 2 of Criminal Justice Act 1993:
   IDO 1994 in relation 8.26
   text Appendix 2C
search warrants, FCA enforcement powers 22.34–22.39
secondary insiders 6.39–6.41
secondary offences, *see* Section 52 of Criminal Justice Act 1993 (offences)
Section 52 of Criminal Justice Act 1993 (offences):
   dealing defined (s 52(3)) 9.02–9.10
   defences, *see* Section 63 of Criminal Justice Act 1993

Index

Disclosing offence (s 52(2)(b)) 5.26–5.34, 5.33
Encouraging offence (s 52(2)(a)) 5.21–5.25, 5.27
insider dealing (s 52) 5.06–5.15, 9.01
primary offence (s 52(1)) 5.16–5.20, 5.22
secondary offences 5.21–5.34
territorial scope, *see* Section 62 of Criminal Justice Act 1993

Section 53 of Criminal Justice Act 1993 (statutory defences):
belief that information disclosed widely enough 11.07–11.11
burden of proof 11.42–11.49
dealings to facilitate accomplishment of acquisition or disposal/nl (Sch 1(3)) 11.33–11.34
Disclosing offence (s 52(2)(b)) 11.19–11.22
Encouraging offence (s 53(2)) 11.17–11.18
introduction to 11.01
market makers (Sch 1(1)) 11.25–11.27
persons in possession of market information (Sch 1(2)) 11.28–11.32
price stabilization (Sch 1(5)) 11.35–11.38
primary offence (s 53(1)) 11.02–11.16
profit not expected (s 53(1)(a)) 11.03–11.06
same action without information 11.12–11.16
secondary offences 11.17–11.22
special defences (s 53(4)) 11.23–11.41

Section 56 of Criminal Justice Act 1993 (inside information):
alleged secondary insiders 6.39–6.41
analysts 6.36–6.38
circumstantial evidence of information communication 6.48–6.61
company directors and inside information 6.33–6.35
direct evidence of information communication 6.42–6.47
fund managers 6.36–6.38
identification of inside information 6.03–6.09
information likely to have significant effect on price (s 56(1)(d)) 6.109–6.126
information not made public (s 56(1)(c)) 6.62–6.108
information relating to particular securities or issuers (s 56(1)(a)) 6.10–6.21
information which may affect a company's business prospects 6.17–6.21
'inside information' defined 6.01–6.02
Insider Dealing Directive in relation 6.02
introduction to 6.01
price-affected securities defined 6.127
proof that information not made public 6.65–6.67, 6.93–6.108
significant effect defined 6.113–6.126
'specific or precise' defined 6.25–6.32
'specific or precise' information requirement (s 56(1)(b)) 6.22–6.32, 6.39–6.41

Section 57 of Criminal Justice Act 1993 (insiders):
categories of insider (s 57(2)) 7.19–7.41
directors as insiders 7.21–7.22
employees as insiders 7.23
inside information at time of dealing 7.10–7.16
inside source defined 7.15–7.18
insider defined 7.01–7.02
insider inner circle (s 57(2)(a)(i)) 7.21–7.24
insider middle circle (s 57(2)(a)(ii)) 7.25–7.32
insider outer circle (s 57(2)(b)) 7.33–7.41
introduction to 7.01
knowledge requirement 7.03–7.09
liability under s 57(2)(b) 7.36–7.41
shareholders as insiders 7.24

Section 62 of Criminal Justice Act 1993 (territorial scope):
introduction to 10.01
primary offence (s 62(1)) 10.02–10.04
scope of 10.06–10.11
secondary offences (s 62(2)) 10.04–10.05

Section 118(2) of Financial Services and Markets Act 2000 (insider dealing behaviour):
dealing defined 16.14–16.15
'dealing' offence 16.02–16.04
elements of offence 16.03
insider defined 16.05–16.13
introduction to 16.01
'on the basis of' defined 16.16–16.22
safe harbours, *see* safe harbours

Section 118(3) of Financial Services and Markets Act 2000 (improper disclosure):
disclosure offence 17.04
improper disclosure behaviour 17.02–17.09
introduction to 17.01
safe harbours 17.10–17.12; *see also* safe harbours

Section 118(4) of Financial Services and Markets Act 2000 (misuse of information):
behaviour 'on the basis of' inside information 18.19
example cases 18.08–18.16
generally available information 18.18
introduction to 18.01
misuse of information defined 18.02–18.16
regular user defined 18.17
'regular user' offence 18.06
relevant information 18.20–18.21
safe harbours 18.23
standards of behaviour 18.22

Section 118C of Financial Services and Markets Act 2000 (inside information):
commodity derivatives 16.61–16.63
information not generally available 16.38–16.45
information of a precise nature 16.30–16.37

Index

Section 118C of Financial Services and Markets Act 2000 (inside information): (*cont.*)
  information relating directly or indirectly to issuer of qualifying investments or to qualifying investments 16.46
  inside information defined 16.28–16.29
  likely to significantly effect price of qualifying or related investments 16.47–16.60
  market rumours 16.41–16.45
  persons charged with execution of orders 16.64–16.65
securities:
  bid price 2.23
  CJA 1993 regime introduced 8.01
  contracts for difference, *see* contracts for difference (CFDs)
  debt securities (bonds) defined 8.04–8.05
  depositary receipts defined 8.06–8.07
  example of trade 2.25
  further issue of 2.03
  futures contracts defined 8.10–8.13
  IDO 1994, *see* Insider Dealing (Securities and Regulated Markets) Order 1994 (IDO 1994)
  Initial Public Offering (IPO) 2.09
  Insider Dealing Directive proposals 4.19–4.21
  investors, *see* investors
  issue of 2.02
  mid price 2.23
  offer price 2.23
  options defined 8.07–8.10
  ordinary shares 2.04–2.05
  preference shares 2.06–2.07
  price-affected securities defined 6.127
  price of 2.23–2.25
  private company 2.09
  public offering (placing) 2.10
  redeemable shares 2.08
  security defined 8.28
  shares defined 8.04
  spread bets, *see* spread bets
  trading, *see* trading
  types introduced 2.03
  warrants defined 8.05–8.06
self-incrimination in market abuse proceedings, privilege against 20.11
sentencing, *see* penalties
Serious Organised Crime and Police Act 2005 (SOCPA 2005):
  full immunity from prosecution (s 71) 23.19
  plea agreements and reduction in sentence (s 73) 23.21
  restricted use undertakings (s 72) 23.20
Settlement Discount Scheme 24.50–24.55
settlement of confiscation proceedings 13.28
shareholders as insiders 7.24; *see also* investors
shares, *see* securities
short selling defined 2.30–2.32

short trading:
  going short 2.52
  short selling defined 2.30–2.32
slippage defined 2.44
Smith, Jason, misuse of information 18.08
specific or precise information, *see* Section 56 of Criminal Justice Act 1993
spread bets:
  basis of spread 2.49
  down (closing) bet 2.51–2.52
  example trades 2.53
  going long 2.51
  going short 2.52
  growth of 2.47
  placing of 2.50
  point defined 2.50
  risk 2.54
  Schedule 2 of CJA 1993 8.15–8.24
  spread defined 2.48
  taxation 2.53
  up bet 2.51
standard of proof in market abuse proceedings 20.13–20.25
statutory defences, *see* Section 53 of Criminal Justice Act 1993
stock, *see* shares
stock exchanges:
  Alternative Investment Market (AIM) 2.14
  electronic trading 2.11
  ICAP Securities and Derivatives Exchange (ISDX) 2.15
  London Stock Exchange (LSE), *see* London Stock Exchange (LSE)
  market makers, *see* market makers
  principal UK markets 2.12
stop loss defined 2.42–2.43
summary proceedings, venue and time limit 12.21
supervision, *see* enforcement
'Surveillance Analysis of Business Reporting' (SABRE II) use by FSA and FCA 21.23
suspension orders for market abuse 24.20
suspicious transaction reporting by FCA 21.25–21.28

takeovers and mergers; *see also* acquisitions and disposals (s 55(1)–(3) CJA 1993):
  City Code, *see* City Code on Take-Overs and Mergers
  Panel, *see* Panel on Takeovers and Mergers
  safe harbour 16.82–16.84
taxation:
  Contracts for Difference (CFDs) 2.38
  spread bets 2.53
  tribunal, *see* Upper Tribunal (Tax and Chancery Chamber)
technical (chartist) analysis defined 2.28

Index

telephone calls, FCA policy statement as to recording 21.30–21.31
timetabling of deals, requirement on firms 21.32–21.33
trading:
  deal timetables, requirement on firms 21.32–21.33
  defined 2.29
  electronic trading, *see* electronic trading
  fundamental analysis 2.28
  long trading, *see* long trading
  short trading, *see* short trading
  strategies 2.28–2.32
  technical (chartist) analysis 2.28
trailing stops defined 2.45
transferable securities defined 15.26
tribunal decisions as precedent 14.17
Tribunal References as to market abuse 24.43

United States, legislative developments 3.02
up bet defined 2.51
Upper Tribunal (Tax and Chancery Chamber):
  burden and standard of proof in market abuse cases 20.11–20.23
  transfer of functions to 14.18
  Tribunal References 24.43

Warning Notice Meetings 24.31
Warning Notices for market abuse 24.29
warrants defined 8.05–8.06
withdrawal of person's approval 24.15–24.17
witness statements, FCA enforcement powers 22.51–22.53

ZEN, use by FSA and FCA 21.24